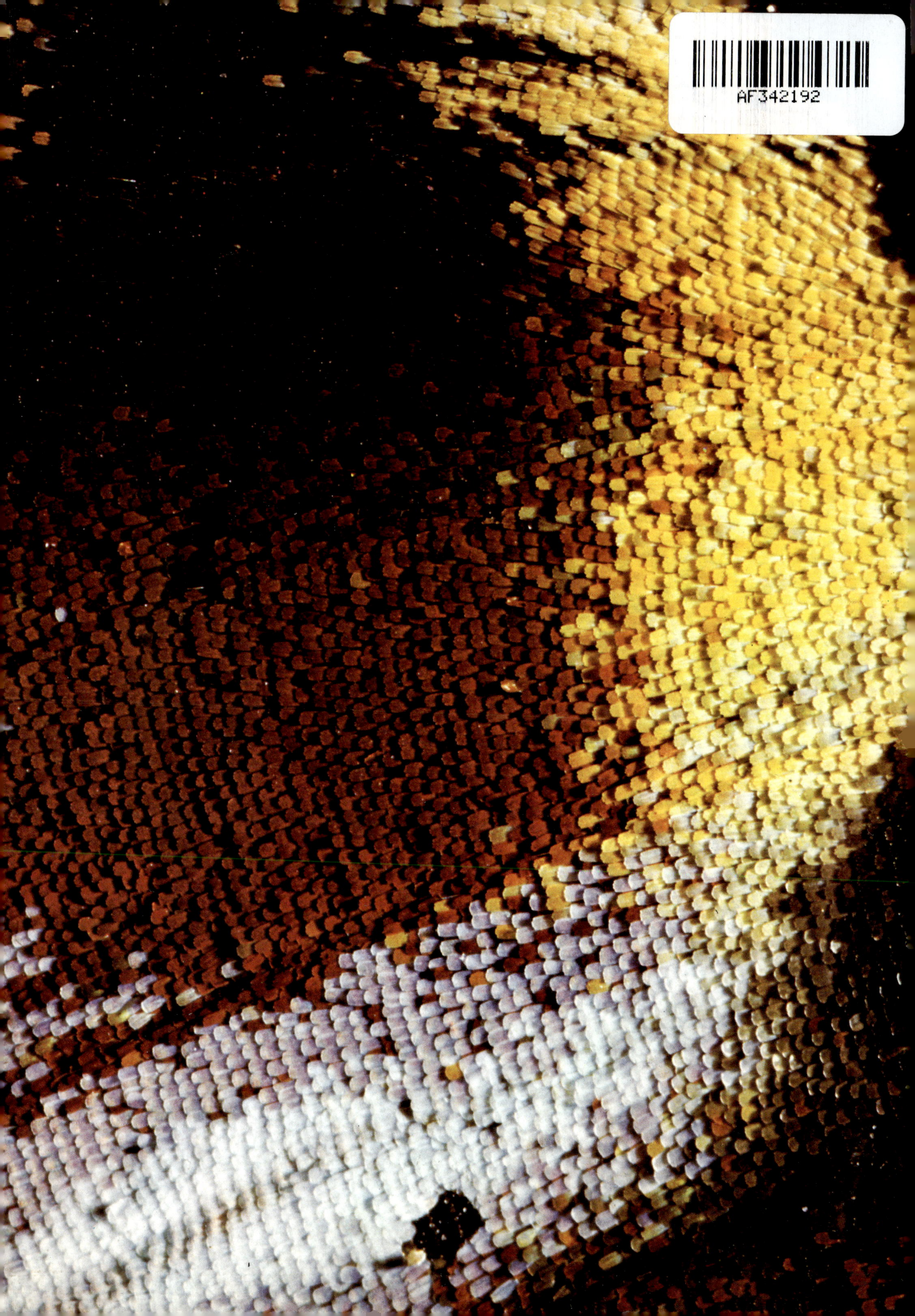
AF342192

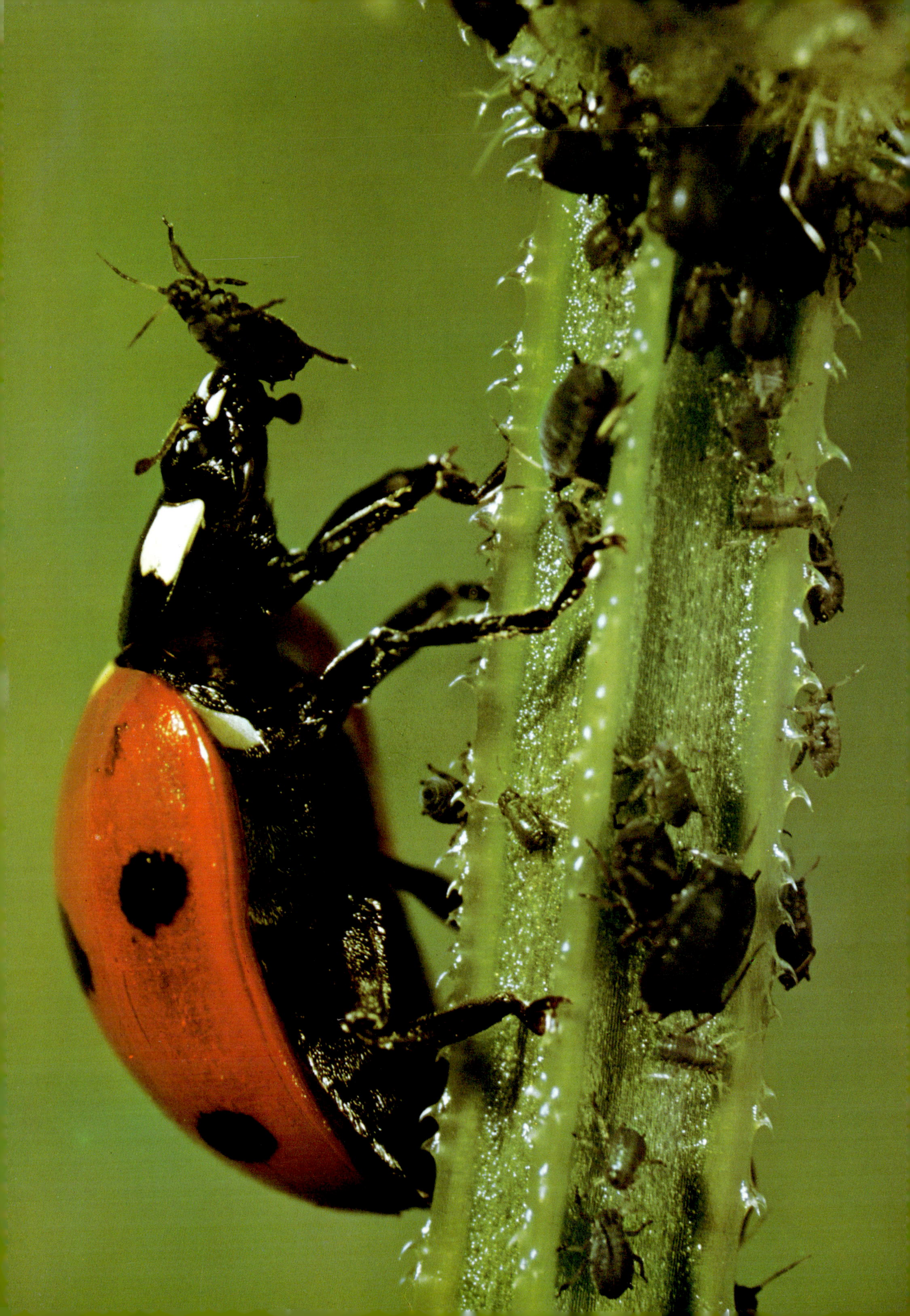

Text and photographs by
Claude Nuridsany and Marie Pérennou
Translated by J. W. Steward

PHOTOGRAPHING NATURE

KAYE & WARD · LONDON
OXFORD UNIVERSITY PRESS · NEW YORK

Endpapers: Peacock Butterfly, detail of eye-marking on rear wing (x 40); reproduction ratio: 3·6; Macro-Summar 24 mm lens on bellows; aperture f/8; electronic flash directed across surface.

Frontispiece: Ladybird devouring a plant-louse (x 20); reproduction ratio 2·4; Macro-Luminar lens on bellows; aperture f/11-16; electronic flash.

Page 144: Burnet Moth, at sunset (x 15). Limestone plateau of Rouerge in France, at the top of a ledge; reproduction ratio 0·7; Macro 55 mm lens with automatic extension ring; aperture f/3·5; exposure time 1/250th of a second; natural light.

Page 146, from top to bottom: Pale Clouded Yellow Butterfly drinking from a Scabious flower (x 4); reproduction ratio 1·8; Macro 55 mm lens mounted on bellows; aperture f/16-22; electronic flash. Head of Spotted Mud-frog (x 2); reproduction ratio 2; 55 mm lens mounted on bellows; aperture f/22; electronic flash. Leaf of Plane-tree (x 8); reproduction ratio: 3·3; Macro-Summar 24 mm lens; aperture f/8; electronic flash positioned behind the leaf.

Page 155: Praying Mantis in an expectant attitude (it has just caught sight of the photographer's lens) (x 12); reproduction ratio 1·6; Macro 55 mm lens mounted on bellows in reverse position; aperture f/16-22; electronic flash.

First published in Great Britain 1976
by Kaye & Ward Ltd
21 New Street, London EC2M 4NT

First published in the USA 1976
by Oxford University Press Inc.
200 Madison Avenue, New York, NY 10016

Copyright © Librairie Hachette 1975

ISBN 0 7182 1138 3   (Great Britain)
ISBN 0 19 519885 9   (U.S.A.)
Library of Congress Catalog Card Number 76–9256

Colour reproduction by Rito AG, Zurich
Filmset by Computer Photoset, Birmingham, England
Printed and bound in Great Britain by
Cox & Wyman Ltd, London, Fakenham and Reading

Contents

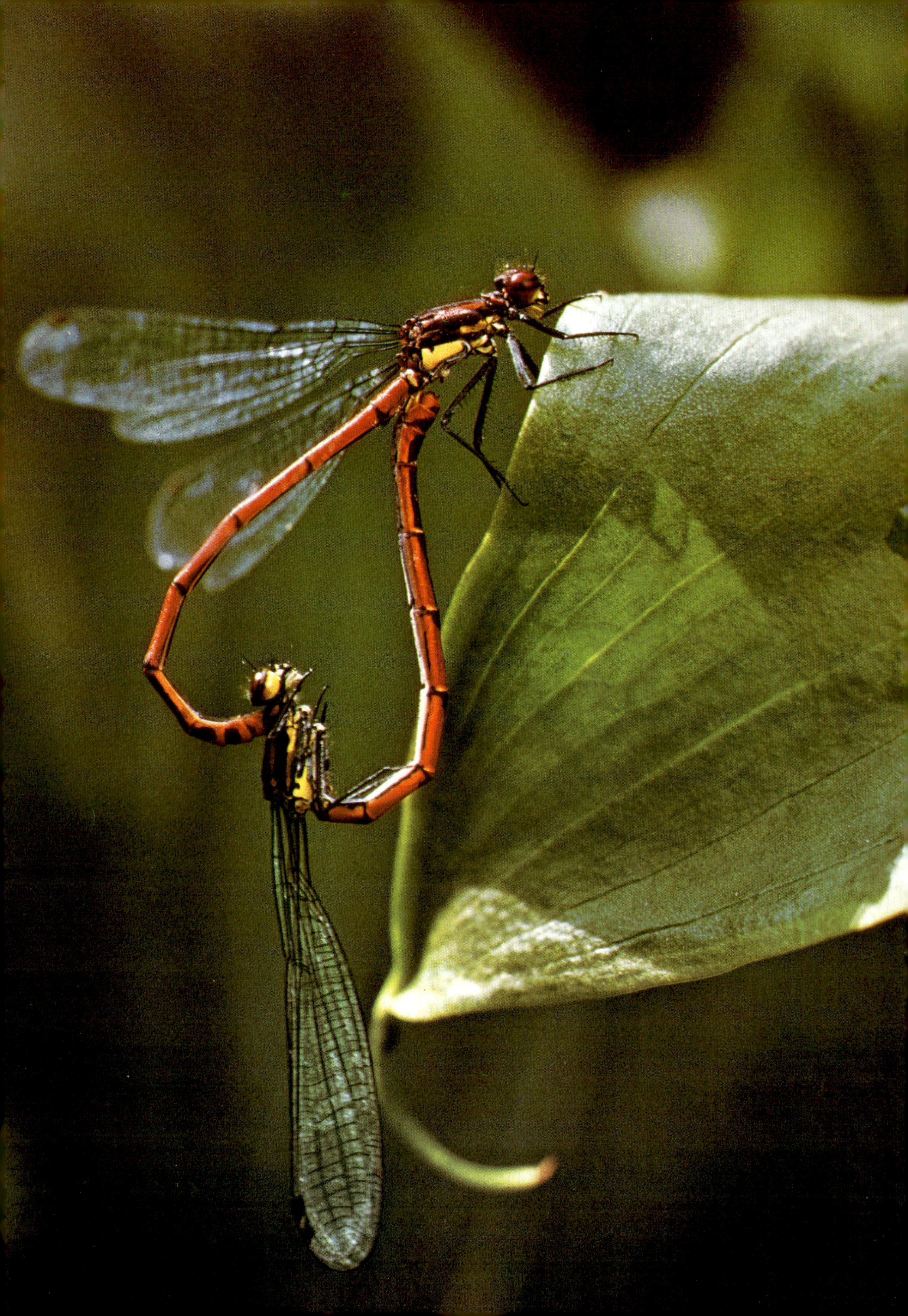

Preface

Not so long ago, observing nature was regarded as a contemplative activity too far removed from our everyday life to be taken seriously.

When, in the middle of the 19th Century, Fabre started to study the habits of insects, he was met by amused smiles from those around him and it was among children that he found his most ardent helpers. In his own racy language he described the rebuffs he met with during his studies of the Sacred Scarab. In order to obtain food for this dung-loving insect, he approached the servant of his neighbour, who owned a horse. When the owner found out about the strange trade which was taking place every day without his knowledge, he thought Fabre's explanations of his experiments were ludicrous lies invented to hide the real motive behind this trade – a means of obtaining manure at a cheap price! The observation of nature nowadays constitutes a pastime or a special branch of scientific research. For us, it has become an occupation which might be located half-way between these two extremes.

When we are hard at work, kneeling in a field for hours on end, passers-by and local people watch us from a distance with a mixture of astonishment and concern. But finally, succumbing to their curiosity, they draw near and discover our photographic equipment spread out on the ground. A long conversation then takes place which is divided between discussion of photographic techniques and recollection of the most amazing habits of ants.

Well, there has certainly been a change in attitude and, even if people tease us a little about our ubiquitous 'little animals', they admit that we are doing a proper job and, what is more, an interesting one.

Moreover, this recent feeling for the things of Nature is by no means a passing fashion or a meaningless fad; it is based on a growing awareness by man of the serious threats to his environment which are now emerging. The population explosion, the squandering of natural resources, pollution, the dizzy increase in production and consumption – these are some of the sad realities of our time which have faced man with the brutal necessity to open his eyes and look at what is taking place.

At the beginning of this century there timidly emerged a new synthesising science – ecology – the intended purpose of which was to study organisms living within the relationships which they maintain between themselves and their environment. Ecology is now one of the most important scientific disciplines. This is because, without pretending to find miraculous solutions to the problems which concern us, it presents the current situation in new and revealing terms which facilitate a more accurate estimate of the actual needs of man. In line with this, the rapid development of societies for the protection of Nature, of ecology groups, and of specialized works and periodicals seems to be evidence – even if it is behind an outburst of ideas which are sometimes disconcerting, though their vitality augurs well for the future – of a desire for new contacts with Nature.

Although this book deals only with a small part of the natural

Red Agrions (x 3).
While mating, these two dragonflies look astonishingly like an upside-down heart.

With the aid of a pincer-like claw at the end of his abdomen, the male – in the upper position – has seized the female behind her head. The latter has curved her body upwards in order to receive the semen from her partner.

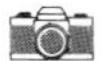

Reproduction ratio: 0·4.
Lens: Macro 55 mm.
Aperture: f/5·6.
Exposure time: 1/125th of a second.
Natural light filtering through the leaves of Arum Lillies, with slight backlighting.
Film: Kodachrome 64.

Note: The first figure (x) indicates the magnification of the illustration in relation to the actual size of the animal or plant.

The reproduction ratio applies to the size of the image on the original record (24 x 36 slide) in relation to the actual size of the subject.

The photographs with electronic flash were taken on Kodachrome 25 film. The daylight photographs were generally taken on Kodachrome 64 film.

universe, we were determined not to remain on the fringes of these movements, feeling ourselves to be directly concerned with them.

So, if in places we seem to linger on some loss to the natural environment for which man is responsible, or on some elementary precaution which should be observed on the ground, this is because in our field also it is necessary to assess the consequences of our acts, knowing that we are dealing with delicate states of balance.

We wanted to make this book a practical guide which would enable the amateur to take his first steps (or to perfect his knowledge) in the field of close-up photography. However, we would certainly have regarded it as incomplete if it had been limited to a simple description of the technical procedures which have to be mas-tered: without any doubt, the main purpose would have been missing. The practice of photomacrography seems to us, in effect, to be inseparable from an enthusiastic knowledge of the living world. We have also made a point of describing – sometimes at some length – certain species, because of their appearance or their particularly interesting behaviour.

The examples we have chosen do not pretend to be representative of all the subjects which might be encountered in the world of small animals. Their main purpose is to persuade the reader to make further advances in the exploration of this universe by holding out to him, we hope, the promise of a thousand-fold increase in the wonders that he will personally experience 'in the field'.

Opposite page: Tulip (x 4). Opening out the corolla will reveal the reproductive organs – the yellow pistil in the centre surrounded by black stamens carrying grains of pollen.

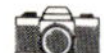

Reproduction ratio: 0·5.
Lens: Macro 55 mm.
Aperture: f/16.
Electronic flash positioned behind the flower.

Right: Tulip bud (x 7·5). Transverse section, seen from above. Petals and sepals are still coiled, tightly overlapping, surrounding the reproductive parts with an impenetrable hood.

Reproduction ratio: 1·5.
Lens: Macro 55 mm mounted on bellows.
Aperture: f/22.
Lighting: 2 electronic flashlights providing backlighting on either side of the subject.

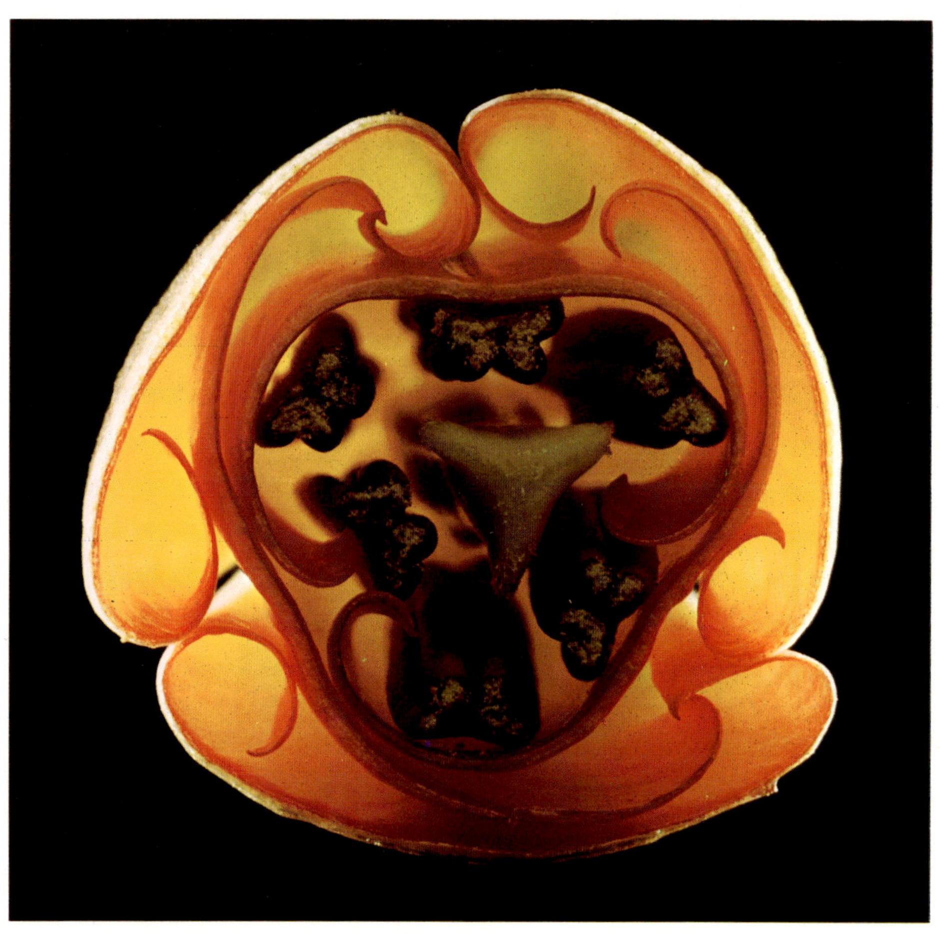

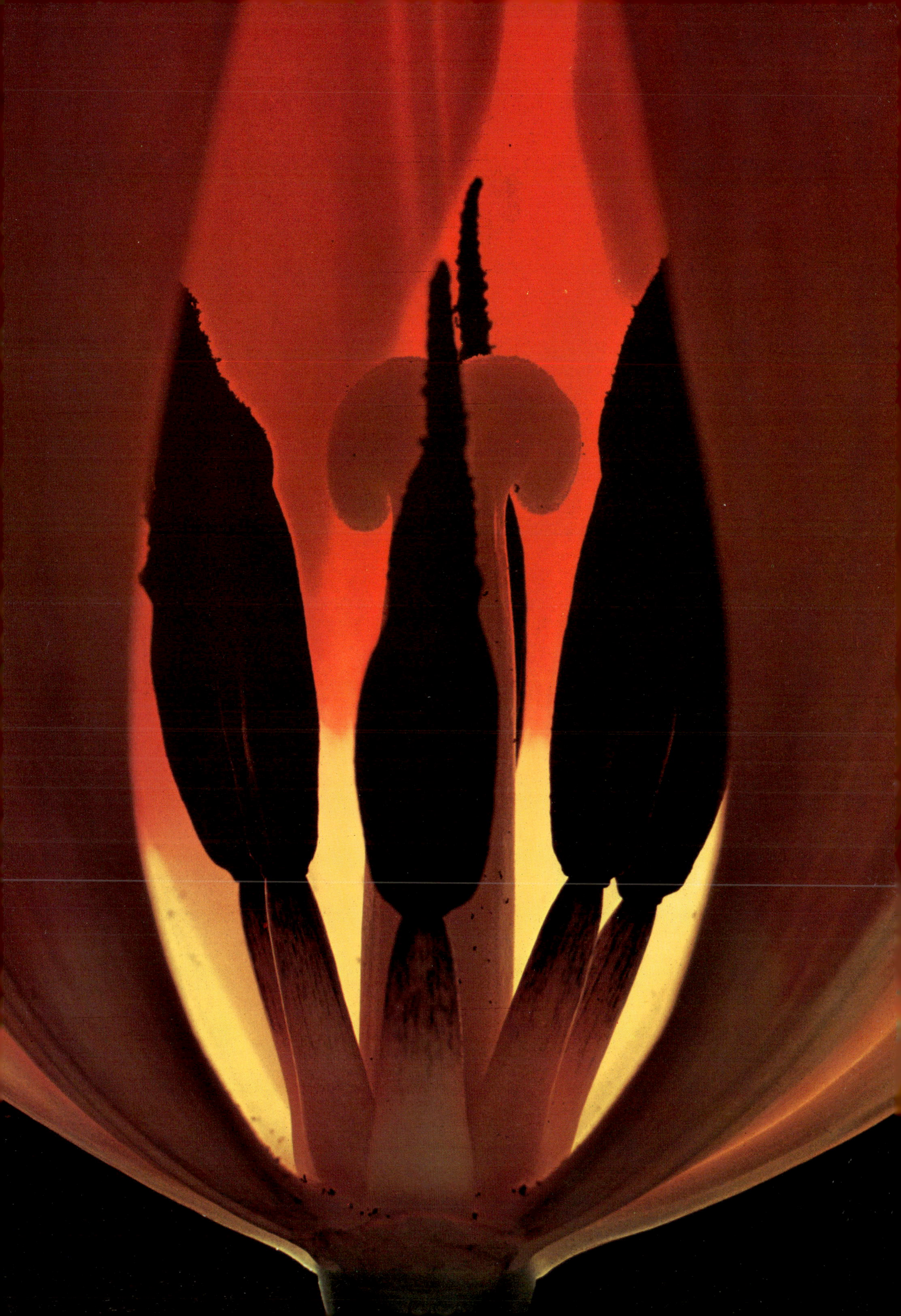

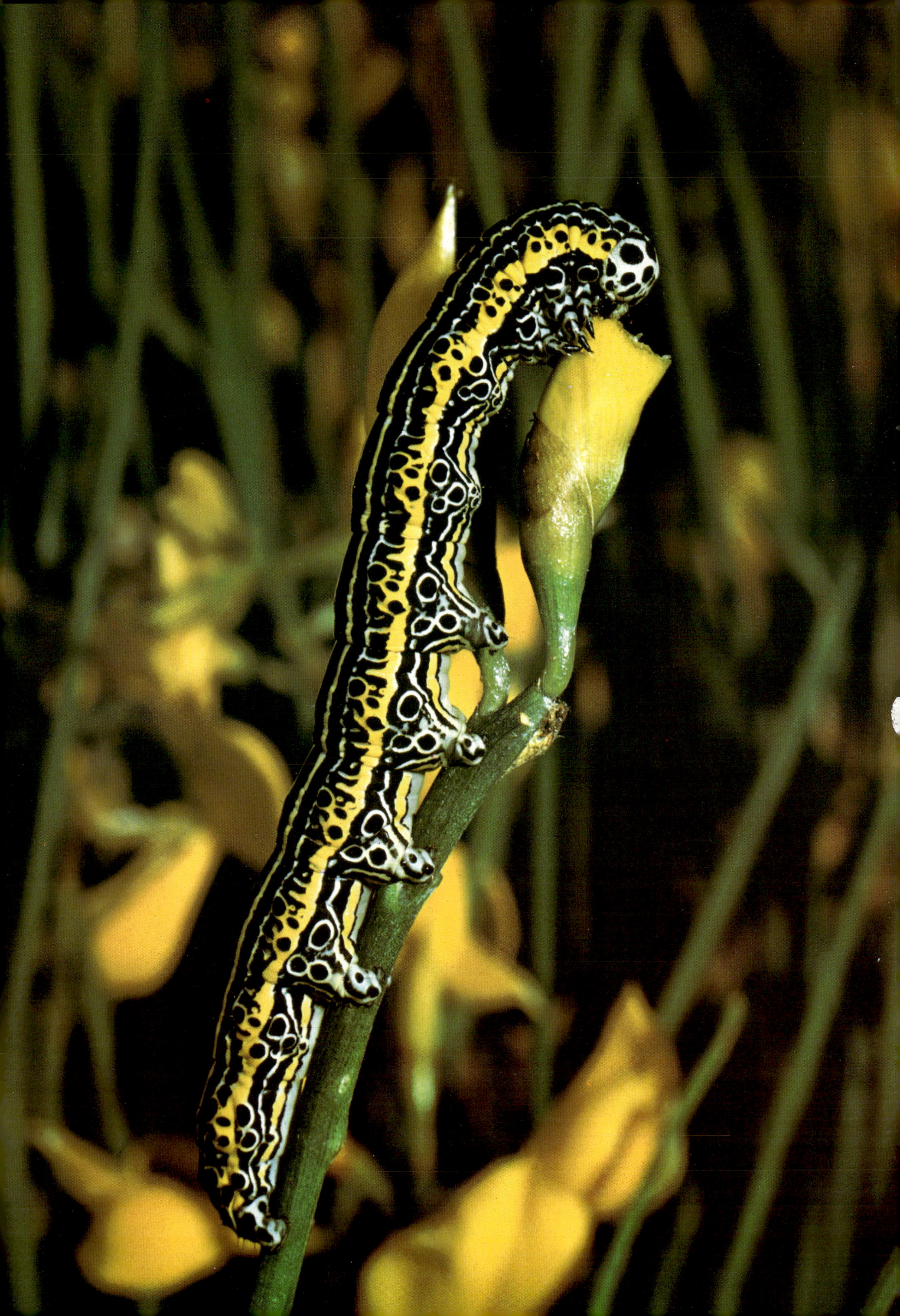

Drawing attention to things

The animals and plants we shall deal with in this book are not rare or isolated subjects. They are not found in protected or inaccessible places. A large number of them can be found in the countryside nearby or even in the smallest gardens. The particular feature which certainly marks them out is that they belong to a different order of size. They are all quite small creatures. In order to find them it is necessary to adopt a new method of looking; this is where our approach to the subject starts.

However, the small size of our subjects is not alone responsible for their unobtrusiveness, for, while certain marvellously coloured insects draw attention to themselves, the majority of them on the other hand are difficult for us to see owing to a further accomplishment they have – the adoption of camouflage.

Easily visible prey: warning animals

Certain creatures of particularly striking appearance attract the attention of the passer-by at first glance: their brilliant colours, ornamental patterns or peculiar shapes intrigue and attract. Such astonishing animals are often regarded as trophies by the amateur naturalist engaged in his first studies (and thus sometimes form the basis of later collections). However, his curiosity might lead him to ask the reasons for these displays of colour, which hardly constitute efficient protection against attack. Such bold display involves the danger of becoming the target of predators, always on the look-out for easy victims. It would be labouring under a delusion to imagine that the 'livery' of small animals is the result of an aesthetic purpose or of blind chance allotting shapes and colours at random. The survival of a species is far too serious and delicate a matter to take into account such trivialities.

Uniforms which command respect

The 'warning animals' – as these flamboyant living displays might be called – are in the minority among small animals. Moreover, species endowed with conspicuous colours are generally provided with an efficient system of defence against their enemies. The common ladybird which, in spite of its small size, attracts attention by reason of its unusual colour pattern, can exude from its sides when provoked a yellowish fluid the unpleasant odour of which drives away its attackers.

The caterpillar of the Large Swallowtail sports a by no means unobtrusive pattern of alternating black and green rings adorned with red and black spots. When attacked, it protrudes from behind its head an orange-coloured forked organ which startles its adversary and overwhelms it with a strongly repulsive odour, discouraging all further attack.

With its colour pattern of black dotted with irregularly distributed bright yellow patches, the European Fire Salamander is one of the most highly-coloured amphibians in Europe; its attractively pigmented skin hides a large number of poison glands distributed over the entire

Caterpillar of the Owlet Moth (x 4).
Its colour pattern of bright yellow strewn with black dots and lines makes it completely invisible among Gorse and Broom flowers. While providing an ideal refuge, the flowers and leaves of these plants also constitute the sole nourishment of this caterpillar.

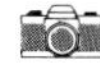

Reproduction ratio: 0·5.
Lens: 105 mm mounted on bellows.
Aperture: f/16.
Electronic flash, with reflector to reduce the shadows.

surface of the body. They are particularly abundant on the two prominences which can be seen behind the eyes. Harmless to man (who does not make a practice of swallowing the animal!), these skin secretions are extremely effective against predators, which hastily disgorge the nauseous prey that causes such irritation to the mucous membranes of their buccal cavities.

Certain vividly coloured animals have even more violent means of dissuasion at their disposal. The wasp, for example, which openly warns its enemies by means of yellow and black rings around its abdomen, is armed with a formidable venomous sting.

All these animals have one thing in common – they combine strongly contrasting colours with means of defence varying from simple unpalatability to a capacity for powerful counter-attack. This combination of characteristics offers valuable advantages. In practice, after a few unpleasant attempts, the predator quickly learns to avoid such over-conspicuous items of prey. The colour patterns quickly become associated in its mind with unpleasant experiences. The motley dress of the previously sought-after animal has become a warning signal which says, 'Do not eat'. Far from being fanciful decorations, the 'liveries' of warning animals are the equivalent of the red labels used to mark bottles containing poison. Such warning 'liveries' thus constitute an important advantage for the success of the species. At a cost of sacrificing a few individuals, the majority is protected against untimely attack. The mechanism of natural selection, which does nothing without cause, has been able to promote the development of these 'live warnings' endowed with an original but effective means of defence, which gives them a head-start in the struggle for existence.

Crab Spider on a Marguerite (x 2). Capable of changing its colour to match the flower in which it is sheltering, this spider catches its prey by lying in wait. With its front legs spread wide and apparently motionless, it awaits the arrival of an insect in search of honey, which does not realize its danger until too late.

Reproduction ratio: 0·4.
Lens: Macro 55 mm.
Aperture: f/8.
Exposure time: 1/125th of a second.
Natural light, towards midday.

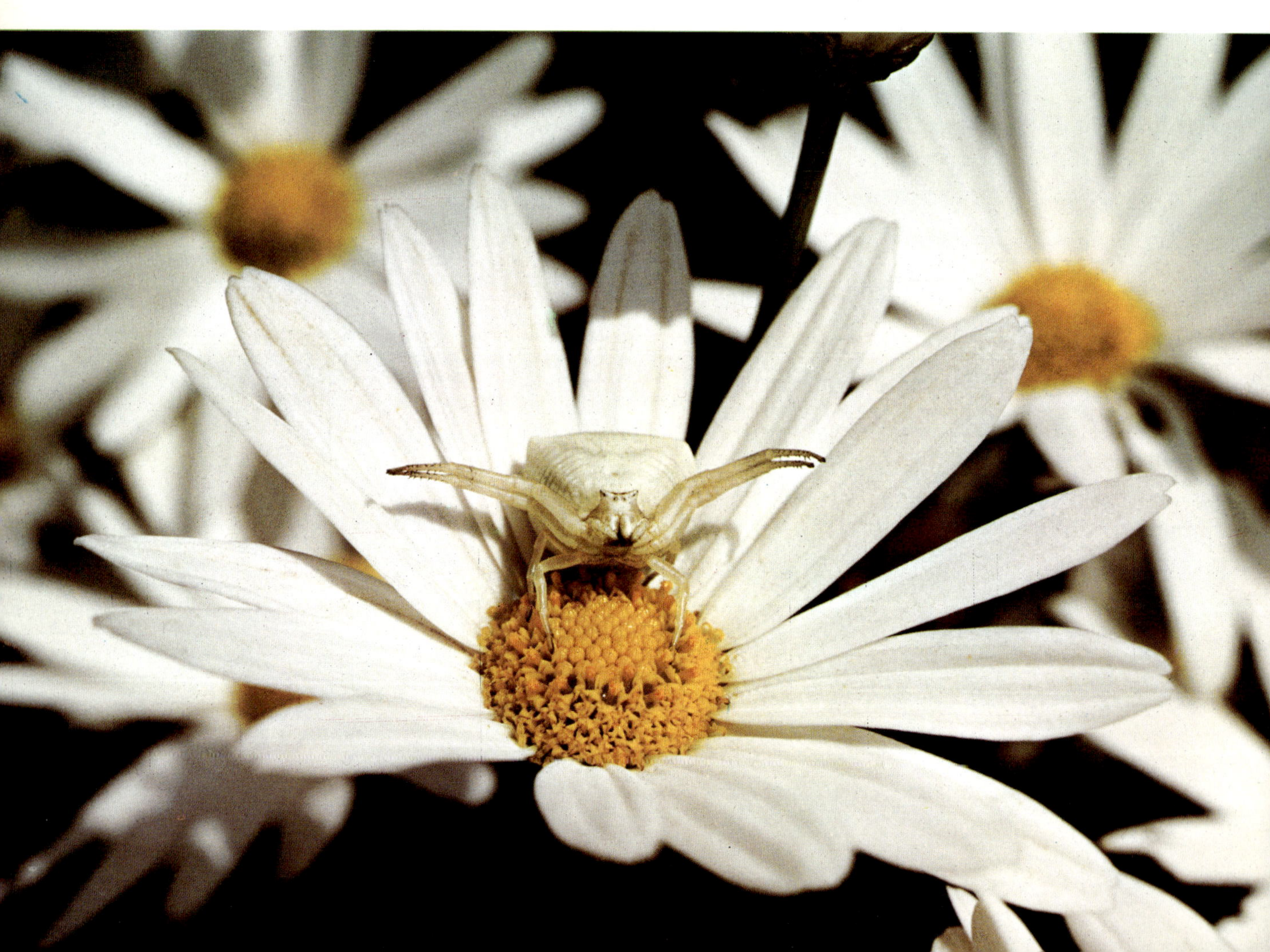

Predators put to the test

Repeated observations have made it possible to confirm these attractive theories. With the Common Toad, for example, it has been found that easily identifiable insects with stings, such as humble-bees, were swallowed the first time and immediately spat out again. After this, the amphibian systematically avoided exposing itself to such a painful disappointment. Other observations on birds confirm these results. Wild birds offered a choice of brightly coloured insects mixed with other more soberly coloured ones invariably chose the latter. The experimenters even invented new warning animals by painting green stripes on mealworms (the larvae of a small beetle, the Flour Beetle) made inedible by impregnating them with quinine. Although normally fond of this juicy prey, starlings quickly learned to put the newcomers on the list of inedible objects.

The colours of small animals thus act as visual warnings, the mere appearance of which discourages attack by predators.

Although in the minority among small animals, the species which have recourse to such an artifice are none the less numerous: if each of them made use of a particular warning, the predators would have to remember an impressively large number of colour patterns, associated with an equal number of disagreable experiences. If, on the other hand, several species had recourse to similar methods of warning, the predator would no longer have to test each of them to confirm that it was inedible. A single test would be sufficient to teach it this and to protect the entire group against its attack.

Nature provides numerous examples of such standardization. Among the night-moths of the genus Arctia, several species have adopted the same method of warning. The front wings are black with white spots or stripes. When at rest, they almost completely cover the rear wings, which are red or yellow dotted with black. The body, which is thick and heavy, has the same bright coloration. These insects never try to hide. On the contrary, they select exposed positions where they can be seen by all, like any warning to which attention should be paid.

If it is approached by an inexperienced predator, the moth gives a warning signal: opening its front wings, it suddenly reveals the red colour of its rear wings and abdomen. To discourage its adversary com-

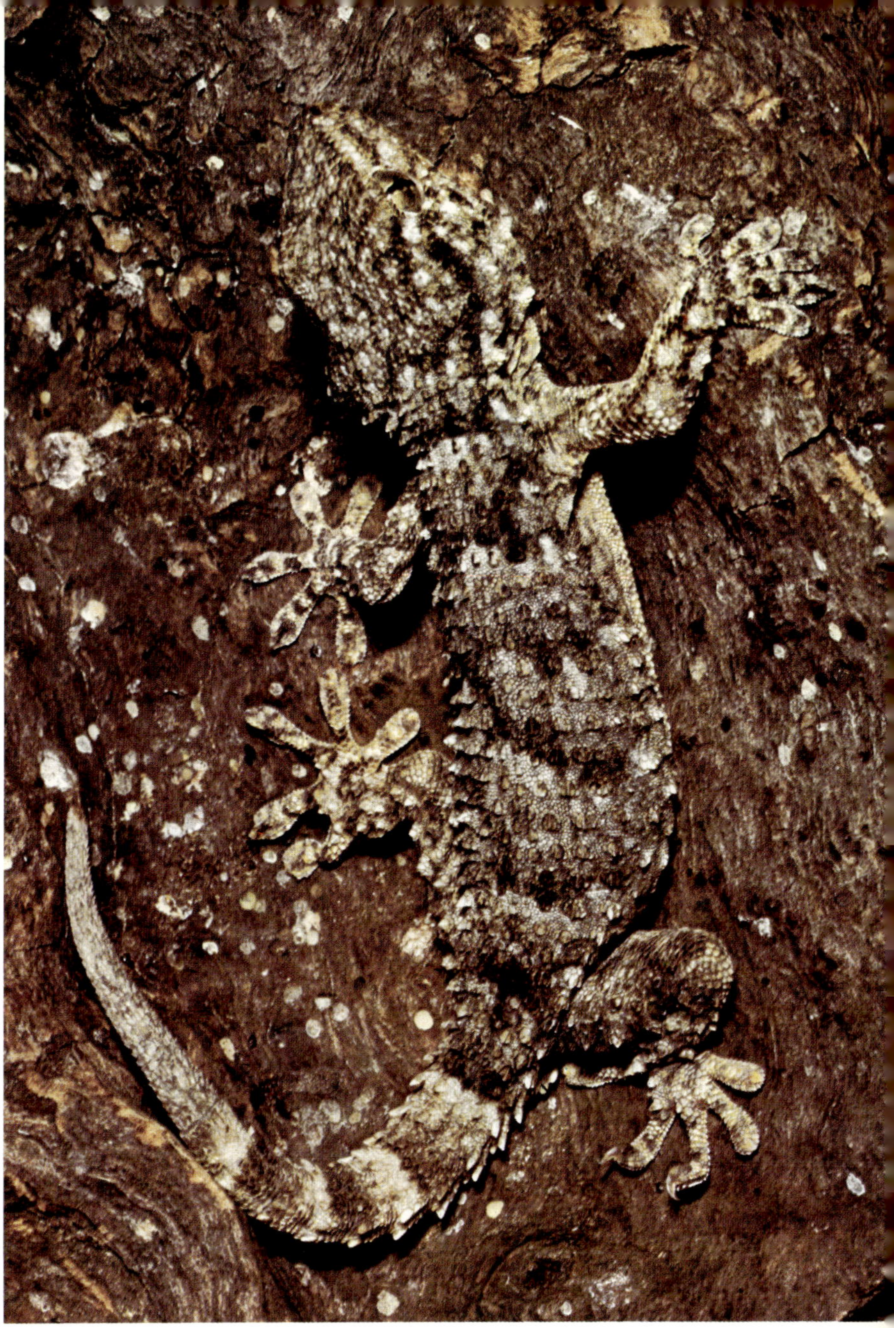

Mauritanian Gecko (x 1·5). Abundant around the Mediterranean, this small lizard can alter the colouring of its skin to match the surface to which it is clinging. The Cork-oak bark dotted with bird-droppings is faithfully imitated by the animal.

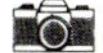

Reproduction ratio: 0·3.
Lens: 105 mm + extension ring.
Aperture: f/22-32.
Electronic flash.

Tiger Moth (x 14).
Suddenly drawing forward its
front wings, it reveals the bright
red pattern of its rear wings to its
surprised and alarmed assailant.
At the same time, it secretes a
toxic substance which also helps
to drive off the unwelcome
intruder.

This type of intimidation is used
as a means of defence by certain
insects which, like the Tiger
Moth, have very conspicuous
colours often called 'warning
colours'. A bird which has tried to
catch the moth will remember its
unpleasant experience and learn to
avoid the insect with gaudy wings
at the next encounter. Protected
by their variegated colours, these
'warning animals' do not attempt
to hide from predators. This is why
the Tiger Moth is always found in
a prominent position, as befits one
whose warning signal deserves
respect.

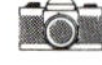

Reproduction ratio: 1·4.
Lens: Macro 55 mm mounted on
bellows.
Aperture: f/22.
A flash, positioned to provide
high-angle illumination from
behind the subject, shines through
the wings of the moth.

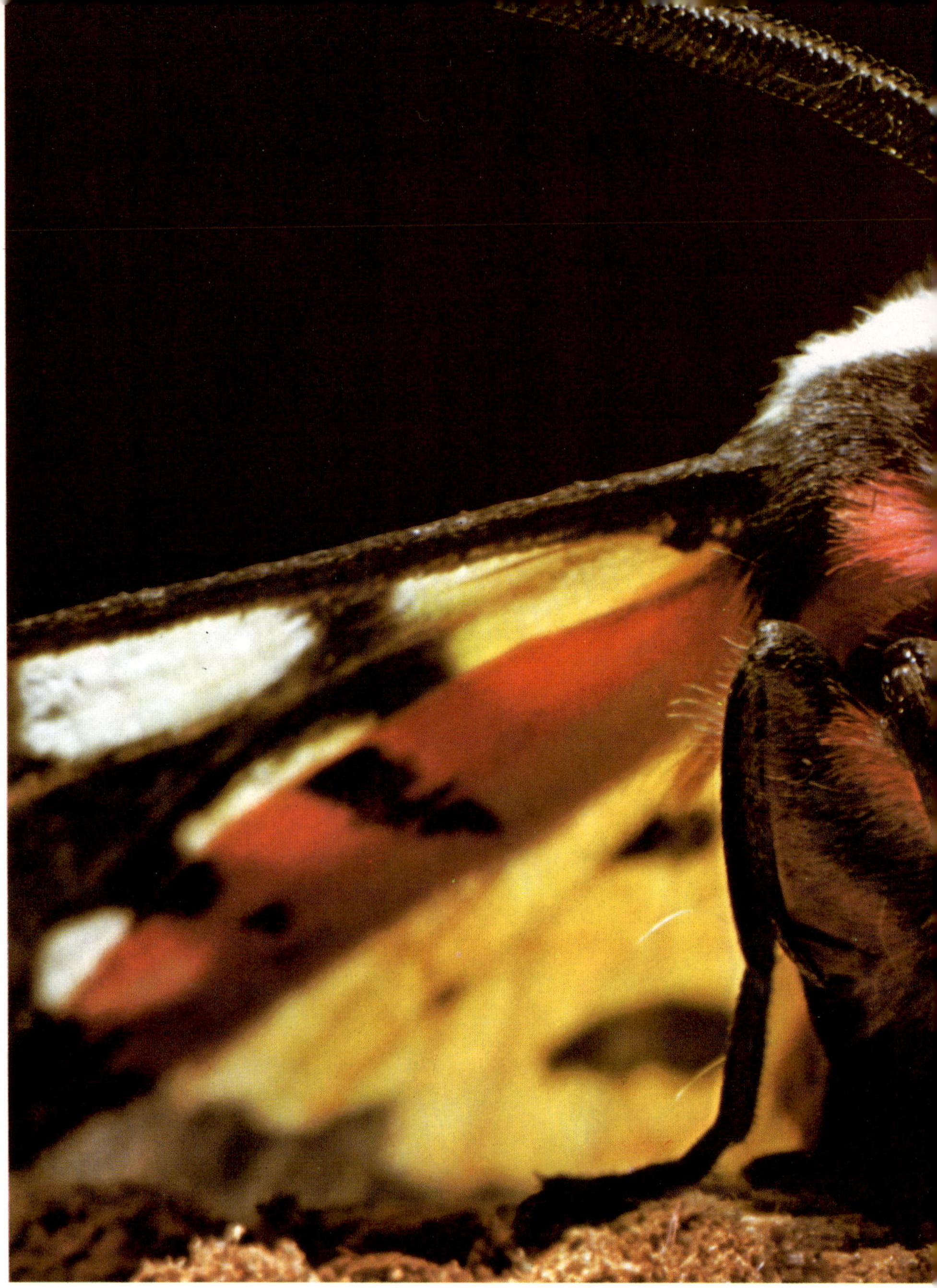

pletely, it simultaneously emits a
toxic substance secreted by its
thoracic glands.

Burnet Moths, although they have
the anatomical characteristics of the
moths, among which they are classified, are active only in the daytime.
Their warning 'code' is made up of
red and black front wings, red rear
wings and a black body. They have a
chemical discouragement device
which can call upon a veritable
'cocktail' consisting of, among other
substances, the redoubtable hydro-
cyanic acid.

During the process of evolution,
these defensive warning procedures
have given proof of their efficacy.
This is so much the case that certain
animals which present no dangerous
features for predators nevertheless
bear the colours of 'warning animals'
and have been able to evolve by
benefitting from the advantages ac-
quired by their models. This is the
phenomenon of mimicry. It is thus
possible for completely harmless
insects to obtain protection to the

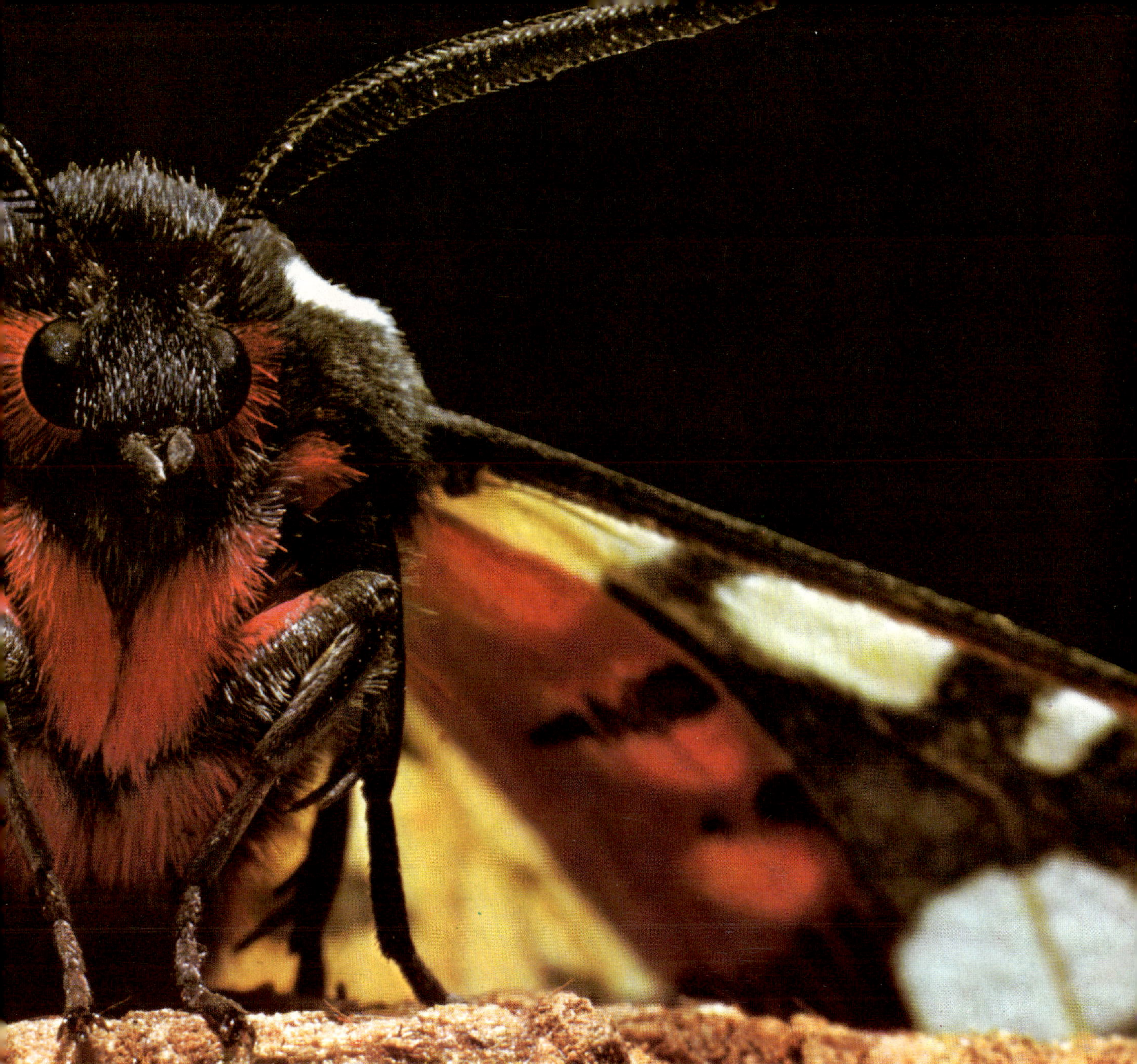

same degree as the wasp, since they show a similar alternation of yellow and black stripes on their abdomens. Among the flies, the Syrphids have adopted this warning disguise. The Lepidoptera (the butterflies and moths) also include such mimics: the Bee Hawk-moths, not content with merely adopting the character-istic abdominal stripes of the wasp, have carried the imitation further to the extent of providing themselves with narrow transparent wings which are completely aberrant for a moth.

All is not what it seems – animal camouflage

It is, however, possible for the rambler to make much more subtle discoveries than of those animal forms which are so ready to attract attention. To do this he should interrupt his walk and simply crouch down in the grass. He would then

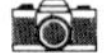

have adopted the customary position of a naturalist, a little strange perhaps, but it has its advantages. He rapidly reduces his normal height to something which approaches the scale of the creatures he is studying.

He will discover amidst the static vegetation a swarming mass of animal life, unobtrusive but very active. Fascinated by the incredible diversity of their shapes and by their complex behaviour, the laws of which he knows nothing about though sensing their faultless logic, he stops to watch them. He has just taken the first step in exploring a new world — that of short distances.

Numerous creatures he had never before noticed gradually appear before his eyes. He might overlook them several times before noticing their presence, so well do they blend, in appearance and posture, with their surroundings. However, a closer examination reveals the extraordinary ingenuity of the ornamental patterns which, though sober at first sight, hide a wealth of dazzling colours.

The vital necessity of being inconspicuous

The need for this persistent quest for inconspicuousness is dictated by the basic forces on which the survival of the species depends. Not all animals have the advantage of possessing the convincing means of defence of the 'warning animals', and only a comparatively limited number of species practise mimicry.

The strict but effective law of the struggle for existence presents living creatures with a double imperative — to eat and not be eaten. Flight or discouragement are often sufficient to ensure the safety of the animal. The more subtle method of camouflage offers the advantage of satisfying on occasion both conditions for survival. Being better concealed, the predator lying in wait has a greater chance of surprising his prey, and of

escaping from predators of larger size. During the long process of evolution, the conditions of life on earth have resulted in the selection of the species best fitted to avoid detection, thus encouraging the evolution of the most varied methods in the progress towards invisibility.

Cloaks of invisibility

Animals which spend most of their time among abundant vegetation quite naturally obtain inspiration from plant-life for their disguise. Mantises, grasshoppers, frogs and lizards have thus adopted 'chlorophyl' hues to hide their animal nature. Biologists have given the name 'homochromy' (etymologically 'of the same colour') · to these methods of camouflage which are based on coloration. The efficacy of such disguise is often reinforced by behaviour. The frog remains motionless among the water-plants, allowing only its nostrils and its two large eyes to protrude above the surface of the water. The Great Green Grasshopper, the delicate green colour of which harmonises perfectly with the long grass, has recourse to a curious stratagem reminiscent of the game of hide-and-seek. As soon as the insect becomes aware of your approach, it changes its position slightly so that the stalk to which it is clinging is between the intruder and itself. If you move to one side to see it better, it will repeat its manoeuvre as often as you move to the other side. Only when it considers you to be dangerously close does it finally leap off to find a new hiding-place.

Unfortunately, vegetation is not consistent as far as its colours are concerned. During early autumn, yellow and brown become the dominant hues. Numerous species do not survive to experience the first cold weather of winter: the rapid replacement of colours does not concern them. For others, less ephemeral or passing through several generations a year, the problem remains. The

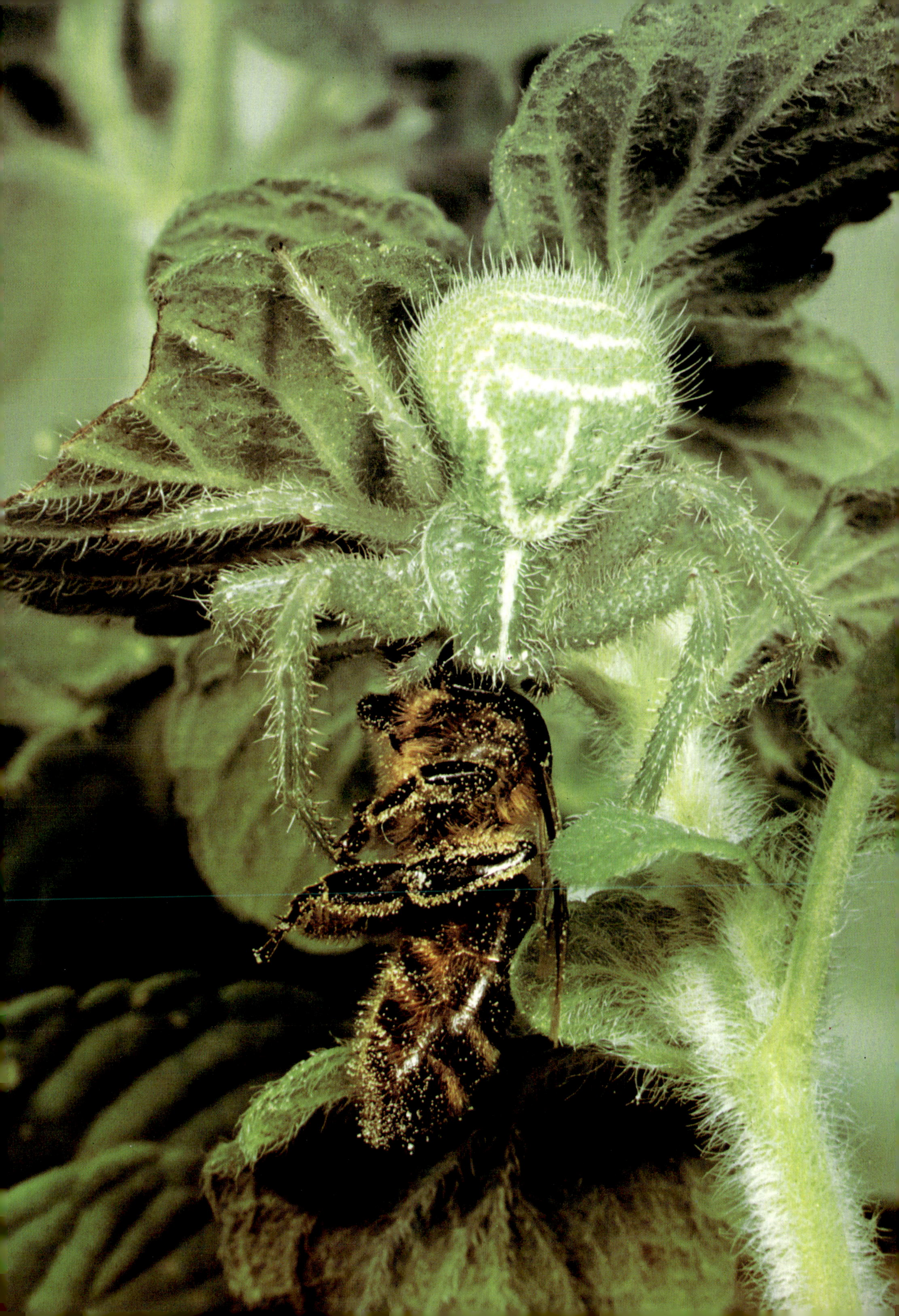

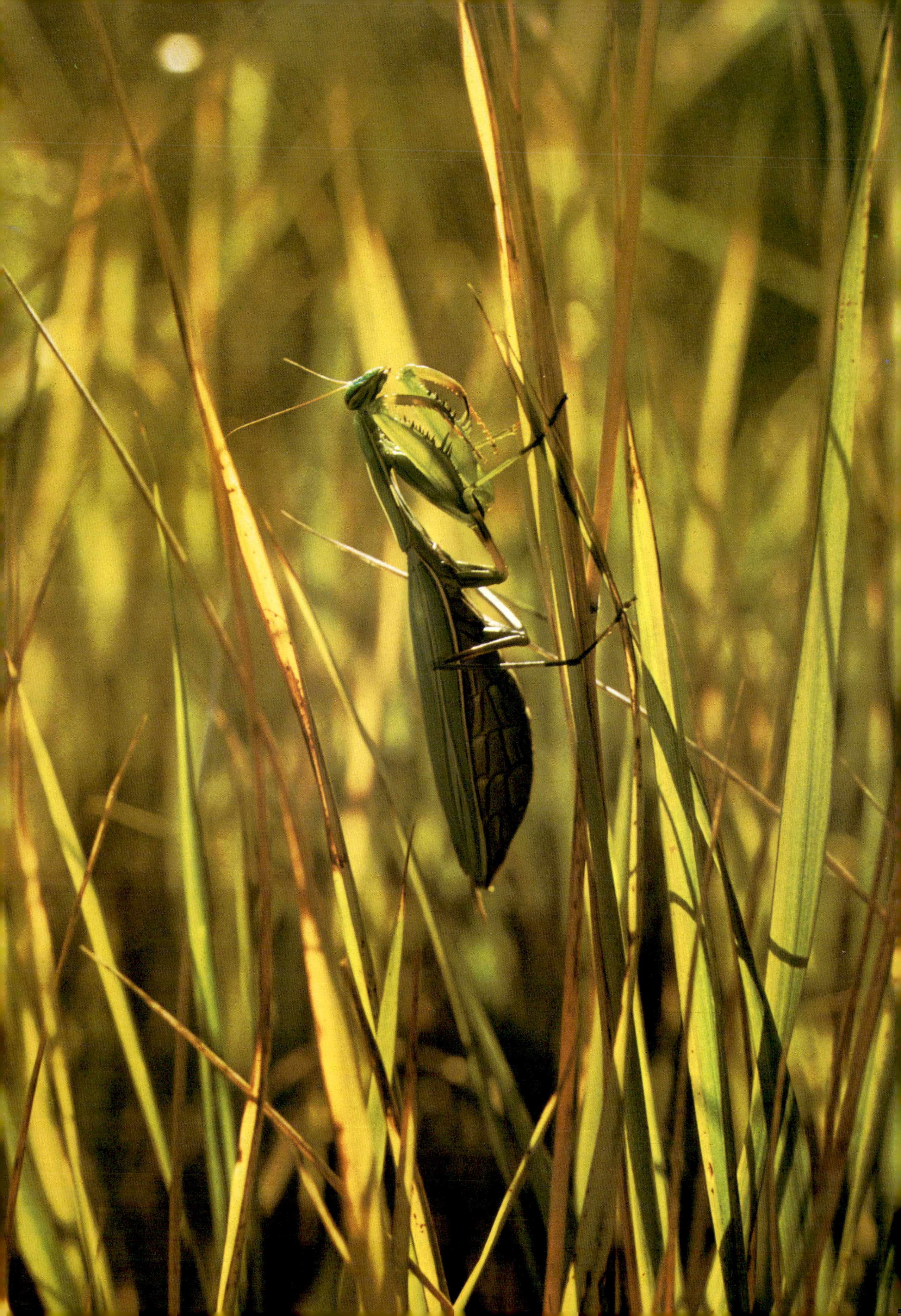

Praying Mantis has for this reason two colour versions: some individuals appear green and others brown, the surroundings dictating which shall be dominant. The 'Truxale' decides its colour according to its generation: this strange Mediterranean cricket has no less than three of them a year. The first, which becomes adult in the middle of summer, is a light green. The second, which appears at the end of the same season, imitates the yellow colour of dry grass. The third, in autumn, is dark green like the vegetation refreshed by the rains.

The same attention to detail is found in the homochromy of the pupae of butterflies. The Swallowtail has two generations a year: the summer pupae are green, but those which have to hibernate are brown.

The chrysalis of the Large Cabbage White Butterfly can adapt much more flexibly: it makes use of a wide range of shades of colour to imitate the surface on which it is found – stone, bark, branch or leaf. The caterpillar, before metamorphosing, actually records the colour to be used in relation to the spot where it has selected to fasten itself.

The large Oedipod Cricket, common in central and southern Europe, shows even greater talent in the art of matching colours. It can appear in a very wide variety of colours but is nevertheless incapable of changing its pigmentation, the precise colour of the insect being fixed permanently at the time it finally moults. After this, throughout its adult life, it must remain at the place which determined its colour in order to benefit from its

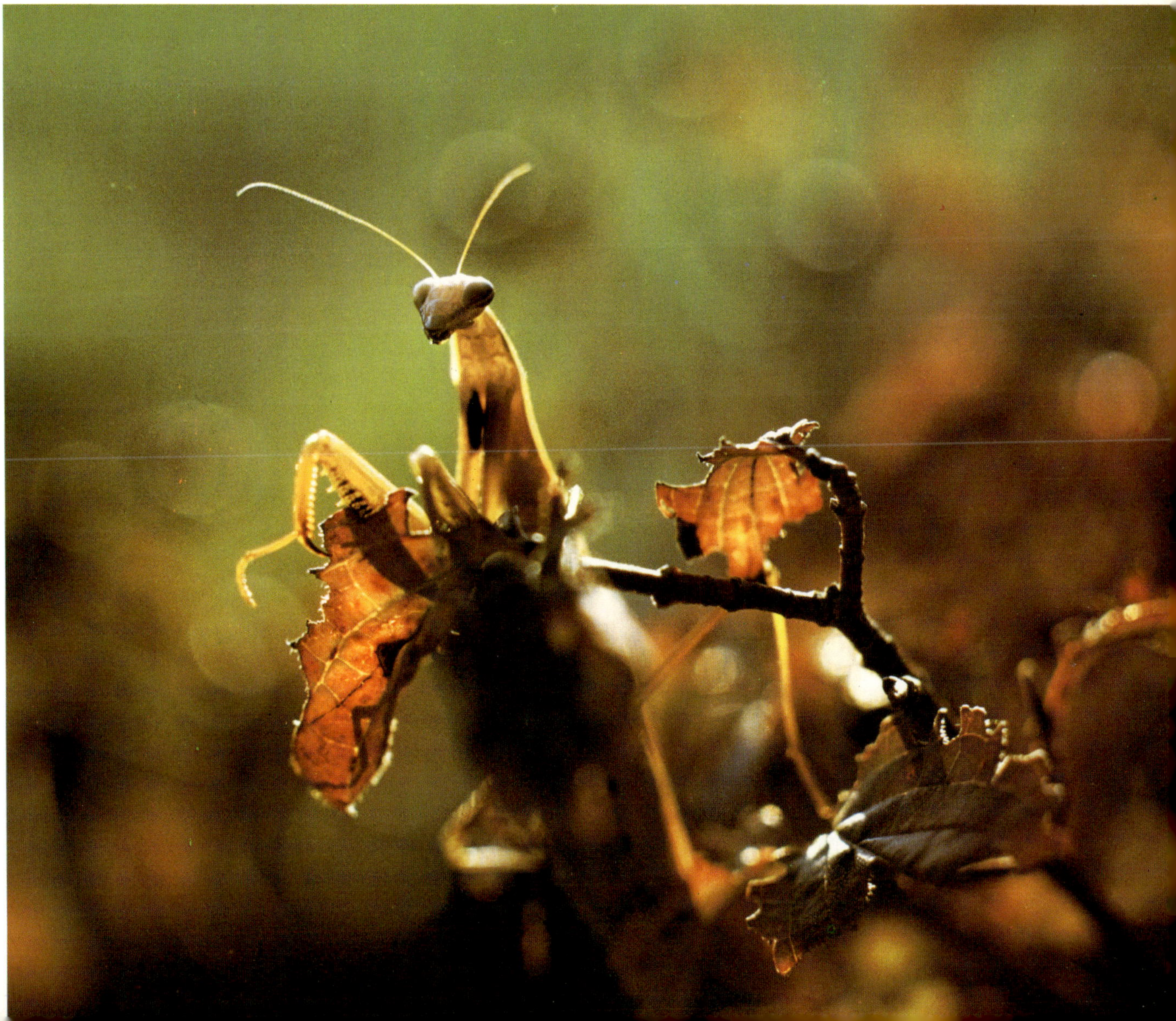

European Tree Frog (x 1·5).
Sitting completely motionless,
with its legs tucked in, on the leaf
of an Agave, it almost escaped our
attention. Like the Chameleon, it
can change its colour to match
its background.

Reproduction ratio: 0·3.
Lens: Macro 55 mm.
Aperture: f/5·6.
Exposure time: 1/125th of a
second.
Natural light.
Film: Kodachrome 25.

astonishingly perfect camouflage. To complete its disguise, it has a further trick up its sleeve, 'flash coloration'. When it is accidentally driven from its position, it takes flight and at the same time uncovers two rear wings vividly coloured red or blue. Like a tracer rocket, it follows a wide trajectory which the eye can easily follow. But on landing all trace of the animal suddenly disappears, and the contrast is so abrupt that the retina, still retaining the impression of the 'flash coloration', is unable to detect the insect in its new guise.

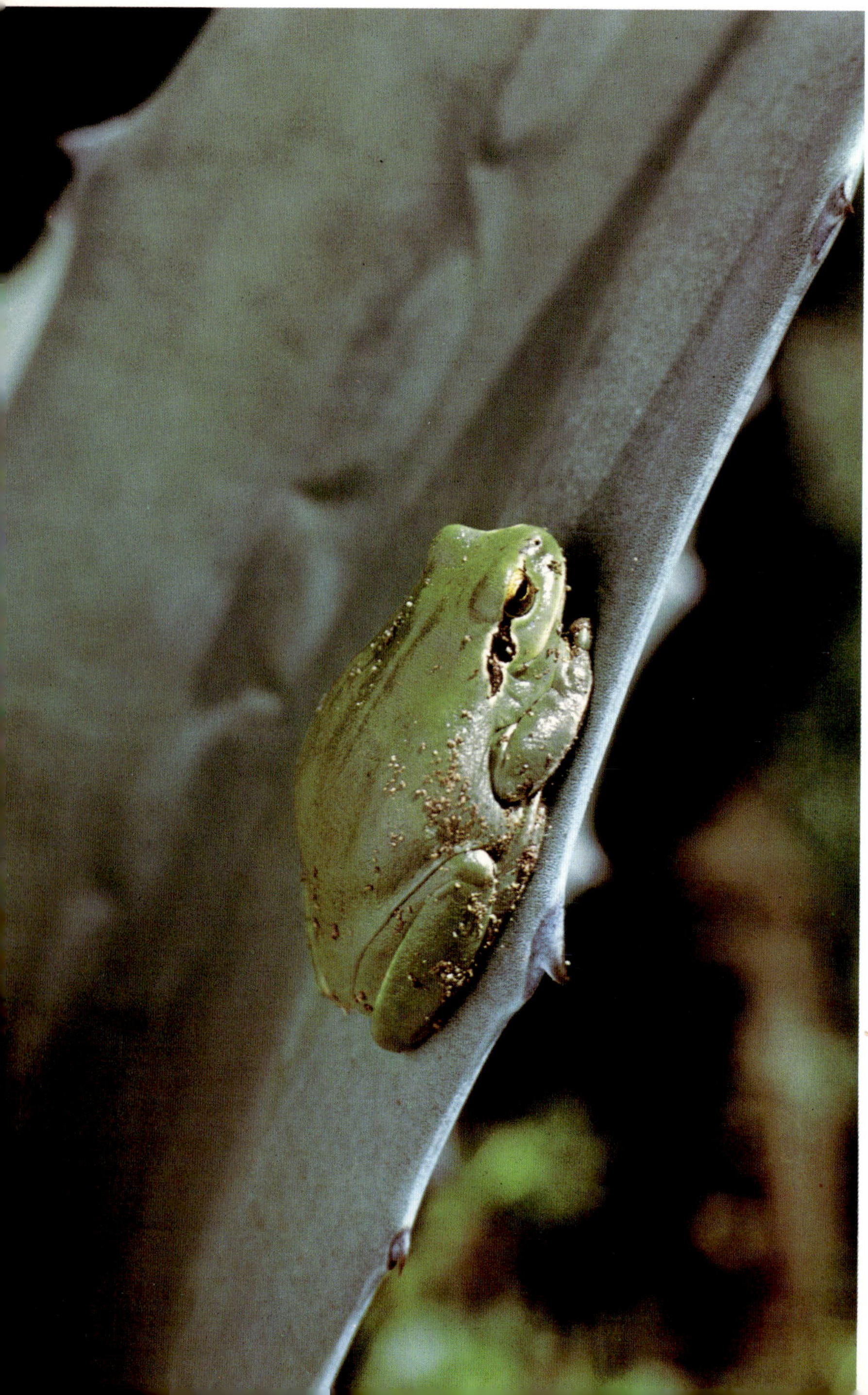

A dress for every occasion

All these methods of camouflage force their users to remain among surroundings of a colour which matches their own. There is, however, a further stratagem which is much more flexible.

It is often thought that the ability to change colour is the prerogative of the famous Chameleon. In fact, a method so capable of ensuring protection could not fail to have evolved a number of times within the world of living creatures. It has, for example, been put to profitable use by a family of spiders known as the Crab Spiders by reason of their occasional sideways method of locomotion.

These spiders do not use a web to catch their prey. All they have to do is lie in wait in the centre of a flower, the colour of which they assume. With their front legs held wide open and their poison fangs ready for use, they quickly seize insects which arrive intent on collecting honey but which fall victim by failing to detect the danger lurking in the object of their desire. By choosing as their post for lying in wait a source of nectar which cannot fail to attract numerous victims, these spiders use the same stratagem as wild beasts which wait for their prey at water-holes. If it changes its resting place, the Crab Spider can change its colour as necessary to take on the exact shade of its model. It requires, however, a few days to achieve a perfect match.

The little European Tree Frog changes colour much more quickly. By virtue of a reflex mechanism which responds to visual signals received by the animal, pigment cells in the skin can become modified in a few minutes. The Tree Frog further enhances this ability by adopting a position of rest which reveals nothing of its real nature. Using the adhesive pads at the ends of its digits to cling closely to the supporting surface, it tucks its four feet in beneath it so that

they melt into the shape of the body and form a completely homogeneous and enamel-smooth whole. It is by no means easy to recognize this plain plant-coloured swelling as an amphibian.

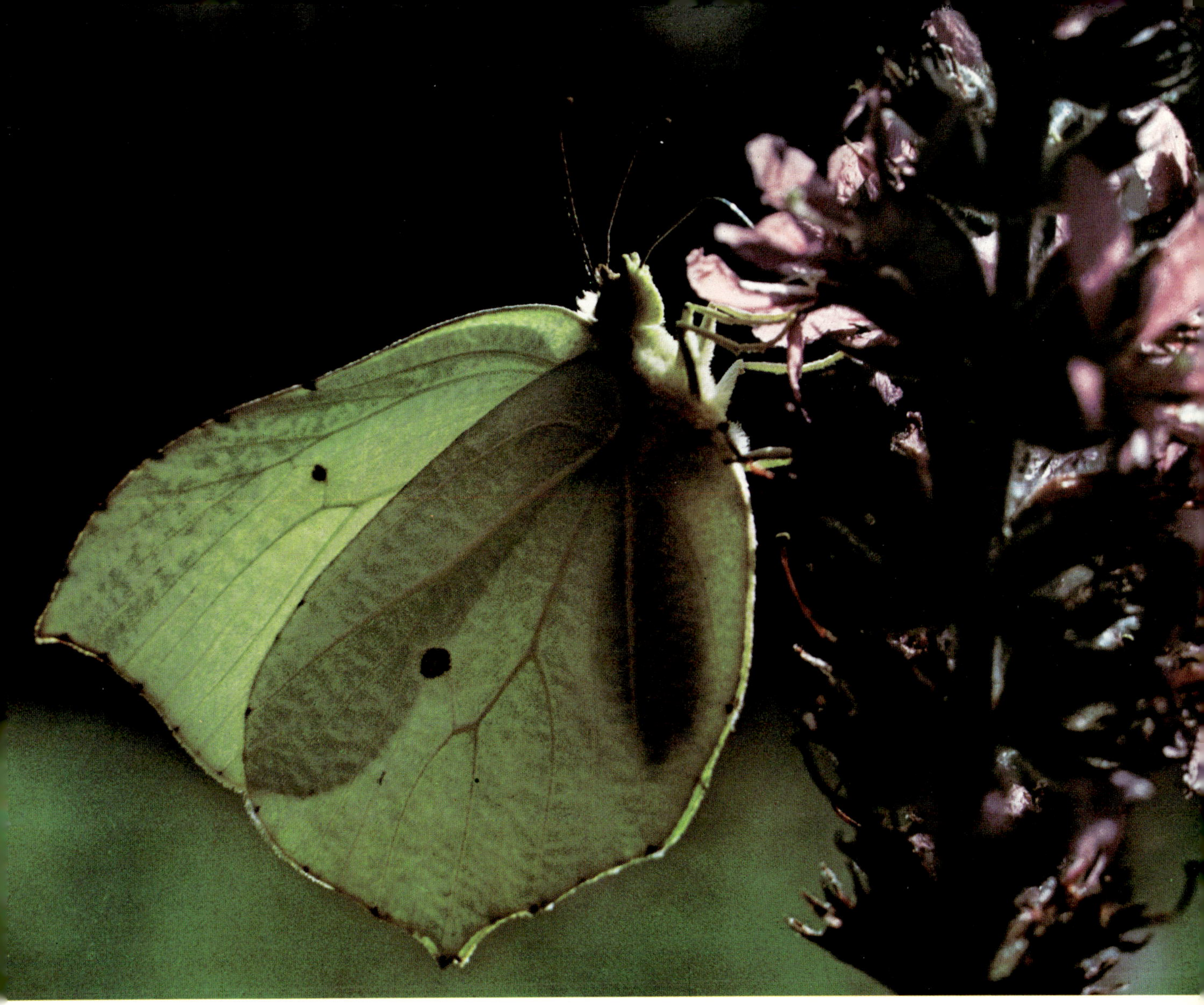

These methods of camouflage would be only partly effective if they were not supplemented by certain artifices. In fact, all these creatures have a characteristic outline which predators could easily identify if their prey were uniformly coloured. To overcome this handicap, they frequently adopt 'disruptive' patterns – stripes, spots or splashes of colour which break up their outline. Their shape is subdivided into small fragments which bear no obvious re-lationship to each other while the animal remains motionless. This is a trick which man has copied for purposes of making war – the parachutist's uniform is an excellent example of disruptive colours.

In the case of the little green Tree Frog, its colour is as uniform as though it had been painted with a coat of gloss paint, except on either side of the head where a wide black stripe encloses the dark pupil of the eye, the only clue which might have revealed the true nature of the animal. Many species use this method of making their otherwise conspicuous eyes 'disappear' by including them in an appropriately positioned stripe. Snakes, which

Brimstone Butterfly (x 2).
Although its wings are reminiscent of fine-veined leaves, the butterfly does not seem to make use of this resemblance in order to hide. This one was found early in the morning, with its proboscis extended, as it was feeding on nectar from the flowers of the Evening Primrose.

Reproduction ratio: 0·4.
Lens: Macro 55 mm.
Aperture: f/4.
Exposure time: 1/60th of a second.
Natural light from behind, so that the abdomen is silhouetted between the rear wings.
Film: Kodachrome 64.

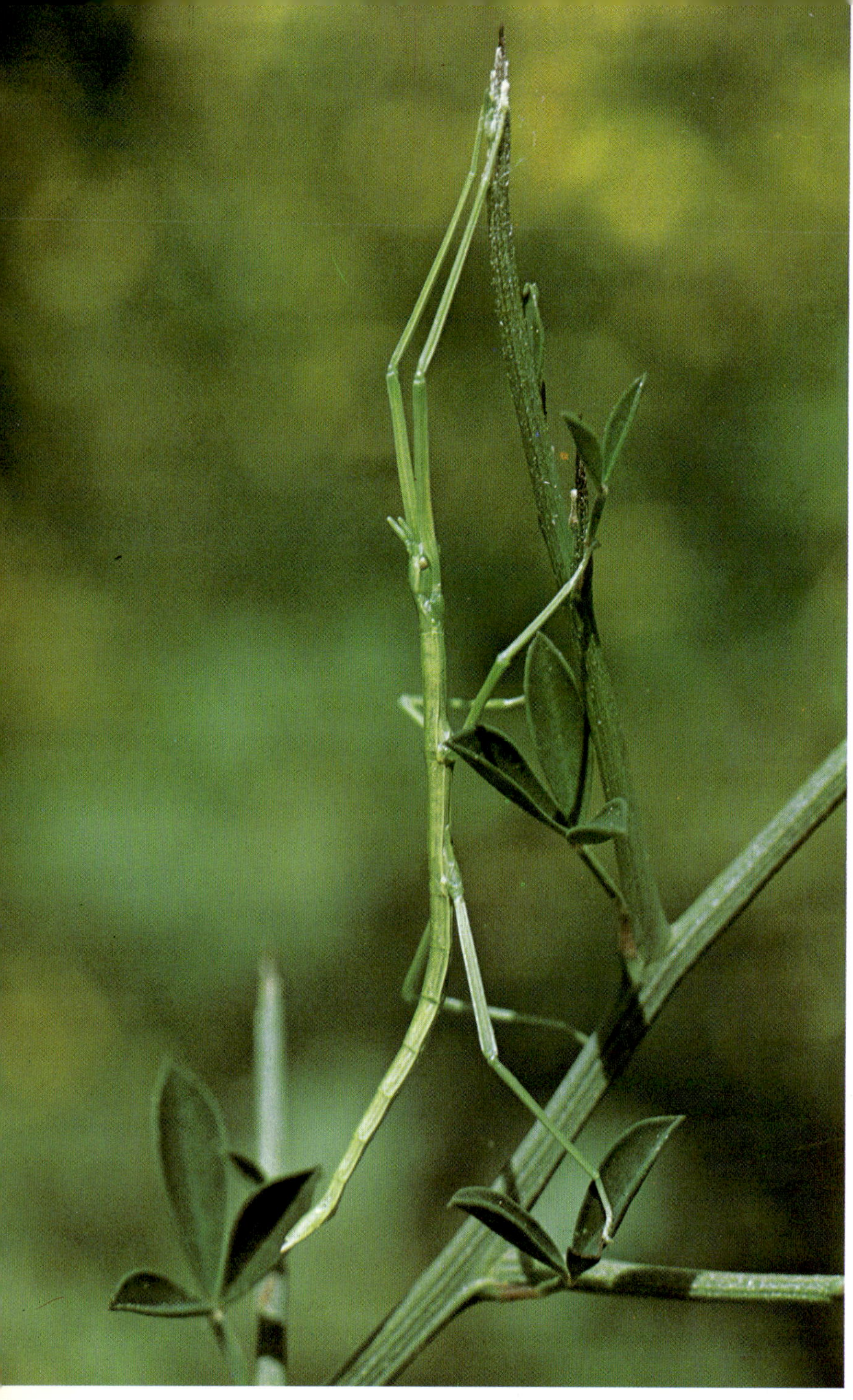

Above: Stick Insect imitating twigs of Broom (x 2). Natural light.

Opposite: The larva of an Empusa (a close relative of the Mantis) lying in wait (x 5). Electronic flash directed downwards on to the subject. A second flash is used to illuminate the background.

could easily be betrayed by their extended shape, make great use of such misleading patterns. Numerous stripes arranged perpendicularly on their sides hide their presence when they are resting in a coiled position.

True copies

In their quest for invisibility, certain animals have evolved to the point of presenting an appearance similar to that of their background support. These are 'true copies' in the real sense. The similarity of colour is supplemented by the similarity of shape: the illusion is complete.

The Looper Caterpillars of the family Geometridae imitate broken twigs. Fastening itself to a branch by means of its two end pairs of claspers, the caterpillar raises its body at an angle, maintaining its position by a fine thread of silk spanning the distance between its head and the branch supporting it. The similarity is further increased by protuberances on its skin, resembling the leaf scars which can be seen on twigs after the leaves have fallen. More than one gardener has been fooled into cutting off a caterpillar with his secateurs, thinking it to be a twig.

However, the champion in this field is without doubt the Stick Insect. In France it is called the Devil's Stick, because its powers of mimicry seem almost supernatural. Just as a slight movement is about to reveal the presence of an insect, all that can be seen a moment later is a lifeless tangle of twigs. However, the insect is certainly there, with its thread-like legs and body invisible among the branches.

If, with practice, you are able to locate it and try to pick it up, it will fall to the ground, as stiff as a rod, with its legs held tightly against its body. Among the twigs which litter the ground, it is very difficult to detect. On many occasions, when breeding Stick Insects, we have picked up small pieces of dead branch to throw them away, only to find them come to life in the bottom of the dustbin, revealing their insect nature at the last moment.

The laws of observation

Anyone who wishes to observe and photograph these living forms might

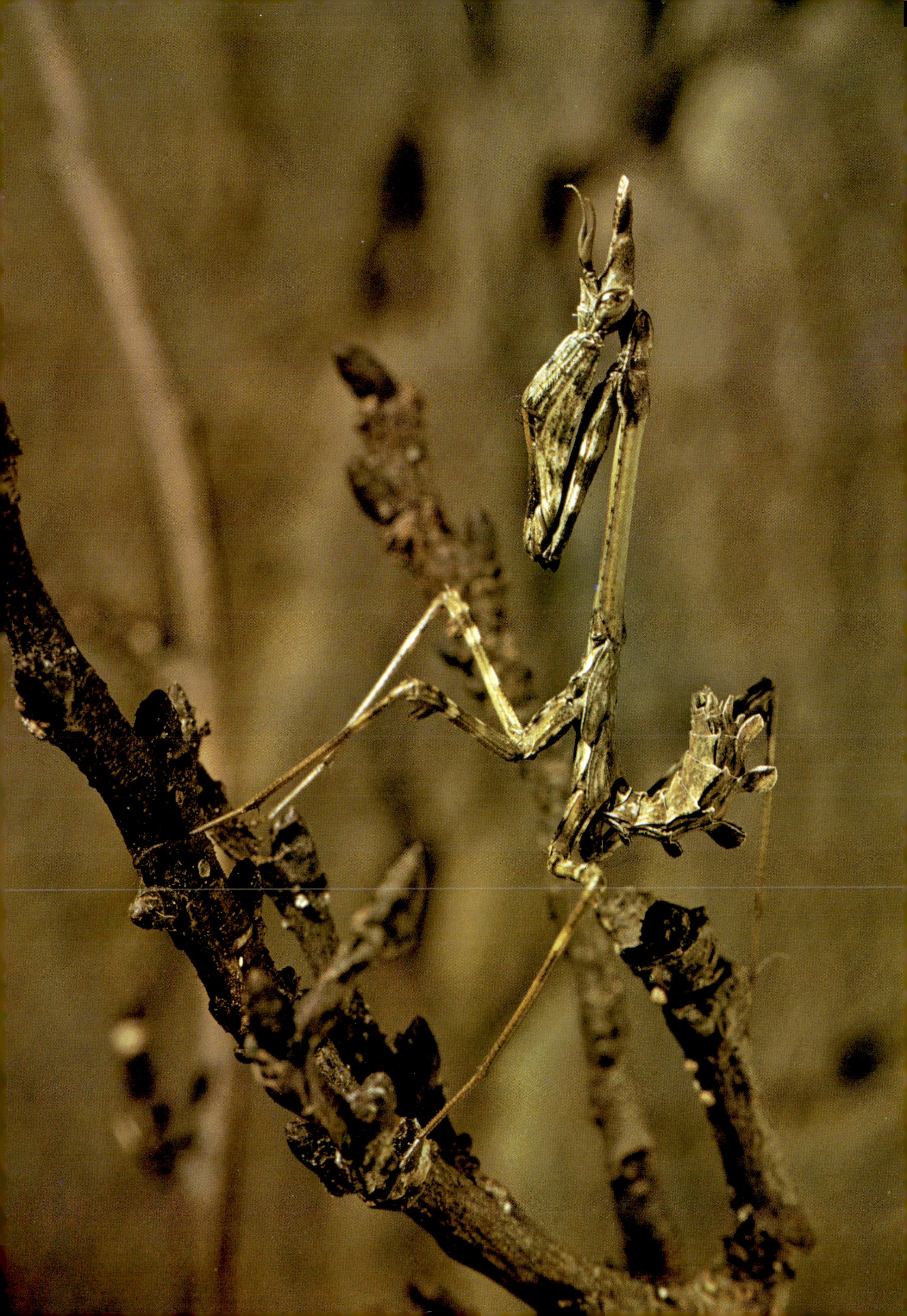

be disturbed by such an accumulation of means of deceiving the eye, but a certain amount of knowledge, supported by resolute determination, makes it possible to overcome these obstacles. Even birds, prompted by the powerful motivation of hunger, have been seen to succeed in detecting motionless stick insects. Cannot the insatiable curiosity of the naturalist generate the same concentration in the search for 'prey'? To guide him in his search, there are numerous reference books which will provide him with information on the time of appearance and the preferred environment of each species. Many insects, for example, are strictly limited to one or more species of food plant. Rossi's Stick Insect from

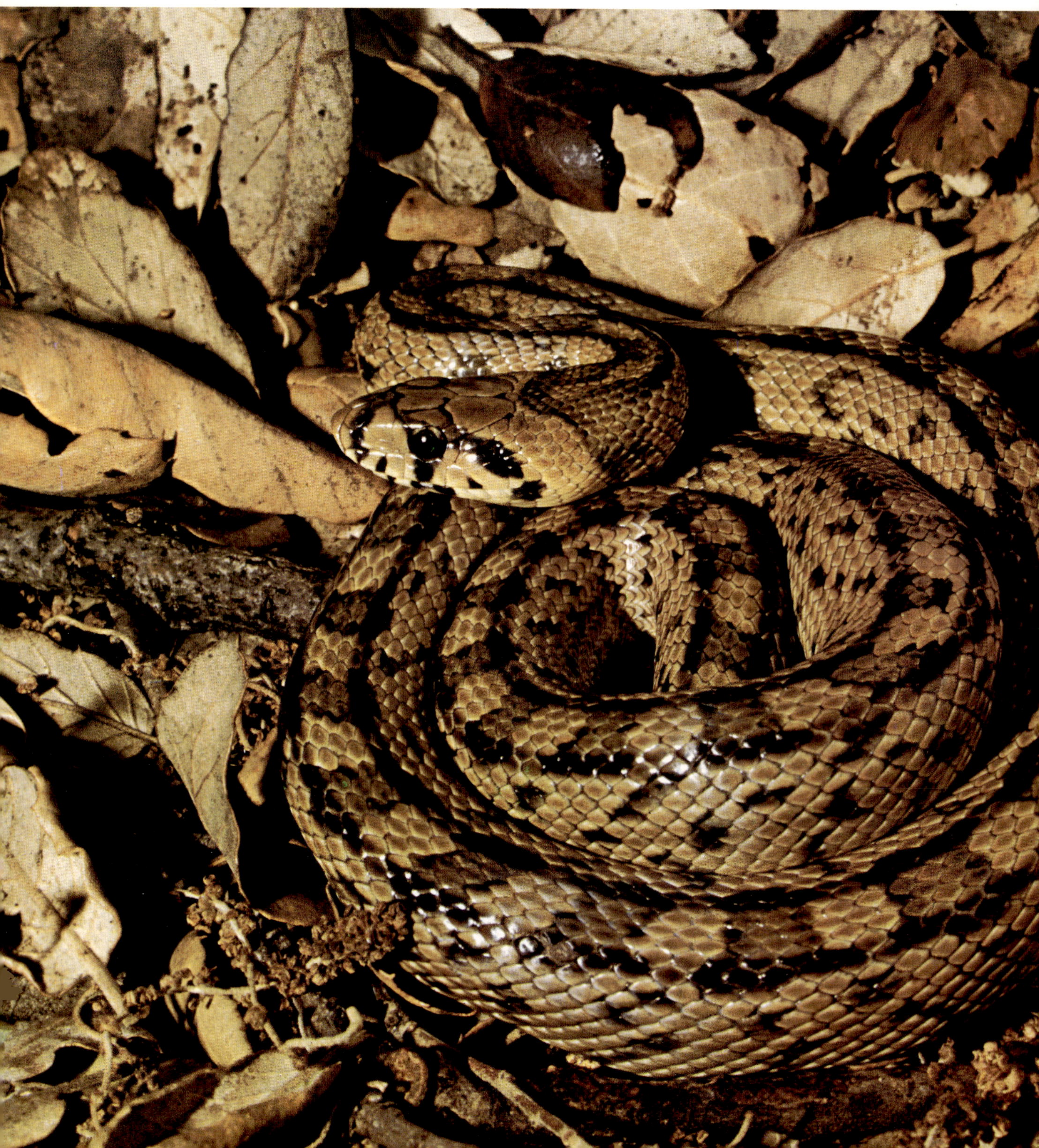

the Mediterranean region lives principally on brooms and gorses. Depending on the time of year and the place in which he finds himself, the naturalist knows which kinds of animal he might expect to find. He has a picture of them in his mind, which cannot fail to sharpen his observation. With the help of experience, the brief descriptions found in books are supplemented by a knowledge – to some extent intuitive – of the habitats favoured by different species. The mushroom-collector may be quite unable to explain exactly where to find chanterelles, for example, but in the field he makes no mistakes when it comes to selecting the area in which to look for them. This is because he makes subconscious use of a large number of insignificant clues, which he has progressively associated in his mind with the presence of this particular plant. Such premeditated investigations do not exclude the possibility of unexpectedly finding a rare species or an individual which has strayed away from its normal habitat. The discovery of a new subject for study is often purely a matter of chance.

The actual method of photography makes it possible to evade the subterfuges employed by animals using mimicry. The strictly limited size of a photograph, which restricts the animal to a small portion of its background, is sufficient to expose the deception. Precise focusing to make the subject stand out more clearly against a less sharply-defined background will accentuate the effect of disclosure. It is up to the photographer to decide whether his exposure should respect the camouflage or unmask it, the ideal solution no doubt being found in a balance between these extremes.

It is difficult to gain a true insight into Nature without making the effort to understand the laws by which its inhabitants are governed. The outward appearance of plants and animals is never a naturally 'pure' one. The interaction between living creatures depends entirely on this consideration. It is the image it receives from others which guides an animal in its attitude – aggressive, conciliatory or indifferent. Can the photographer, ensconced behind his view-finder, afford to ignore such delicate assessments? What facts would his pictures then show other than those everyone knows already?

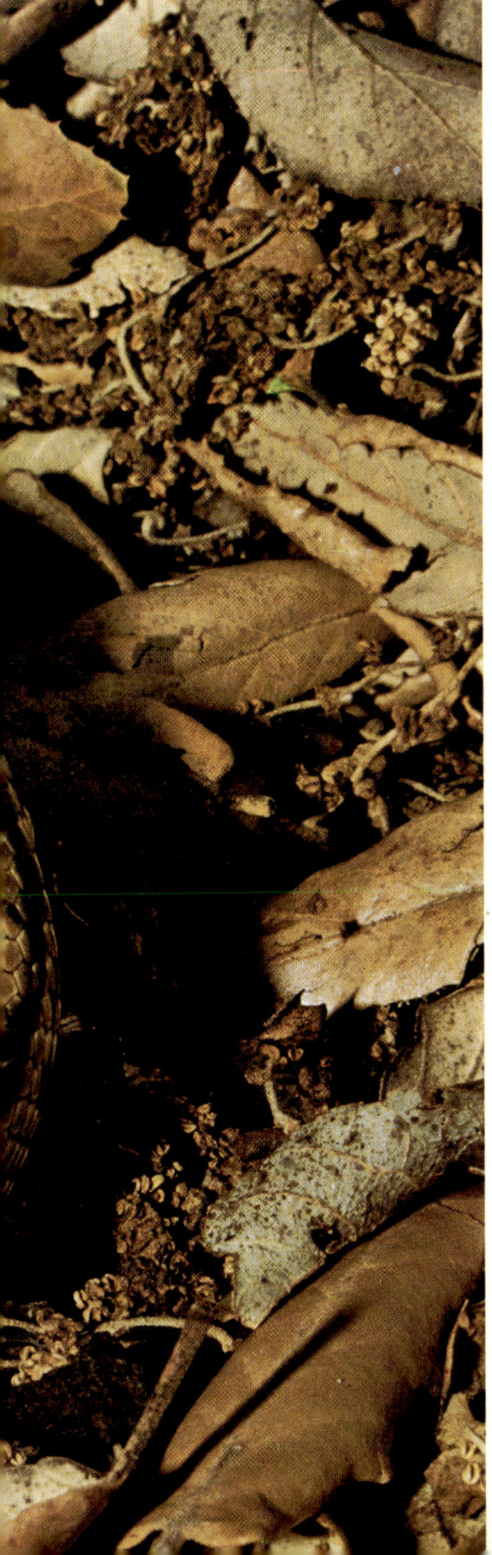

Ladder Snake (x 1·2).
Its colour pattern, consisting of dark cross-bands, breaks up its extended outline. It thus remains unobserved among the vegetable debris strewn on the ground.

Numerous animals — mammals, birds, amphibians and insects — use this method of concealment based on an optical illusion. The 'disruptive' markings — stripes, spots and blotches — and the colour-pattern harmonising with the dominant colours of the habitat obliterate the outlines of the animal when motionless and make it blend into the background.

Reproduction ratio: 0·15.
Lens: 105 mm with extension.
Aperture: f/16-22.
Electronic flash.

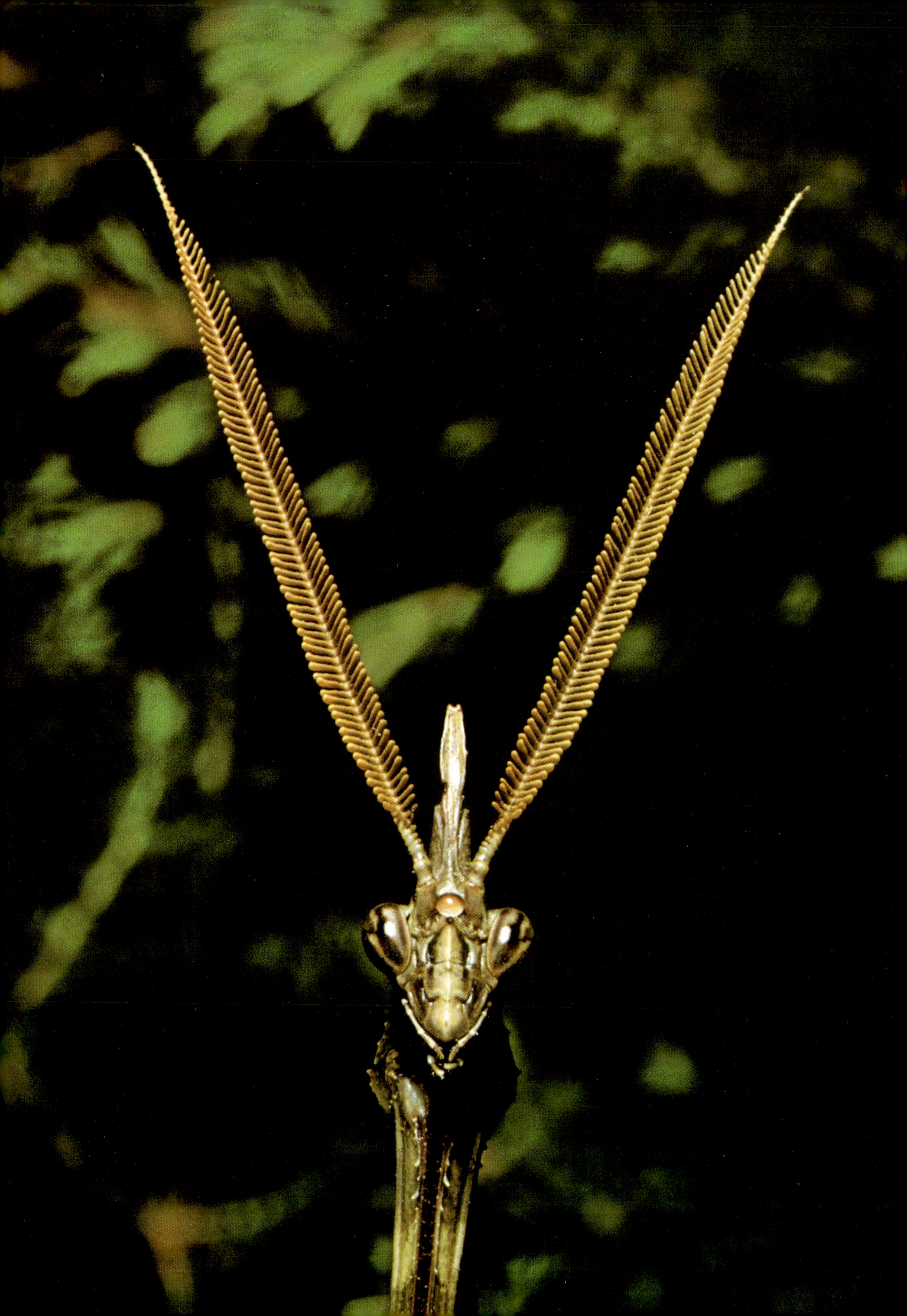

Observer and photographer

Perfecting the human eye

Descartes, in his work on dioptrics, wrote at the end of the 17th Century: 'The entire conduct of our lives depends on our senses, among which that of sight being the most universal and the most noble, there is no doubt whatever that inventions which serve to increase its power are the most useful there can be.'

Within two well-established limits the eye is able, thanks to the process of accommodation, to give a clear image of objects situated at varying distances. By inventing the astronomical telescope on the one hand and the magnifying glass and the microscope on the other hand, man has broken through, or at least pushed back, these barriers of the infinitely far and the infinitely close and has thus been able to increase the power of his sight, just as Descartes had hoped.

In this book we have chosen to devote all our attention to the lower limit, that of short distances. It has to be accepted that the minimum distance at which vision is possible over a period is around ten inches (25 cm). Under these circumstances, the eye is able to distinguish objects measuring ·004 of an inch (1/10th of a millimetre). By altering the shape of its crystalline lens, the eye is still able to achieve accommodation if an object is brought as close as about six inches (15 cm), but the eye then quickly becomes fatigued, so that it is necessary to break off the examination.

Certain individuals are better than others at seeing things very close to them – these are myopic or short-sighted people. This is their compensation for being unable to enjoy distant horizons. With their eyes an inch or two from the subject, they can distinguish minute details which are invisible to others, without suffering excessive fatigue (provided they have taken off their glasses!). Perhaps the mania that short-sighted people have for examining everything at close quarters which is one way of making the best of things – has determined the vocation of more than one naturalist (this is to some extent the case with one of the authors, who is fortunate enough to enjoy myopia).

Quite naturally, man has looked for ways of improving his close-up vision by voluntarily making himself short-sighted with the aid of a convergent lens interposed between his eye and the subject. The use of magnifying glasses of this kind can be traced back to the beginning of the 14th Century in Italy, around which time there also appeared the first corrective spectacles (these received, in fact, only a limited welcome because the number of people who could read was very small!). However it was not until the 17th Century that optical systems of sufficient power to be properly called microscopes were made. A draper of Delft, Antoine Van Leeuwenhoek, an enlightened amateur who had a passion for the creations of Nature, developed the technique of polishing lenses

Head of an Empusa (x 7·5). Like the Praying Mantis, the Empusa lies in wait for its prey and is mainly found on the wastelands of Southern Europe. Only the male has these enormous comb-like antennae.

This strange and fascinating insect, with its extremely elegant movements, bears the name of a highly disconcerting being from Greek mythology. The Empusa was a formidable spirit serving Hecate, the Goddess of Magic. It could appear in a wide variety of forms, sometimes appearing as a seductive maiden who attracted young men in order to devour them – not unlike the nuptial habits of mantises.

Reproduction ratio: 1.
Lens: Macro 55 mm with automatic extension.
Aperture: f/22-32.
Electronic flash.
Film: Kodachrome 25.

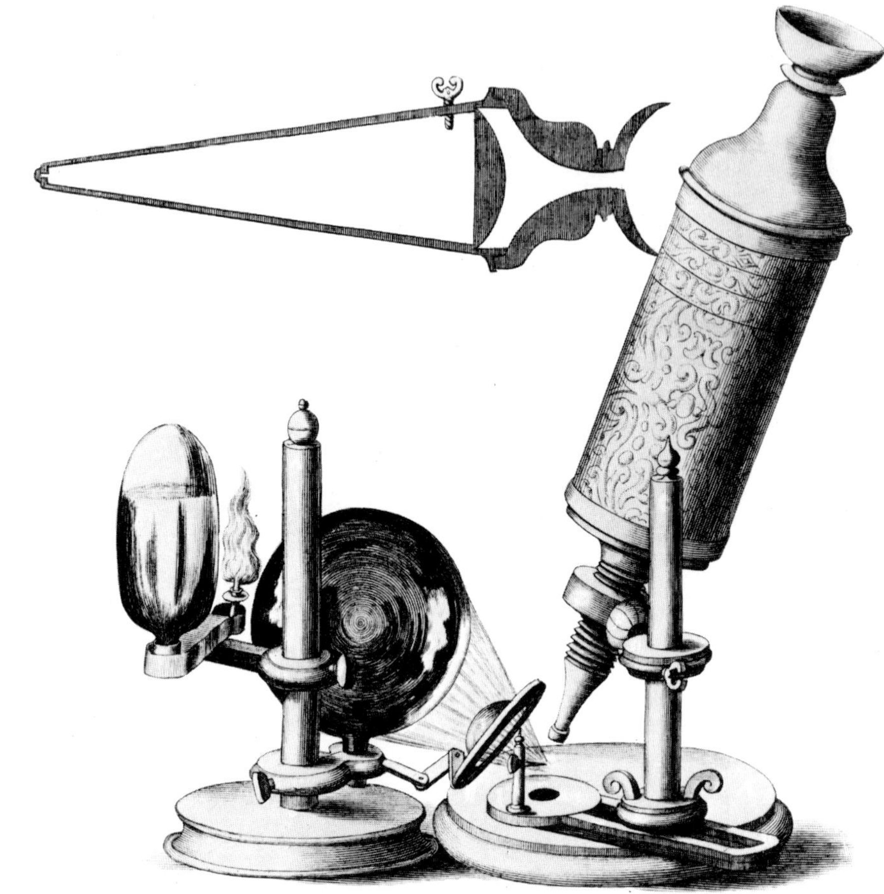

Below: Aplanatic magnifying glasses.

1 Glass of 8-power magnification, with holder which folds over and covers the lens to protect it when closed; for observation in the field.

2 Glass of 10-power magnification, mounted on a hinged arm: for observation in the laboratory.

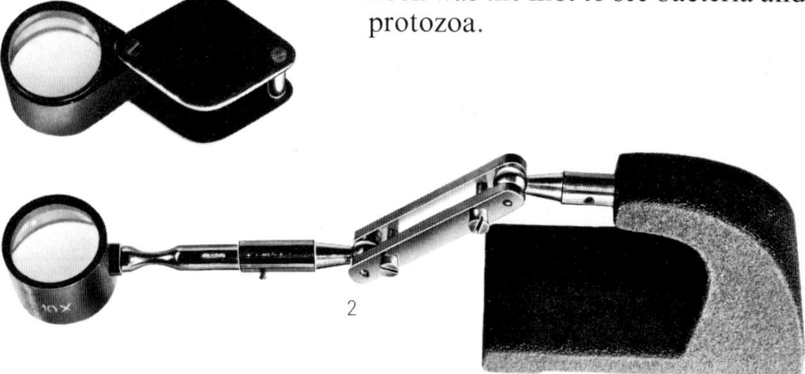

to a degree of perfection which dazzled his contemporaries. Moreover, he kept his methods of manufacture to himself. He built more than four hundred 'microscopes', the most powerful of which provided a magnification of 250 times. They consisted of a simple bead of glass, almost spherical in shape, set in a copper plate. With the aid of this very rudimentary instrument, Leeuwenhoek was the first to see bacteria and protozoa.

Paradoxically, the true ancestors of the modern microscope, consisting of two optical systems, the objective lens and the eye-piece lens, appeared before the simple microscopes of Leeuwenhoek. They were based on the principle that it is possible to increase the power of a magnifying glass by combining a lens with it; this lens, positioned at some distance from the magnifying glass, magnifies the image provided by the latter. Galileo, modifying the principle of his astronomical telescope, was one of the first to build a composite microscope. The image obtained from this was much poorer than that given by a simple magnifying glass; in fact the second glass (the eye-piece lens), by magnifying the image obtained from the first (the objective lens), also increased the optical defects of the latter and at the same time added its own. It was, therefore, not until the beginning of the 19th Century that a microscope was made which was capable of improving on the performance of Leeuwenhoek's small glass bead.

All the early magnifying instruments had one fault in common – they gave the observer terrible eye-strain.

For the amateur naturalist of today, magnifying glasses remain a useful accessory. We can recommend the use of a small aplanatic glass having two lenses (the image obtained is not blurred at the margin like that provided by an ordinary magnifying glass), magnifying 8 or 10 times, mounted on a hinged stand from which it can be removed for use when you need to hold it in your hand. Such hand magnifiers are used by most opticians. Certain kinds furnished with a folding handle are very practical for use in the field. They make it necessary, however, to observe at a distance (about 2 centimetres or 4/5ths of an inch for a magnification of 10 times), which rather limits their use to the examination of plants or small creatures held in the hand. The microscope takes over for higher magnifications (10 to 1500 times) but obviously involves laboratory work (we shall discuss this later in the paragraph dealing with photography using a microscope).

The binocular magnifier (10 to 150 times magnification) provides a stereoscopic view (in relief) of small objects by virtue of its two coupled lenses, mounted so that they slightly converge. Although very easy to use, it unfortunately cannot be employed in photography since it is obviously impossible to record the impression of relief in a single photograph.

However, the lens of a camera equipped for close-up photography is undoubtedly the best form of magnifying glass. In fact, it makes it possible for us to record a given scene of insect life or a particular detail in the structure of a flower at the very moment when we are fascinated by

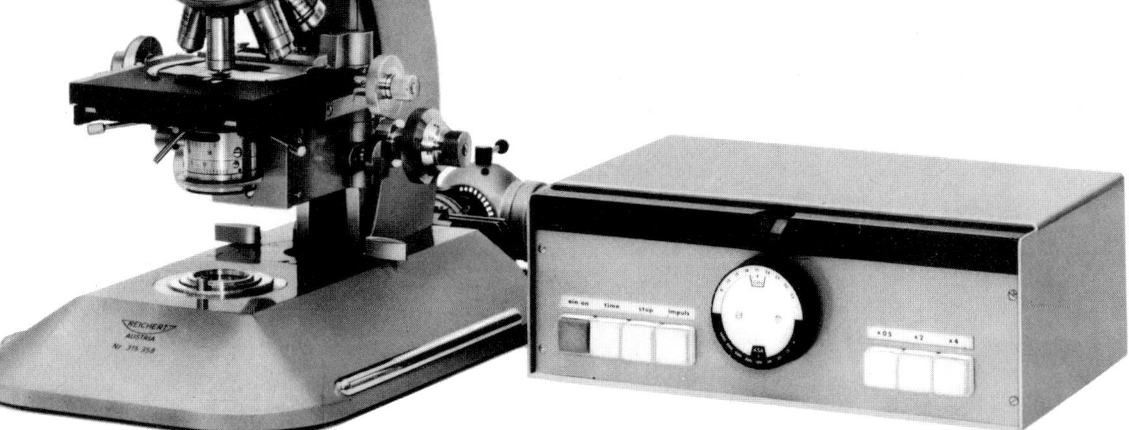

A large modern research microscope. This Zetopan, made by Reichart, provides for multiple lighting techniques and automatic exposure. Six lenses mounted on a rotary turret. Observation by binocular head. Variable-magnification eyepiece (zoom). Automatic exposure with built-in photoelectric cell. Film wound on by electric motor.

its discovery. It is difficult to follow many of the happenings which take place in a world of Lilliputian dimensions. In an area of a few square centimetres or inches, there is often room for only one pair of human eyes. Photography makes it possible to communicate to everyone these wonderful events, so often experienced alone.

Close-up photography

The working tool

Close-up photography has today become associated with the reflex camera. If we had written this book fifteen years ago, we would have discussed other types of camera. Nowadays, there is a very wide range of reflex cameras and the simpler models are reasonably priced. On the other hand, the use of cameras with simple viewfinders for close-up photography involves such complications (with such uncertain results)

that it would take up far too much space to try to explain it here.

In a non-reflex camera, the viewfinder is situated above or to one side of the lens. Under these circumstances, its axis presents a certain displacement (or parallax) in relation to the lens. This displacement – of the order of a few inches – is not significant over distances of more than three feet (1 m). Below this, the frame shown by the viewfinder no longer corresponds exactly with that which will be recorded on the film.

The single-lens reflex camera provides an enormous advantage – the ability to view through the lens. While being very useful in all fields of photography, it has proved of inestimable value in close-up photography.

By its very nature, this method of viewing obviates any problem of parallax. It is achieved by means of a mirror positioned at an angle of 45° in the path of the light-rays passing through the lens. The image is formed on a glass screen, which the photographer generally views through a pentaprism which rectifies the image and magnifies it. When the

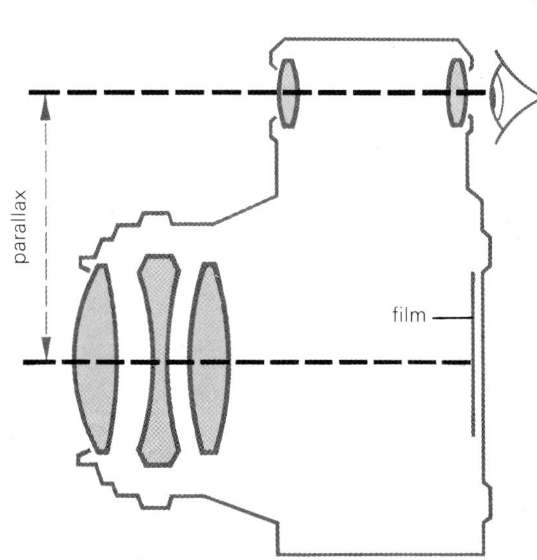

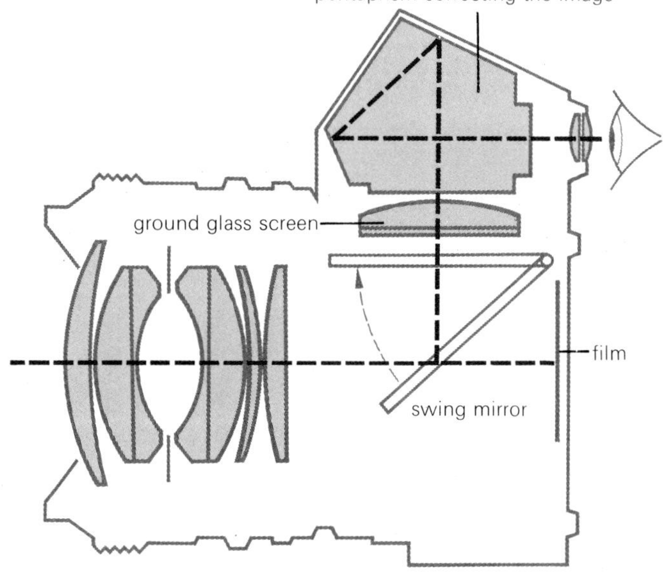

Comparison of paths of light rays in a camera, with a plain viewfinder (left) and a single-lens reflex camera (right).

glass parts shown in light grey

shutter is released, the mirror moves out of the way against the screen, opening the way for the light rays to which the film will be exposed for the period of time determined by the shutter speed. On completion of the exposure, the mirror resumes its viewing position. The entire action takes a fraction of a second, the operator hardly noticing the dimming of the viewfinder as the mirror is raised. The system has one disadvantage – the noise created by all these mechanisms and in particular the vibration associated with the movement of the mirror. However, some progress has been made in these areas, and these slight handicaps have to be accepted.

Apart from the absence of parallax, the strongpoint of the single-lens reflex is focusing. The image formed on the glass screen is an exact duplicate of that which will be recorded on the film; the focusing can thus be checked in the viewfinder at any time. The final trump card is that it is possible to check the overlay of sharp and out-of-focus planes as they will be reproduced on the photograph, which cannot be done with simple viewfinders in which the image does not show any gradation of sharpness (it is always sharp over its entire surface).

About equipment

You cannot make your own camera. You have to buy one, choosing it from an impressive range of models. Like a car, certain types of camera constitute an object of prestige rather than a working tool. Everything depends on the attitude of the purchaser, and on how susceptible he is to the insidious appeal of advertising.

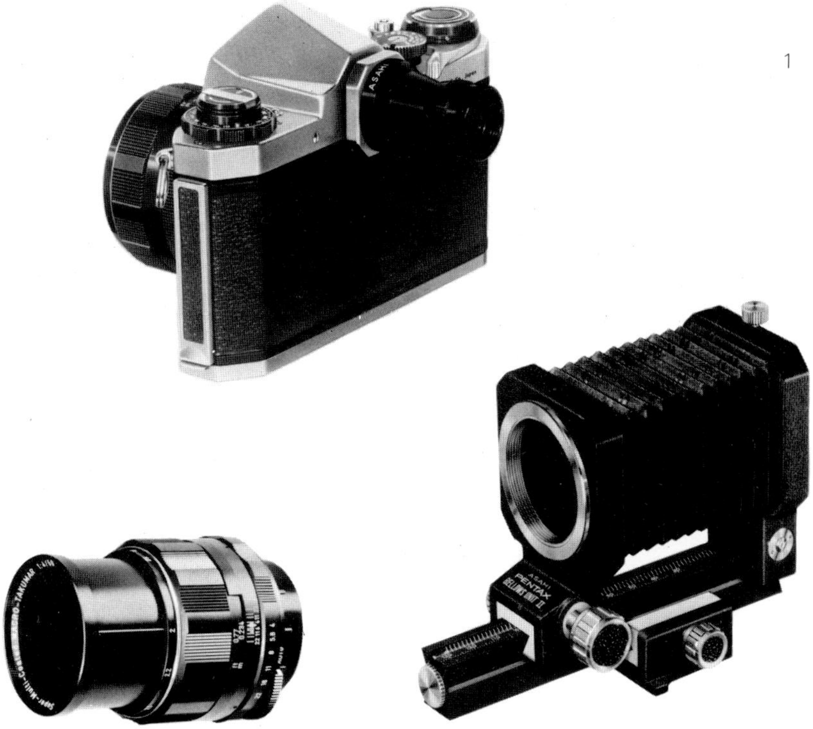

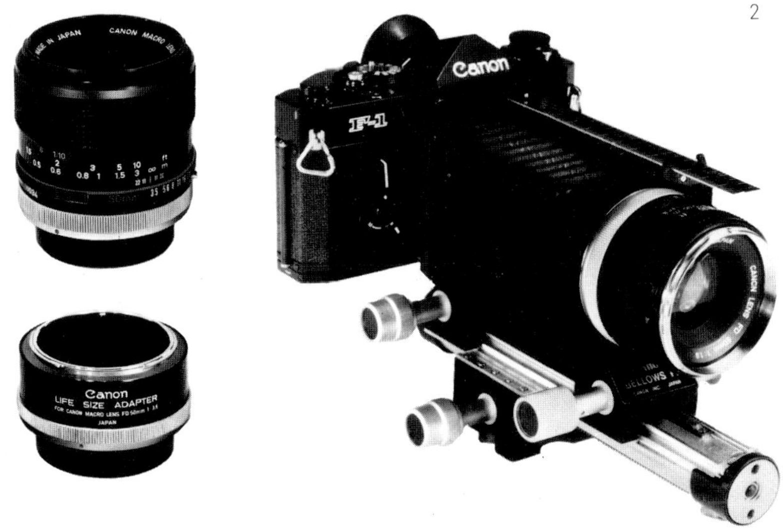

We started doing close-up photography using very modest equipment – an Edixa Mat Flex equipped with a 50 mm lens and a set of four extension rings – which we bought in a sale about ten years ago. It is, however, thanks to this equipment that we

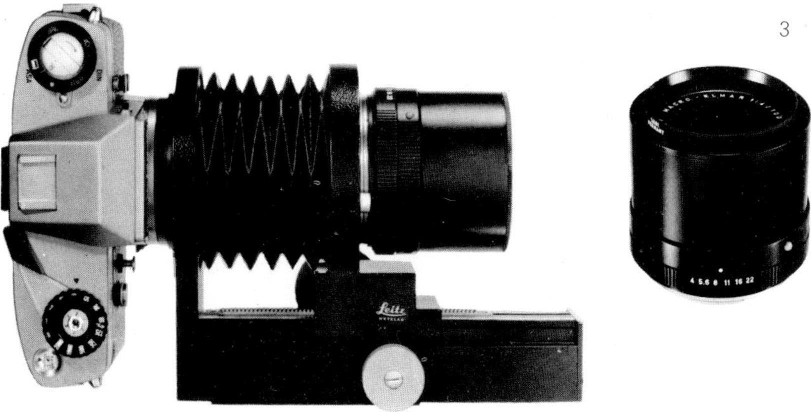

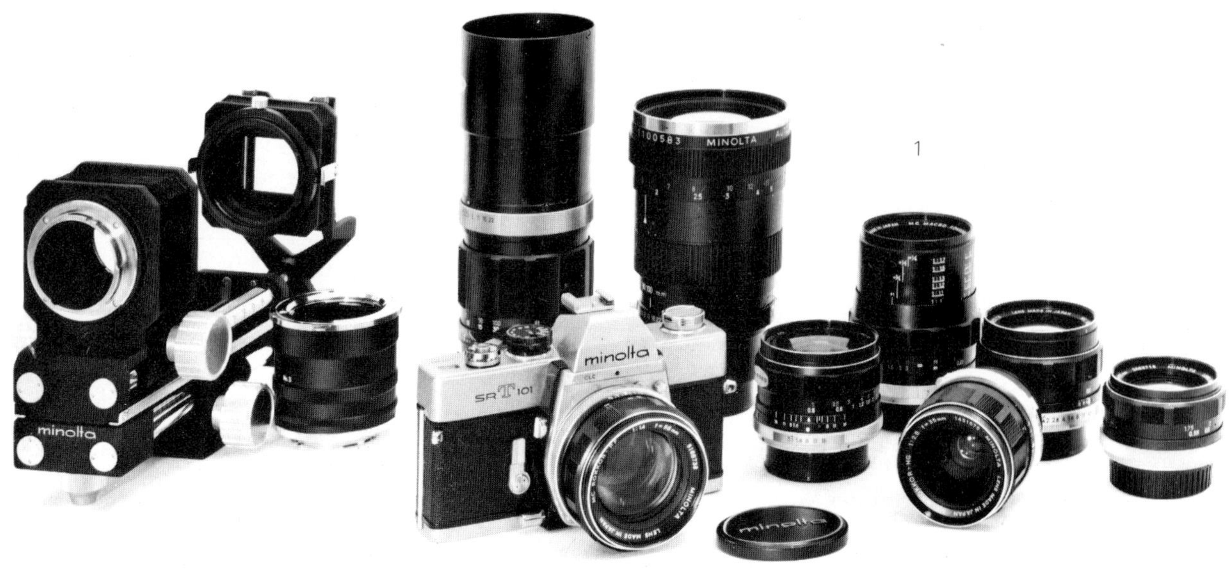

decided after a few years to devote ourselves exclusively to this activity. It must be admitted that this equipment was neither inefficient nor difficult to operate (a few of the photographs obtained at the time are still some of our favourite pictures). A good quality reflex camera can now be obtained for about £50 (U.S. $100). This applies, for example, to the Zenith (see the list of cameras at the end of the book). There are, of course, more sophisticated cameras which can take an impressive list of accessories and the lenses of which are of higher optical quality.

However, the method of illumination chosen is often more decisive than optical quality in obtaining a 'sharp' picture (meaning one with great clarity of detail). An amateur who has paid a great deal of money for a well-known make of lens might find himself disappointed in obtaining 'flat' photographs with insufficient definition through having, for example, used front lighting which has destroyed all the relief provided by the subject. What is more, the policy of systematically amassing a collection of photographic accessories gives the person who does this an acute sense of insufficiency, which in the end inhibits his creative ability: just as he is about to take a photograph, he has the frustrating feeling

1 Minolta system (24 x 36 reflex). SRT 101 camera, with fixed prism and photoelectric cell behind the lens, and interchangeable lenses. On the left, extension rings and automatic presetting bellows.

2 Nikon system (24 x 36 reflex). F2 camera equipped with Micro Nikkor f/3·5 55 mm and prism with photoelectric cell. Six interchangeable viewfinders, nineteen different viewing screens.

3 Olympus OM 1 camera, miniaturized 24 x 36 reflex, mounted on bellows and equipped with f/3·5 50 mm Macro lens. In front, from right to left: 38 mm and 20 mm Macro lenses for high reproduction ratios and adapter ring.

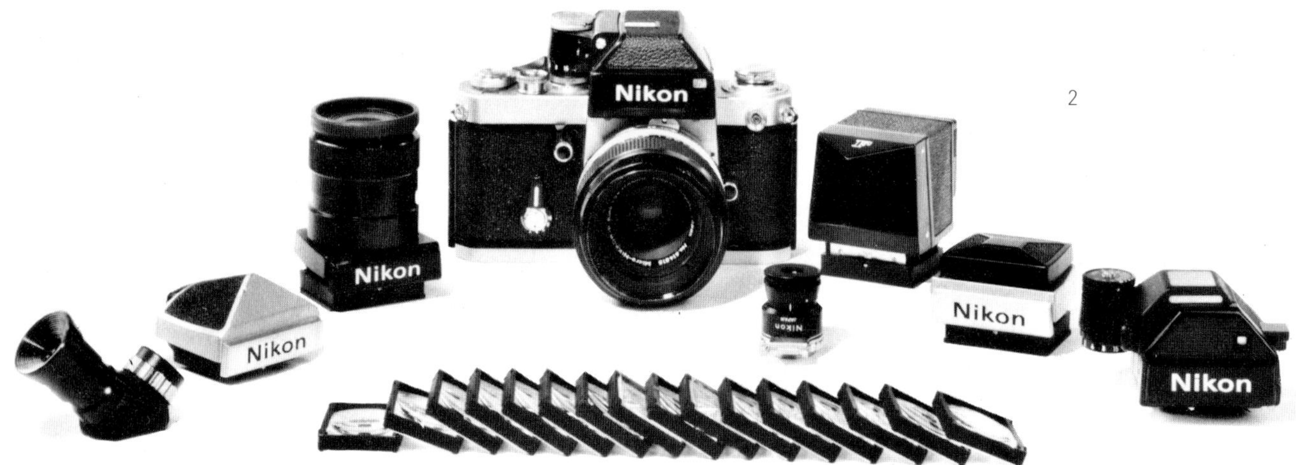

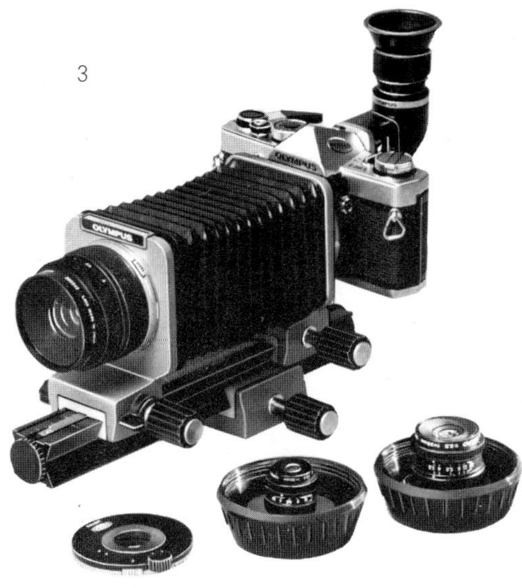

that he lacks some necessary piece of equipment. Excuses of this kind can spoil many a good exposure.

Experience shows that in close-up photography, as in all fields of photography, whatever may be the financial resources of the photographer, he generally ends up using only a limited number of optical systems and accessories of his own preference; he has systematically adopted them because they relate to his personal work style and enable him to interpret his view of things without saddling him with the annoying factual difficulty of badly planned equipment. For our part, we take most of our pictures with the aid of 50 mm and 105 mm lenses only. In a few special cases we have recourse to other lenses (300 mm telephoto lens, 24 mm wide angle). (See paragraph on focal length.)

A few technical terms

Photomacrography. Strictly speaking, this is the exposure technique which makes it possible to obtain on a photographic film an image the size of which is equal to or larger than that of the object reproduced. We then say that the reproduction ratio R is equal to or greater than 1, R being defined by the ratio between the size of the image and the size of the object. Following the widespread use of minature-size film (particularly 24×36 mm) in this field, this definition must be corrected. In fact, a 24×36 mm photographic record is never looked at other than enlarged (printed on paper or projected onto a screen). Photomacrography should, therefore, be understood to mean any form of exposure making it possible to obtain photographic records which, looked at under customary conditions, provide an enlarged image of the subject (see adjoining sketch).

Focal length. The focal length of a lens is the distance separating the

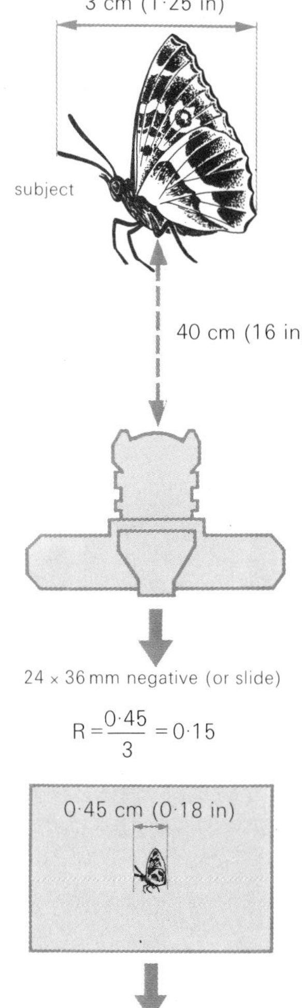

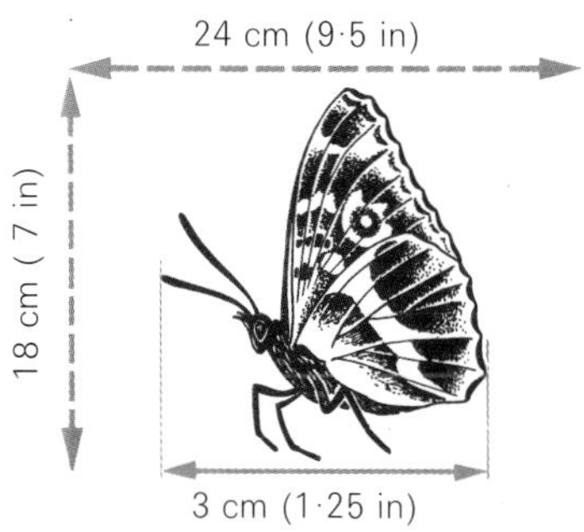

On a print enlarged to 18 × 24 cm, the image appears the same size as the subject.

REPRODUCTION RATIO AND PHOTOMACROGRAPHY

For prints on paper size 18 × 24 cm from 24 × 36 mm negatives, close-up images will be obtained since the R, when taking the picture, will be equal to or greater than 0·15, or a focusing distance equal to or less than 40 cm for a standard 50 mm lens.

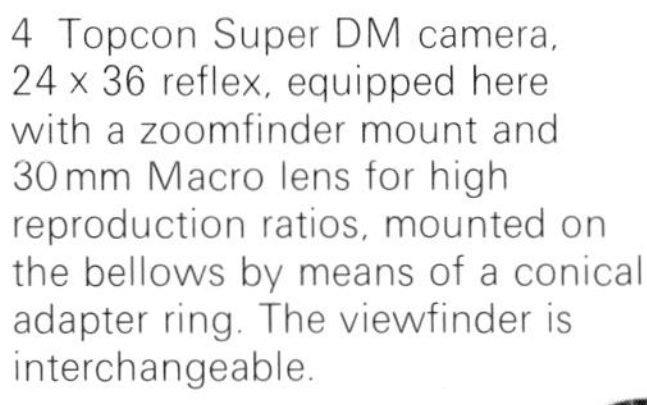

4 Topcon Super DM camera, 24 × 36 reflex, equipped here with a zoomfinder mount and 30 mm Macro lens for high reproduction ratios, mounted on the bellows by means of a conical adapter ring. The viewfinder is interchangeable.

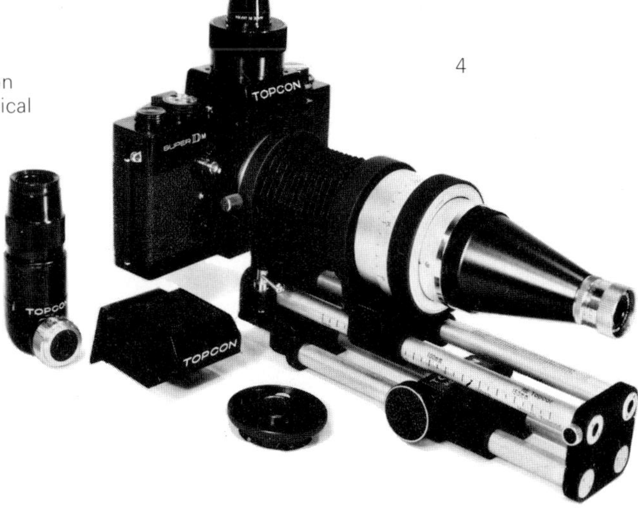

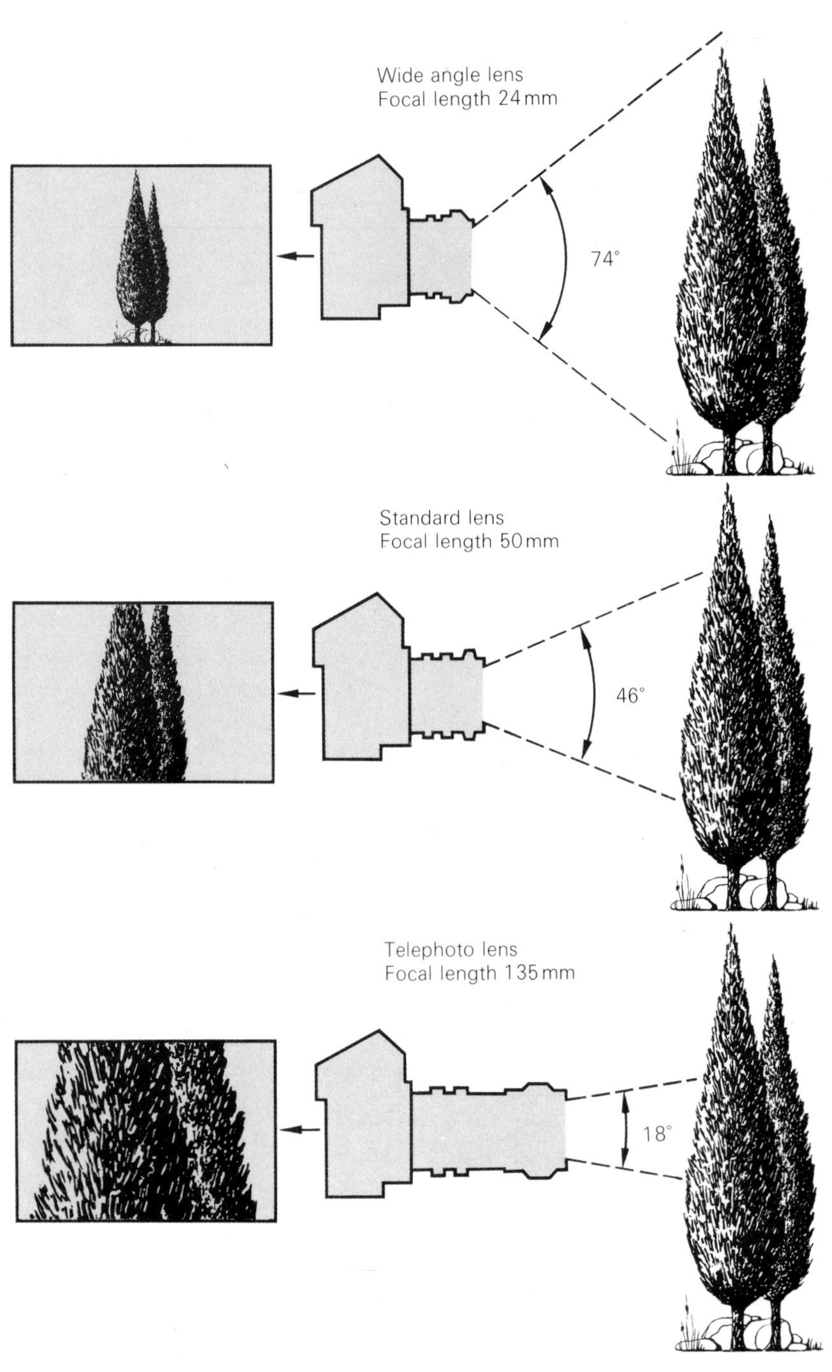

optical centre of the lens (where the lens diaphragm is generally located) and the plane of the film when the focus is set at infinity.

A lens is said to be 'standard' when its focal length is more or less equal to the length of the diagonal of the film size used. Its angular field is then close to the human field of vision (47°). For 24×36 mm film, standard lenses have a focal length of 45 mm to 55 mm.

Telephoto lenses (from 100 mm to 1000 mm for 24×36) have a focal length greater than that of a standard lens and a narrower angular field: they give a close-up image of the subject in the same way as a telescope. (The 100 mm, in relation to the 50 mm, magnifies the image by $100/50 = 2$ times, and the 300 mm by $300/50 = 6$ times, etc.)

Wide angle lenses (approximately 35 mm to 15 mm for 24×36) cover, on the other hand, a much wider angular field than a standard lens: they have a reverse perspective effect like a telescope used the wrong way round. (A 25 mm lens gives a subject image which is $25/50 = 0.5$ or half the size of that given by a 50 mm lens at the same distance.)

Aperture and diaphragm. The relative aperture of a lens is defined by the ratio between the focal length and the maximum diameter of the diaphragm. It expresses the transmitting power or speed of a lens. The smaller the f-number of a lens, the larger is its effective diameter and the higher its speed.

By varying the aperture, the diaphragm makes it possible to modify the speed. The sequence of f-numbers is such that when changing from one number or 'stop' (f/8 for example) to the next higher number (f/11), the amount of light transmitted to the film is reduced by half.

Automatic presetting. Since viewing takes place through the lens in reflex cameras, it is useful to be able to use full aperture in order to benefit from maximum light transmission. The process of automatic presetting makes it possible to set the required f-stop in advance, while maintaining full aperture. At the moment of exposure, the diaphragm closes automatically to the selected stop and reopens fully immediately the exposure is completed. This mechanism, which makes it unnecessary to close the diaphragm ring just before taking the picture, represents a great advance in terms of speed and precision.

Extension tube and exposure factor. If the focusing ring of the lens is turned from infinity to minimum distance, the entire lens mount moves forward, increasing its distance from the film: this movement corresponds to extending the bellows.

For very close photography, considerable additional extension is necessary: extension pieces or a bellows, inserted between the lens and the camera body, enable this to be achieved.

The additional extension (A) varies according to the reproduction ratio (R) it is intended to use. It is determined in each case by the formula:

$A = R \times F$ (in which F is the focal length of the lens used).

To obtain $R = 1$ with a 50 mm lens, A must be 50 mm; for $R = 2$, A must be 100 mm, and so on.

Extending by a large amount involves a decrease in light passing through the lens, which must be compensated for by applying an exposure factor F exp.:

$$F \text{ exp.} = (R + 1)^2$$

For $R = 1$, for example, F exp. $= 4$, which means that 4 times as much light is required as for a normal exposure under the same light conditions. It is, therefore, necessary in this case to open the diaphragm by two or more stops, or even, if artificial lighting is being used, to bring the light source closer to the subject (see electronic flash).

Depth of field. The depth of field is the permissible zone of sharpness available in front of and behind the plane on which the camera has been focused. In the field of close-up phtography the depth of field is independent of the focal length of the lens used. On the other hand, it depends on R and on the aperture selected. For a given aperture, it decreases as R increases. For the same value of R, it increases as the diaphragm is closed.

The depth of field falls to very low values in photomacrography: for $R = 1$, with aperture f/22, it is reduced to 3 mm (see the general table of depths of field on page 151).

Resolving power. The resolving power or definition of a lens is the smallest distance separating two discernible points of the image obtained on the plane of the film. It thus corresponds to the ability of a lens to cope with the finest details of a subject. The resolving power varies with the aperture used: it is generally greatest for f/8 or f/11. Under these conditions most modern lenses achieve a resolving power of 1/100 mm.

Another property of the lens which is almost as important is its ability to express contrasts. The treatment known as 'multi-coating', which has been applied for some years to the surfaces of lenses, does noticeably

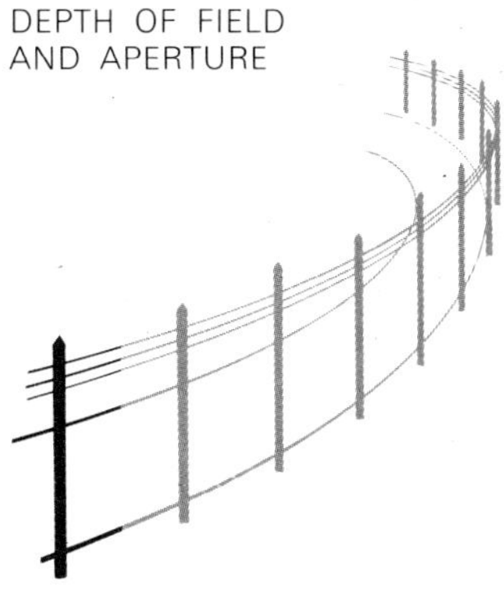

1 Full aperture, minimum depth of field

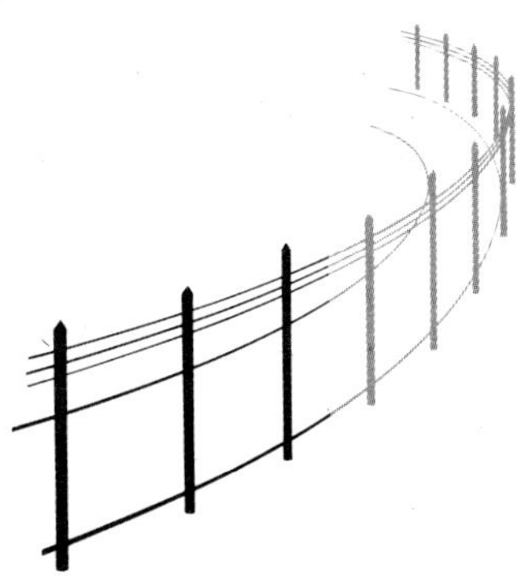

2 Medium aperture

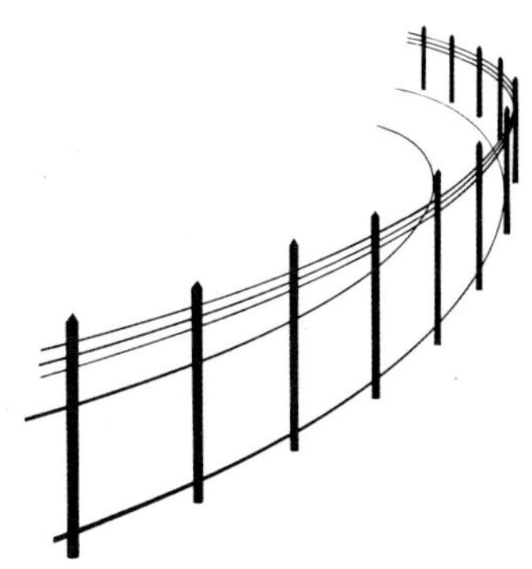

3 Minimum aperture, maximum depth of field
(In all three cases, focusing is carried out on the foreground.)

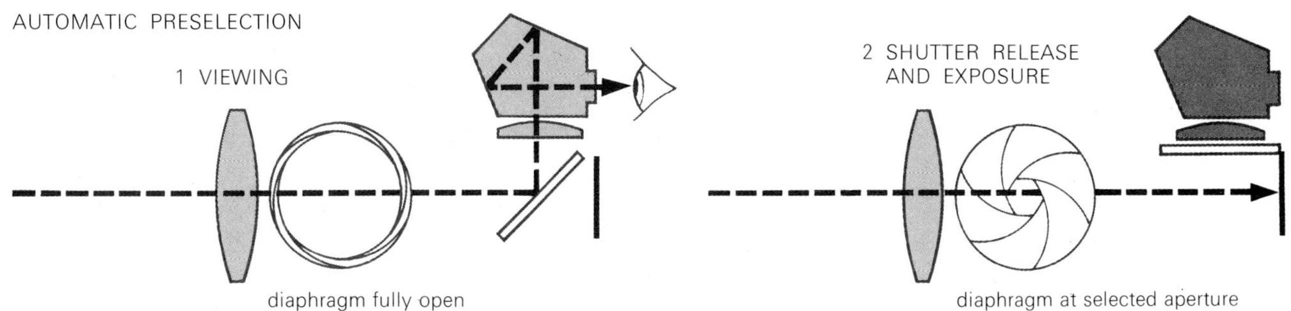

Venus's Fly-trap.
A carnivorous plant from the
marshlands of Carolina.

1 A fly settles on the trap at the
end of a leaf, attracted by the
sugary secretions of its walls
(× 6).

Reproduction ratio: 1.
Lens: Macro 55 mm, with
automatic ring extension.
Aperture: f/22.
Electronic flash, with reflecting
screen to reduce the shadows.

2

1

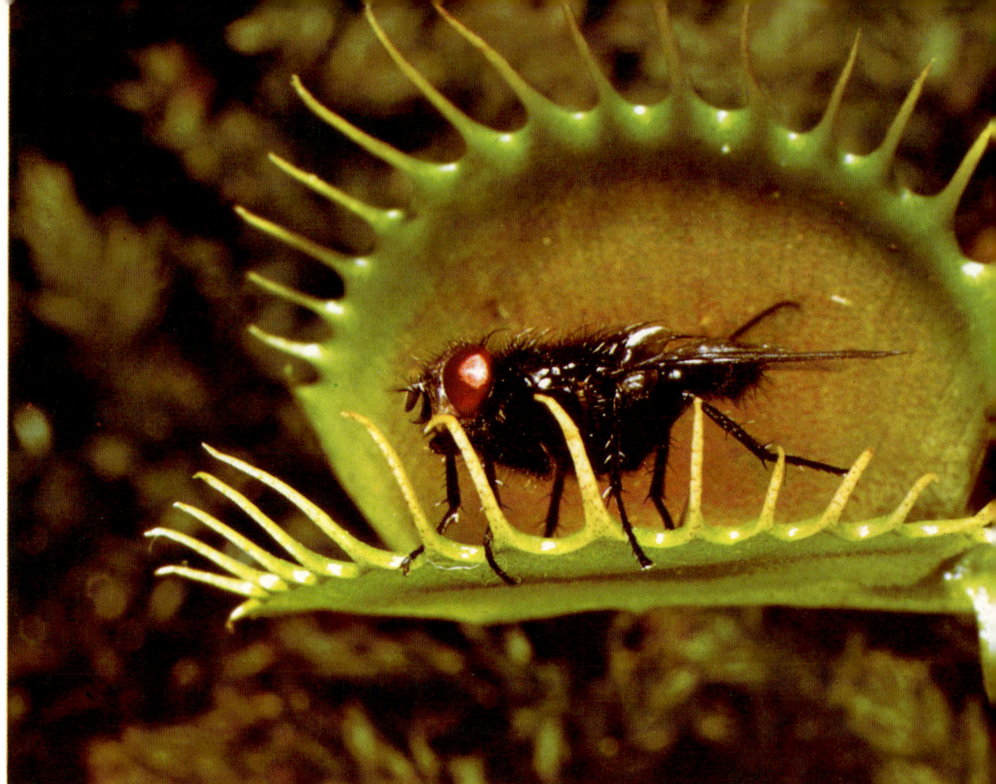

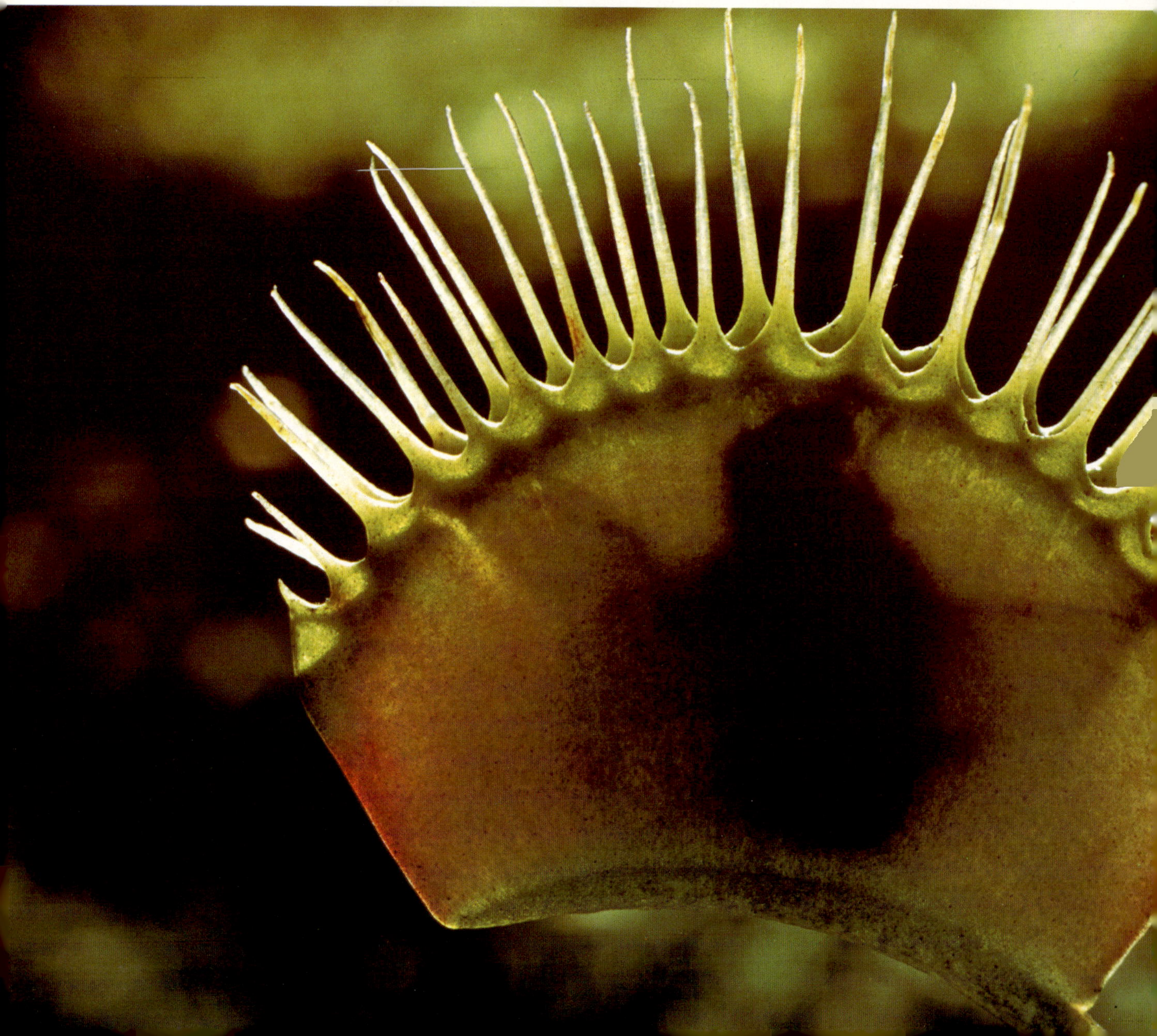

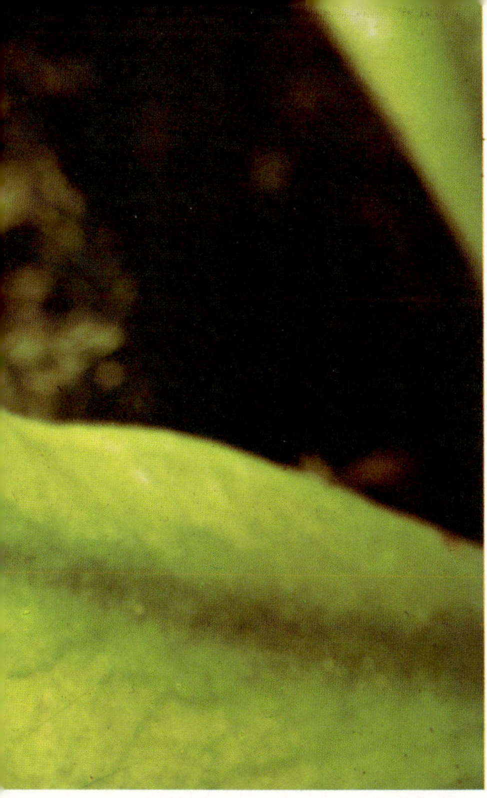

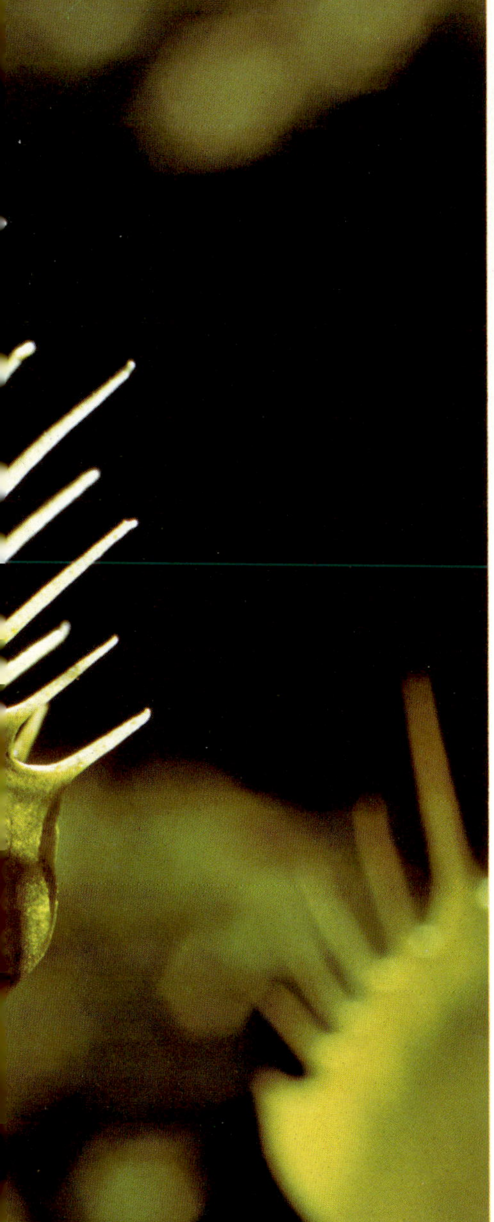

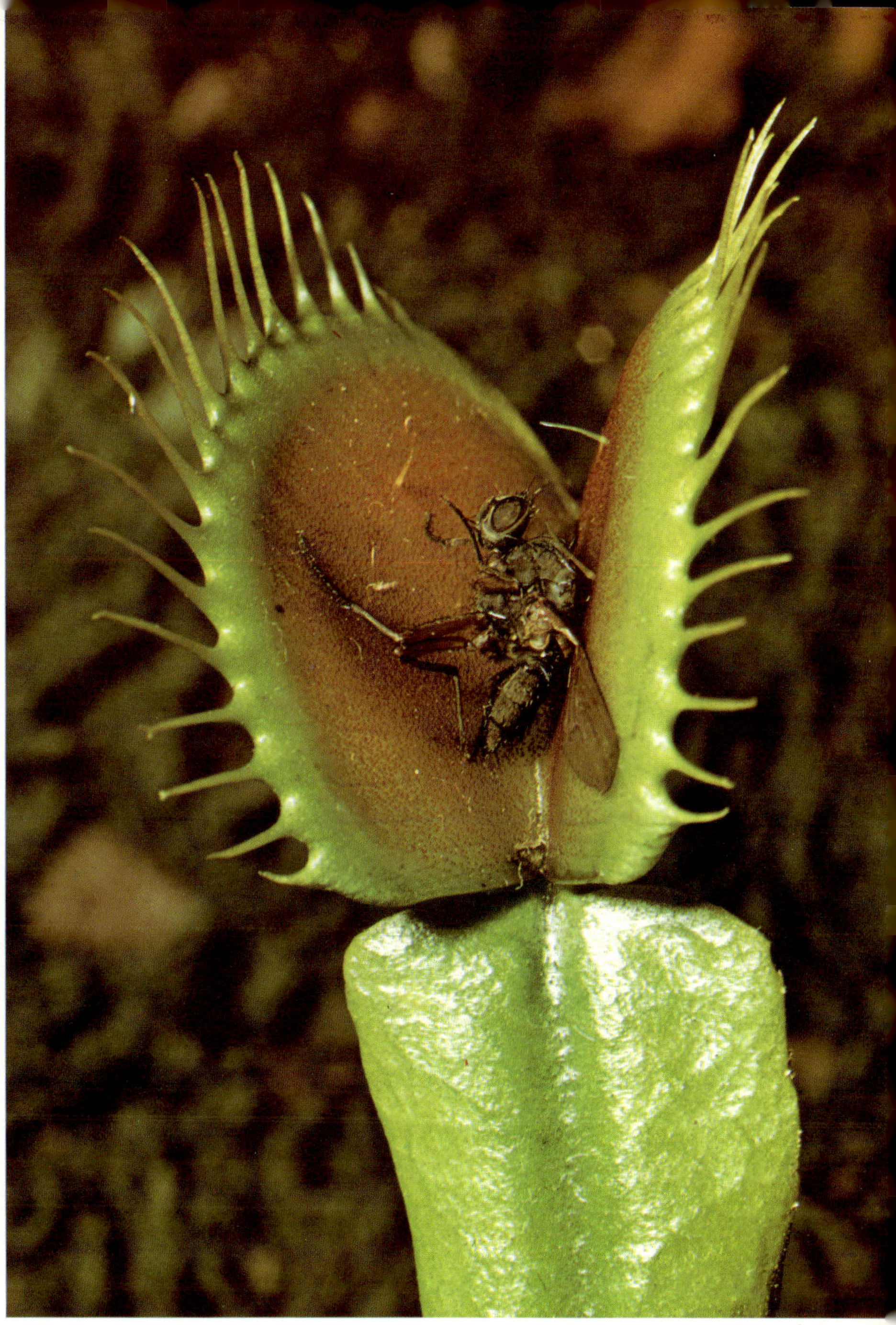

3

2 A fraction of a second later the 'jaws' close on the insect, which can be seen silhouetted with its wings outspread (x 9).

Reproduction ratio: 1·2.
Lens: Macro 55 mm mounted on bellows.
Aperture: f/11-16.
Electronic flash with backlighting.
Film: Kodachrome 25.

3 Ten days later, digestion has finished. The trap reopens, releasing the carcase. On the inside walls can be seen the sensitive hairs which, when brushed against, trigger the mechanism that closes the jaws on the victim (x 6).

Reproduction ratio: 1.
Lens: Macro 55 mm with automatic ring extension.
Aperture: f/22.
Electronic flash with reflecting screen to reduce the shadows.

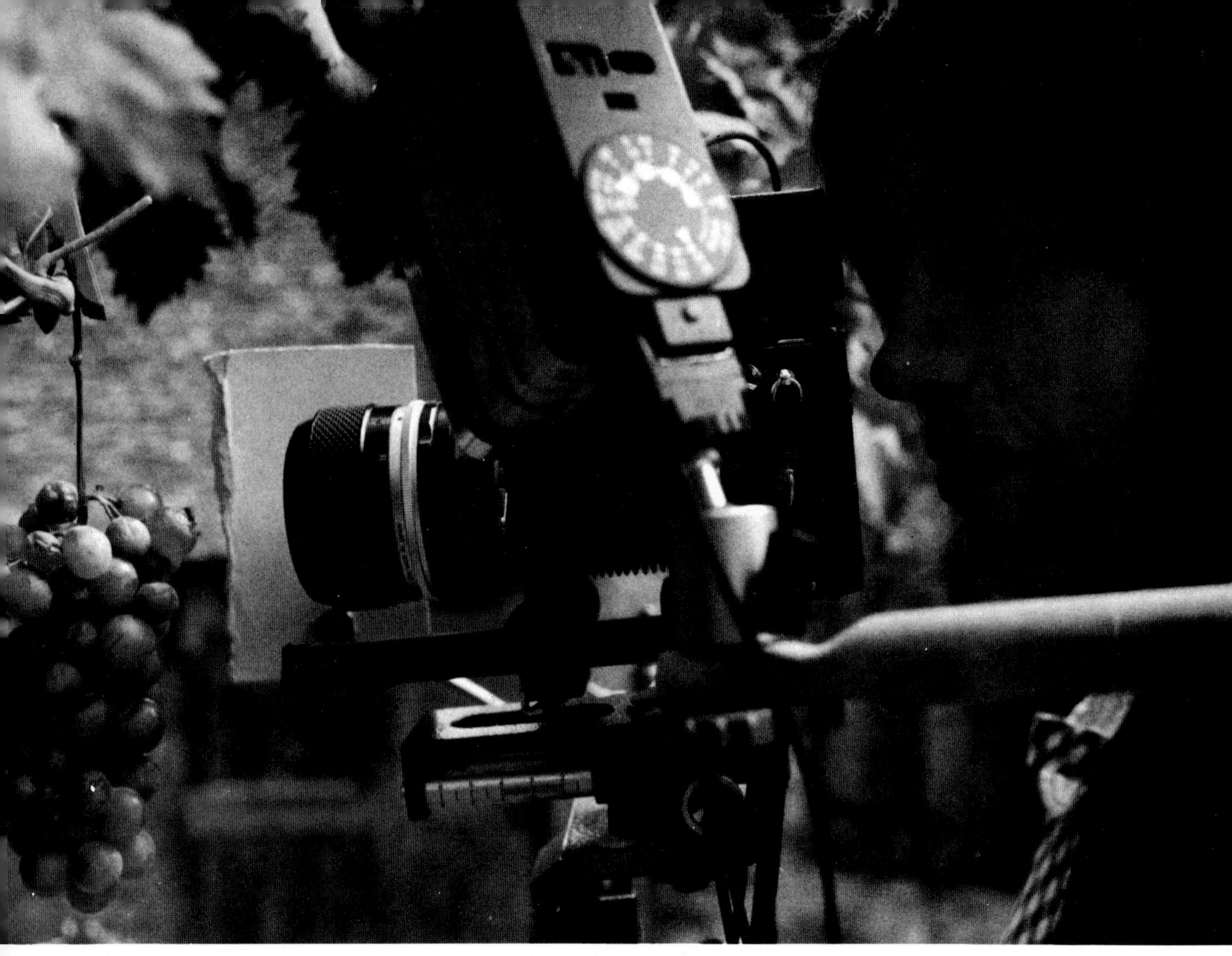

Outdoor shot using electronic flash. A wasp is being photographed eating a grape.

A bunch of grapes has been cut from the vine and fastened at an easy height for photographing.

Equipment used:
Nikon F camera equipped with a sports-type viewfinder. 55 mm Micro Nikkor lens. Novoflex focusing rail mounted on tripod. The electronic flash (Metz 184) on the left is mounted on a swivel joint, which can be turned in all directions. On the right, a reflecting screen (of white cardboard) makes the shadows less strong, taking into account the lateral position of the flash.

improve lens performance in this respect.

The term 'resolving power' is likewise used in respect of photographic films. The greater the sensitivity of the film, the more noticeable is its grain and the weaker is its resolving power.

Exposure guide number and electronic flash. Electronic flash is the source of artificial light most used in photomacrography. It emits a very short flash, generally not lasting longer than 1/1000th of a second. Used with a reflex camera, which has a special kind of shutter called a 'roller-blind' shutter, a comparatively slow shutter speed (1/30th to 1/125th of a second, depending on the model) is required to ensure perfect synchronization between the opening of the shutter

and the flash. The actual time of exposure, however, corresponds to the period of the flash: in most cases, in photomacrography, the amount of natural light entering the lens over a period of 1/60th of a second is negligible compared with that emitted by the flash in 1/1000th of a second.

The lighting power of a flash is expressed by its guide number (G.N.). G.N. = aperture setting × distance between flash and subject (in metres). The G.N. is always indicated for a given film sensitivity. The manufacturers have chosen for this reason a colour film having a sensitivity of 50 ASA (18 DIN according to the other scale used for measuring sensitivity), or more often 100 ASA (21 DIN). A flash having a G.N. of 22 makes it possible to photograph a subject at a distance of 2 metres (7 feet) with an aperture of 22/2 = f/11. The G.N. is merely a guide provided by the manufacturers – often noticeably inflated – which it is wise to check with the aid of a test film and then correct.

Film size. Looking at the two sizes generally used for film on spools – 6 × 6 cm and 24 × 36 mm – the question arises as to which should be used for close-up photography. For both sizes there are, in fact, reflex cameras with interchangeable lenses, which can be used with numerous accessories for photomacrography. The advantage that the 6 × 6 provides over the 24 × 36 lies in the picture area, which theoretically makes it possible to obtain much more detail in the negative. However, the 6 × 6 camera case is heavier and more inconvenient, and it is more expensive to buy. In other respects, the advantage of the 6 × 6 area compared with 24 × 36 is a real one only when the subject occupies the same relative area on the negative. The use of 6 × 6 thus involves higher reproduction ratios on exposure (60/36 = 1·66 times higher), which has disadvantages – considerable extension requiring inconvenient accessories, weak depth of field, restricted conditions of operation for the lens (with reduced definition), etc.

We can conclude this assessment by stating that the 6 × 6 cm size is a somewhat unnecessary luxury in the field of photomacrography (one last detail – Kodachrome 25, which is the emulsion having the greatest definition, cannot be obtained in size 6 × 6).

Lenses and their accessories for short-distance work

The camera lens seems to be no better designed for short-distance work than does the eye – the former has, in fact, largely been based on the latter. Most lenses are restricted to a close focusing distance of about twenty inches (50 cm). However, not all photographers necessarily want to keep their distance. What facilities are available to those who indulge in close-up photography?

The supplementary lens. There are readily available accessories which make it quite easy to break through the fifty centimetre barrier.

The first of these, the supplementary lens (or close-up lens), is a form of spectacle-lens which is fastened over the lens proper. We shall not waste time on this; it is purely a make-shift solution which does not improve the performance of a lens (you cannot merely add a supplementary lens to an objective lens the optical design of which is the result of advanced research), and is hardly likely to make it possible to take pictures at a distance of less than about eight inches (20 cm).

Extension rings. These provide a much more rational solution to the problem of close-up focusing. Inserted between the camera body and the lens, they increase the focus of the latter so that it is possible to obtain satisfactory images of objects situated at a short distance, without altering the definition.

A lens especially designed for photomacrography – the 55 mm Micro Nikkor f/3·5.

Right: The lens, without its ring, which, because of its high-reduction helical focusing mount, makes it possible to take pictures down to a distance of 24 cm (or a reproduction ratio of 0·5).

Left: Fitted with its special ring to ensure automatic presetting, it allows the subject to be approached to a distance of 11 cm (or a reproduction ratio of 1).

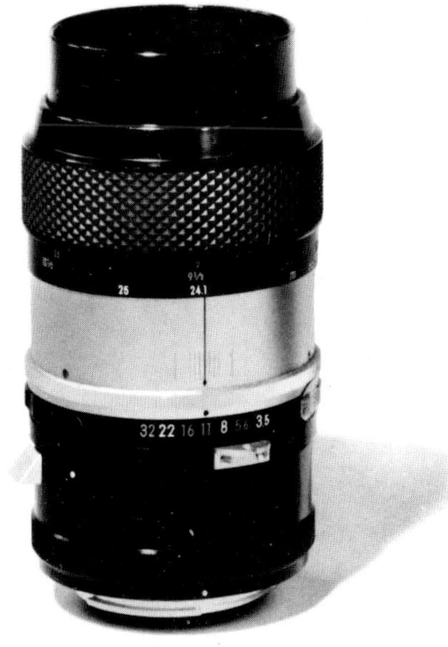
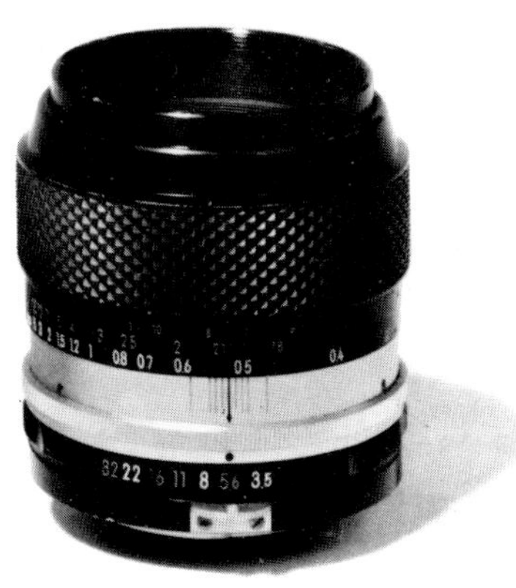

Sundew (x 7).
A colony of 'carnivorous' plants discovered in a half-flooded peat-bog on the Aubrac plateau (Massif Central of France).

Opposite: The plant, greatly enlarged, with its numerous tentacles tipped with transparent drops that catch the rays of the sun.

Below: Attracted by the sparkling lights, a winged plant-louse settles on the trap. Its wings are quickly caught in the viscous liquid of the drops. The tentacles slowly bend over towards the victim, which is already paralyzed. A long period of digestion commences.

Opposite:
Reproduction ratio: 1·2.
Lens: 100 mm Macro Luminar, mounted on bellows.
Aperture: f/11-16.
Electronic flash with backlighting.

Below:
Reproduction ratio: 2·6.
Same lens and aperture.
Electronic flash.

Extension rings are supplied in sets of three to five. They can be used separately or combined, which allows quite a wide range of reproduction ratios. All the rings screwed end to end generally measure fifty milli-metres. This makes exposures pos-sible up to a ratio of 1 (with a 50 mm lens), the subject being then about four inches (10 cm) from the lens.

The double release. Detaching the lens from the camera breaks the mechanical connection between these two items which is necessary for diaphragm presetting. Many design-ers nowadays suggest rings capable of transmitting the presetting by means of a set of built-in moving rods.

When such a mechanism is not provided, recourse must be had to a double release which terminates on the one hand at the body release and on the other hand at the diaphragm socket located on the lens or on a special ring provided for this purpose (Nikon system, ring E2 or PW 1). Simply pressing the terminal push-button causes the diaphragm to close, synchronized with the shutter.

The bellows. The bellows permits continuous variation of extension where the rings extend by stages. What is more, it goes even further in the approved reproduction ratios, often three or four times with a 50 mm lens. It has, however, one dis-advantage: in its position of mini-mum extension, the bellows extends the focus to a not inconsiderable degree, often by an inch or so, by reason of the actual thickness of its uprights. There is thus a sudden jump between the minimum focusing distance of the lens on the camera and the maximum focusing distance which makes it possible to insert the bellows in its position of minimum extension. For these intermediate distances one would then need to use

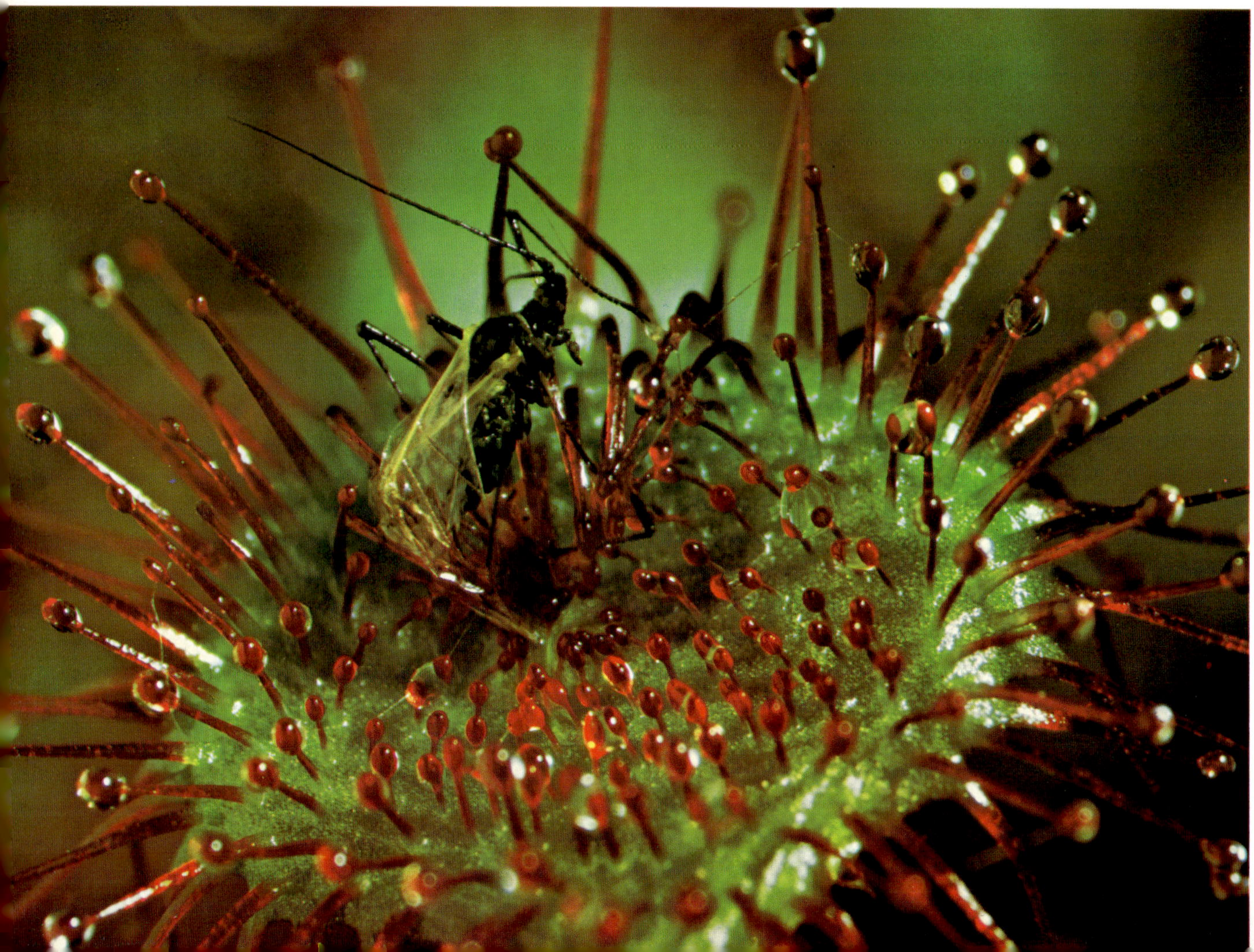

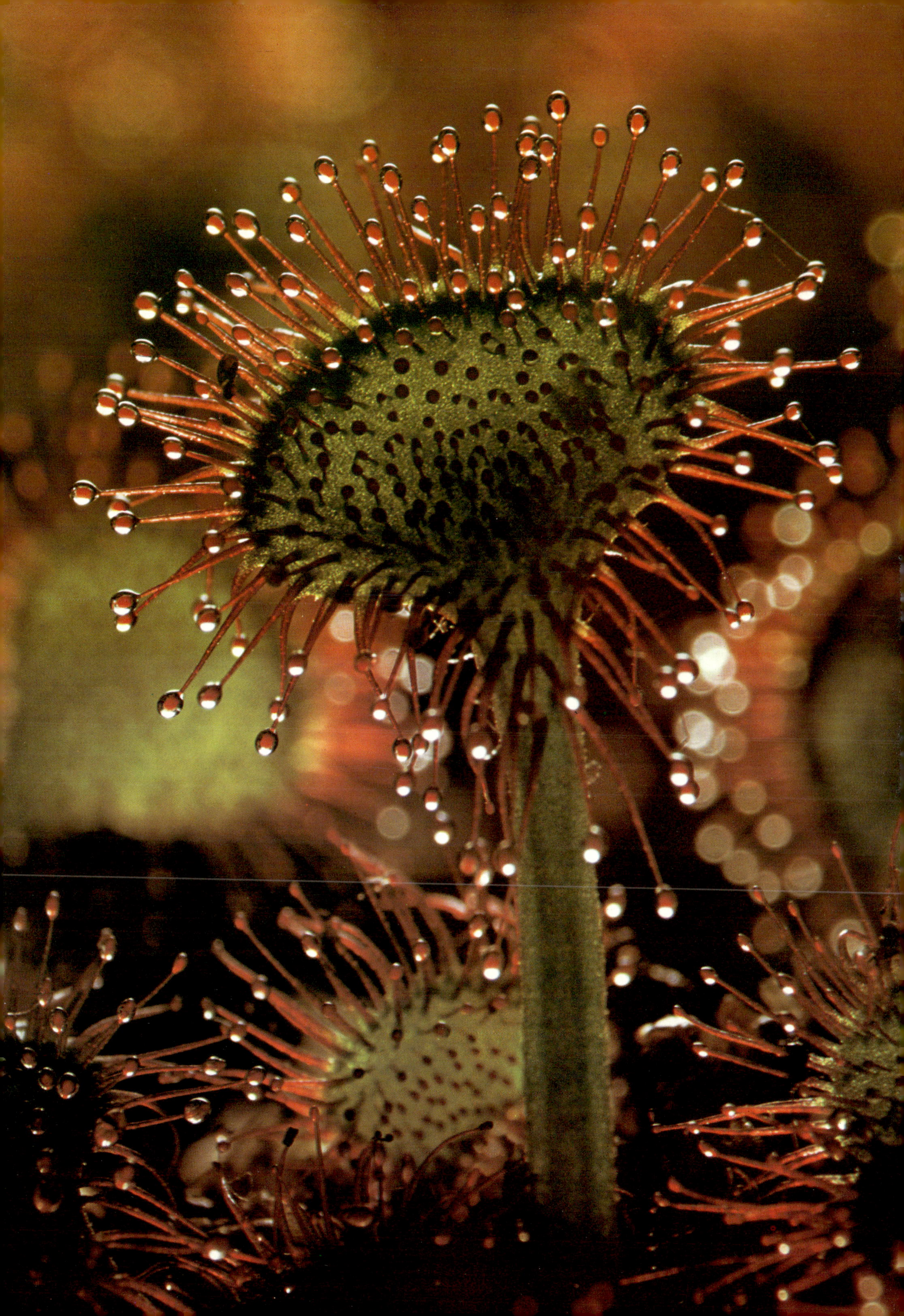

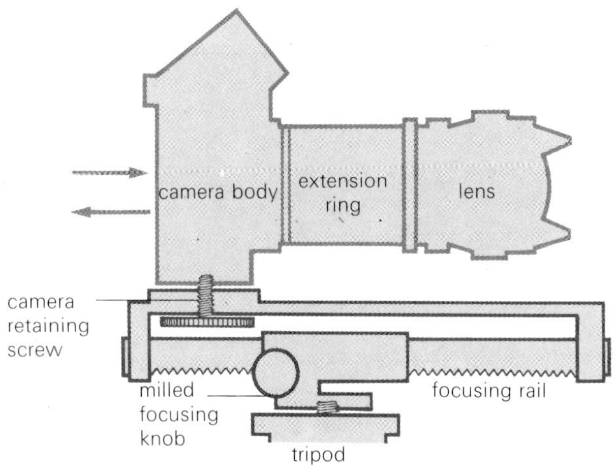

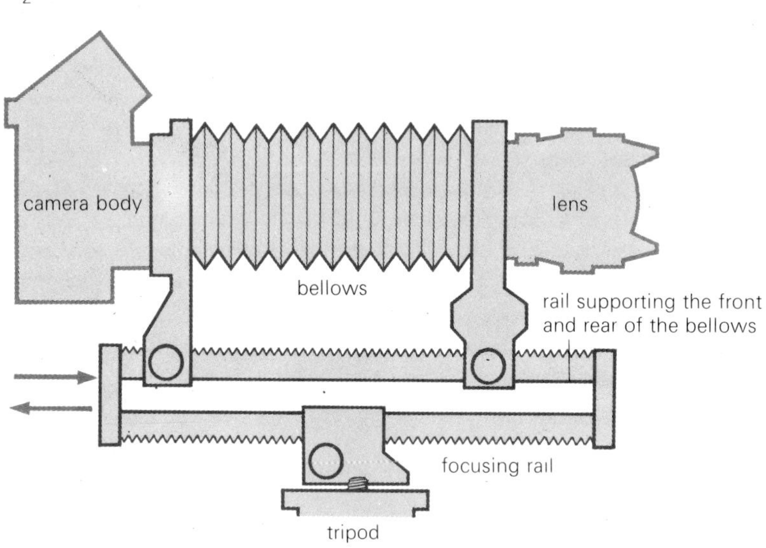

Focusing systems used in photomacrography.

1 Focusing rail. The assembly consisting of camera body, extension rings and lens can be moved back without altering the length of extension.

2 Bellows with a double set of rails. The two lower rails act as the focusing rail.

the distance between the subject and the lens is always much greater than the distance between the image and the lens. The complex calculations involved in the design of a lens take this fact into account.

If a picture is taken at a ratio of 1, these two distances are equal. Beyond this, the ratio between the two distances becomes reversed. The lens then operates under aberrant conditions not foreseen by the designer. To avoid any loss of definition, recourse is had to a simple trick, that of reversing the lens, turning its front face towards the housing. All makes include among their accessories a reversing ring which enables the lens to be installed in this unusual but, under the circumstances, logical position.

Diffraction. Depth of field is the weak point in photomacrography. It might, therefore, seem advantageous to use the smallest possible aperture. However, it is necessary to guard against the fact that beyond a ratio of 1 the phenomenon of diffraction may occur – connected with the wave-form structure of light – which affects the quality of the definition by surrounding the finest details with a faint halo. It is possible to stop down to f/22 or even f/32 for a ratio of up to 1/2; between 1/2 and 1 it is better to keep to f/22, and between 1 and 4 to f/16 or even f/11.

the shortest possible extension rings.

There are bellows which are equipped with a presetting transmission system. Nevertheless, this device cannot always be used. If the lens is used in reverse position (with its front face fixed to the bellows), the transmission system becomes inoperable, since mechanical connection by means of a rod located behind the lens is no longer possible. The double release, on the other hand, can be used in all cases.

The reversing ring. Under normal conditions of use of a camera lens,

'Macro' lenses. The inestimable flexibility in use of these establishes them as all-purpose lenses for amateur photomacrography. Nearly all makes offer one or more 'macro' lenses in their range of lenses. With a focal length of 50 mm or 55 mm, they are furnished with a geared-down focusing ring which permits exposures up to a ratio of 1 or 1/2 (in the latter case, an automatic extension ring is supplied with the lens for ratios of 1/2 to 1). In the field, they enable the interminable manipulation of extension rings to be dispensed with, and the saving in time thus achieved makes it possible to obtain pictures of restless animals which are not used to posing. We would point out that 'macro' lenses generally benefit from an optical formula calculated with short-distance use in mind: their sharpness in extreme close-up is noteworthy. Their design makes it necessary to restrict the maximum aperture somewhat (f/3·5 or f/4), which is a minimal disadvantage with the small apertures used in photomacrography; at the worst, there is a little less light available for viewing.

Small telephoto lenses (85mm to 105mm). These are likewise very useful for photomacrography (there are few 100mm 'macro' lenses). They permit a working distance between the subject and the camera double that for a 50mm lens. Thus, for a ratio of 0·5, a 100mm lens is positioned twelve inches (30cm) from the subject and a 50mm lens six inches (15cm) away. These few inches of extra distance can sometimes be an advantage; they may be sufficient to avoid frightening away a nervous animal such as a snake, lizard, frog or butterfly. In addition, this extra distance reduces the risk of the shadow of the lens or the photographer falling on the subject (which obviously makes it impossible to take the photograph and almost invariably results in the animal taking flight).

Telephoto lenses (200mm to 300mm). These are more rarely employed. Used in conjunction with short extension rings, they make it possible

Use of the double release. This makes it possible to maintain the automatic setting when the lens is separated from the body. Here a 55mm Micro Nikkor is mounted in reverse position on a Nikon PB 4 bellows.

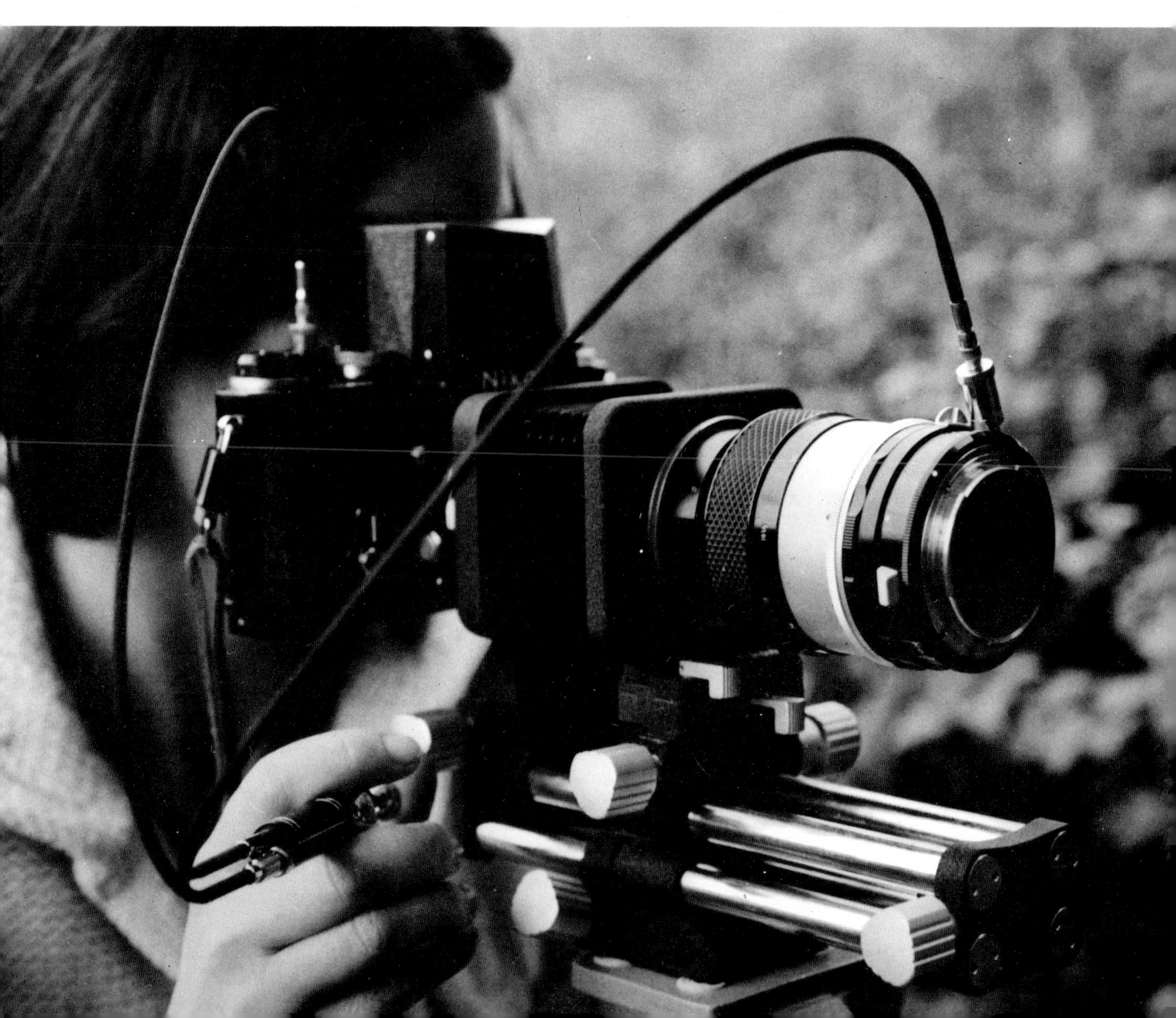

to photograph small creatures which cannot be approached either for reasons of topography (such as an isolated frog on a water-lily in a pond or a dragon-fly resting on a reed) or because they are particularly timid (such as snakes, lizards and certain large butterflies).

Wide angle lenses (24mm to 35mm). These should be avoided. They are the least accurately corrected of all lenses for short-distance work. In addition, they merely serve to increase the photographer's difficulties, since using them involves taking pictures at distances even shorter than with the 50mm. They can be used for high reproduction ratios (from 3 to 5) in order to avoid having to manipulate an unduly long bellows, which would affect the stability of the camera.

Large ratios. For those who are always wanting to take magnification a stage further, ordinary lenses or even 'macro' lenses can possibly be misleading. Starting with a reproduction ratio of 2, definition quickly shows a noticeable decrease in quality (it must be admitted that this

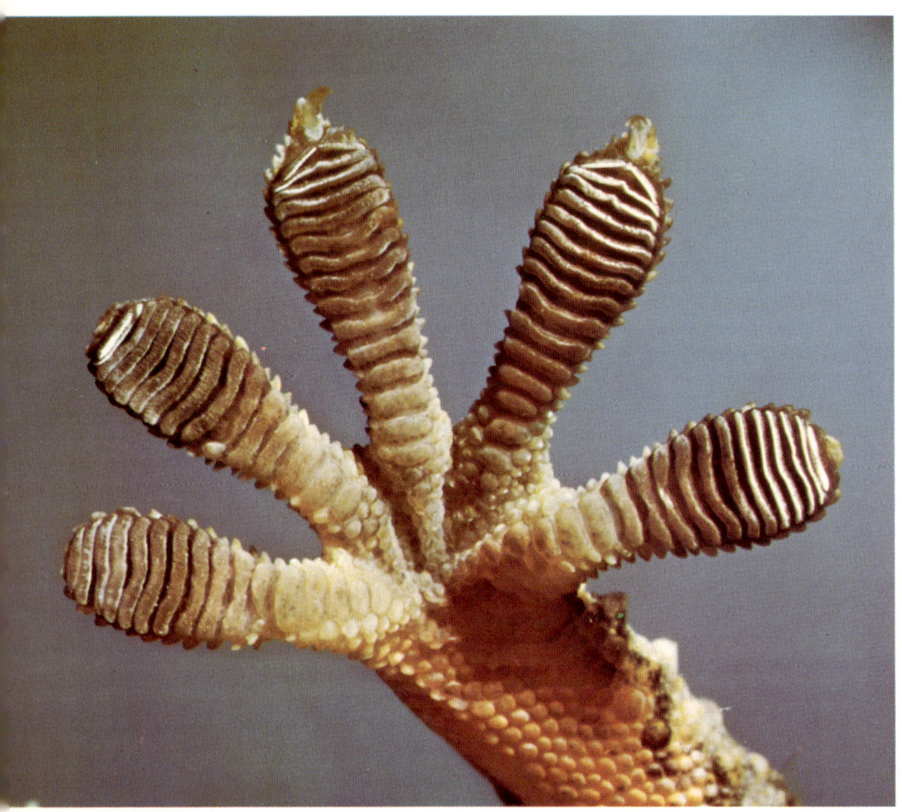

Foot of a Mauritanian Gecko (x 12).
With the aid of the flexible lamellae running across the underside of its digits, this lizard can run on surfaces as smooth as glass. Each of these lamellae has innumerable growths round the edge, which divide into a number of branches ending in a pair of minute 'fingers'. The size of these terminal organs is much less than a 1/1000th of a millimetre, and only examination under an electron microscope has made it possible to discover their existence.

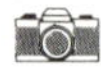

Reproduction ratio: 2.
Lens: 55mm Macro mounted on bellows in reverse position.
Aperture: f/22-32.
Electronic flash. A second flash is used to lighten the background.

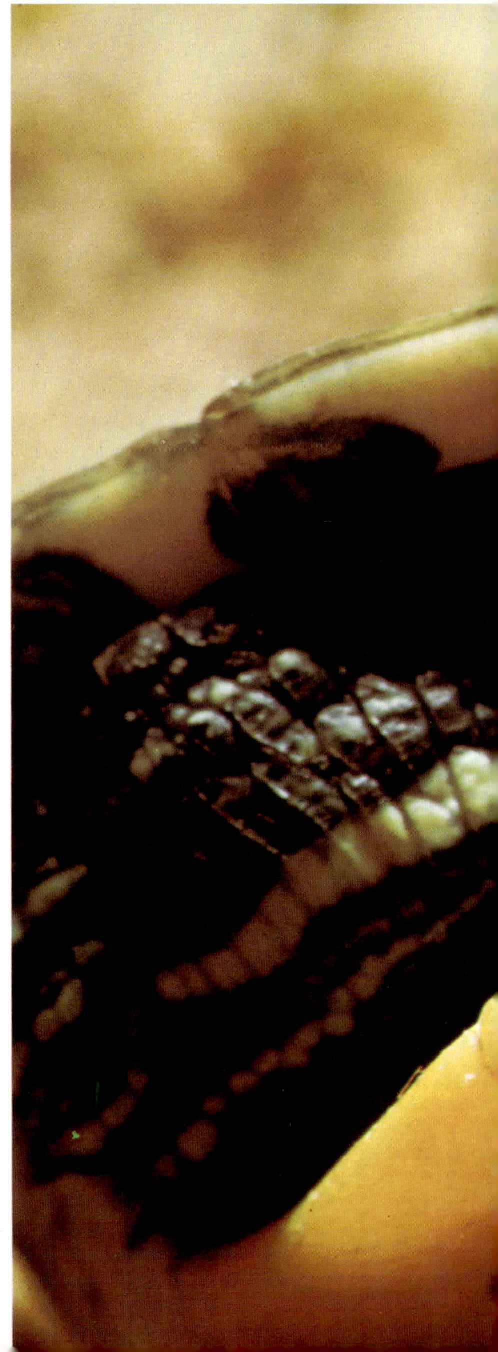

is expecting lenses to function under decidedly abnormal conditions). For ratios of 3 to 25 (beyond this the microscope takes over), there is quite a large range of lenses, generally of fairly short focal length (which avoids too much extension), especially designed to give strongly magnified images of very small subjects. These were originally photographic lenses intended for use in microscopy, so that their mountings have a standard microscope thread. Using them on the bellows of a reflex camera therefore requires an adapter ring, which one can easily have made by a specialist fitter. No presetting system is provided: the diaphragm must be closed by hand before taking the picture, a minor inconvenience in relation to the handling time and high precision inherent in this type of exposure. The Summar 24mm by Leitz, for example, allows pictures to be taken at ratios ranging from 4 to 25, and the Luminar 16mm by Zeiss from 10 to 40. Each make offers a whole series of focal lengths (16mm to 100mm for Zeiss and 24mm to 120mm for Leitz), each covering a specific range of reproduction ratios.

Florida Terrapin (or Florida Turtle, as it is called in the U.S.A.) (x 12).

Reproduction ratio: 1·6.
Lens: 55mm Macro mounted on bellows in reverse position.
Aperture: f/16-22.
Electronic flash positioned above the subject. Reflecting screen under the animal to open up the shadows.

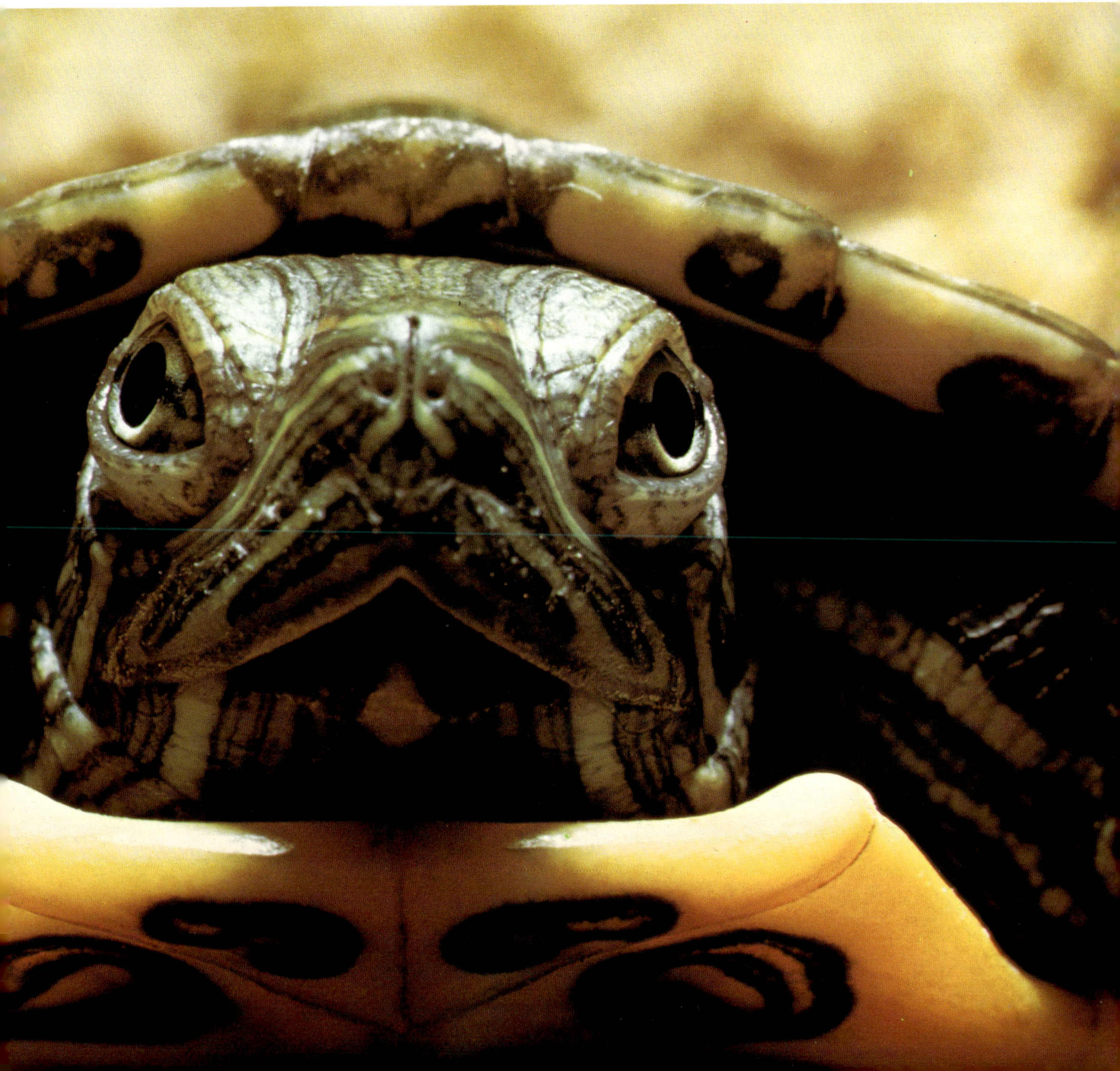

Measuring the light with the aid of a separate photoelectric exposure meter; in this case a Lunasix 3, provided with a 'tele' accessory to give a narrow field of measurement (15° or 7·5°), which can be controlled by the reflex viewfinder on the top.

Nearly all present-day 24×36 reflex cameras are equipped with one or more photoelectric cells powered by battery and positioned inside the viewing prism or behind the swing mirror.

These cells measure the quantity of light available behind the lens; there is, therefore, no need to apply an exposure factor, since the effect of altering the extension tube or bellows is automatically taken into account. The cells behind the lens (also called TTL = through the lens) generally permit measurement at full aperture. Coupling the cell to the diaphragm ring makes it possible for the measuring system to allow for the indicated aperture.

When extension rings or a bellows are interposed, this coupling is generally interrupted. The light must then be measured with the diaphragm closed, and the advantage of automatic preselection is lost when the measurement is taken.

Separate exposure meters are still unsurpassed for reliability and sensitivity. In very weak light conditions, they are the only ones which can still provide usable data. It is, therefore, still a good idea to check and calibrate a TTL measuring system with the aid of a good separate photoelectric exposure meter.

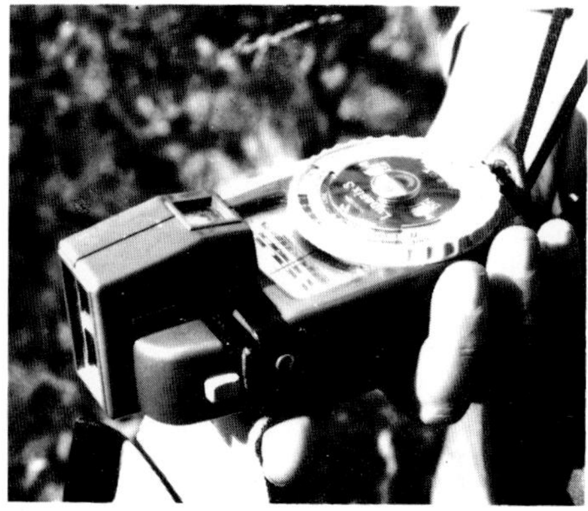

Light

Daylight. Compared with its artificial competitors, daylight has for the photographer a quality which cannot be matched. It offers the advantages of directional lighting (with a 'modelling' effect caused by the shadows which make the surface relief stand out) without having its disadvantages, thanks to the presence of atmospheric haze of greater or lesser opacity which reduces the contrast and bathes the subject in diffused light.

These advantages still hold good in close-up photography. However, the decrease in image brightness due to the lens extension (see page 37) must be offset by strong lighting. Since the intensity of the light source cannot be modified, it is necessary to use slow shutter speeds and relatively large apertures, which diminish the depth of field. In practice, daylight can be used for exposures up to a ratio of 0·5 (exposure correction = 2·3 or a little more than one stop) with an 18 DIN (50 ASA) film. Within these limits the photographer benefits from considerable flexibility of operation – no inconvenient flash and little or no calculation – when it is necessary to capture certain fleeting scenes. In the case of side lighting which is too harsh – with a clear sky and the sun low down – it is necessary to position a reflector (white card) on the shadow side in order to reduce the shadows (colour film in particu-

lar cannot cope with very strong contrasts).

Most modern reflex cameras are equipped with a photoelectric cell which measures the brightness of the image provided by the lens. Such a device will record the decrease in light resulting from extending the lens for purposes of photomacrography; it is then only necessary for the photographer to make allowance, without correction, for the data provided by the cell. On the other hand, if he uses a photoelectric cell not incorporated in the camera, he must correct the exposure data with the aid of the exposure factor (see page 37 and the table at the end of the book).

Electronic flash. Electronic flash has the advantage of being a light source which can be controlled for intensity and direction. Placed at a short distance from the subject, it emits a considerable quantity of light which makes it possible to use the smallest apertures (greatly improving the depth of field, which is of considerable value in photomacrography). Its very short duration (generally 1/1000th of a second) prevents any risk of blurring the picture by shaking the camera.

Electronic flash is thus a preferred form of lighting for the close-up

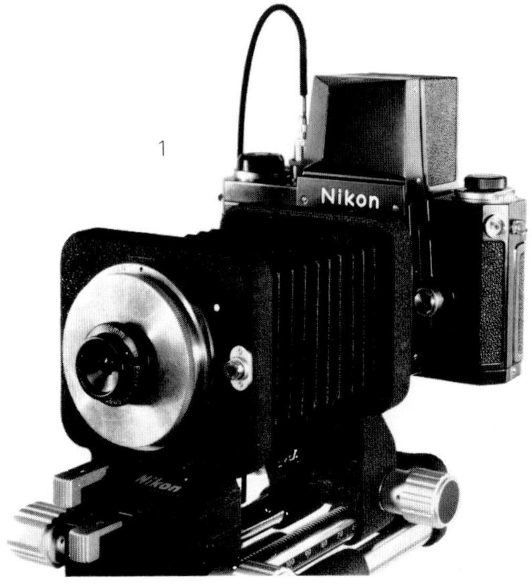

photographer. It gives his pictures spectacularly improved accuracy of detail. It becomes indispensible for exposures with high ratios of reproduction; its use is advantageous from $R = 0.5$.

All these benefits are offset, however, by a few annoyances. In the first place, the photographer finds that having to cope with all this relatively cumbersome equipment – electronic flash, connecting bar, synchronizing cable, etc. – can sometimes distract his attention from the subject he is trying to photograph.

Moreover, the light from a flash, being highly directional, generates strong contrasts between the shadow areas and those which are illumina-

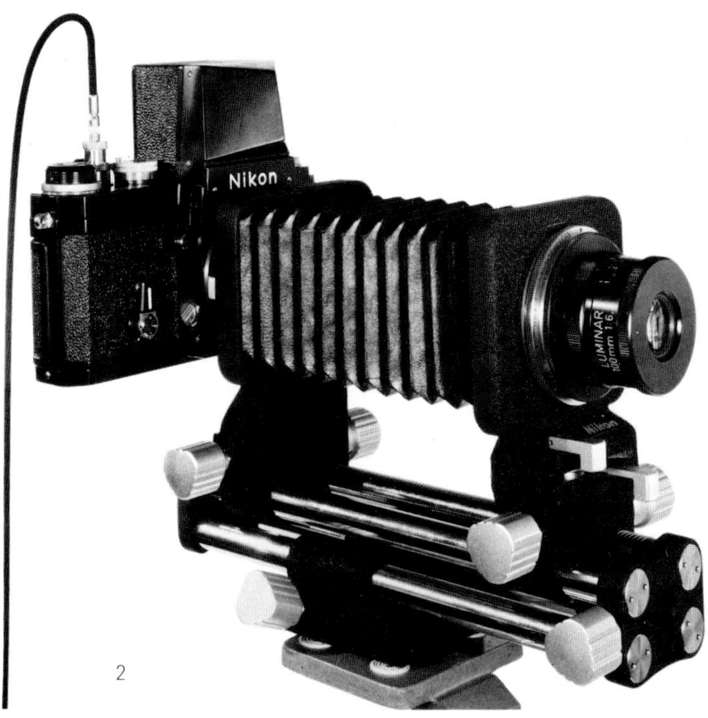

2

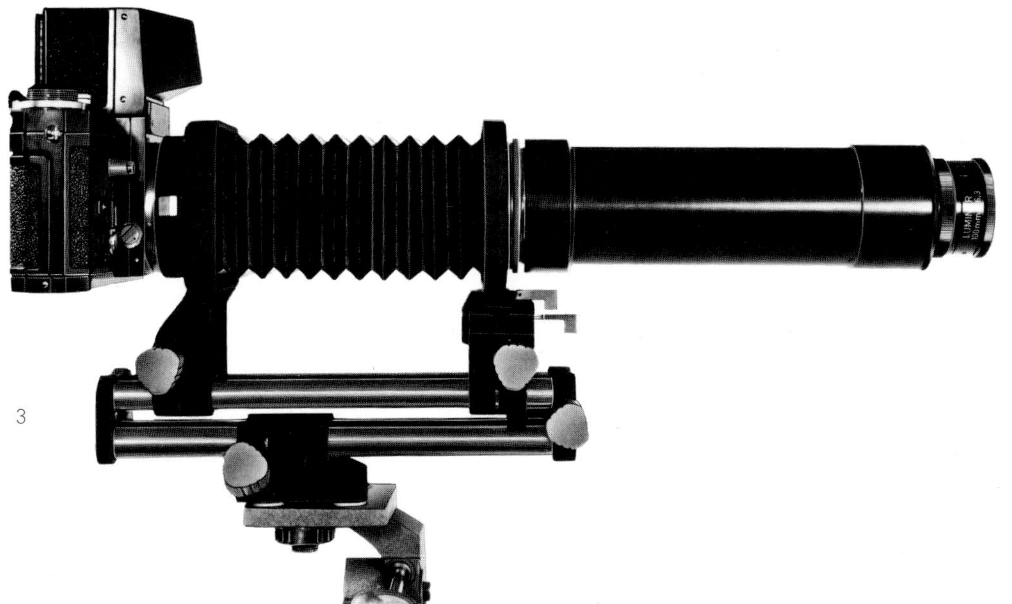

3

ted. To obviate this fault it is necessary to use reflecting screens – simply pieces of white Bristol board – positioned on the side opposite the flash and held fairly close to the subject. The same result can be obtained by using two flashes positioned on either side of the camera. It is then necessary, in order to ensure sufficient clarity of detail, to be careful to introduce a measure of asymmetry in the layout of the lighting, either by choosing two flash units of different luminosity or by positioning one of them closer to the subject.

Another disadvantage of using an electronic flash is that it is difficult to evaluate the quality of the lighting, since the light is emitted for only a short period. When taking photographs indoors, it is possible to visualize approximately the result that will be obtained by placing a

1 Summar 24 mm lens by Leitz, designed for very close photography (reproduction ratios of 4 to 5). A flat adapter ring has been specially made for connecting to the bellows.

2 Luminar 100 mm lens by Zeiss, designed for reproduction ratios between 1 and 8, mounted with the aid of a special adapter ring on a Nikon PB 4 bellows.

3 An 18 cm extension ring fitted to the end of the bellows makes it possible to obtain a maximum reproduction ratio of nearly 4 (the rather long focal length of the lens entails considerable extension).

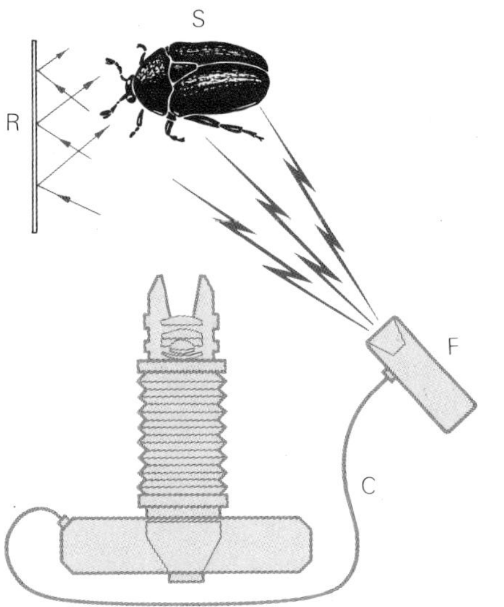

PHOTOGRAPHY USING A
SINGLE FLASH UNIT

R — Reflecting screen (of white
cardboard) to reduce the shadows.

F — Flash in lateral position
(ensuring definition of details).

C — Flash-synchronizing cable.

S — Subject.

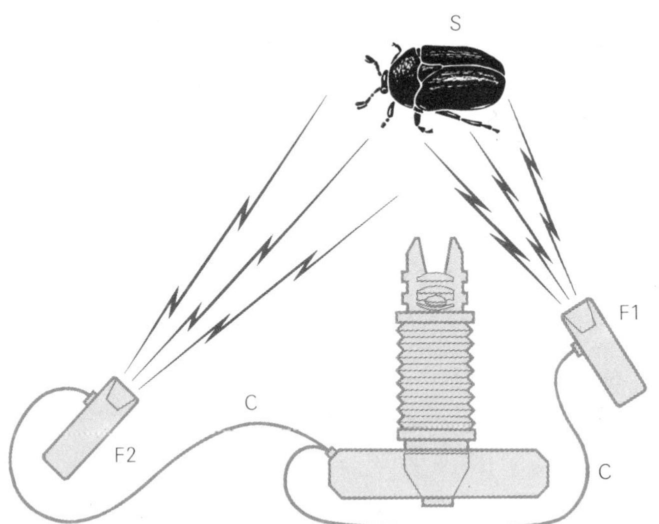

PHOTOGRAPHY USING TWO
FLASH UNITS

F1 — Flash providing main
illumination. This is positioned
closer to the subject and nearer
the axis of exposure.

F2 — Flash reducing the shadows
resulting from illumination by F1.
This is positioned further away
and more to one side.

C — Synchronizing cables.

P — Multiple socket enabling
several cables to be connected to
the camera.

S — Subject.

It is preferable to direct the main
lighting on to the head of the
animal.

modelling light (a 60 W krypton lamp
will do) in front of the flash or
flashes; the operation should be
carried out in as dim a light as
possible (with the blinds drawn).
This will make it possible to correct
the position of a flash which might
cause unwanted shadows, and to
ensure that the reflecting screens are
in the best position.

The final disadvantage of the
electronic flash is that it produces a
very noticeable fading-off between
the lighting of the foreground, which
corresponds to a correct exposure,
and that of the background, which
appears increasingly dark until it
becomes completely black. This
effect is emphasized all the more
when a low-power flash is used. To
mask it, one can arrange a more or
less flat background behind the
subject, either natural (a piece of
bark or a large leaf) or artificial (a
sheet of coloured paper), which, by
blocking the perspective, prevents the
appearance of extensive dark zones.

A low-power flash (G.N. 18 to 22)
is practical for photography in the
field. Its weight and small size enable
it to be attached to a lateral bar
forming an integral part of the
camera body. For studio photography it is better to use a more
powerful flash (G.N. 25 to 32, with
which there is less reduction in background lighting) mounted on a stand
and completely separate from the
camera.

'Computerized' flashguns. These can
be used for subjects at distances of
down to about eighteen inches
(50 cm). They are thus of no advantage in photomacrography, where in
order to use them it is necessary to
disconnect the automatic device con-
trolling the duration of the flash.

Ring flash units. These have a ring-
shaped flashtube which is positioned
around the lens like a crown. It gives
'flat' lighting (without any shadow)
which is not very attractive but might
be useful with high reproduction
ratios, when the short distance between the lens and the subject makes
it difficult to position an ordinary
flashgun (when there is a risk of the
shadow of the lens falling on the
subject).

When a flash unit is used, determining the correct exposure is a
matter of determining the distance
to be used from the flash to the
subject, allowing for the 'aperture
selected (generally f/16 or f/22). This
distance depends on the intensity
(guide number) of the flash, the
reproduction ratio and particularly

the speed of the film used. All these variables necessitate complicated calculations in order to obtain the all-important distance. It is easier, and above all quicker, to make use of a previously prepared table giving the distances for each aperture, as a function of a range of ratios and guide numbers (see the tables at the end of the book).

Nevertheless, it remains necessary to determine once and for all the precise guide number of the flash used. The G.N. provided by the manufacturer – which, it must be remembered, is often optimistic – is valid only for distances of about three to sixteen feet (1–5 m). Below this it rapidly decreases as the flash is brought closer to the subject (the effective performance of the flash reflector being reduced at short distances). With the aid of a test colour film a series of pictures can be taken with different ratios (0·1, 0·5, 1, 2) using the same aperture (f/22 for example). The subject chosen must have an average colour shade, neither too light nor too dark. For each reproduction ratio, several photos should be taken progressively decreasing the distance between the flash and the subject, commencing with the distance corresponding to the theoretical G.N. of the flash as shown on the table, and continuing down through at least the next five numbers. The results make it possible to find the actual G.N. of the flash and its variations as a function of R (the latter being that for the speed of film used), following which reference can be made to the distance charts. In each case the G.N. corresponding to the reproduction ratio used is taken, extrapolating for the intermediate ratios: for an exposure at R = 0·7, for example, the G.N. would have a mean value between the G.N. for R = 0·5 and the G.N. for R = 1 as determined by the tests. The values shown in the tables are valid for subjects of average colour characteristics. For light-coloured subjects it is necessary to correct the exposure by closing the aperture by half a stop (or multiplying the distance from the flash to the subject by 1·2 to 1·4, which comes to the same thing). If, on the other hand, the subject is dark-coloured, it is necessary to open the aperture to the same extent or divide the distance by the same figures.

Photographic film

The main characteristic of a film is its sensitivity or speed (the higher the speed, the less light it requires). This is assessed according to two different scales:

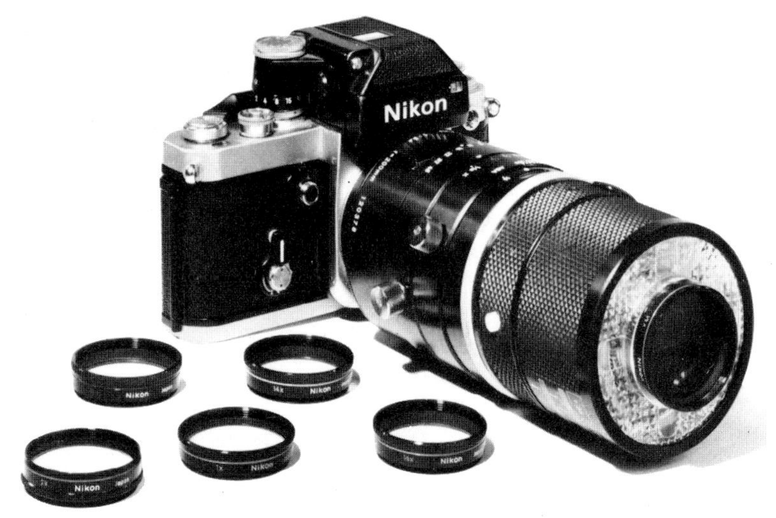

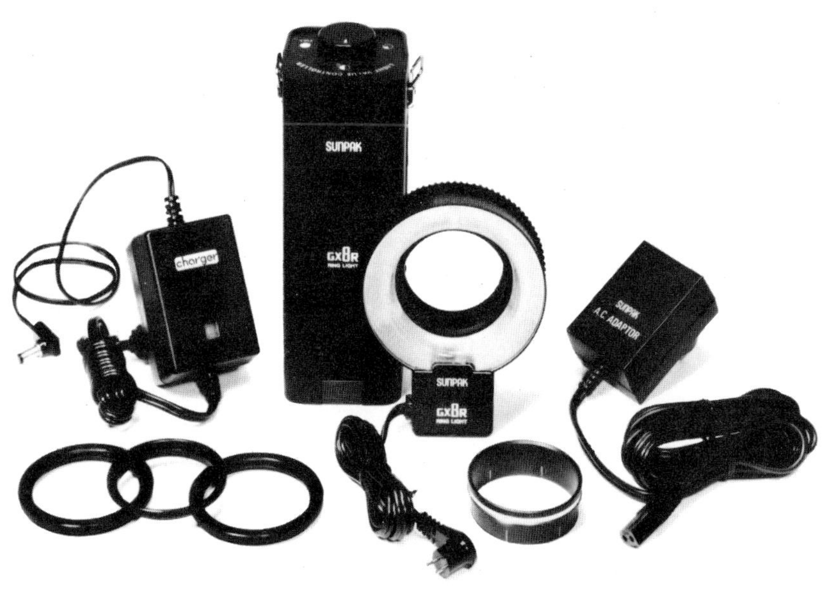

Nikon F2 with Nikkor f/5·6 200 mm medical lens and its set of 6 supplementary lenses. Built-in ring-type electronic flash, incorporating 4 modelling lamps. The diaphragm closes automatically to the required stop in relation to the speed of the film and to the reproduction ratio (from 1/15 to 1). Used for difficult exposures requiring very rapid action. The illumination provided is devoid of shadow.

At the bottom of the page: Sunpak electronic flash, adaptable to different types of lens. Three intensities of flash are available.

(a) on the ASA (American Standards Association) scale the speed is proportionate to the number: a 100 ASA film is twice as fast as a 50 ASA film;

(b) on the DIN (Deutsche Industrie Normen) scale, the speed doubles for every three numbers: an 18 DIN film is twice as fast as a 15 DIN film.

When there is sufficient light (daylight with a low reproduction ratio or electronic flash), it is an advantage to use low-speed films (25 to 50 ASA or 15 to 18 DIN), the fine grain of which gives a picture with well-defined detail. Among the colour films Kodachrome 25 at present holds the record in its class with a resolving power of 1/100 mm. Agfachrome (50 ASA) similarly gives very good results.

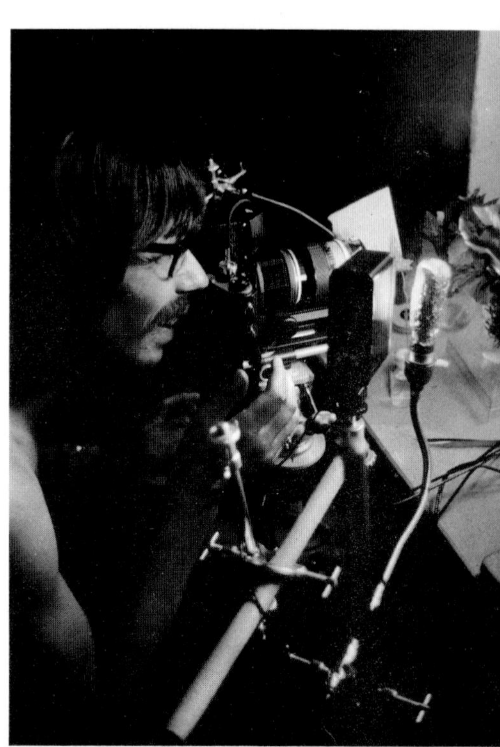

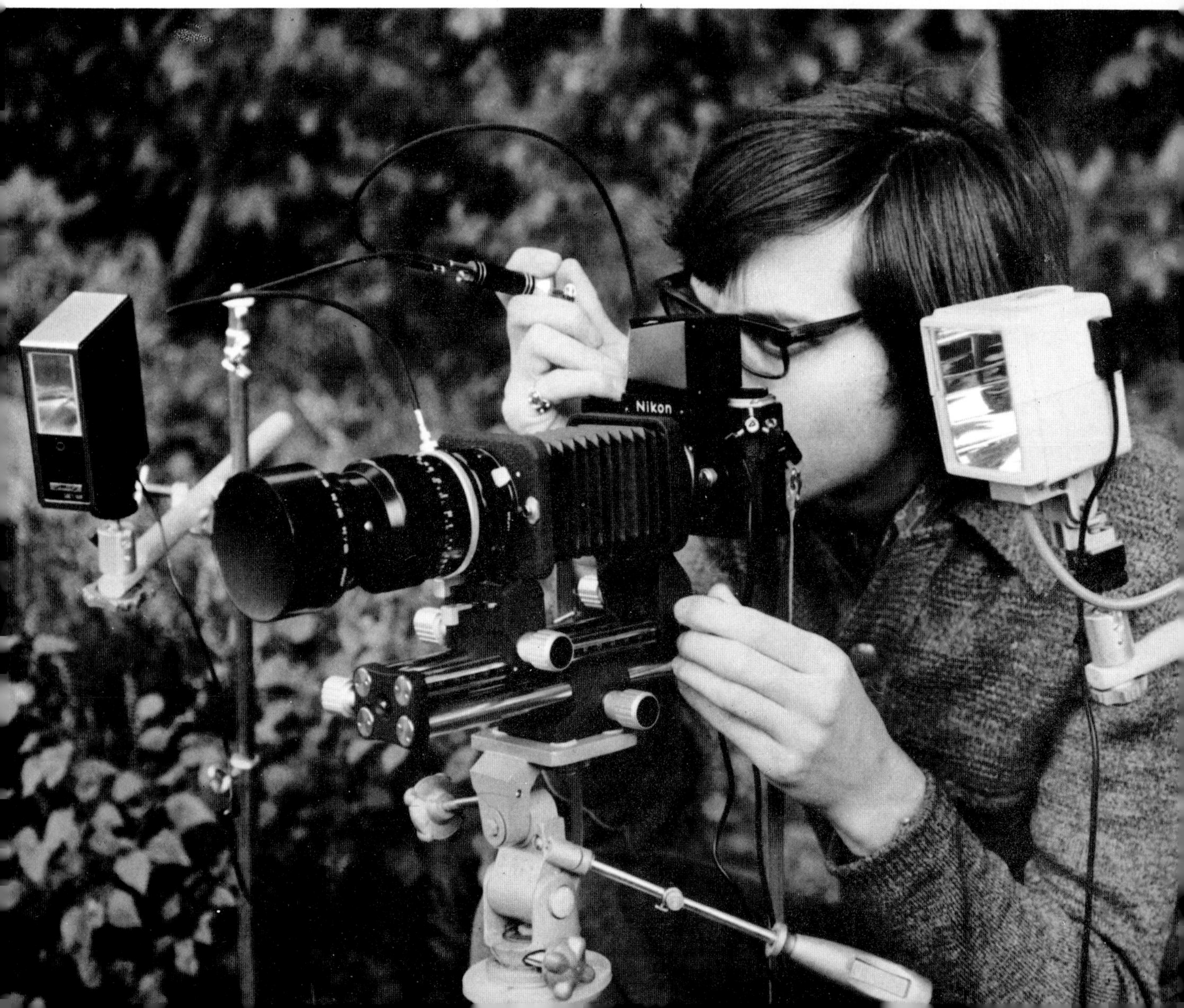

Under poor lighting conditions (daylight, ratios around 0·5 or more), use must be made of fast films (100 to 400 ASA), which can cope with almost everything because of their high sensitivity. Examples of these are 3M Color Slide (100 ASA), Fujichrome R (100 ASA), or High Speed Ektachrome (160 ASA), which can be 'pushed' to a speed of 400 ASA if given appropriate laboratory treatment. The images obtained with this type of film are more grainy but have greater softness of contrast.

Useful accessories

A tripod is especially useful for indoor photography. For short-distance exposures, it permits very accurate framing and focusing. For the latter operation, a very useful accessory is the focusing track; by means of its rack rail, it is possible to move the combined camera and lens forward or backward. Certain types of bellows are equipped with a double set of rails, the lower rails acting as the track.

Outdoors, when using a large range of shooting distances, it is often preferable to hold the camera in the hand; the framing can then easily be adjusted as necessary.

With 200 mm or 300 mm telephoto lenses, the use of a gunstock mount reduces the risk of camera shake, when using a medium shutter speed. With a 300 mm lens it is possible to take photographs down to 1/60th of a second.

Most modern reflex cameras are equipped with a ground glass screen with which is combined a central optical system – a split-image range-finder or micro-prisms – to facilitate focusing. These devices – the use of which in present-day photography seems to us somewhat doubtful – become completely inoperable, and thus a nuisance, in close-up photography; their presence in the middle of the field is a disturbing factor when framing. If the design of the camera makes it possible to replace the viewing screen, it would be wise to choose a plain ground glass screen or one of the Fresnel ring type (the

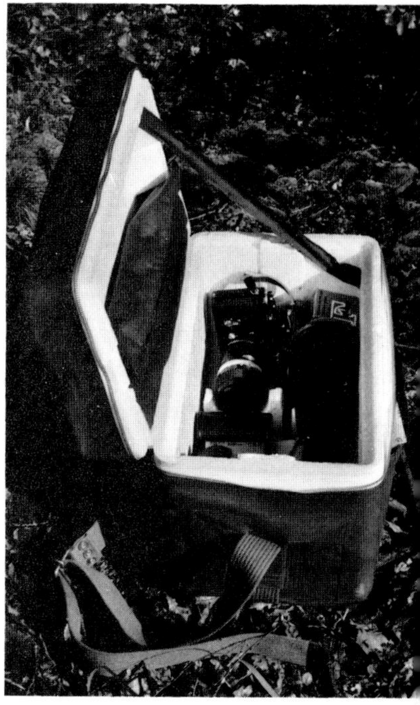

Above: An example of a hold-all, made from a camping 'fridge' of expanded polystyrene enclosed in a cloth bag with a zip-fastener. The equipment is very efficiently protected against knocks and heat. Polystyrene partitions have been glued inside the box to provide compartments for the various accessories.

Left: Using an angle-finder, fitted on to the prism viewfinder, for photography at ground level.

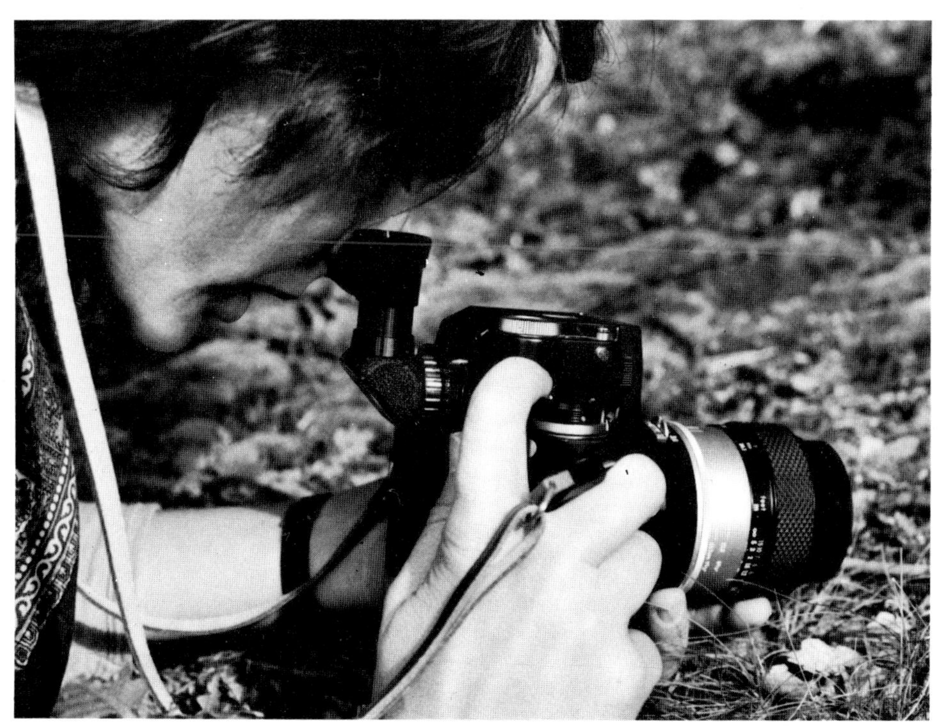

latter being more luminous). When photographs are taken at a high reproduction ratio (2 to 10, or microscope photograph) the small quantity of light reaching the ground glass screen – the grain of which becomes very clear – makes viewing difficult; in this case a viewing screen with a clear reticulated picture area will provide a considerable increase in brightness and make focusing easy.

vertically. If the viewfinder is removeable, the prism can be replaced by a waist-level viewfinder, which also makes viewfinding possible over the camera (in both cases the image is reversed from right to left).

Finally, the use of a motor can be of assistance in photomacrography. The main function of this accessory is to obtain photographic sequences in bursts (one to five photos per second). Unfortunately, photo-

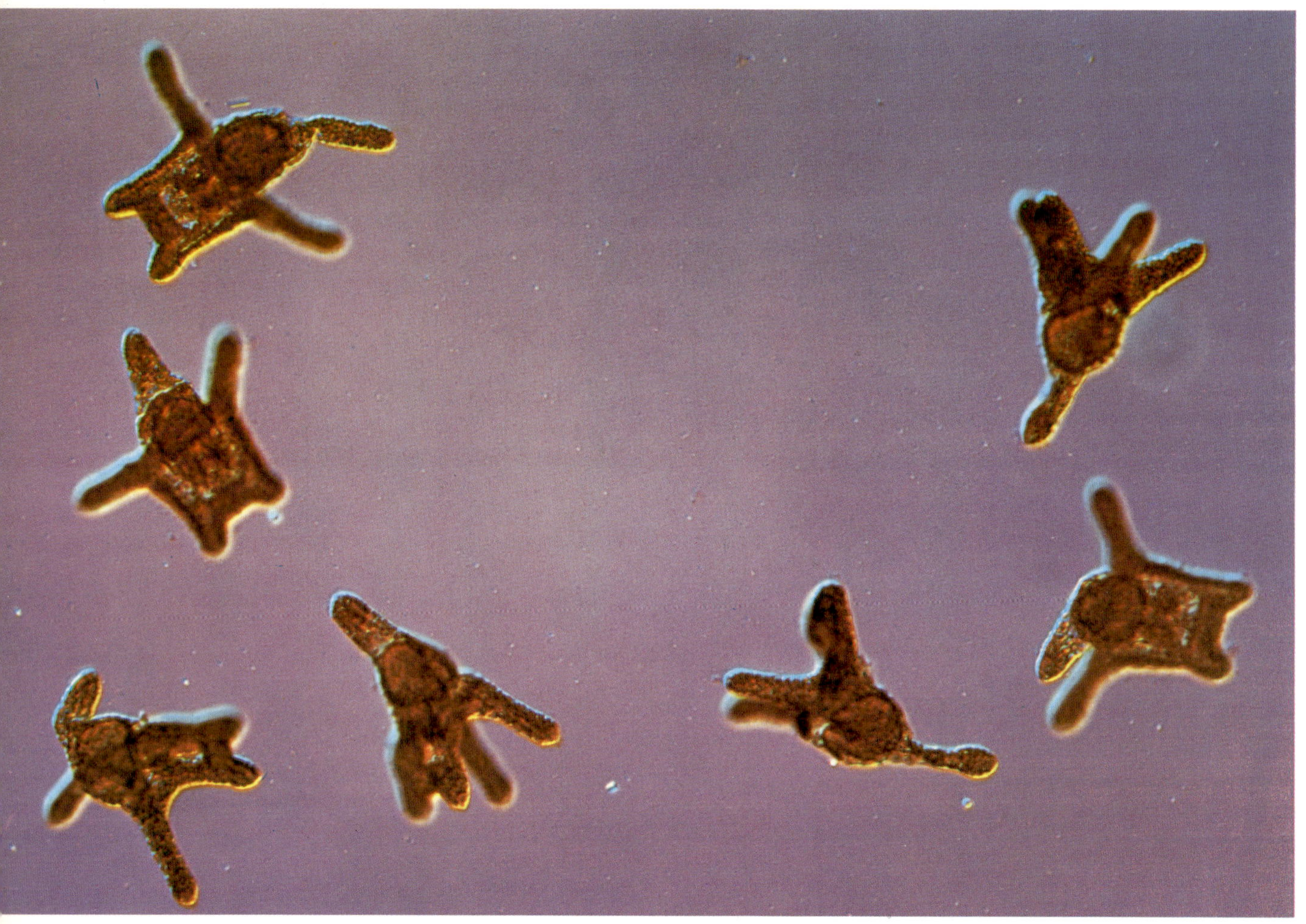

Photographing small creatures often makes it necessary to work at ground level. In this situation, to avoid too many contortions in reaching a position with the eye behind the viewfinder, one can use a right-angle finder which is fitted to the back of the prism and reflects the image

macrography usually requires the use of a flash unit, and the photographer is forced to observe a period of delay between each picture corresponding to the flash unit recovery time (three to eight seconds). Under these circumstances the motor becomes a useless luxury. On the other

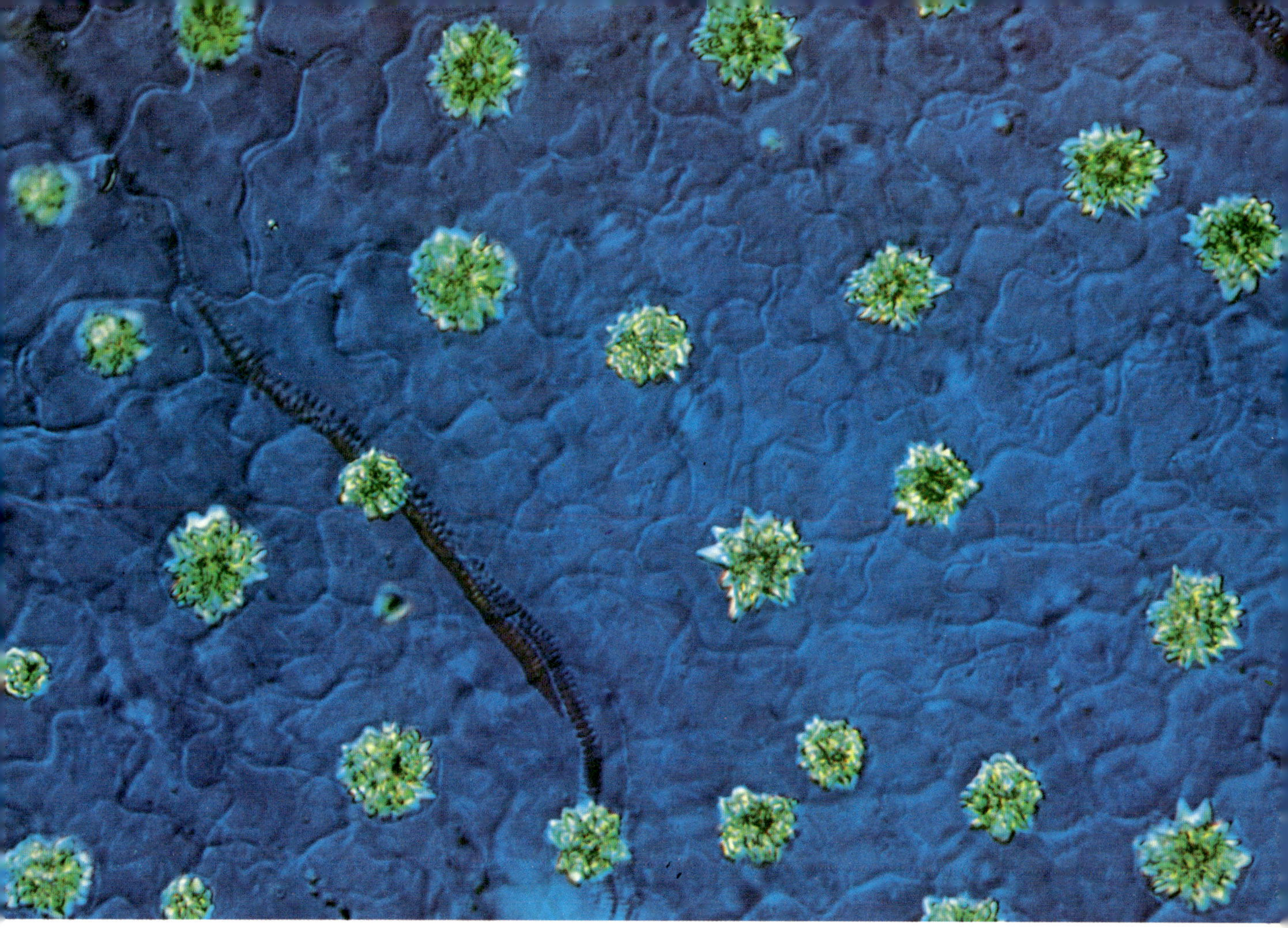

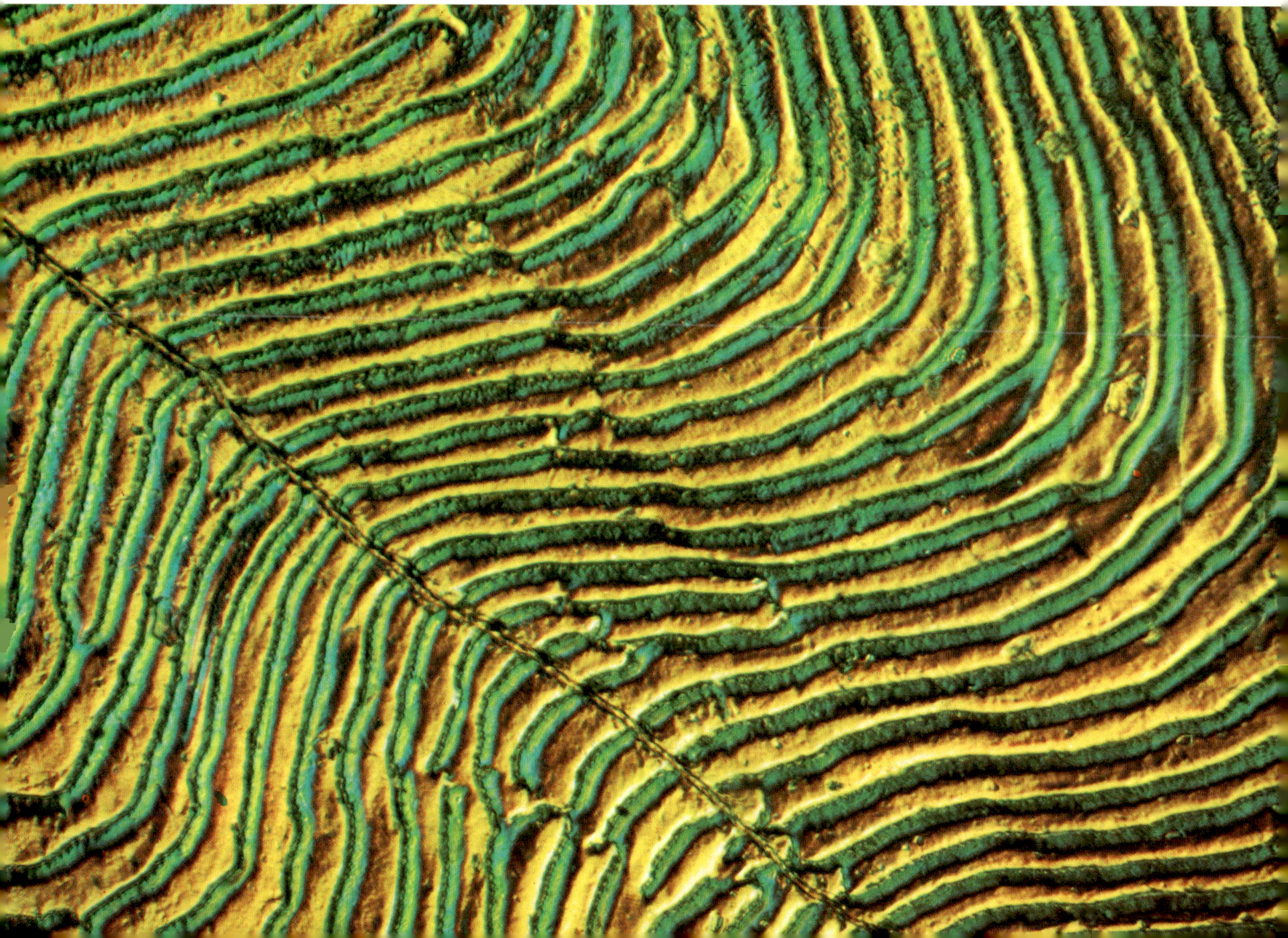

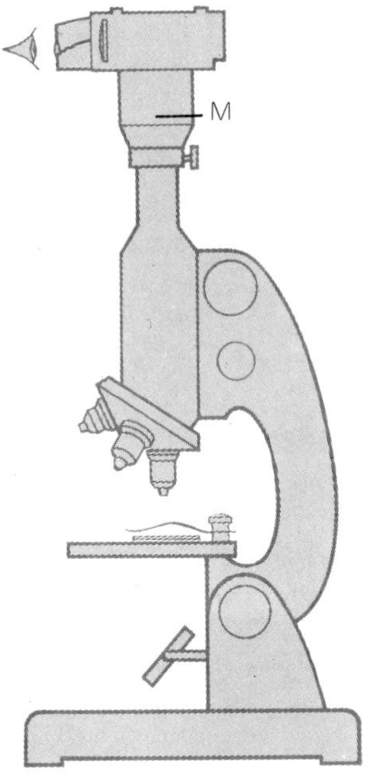

24 x 36 reflex camera fitted to a microscope. Using a 'micro' connecting piece (M), the camera body becomes an integral part of the eye-piece support tube.

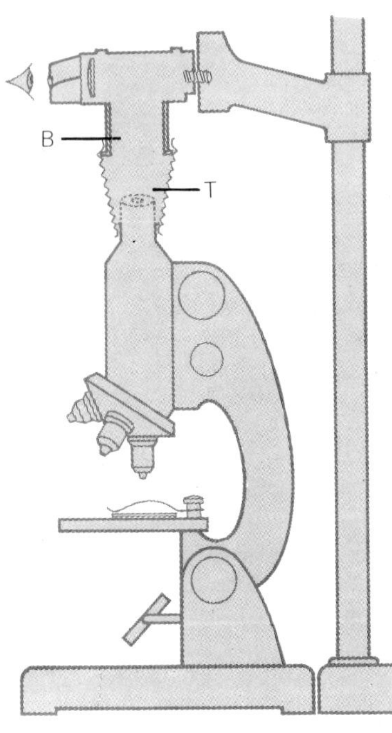

Camera fastened to a stand and connected to the microscope by means of a flexible sleeve of lightproof cloth (T).
B – extension ring.

hand, when used as required it avoids the need for resetting by hand and all the drawbacks this involves: certain insects which allow themselves to be approached closely will take flight at the moment of resetting, frightened by the sudden movement of the thumb; in the case of high-precision work (with high ratios or microscope photographs), resetting by hand might alter the focusing or framing.

Microscope photography (Photomicrography)

It is much easier than one might think to obtain black and white or colour photographs with the aid of a microscope, at least if one limits oneself to relatively small magnifications. In this instance, too, a reflex camera is the ideal instrument.

The camera must be used without its lens; this is replaced by the combined objective lens and eye-piece lens of the microscope. The camera is firmly attached to the microscope by means of a special connecting tube – manufacturers provide this accessory – which can be adapted to all eye-piece lenses of standard diameter. The camera can also be furnished with extension rings and the end of the tube connected to that of the microscope by means of a completely lightproof sleeve of black cloth, the camera being held in position with the aid of a stand (a copying stand or a tripod). The latter ensures that vibrations produced at the moment of release are not transmitted to the microscope.

Focusing is carried out by means of the geared rail of the microscope. It is controlled on the ground glass screen (or better, on a clear screen substituted for the ground glass screen, if the viewfinder screen is removeable).

For black and white photography, a simple opal lamp constitutes the best source of light. Inserting a yellow-green filter makes it possible to use the capacities of lenses to the greatest possible advantage.

For colour photography, a slide projector will provide a light which is both powerful and well-balanced (3,200 K). Inserting a ground glass screen will provide more uniform lighting. Films for artificial light can be used or daylight films, in which case it is advisable to fit an 80-A filter (see working data on page 152).

An electronic flash – preferably of low power – can equally well be used under the same circumstances, with a daylight film and without a filter. A modelling light placed in front of the flash opening makes it possible to adjust the angle of the mirror and its focus. It should be swung out of the way immediately before the flash is fired.

The use of polarised light often gives spectacular results in colour photography through the microscope. This kind of lighting is easily obtained by using two sheets of polarising film, which can be bought cheaply from dealers specializing in microscopy. One of them is placed horizontally under the stage of the microscope, and the other, cut into a small piece of appropriate diameter, inside the eye-piece. The latter is then rotated on its own axis, and objects capable of polarising light (micro-crystals, plant structures, etc.) can be seen to light up with bright colours on a dark background.

In all cases, the exposure is determined by tests, varying the exposure time from single to double (for example, going from 1/30 to 1 second – 1/30, 1/15, 1/8, 1/4, 1/2, 1), or using flash, by inserting neutral grey filters of densities increasing from single to double (50%, 25%, 12%, 6% and 3% light transmission)*.

The results obtained from a typical set-up with a given method of lighting and magnification can then be

*The Kodak Wratten No. 96 series of fourteen neutral filters ranges from 90% to 0·01% transmission.

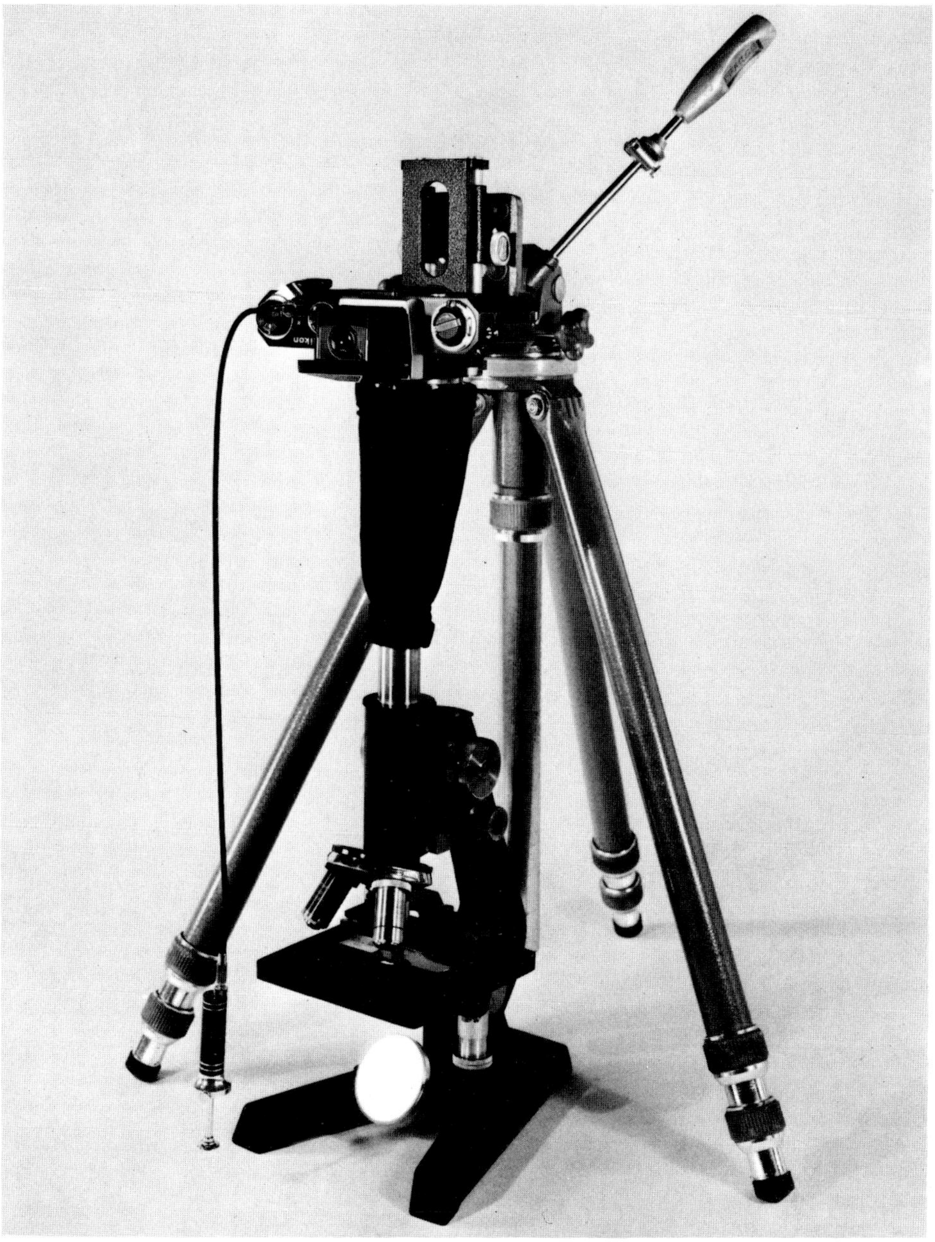

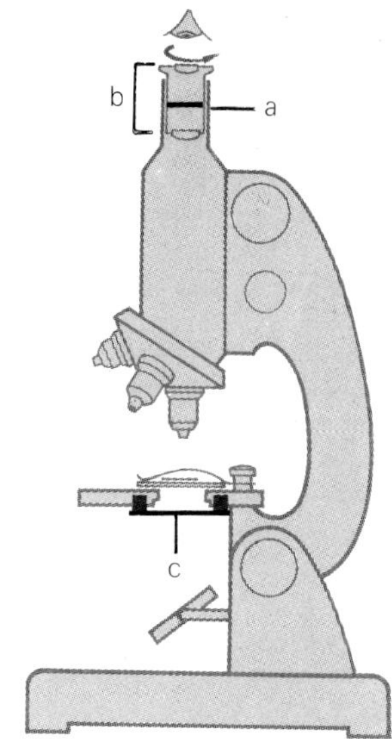

used for other photographic subjects under the same conditions (it is, however, wise always to take three pictures – typical exposure, this exposure divided by 2 and then multiplied by 2).

Certain sufficiently sensitive independently-used photoelectric exposure meters (Lunasix-3 with Micro attachment), used at the eye-piece, can indicate the intensity of light available and, after being calibrated, can define the correct exposure.

(Meters installed behind the lens of the camera are generally not sensitive enough to operate under these conditions.)

All these data are valid for low magnifications (lenses × 2·5, × 4 or × 10; eye-pieces × 5 to × 10). Higher magnifications (lenses from × 25 to × 100) require sophisticated lighting techniques which are explained in specialized books on microscopy (the use of a condenser, Köhler lighting, collector and field stop, etc.).

Above: Use of polarised light in microscopy.

(a) Round disc of transparent polarising sheet placed on the central diaphragm of the eye-piece. This is called the analyser.

(b) Eye-piece. The analyser can be inserted by unscrewing the upper component.

(c) Square piece of transparent polarising sheet, held under the stage by adhesive tape (shown in dark grey). This is called the polariser.

By rotating the eye-piece inside the tube, a position can be found in which the background appears dark (the position of extinction).

If the object observed polarises light, it then appears more or less bright and often in vivid colours.

The effect obtained changes progressively as the position of the analyser is altered.

Top left: A 24 x 36 reflex camera fitted onto a microscope. The use of a waist-level viewfinder makes viewing easier.

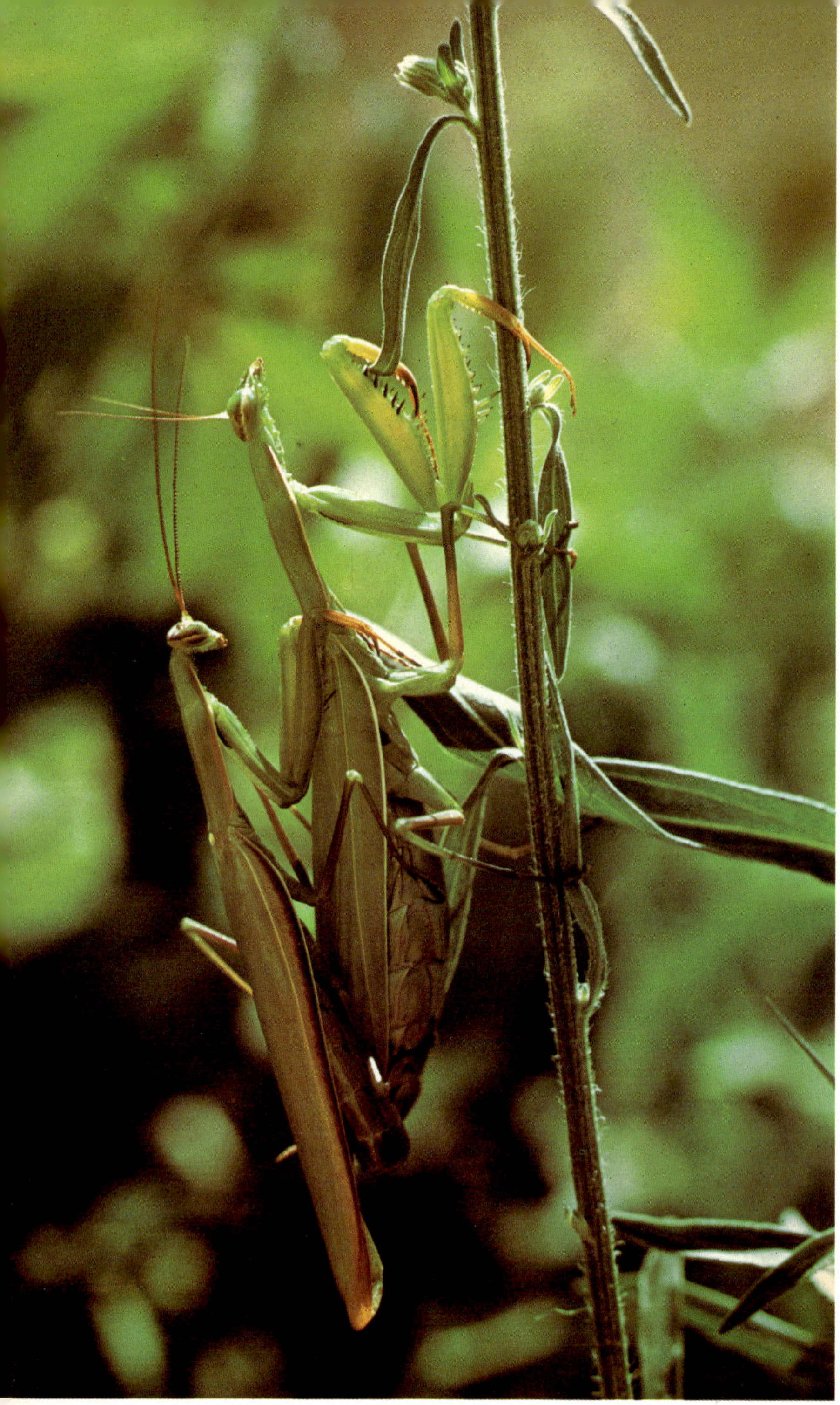

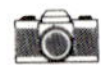

Praying Mantises (x 1·5).
Mating. The male, the smaller of
the two, is clutching his partner
round the middle with his
predatory feet.

Reproduction ratio: 0·3.
Lens: Macro 55 mm.
Aperture: f/5·6.
Exposure time: 1/125th of a
second.
Natural light from behind.

Using the pictures

In order to make satisfactory progress in photographic techniques, it is necessary to make a record card for each completed film, detailing the conditions under which each photograph was taken. It is then possible to avoid repeating certain mistakes and to choose the method of operation best suited to each subject. In the case of slides, the number of the film followed by that of the picture (recorded on the edge of the frame) makes it possible to recover the technical information relating to each photograph with the aid of a card index in which the cards are carefully filed in the numerical order of the films.

Experience shows that the most practicable method of classification is one which uses the conventional subdivisions of zoology and botany. There is a whole series of progressively more detailed subdivisions which make it possible quickly to locate the required picture (and to learn the scientific classifications).

Old slides are too often left to lie neglected in their original boxes. Once classified, they become immediately available. It is then possible to arrange a sequence – a succession of slides projected onto a screen. The projection of photographic sequences – different stages in a metamorphosis, for example – makes the subject-matter appear more alive. It is also possible to alternate between close-ups and more general scenes which show the location of events. This will improve the tempo of the display; close-ups which might not hold the attention of the audience if shown in regular succession will have greater impact.

A sound tape will help even more to reinforce the evocative power of the photographs. A whole range of natural sounds can be used to bring the slides to life – the noise of the wind, of leaves, of running water, of rain; bird-song, insect noises, the croaking of frogs, the buzzing of bees, etc. It is possible to buy commercial recordings of these sounds of the living world. Anyone who has his own portable tape-recorder will find it fascinating to make his own recordings of these sounds, even if they are not always of professional quality.

Recording in the field

A moving coil microphone of directional type should be used if possible: it records sounds only from a limited portion of the area towards which it is directed. This reduces undesirable intrusive noises (vehicles, aircraft or even the croaking of frogs where these are plentiful) which are the bane of outdoor recording.

Moreover, even a light breeze can give rise to unwanted interference (rumble) at recording level. A moderately priced accessory, the 'wind bonnet' – a form of hemispherical hood of foamed plastic used to cover the microphone – will eliminate this nuisance. A fine-fabric handkerchief might even do the job.

Bearing in mind that the sounds made by insects and amphibians are generally of low volume, it will help to position the microphone as close as possible to the source of the sound (without, however, reducing the distance to less than about four inches, as this might result in distorted recording).

A parabolic reflector is a very useful instrument for recording creatures difficult to approach (such as cicadas, frogs and birds). This accessory magnifies the sounds considerably while improving the directional capacity of the microphone (the metallic reflector receives the sound vibrations and reflects them so that they converge on the front of the microphone).

Finally, the faster the magnetic tape is made to run, the wider is the range of sound frequencies which can be recorded. The maximum speed (usually 19 cm/s) is, therefore, recommended in all cases, particularly to capture the very high sound frequencies used by insects.

Common Toads (x 2·5).
During mating, the male remains perched on the back of the female, gripping her tightly behind the front legs.

Reproduction ratio: 0·5.
Lens: 105 mm mounted on bellows.
Aperture: f/11-16.
Electronic flash with reflecting screen to reduce the shadows.
Film: Kodachrome 25.

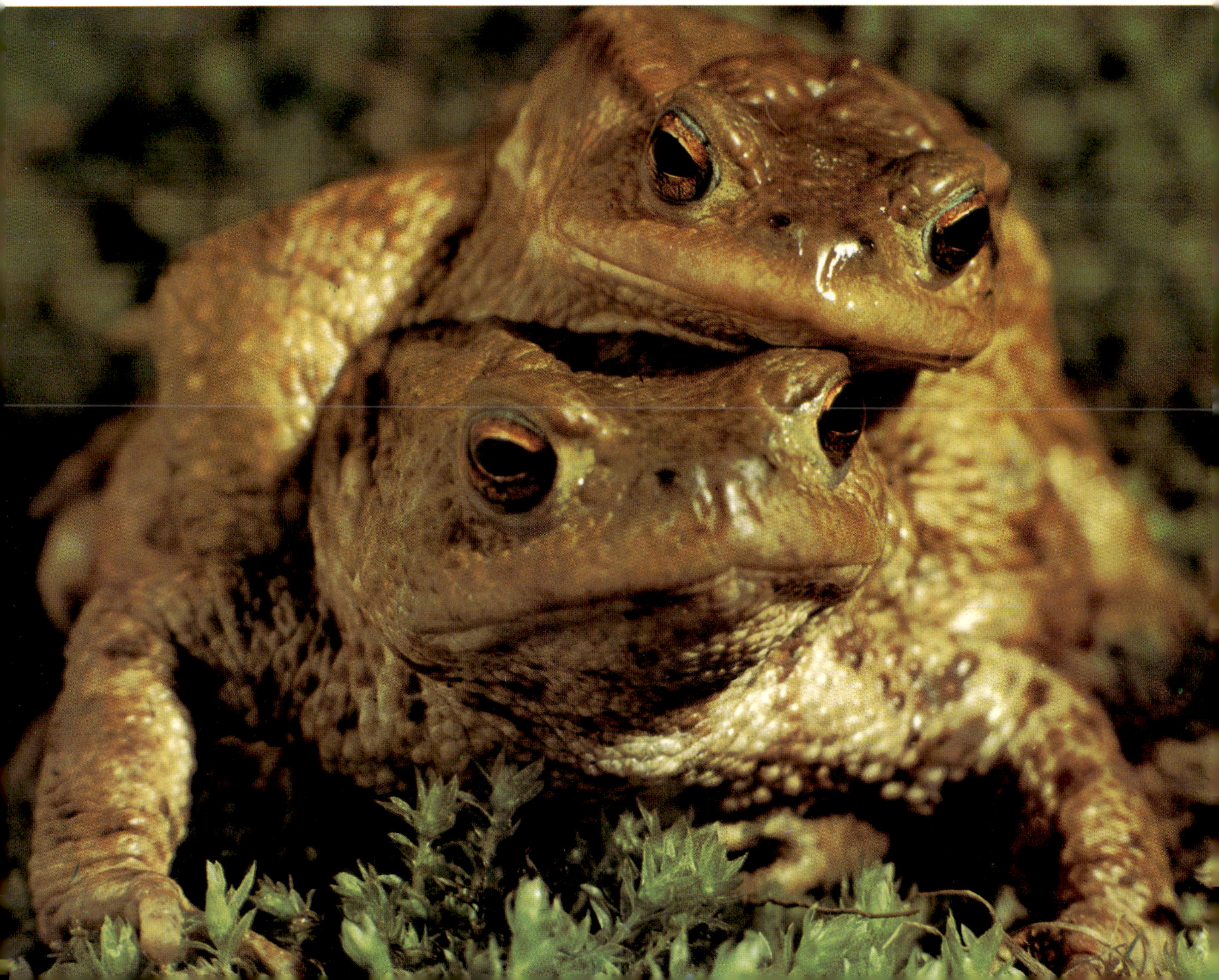

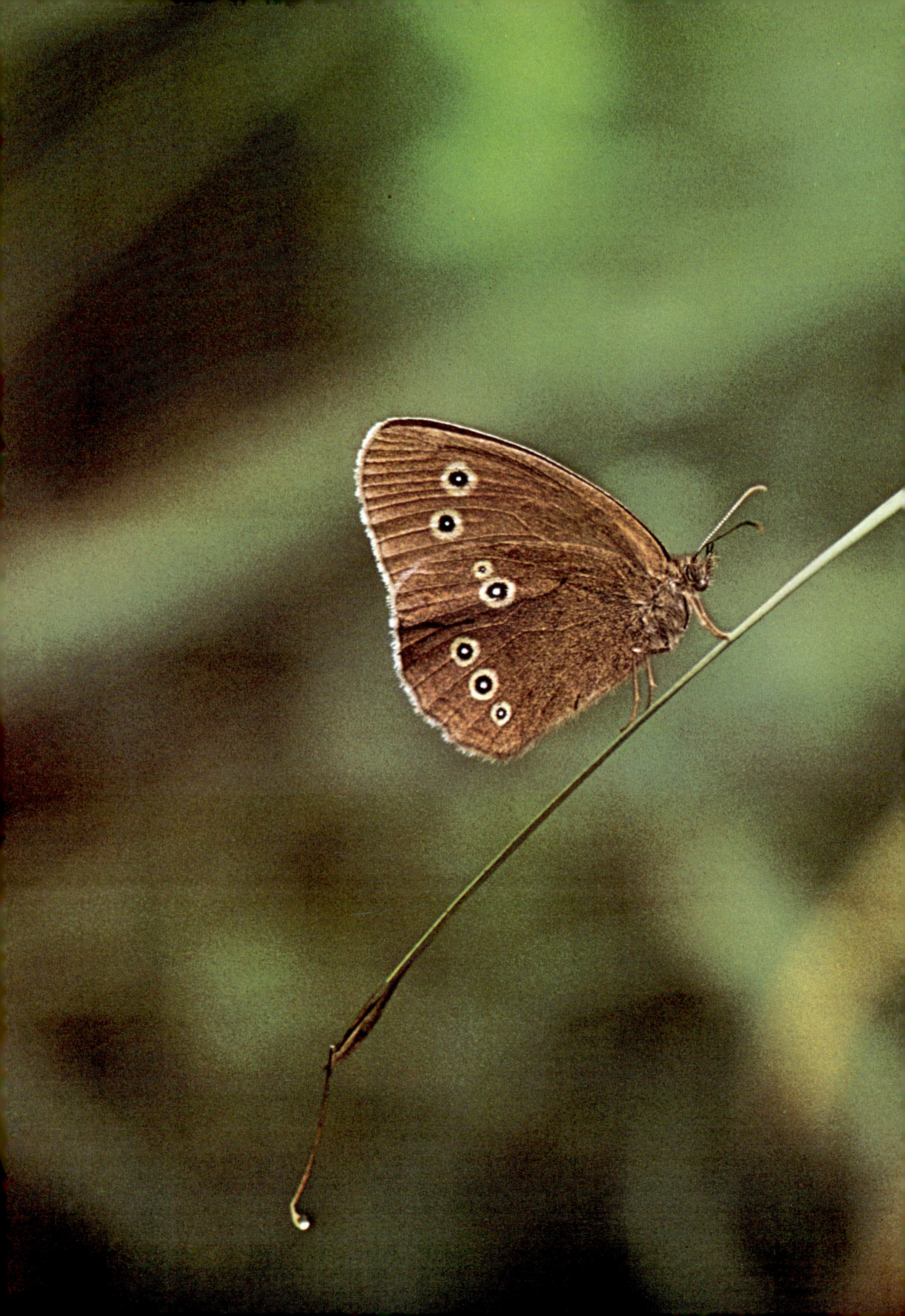

Outdoor exploration

Meadow · Water's edge · Forest

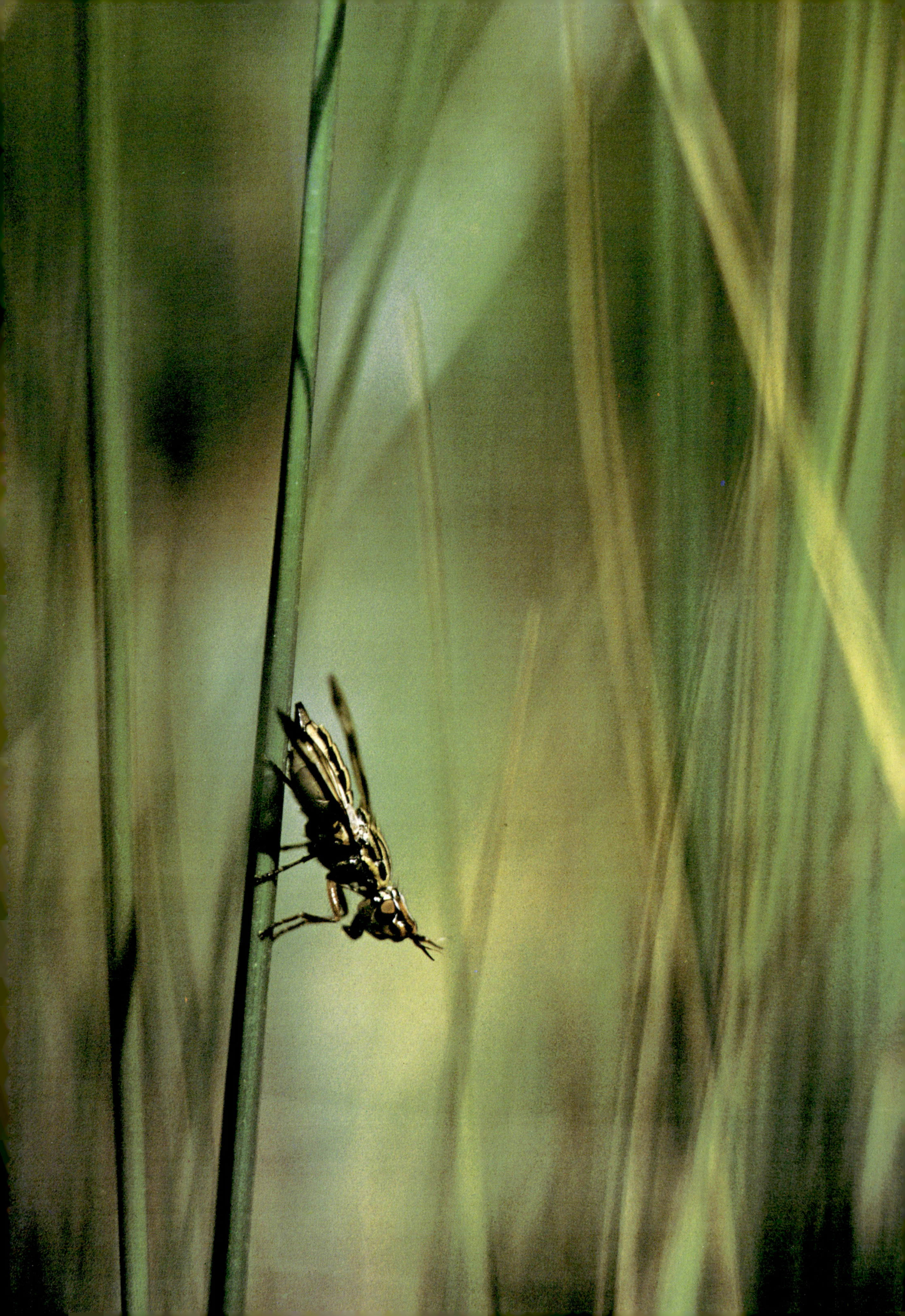

The meadow

The world of flowers

The meadow is without doubt the place where the close interdependence which links the animal kingdom to the vegetable kingdom is most evident.

When the first flowers appear in the spring, quickly followed by an absolute outburst of multi-coloured blossoms, one can at the same time witness the appearance of thousands of honey-gathering insects, the buzzing of which constitutes the familiar music of the meadow. This double event, which recurs punctually each year and is taken for granted by everyone, still represents surviving evidence of a major break-through in the evolution of the living world which took place two hundred million years ago, during the Jurassic period.

In this distant age a revolution occurred in the vegetable kingdom: the appearance of the first plants with flowers. The insects had already been present on this planet for two hundred million years. The 'invention' of the flower, however, was the main factor in their subsequent tremendously successful evolution. The process of improvement of flowers went on continuously: bright colours serving as 'beacons', perfumed substances, the corolla on which to alight – these were the irresistable features which they developed to attract and beguile the insects. In turn, the latter developed a complete arsenal of mouth-parts to enable them to take full advantage of this Heaven-sent supply of food. In exchange for these gifts, the flowering plant was assured of its future generations: the pollen carried by the insects from one flower to another ensured that the ovules would be fertilized and would produce seeds. The incredible diversity of the flowers and honey-gathering insects which can be found in meadow-land today is the result of this very long period of parallel evolution. In a single field of lucerne, with only one kind of flower from which honey can be collected, biologists have up to now been able to count 790 different species of insect.

Midsummer is the time for the umbellifers to flower, and they appear to be the favourite meeting-place of all the honey-gathering insects. A veritable swarm of small beetles, flies, butterflies, wasps and bees brings life to these large white flower-heads, which make such convenient landing platforms. Made up of hundreds of minute flowers, they provide abundant pollen and nectar which are easily available to all; the naturalist-photographer will find them of interest too. Moreover, he will find that they act, as it were, as natural reflectors which illuminate the subjects with light from all directions, without any hard shadows. It is only necessary to be careful to reduce the aperture by one stop when using flash or conversely to open it by one stop when using daylight, relative to what is indicated by the photoelectric exposure meter.

Other flowers do not provide their nectar so freely. Their special structure reserves this precious food for a

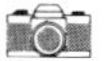

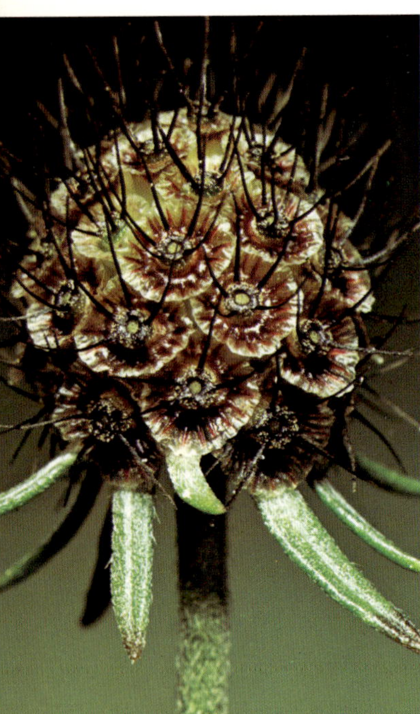

Composite fruit of the Field Scabious (x 6).
Each round head consists of dozens of minute fruits packed closely together. Each has a delicate involucre and five long awns, which act as a parachute when they are carried away by the wind after ripening. This helps to scatter the seeds over a wide area.

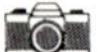

Reproduction ratio: 2.
Lens: Macro 55 mm mounted on bellows in reverse position.
Aperture: f/16-22.
Electronic flash.

few privileged insects the anatomy of which is highly adapted to collecting it.

The Corn Cockle, for example, which keeps its nectar hidden at the bottom of the long tube of its corolla, is visited by the Humming-bird Hawk Moth. This moth, which is equipped with a very long proboscis, is also able to hover seemingly motionless in order to collect the nectar: the combination of these two features qualifies it as the chosen guest of this otherwise miserly flower.

A plant much sought after by bees, the Meadow Sage, with its erect clusters of purplish-blue flowers, has certainly developed a most efficient means of dusting its visitors with pollen. The bee settles on it by clinging to the lower flared lip of the corolla, then moves forward into the flower in its search for nectar. As it does so, two long curved stamens drop rapidly on to the hairy back of the insect. As the latter backs out, these stamens return to their original position in the hollow of the upper lip, where they remain protected. The same balancing movement can be instigated by introducing a twig into the flower. In its search for perfection, therefore, the flower has thus developed highly efficient automatic dispensers of pollen. This surprising ability can form the basis of some fine photographic sequences.

Some flowers have no nectar. They have to use other kinds of bait to attract insects. The Bee Orchid, one of the numerous species of orchid found in Europe, uses a very sophisticated technique: its flower, both in its shape and smell, imitates the female of certain bees. It is, therefore, visited by males which, while trying to mate with it, find their pollen sacs filled before they discover their mistake.

Honey-gatherers

It is difficult to give general directions as to how to find honey-gathering

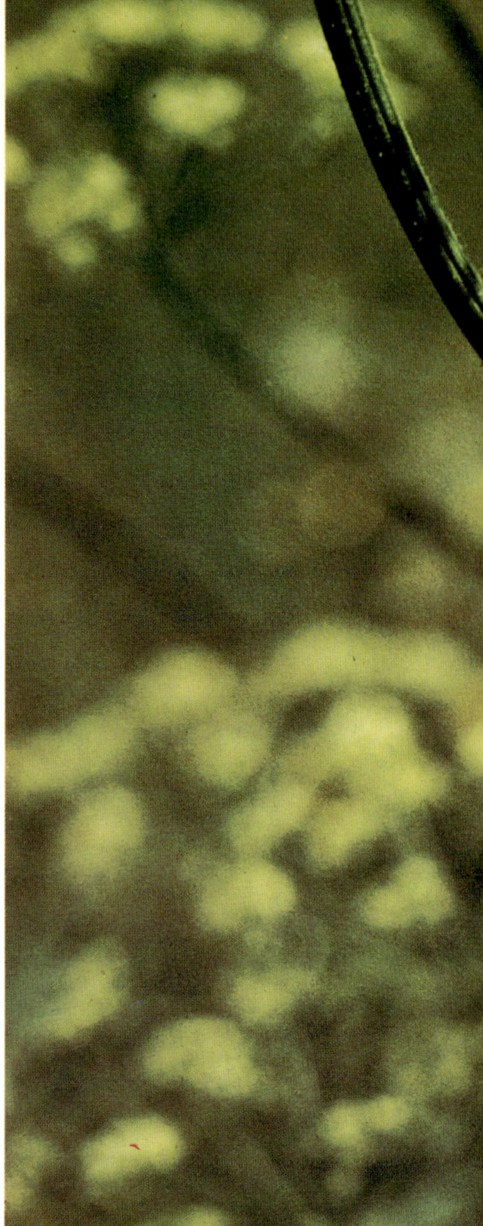

insects. Given the opportunity to spend a little time in a particular district, it is important to record very accurately the locations visited by insects and at what times they visit them.

Even in a garden, such locations are very strictly defined and none of them attracts honey-gathering insects for more than an hour or two a day. An insect operates in a universe on its own scale and is very sensitive to the kinds of 'microclimate' available to it: temperature, humidity and sunlight can vary considerably over a distance of a few feet for a creature of this size. Biologists have even

been able to study the very special microclimates which prevail inside flowers.

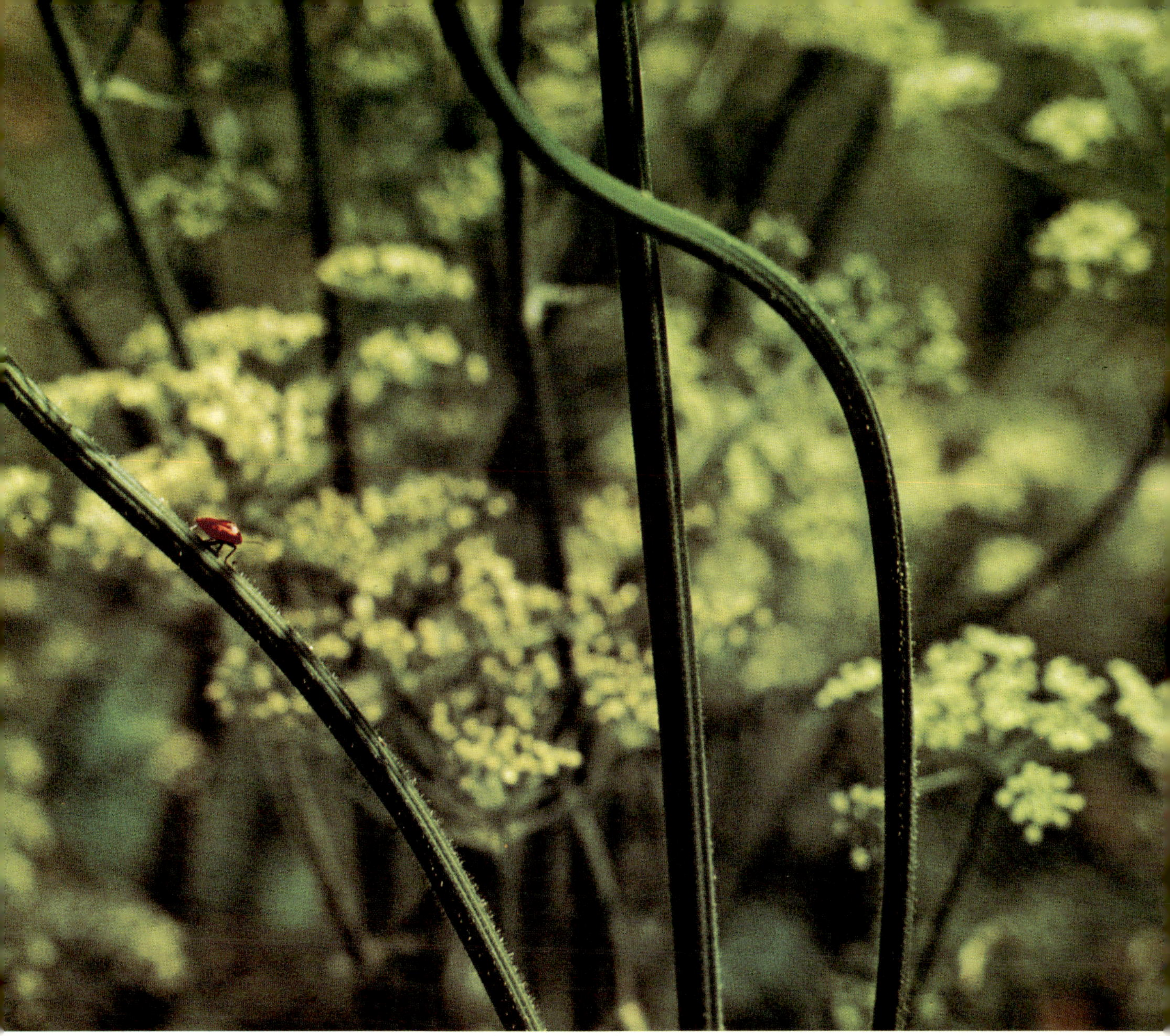

Having recorded this information, it is only necessary on subsequent days to visit all the locations by the clock; the visitors are always very punctual – at least provided the weather remains fine.

Not all flower-visiting insects are good flyers. One of the clumsiest – but also one of the most beautiful – is the Rose Chafer, the carapace of which is a brilliant metallic green. Its tastes are simple: all it likes is pollen, which it devours gluttonously with the aid of its mandibles, leaving the fastidiously arranged flower in disorder. To see it wallowing among the stamens, one might think it slow to react. It is in fact quite shy, and on the approach of a photographer will immediately fly away, buzzing loudly.

Flies, bumble-bees and honey-bees demonstrate better manners, and are more active. This is because they are provided with more elaborate tools to obtain their food.

Flies lap up the nectar with little dabs of their articulated suction-probes, and bees explore the bottoms of the flowers with their long flexible tongues.

Graphosoma italicum (x 0·8). Feeding on the sap of umbelliferous plants, this bug is examining a stem of Giant Hogweed to find a place to insert its proboscis. This organ, rather like a hypodermic syringe, enables it to suck the nourishing liquid.

Lens: 105 mm.
Focusing distance: 1 metre.
Aperture: f/5·6.
Daylight diffusing through the umbellate flowers of the Giant Hogweed.

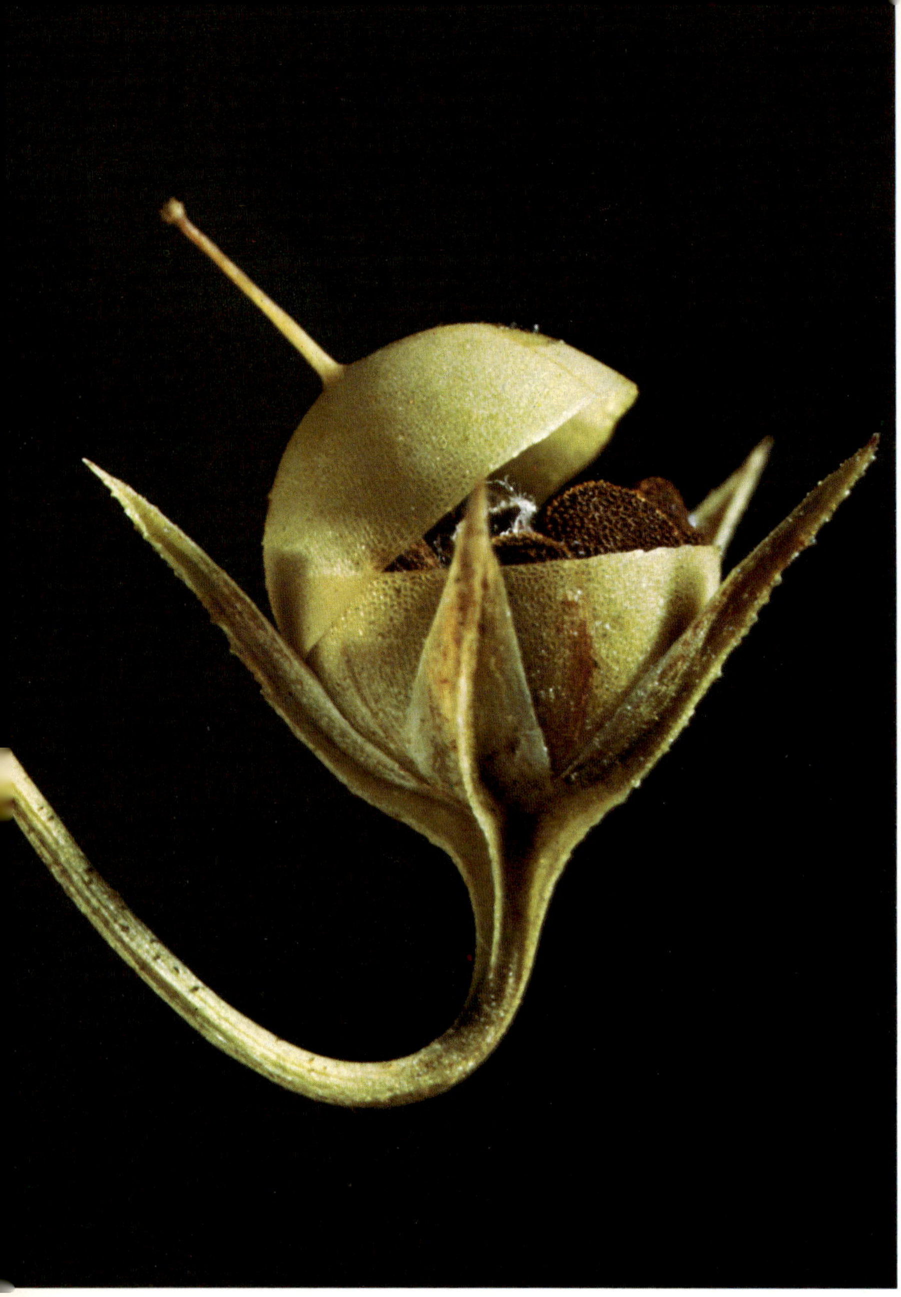

gourmets among the insects which feed from flowers. During hot weather they can be seen gathering in very large numbers on the ground around some minute pool of water, a water-hole for butterflies. The Small Blue, which has a certain propensity for living in groups, often behaves in this way. Liquid manure also attracts clouds of butterflies which exhibit in this respect an unusual form of greed. We have often seen swarms of large Scarce Swallowtails – an imposing butterfly found in France and elsewhere, gathering around patches of cow-dung.

How to photograph flower-loving insects

Photographing these insects involves some special problems. The obviously timid nature of all these insects might discourage the amateur. It is possible to avoid this difficulty by setting out early in the morning before it gets warm. The first insects found visiting the flowers will prove to be strangely slow-moving and disinclined to flee, as though they were torpid: photographing them could not be more easy.

Insects are, in fact, cold-blooded creatures. Being incapable of maintaining a constant internal temperature, they are necessarily affected by external temperature variations. Early in the morning before the rays of the sun have warmed the air, they are capable of only reduced activity, their chilled muscles barely enabling them to beat their wings sufficiently rapidly for flight. The coloured patterns which adorn the wings of butterflies are not merely an incidental form of decoration but play a part in raising the temperature of the insect: depending on their colour, they absorb heat to a greater or lesser extent from the rays of the sun, thus promoting the circulation of the insect's blood. This is why so many butterflies like to spread their wings to face the sun. During cloudy weather, when the temperature

Fruit of the Scarlet Pimpernel (x 11). The ripe seeds are escaping from the upper part of the fruit, which opens like the lid of a box.

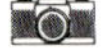

Reproduction ratio: 3.
Lens: Macro Luminar 100 mm.
Aperture: f/11-16. Flash.

Opposite: Fruit of Dove's-foot Cranesbill (x 11). When ripe, the carpels rise suddenly from the base of the pistil, scattering the seeds over a distance.

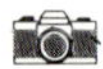

Reproduction ratio: 1·4. Lens: Macro 55 mm. Aperture: f/22. Flash.

Honey-bees are without doubt the most gifted of the pollenating insects. They are able to communicate with each other in order to indicate the best source of food, which is then rapidly invaded. They are likewise capable of telling the time, which enables them to visit at the right moment the many flowers which secrete their nectar only at a given time. Finally, on their rear legs they have pollen sacs in which they carry their booty to the hive in the form of large yellow balls.

With their very long proboscis rather like a straw, butterflies are the

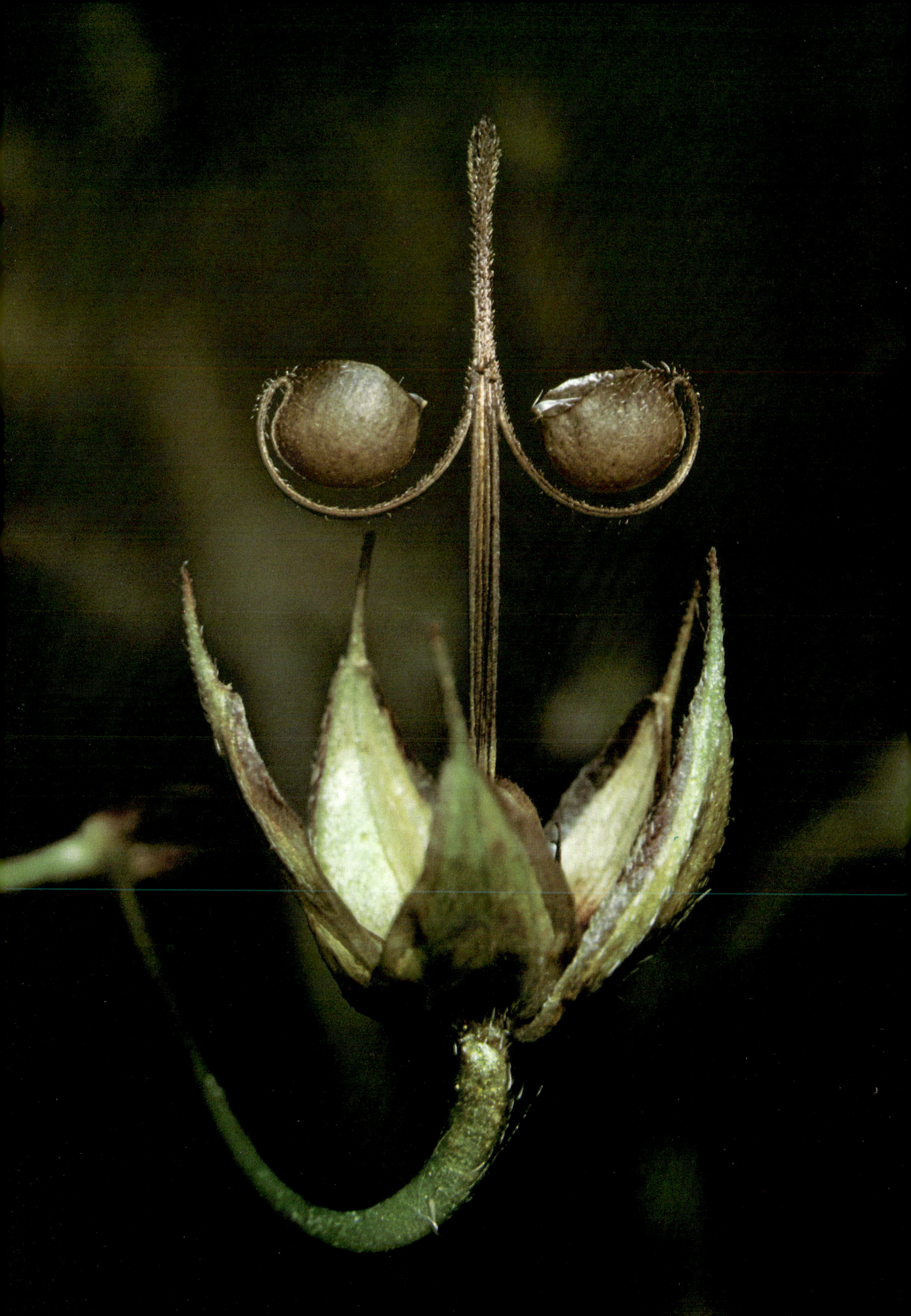

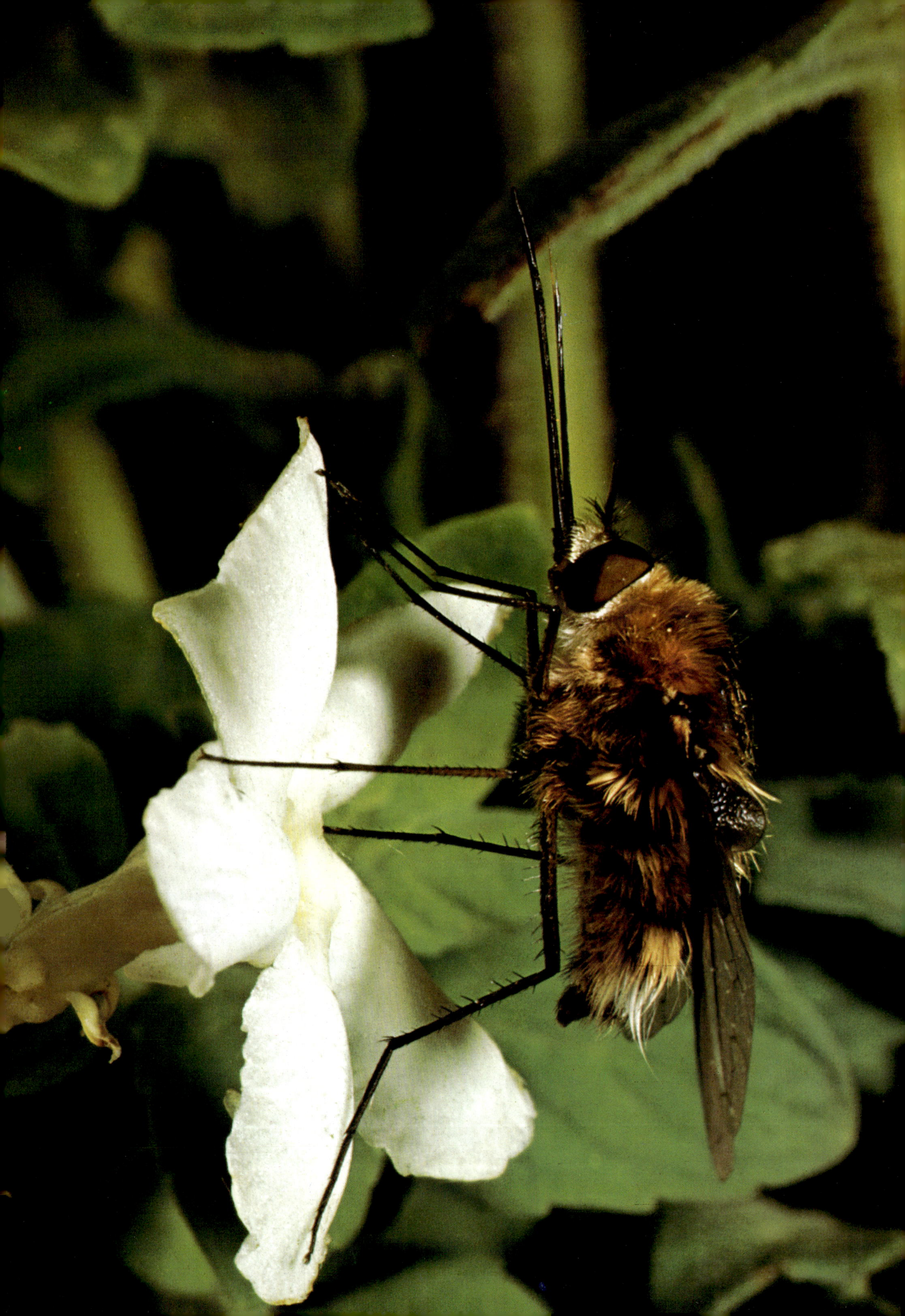

remains cool, these insects display the same enforced indolence, to the great satisfaction of the photographer.

But how can they be photographed when they are in full possession of their faculties during the warm hours of a fine day? There is one helpful factor: they are creatures completely devoted to one vital activity, that of feeding. Once a butterfly has extended its proboscis and started to sip the nectar, it becomes for a moment less shy. Unfortunately, the time spent visiting each flower rarely exceeds a few seconds, which is hardly long enough for the photographer, hampered by his cumbersome equipment. It is possible to improve on nature a little by depositing a few drops of water sweetened with honey at the bottom of the corolla of the flower: the next butterfly to visit will then be found to remain noticeably longer.

When approaching, it is essential to avoid letting your shadow fall on the insect, as the resulting sudden decrease in light and heat is bound to make it fly away. You should, therefore, take care to keep the sun on one side or – why not? – in front of you; with back lighting, the picture will be even better.

When the flowers visited by insects are known in advance, it is similarly feasible to lie in wait for them, perhaps having noted the particular flower which seems to attract most insects because of its reserves of nectar. Framing and focusing are carried out in advance, and readjusted at the moment the visitor arrives. It is best to use a tripod, as the period of waiting might be a long one and you may get cramp. A small telephoto lens (100 mm) is extremely useful, as insects are particularly suspicious of nearby watchers. It is, therefore, better not to approach the flower too closely if you want it to continue to act as a source of attraction.

How about the insect? What view does it have of its environment? How does the approaching photographer appear to it? Man is still a long way from knowing all the peculiarities of the extraordinary facetted eyes with which insects are endowed. Made up of thousands of minute simple eyes placed side by side, these organs hardly seem capable of producing accurate images (the less so when the number of facets is small). At the end of last century, Professor Exner had the idea of taking a photograph using the composite eye of a glow-worm as the lens. The image obtained proved to be a hundred times less sharp than that provided by the human eye. It is very difficult,

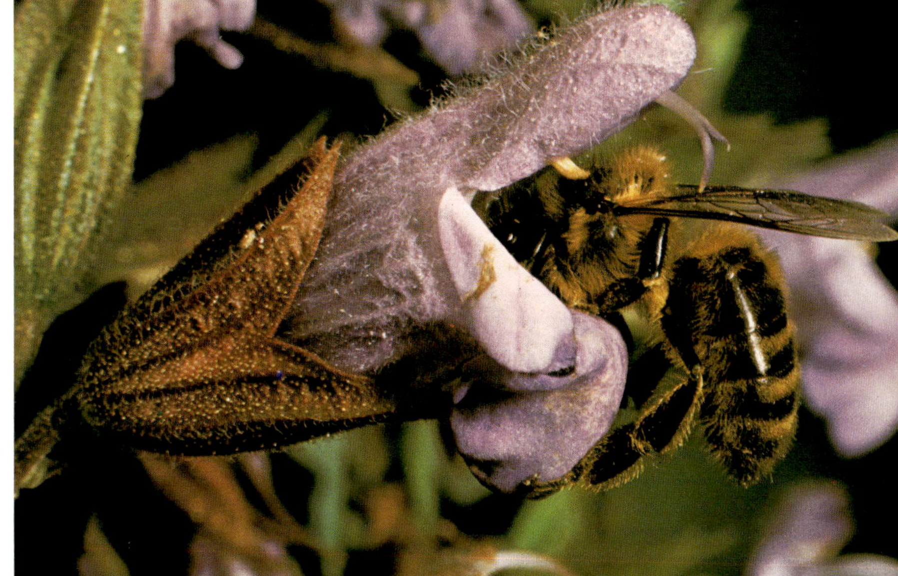

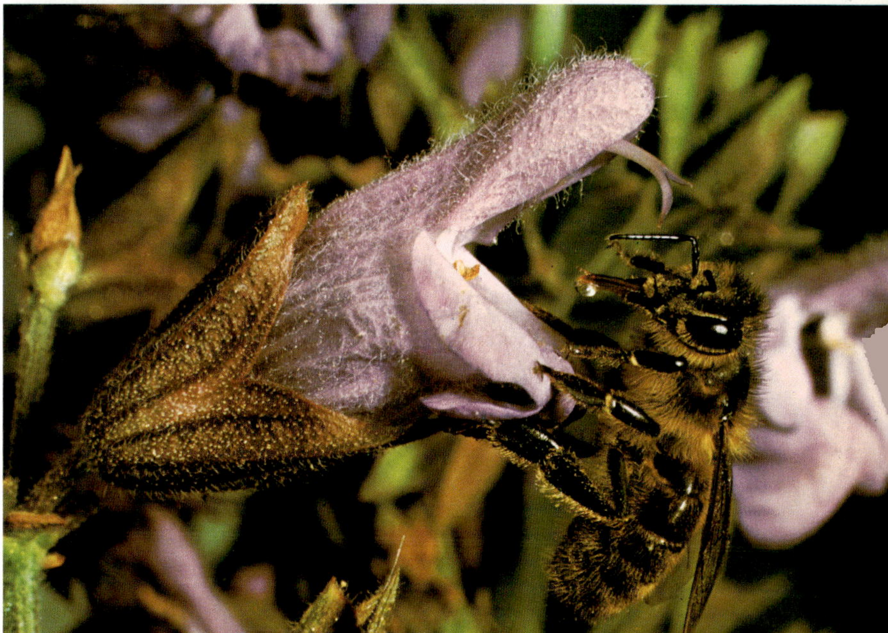

Opposite: Bee Fly (x 7). Its long, rigid proboscis enables it to suck the nectar of the flowers.

Reproduction ratio: 1. Lens: Macro 55 mm. Aperture: f/22. Flash.

Bee and Sage (x 4). Penetrating the flower to obtain nectar, the bee causes the stamens to swing inwards and powder its thorax with pollen (above). Visiting another flower, the insect releases a few grains on to the pistil, thus ensuring that the flower is fertilized.

Reproduction ratio: 1·2. Lens: Macro 55 mm. Aperture: f/22-32 Flash.

however, to know how the brain of an insect interprets this imprecise image. Moreover, it has been shown that the structure and method of operation of the insect eye permits very exact assessment of distances and movements.

All honey-gathering insects seem able to distinguish colours, which is not the case with all insects. Many of them, such as the bee, do not see red but can perfectly well perceive ultraviolet, which is invisible to man; their colour vision as a whole must be greatly modified by this. Thus, no plant bearing red flowers is visited by bees – which cannot tell red from black – unless, like the poppy, it

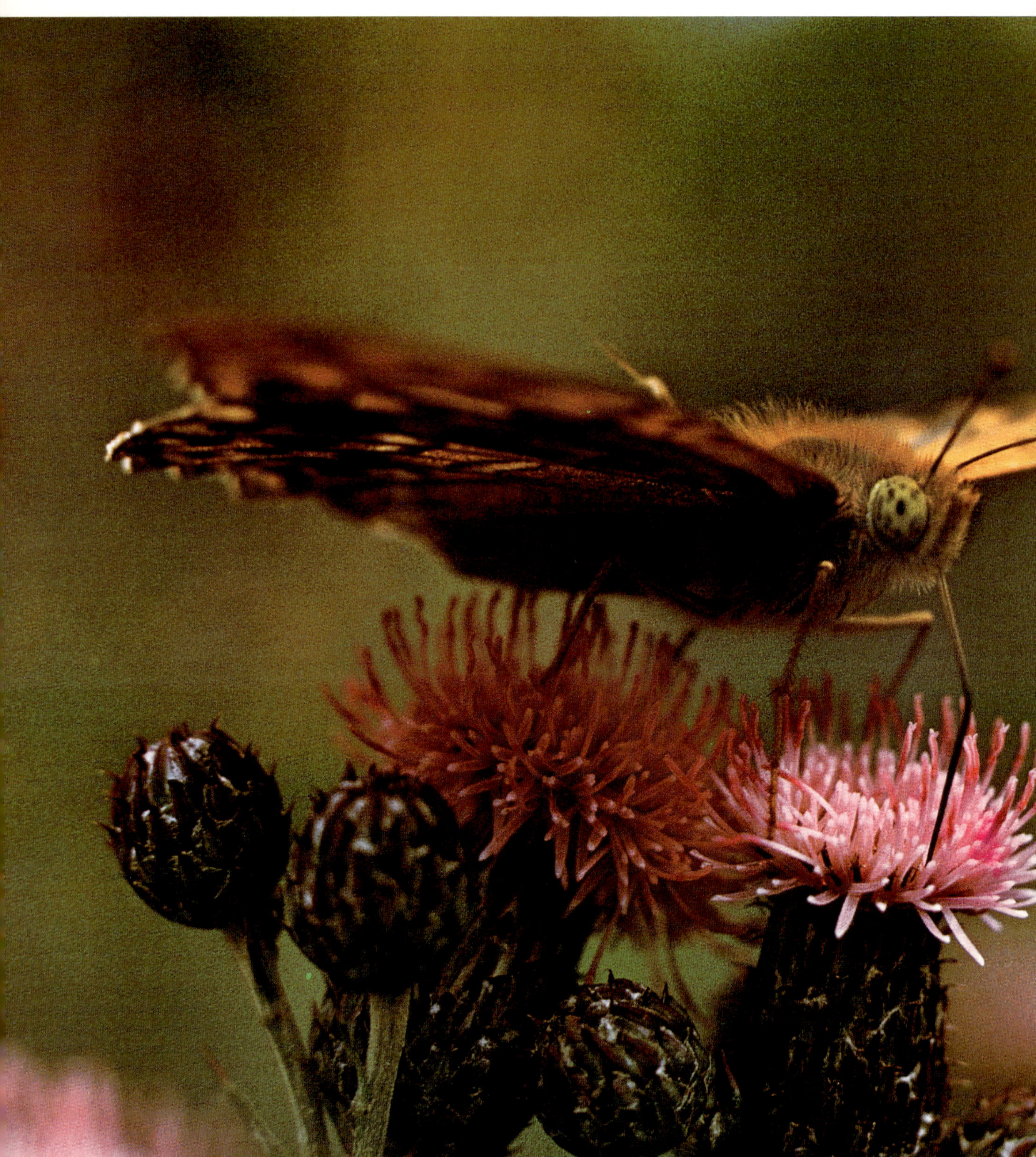

reflects a certain amount of ultra-violet light. On the other hand, the bee can recognize a large number of shades of colour among blue or violet flowers which variously reflect ultra-violet light. Insects have other very acute senses which we do not share with them. Their antennae, as well as the thousands of minute hairs which cover the surface of their bodies, inform them of the slightest air-currents. If you move your hand towards a fly, it will take flight. If it is on the other side of a pane of glass, the same movement will not cause it to fly away. This is because, when you move, the fly can detect the disturbance of the air accompanying the

Silver-washed Fritillary (x 4). While sucking the nectar of a Creeping Thistle, it captures the heat of the sun's rays by spreading out its wings like an aeroplane.

The proboscis of butterflies is an extremely complex organ. When at rest, it is coiled up in a spiral, protected by two labial palps covered with hair, which can be seen in the photograph like a keel on the front of the head.

When a butterfly settles on a flower, it knows immediately whether there is any nectar present: on the ends of its legs it has certain organs of 'taste', which are two hundred times more sensitive to sweetness than a human tongue. When these detectors pick up traces of nectar, thousands of oblique muscles lining the walls of the proboscis contract, causing it to unroll and form, as it were, a long straw. The elbow-bend in the proboscis enables the butterfly to insert it to the bottom of the corolla without having to lower its head.

Reproduction ratio: 0·4.
Lens: Macro 55mm.
Aperture: f/4.
Exposure time: 1/125th of a second.
Natural light, bright interval between showers.

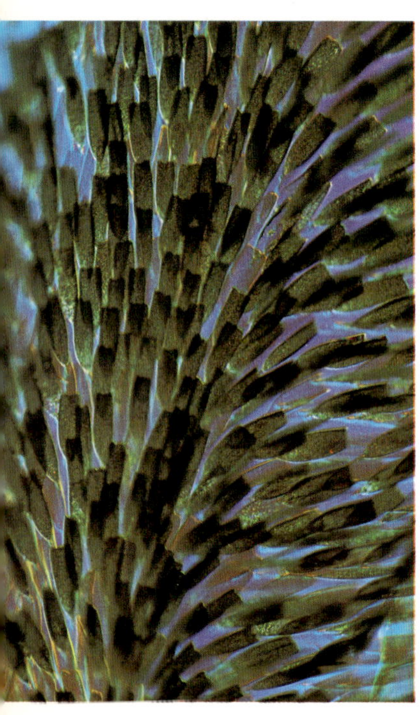

Scales on the wing of a Burnet Moth, observed under a microscope (x 150).

Opposite: Black-veined White Butterflies (x 3). They remain joined for some hours, hidden in the grass. Disturbed, the pair will fly away. The male takes the initiative during flight, trailing the female behind him without releasing his grip.

Reproduction ratio: 0·4.
Lens: Macro 55 mm.
Aperture: f/5·6.
Exposure time: 1/60th of a second.
Natural light, cloudy sky.

movement. This should be a warning to restless photographers!

There are many moments in the life of these insects which deserve to be translated into pictures. In the case of butterflies, mating is preceded by a complex courtship in which pursuit alternates with display. The female attracts the male by adopting the 'attitude of invitation': with her wings lowered and abdomen curved upward, she releases into the air a subtle perfume (undetectable by man) which rouses the male to a state of passion.

During mating, the two partners remain joined together by the ends of their abdomens, with their bodies pointing in opposite directions. They are nevertheless capable of tandem flight and seem perfectly able to control their direction. One might well wonder how they achieve such co-ordination in their movements.

Caterpillars also represent an interesting stage in the life of an insect. It is useful to collect them and raise them so as to be able to witness the unusual spectacle of metamorphosis (see page 134).

The population of the grass

Beneath the bright kingdom of the flowers, which raise their heads towards those lords of the air, their insect visitors, stretches the more secret world of the grasses, which shelter a swarm of animal life.

To enter this world, it is necessary to relinquish one's upright position and to crouch down so as to adjust one's level of vision to that of the ground. This will lead to the discovery of a tangled universe, an endless jungle bathed in a glaucous light, filtered by the network of grasses. A very mixed population inhabits this world. To describe it, we have chosen a method of classification of little scientific pretension, which is simply based on how each particular species appears to the observer.

The jumpers

It is in mid-summer that locusts and grasshoppers invade the meadows. It is impossible to take a step without flushing dozens of them from cover, bursting out one after the other.

Locusts can be distinguished from grasshoppers by the length of their antennae. In the former the antennae are short and straight, while in the latter they are as long as the entire body and flexible.

Locusts are vegetarian while grasshoppers are formidable carnivores which eat other insects. You can prove this for yourself if you take a large Green Grasshopper in your hand: in order to free itself, it will try to bite the fingers holding it by gnashing its two strong mandibles. If these should happen to nip your skin, you will find out for yourself how sharp they are (the pain is nevertheless on the same scale as the insect which causes it). Female grasshoppers have at the end of the abdomen a sort of long, tapering blade, which is never present in the case of the locust. This impressive feature is quite harmless, since it serves as a dibble. When laying its eggs, the female drives its ovipositor (this is the correct name of this organ) vertically into the ground, so that the eggs are immediately buried and can enjoy the temperature and humidity conditions necessary for their proper development.

All these jumping insects make capricious subjects for the photographer. For anyone recording sound, on the other hand, they are one of the best of all subjects. Locusts 'sing' by moving their rear legs rapidly against their wings, and grasshoppers and crickets by rubbing their front wings together. Each species produces a specific song characterized by its rhythm and pitch.

Biologists have learned to recog-

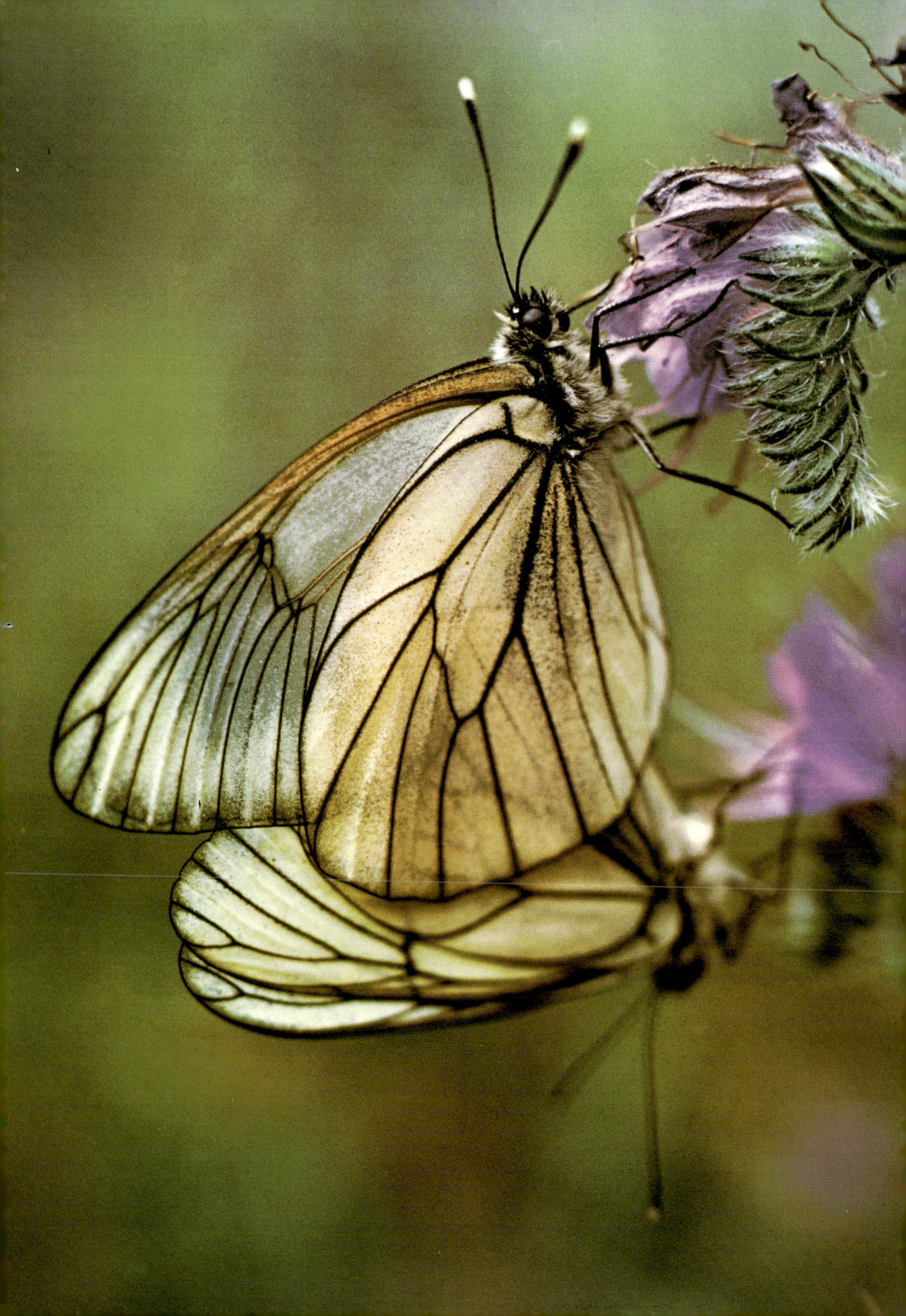

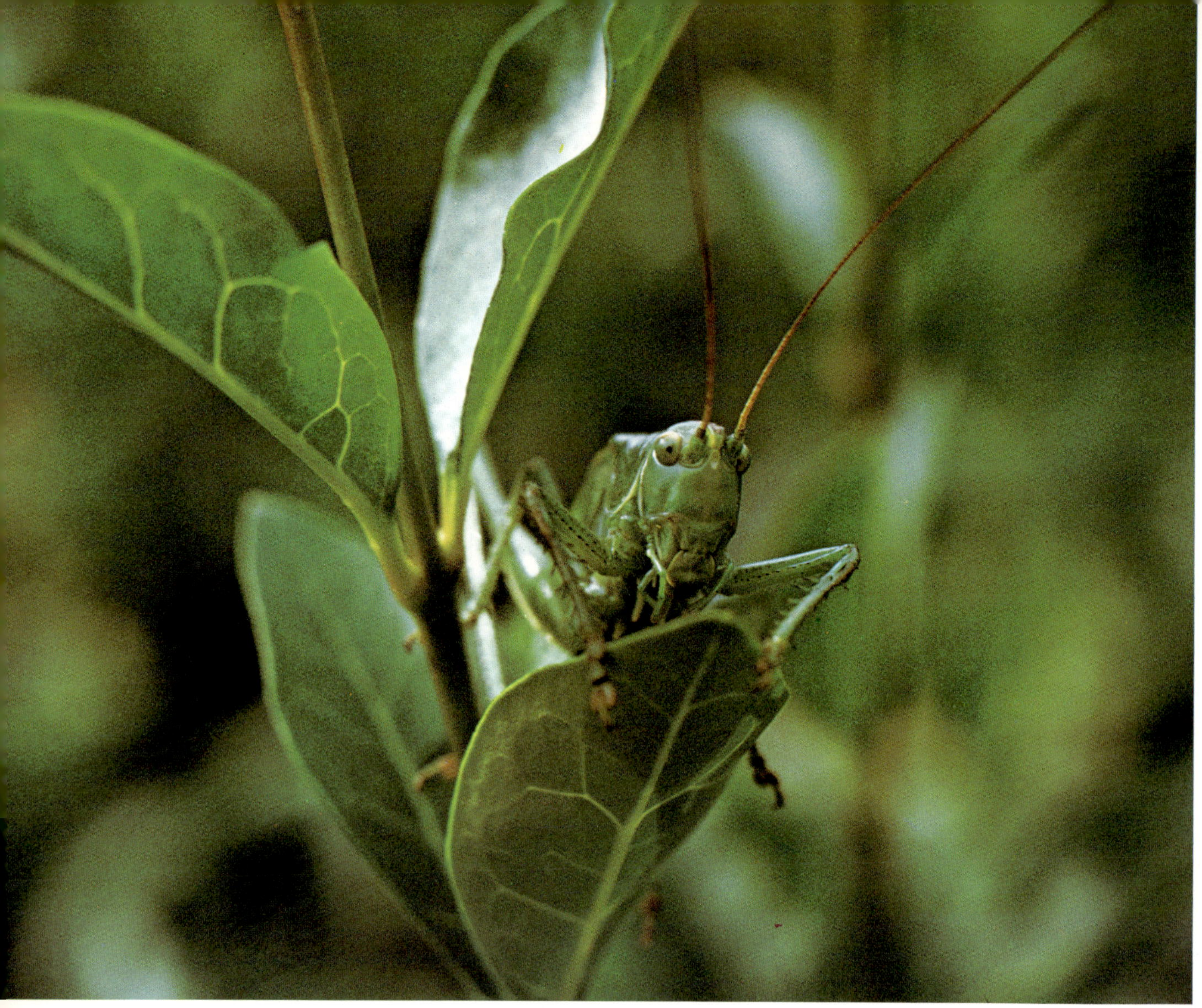

nize a varied repertoire for each of them – a spontaneous call, a love call, and calls indicating rivalry between males, and triumph. It is intriguing to listen to these endless exchanges of dialogue in the grass. Moreover, these musicians are quite capable of detecting the sounds made by their kin. They are provided with auditory organs which, though located in bizarre places (on the front legs in the case of grasshoppers and on the sides of the abdomen in the case of locusts), are none the less very sensitive. They are thus perfectly capable of hearing very high-pitched (ultrasonic) sounds to which we are deaf.

A more portly 'jumper' often driven from cover in the meadow is the Common Frog. Although of terrestrial habits, it requires moisture like all other members of its group. It is, therefore, never found during the hotter part of the day, when it takes cover in the shade.

The climbers

Most of the creatures who live in the grass use a more circumspect method of locomotion than the hasty leaps of locusts and grasshoppers. They climb cautiously, stopping or going faster at the slightest sign of danger. Thus low vegetation gives shelter to large numbers of small creatures, which often find in it a source of food and a refuge at the same time.

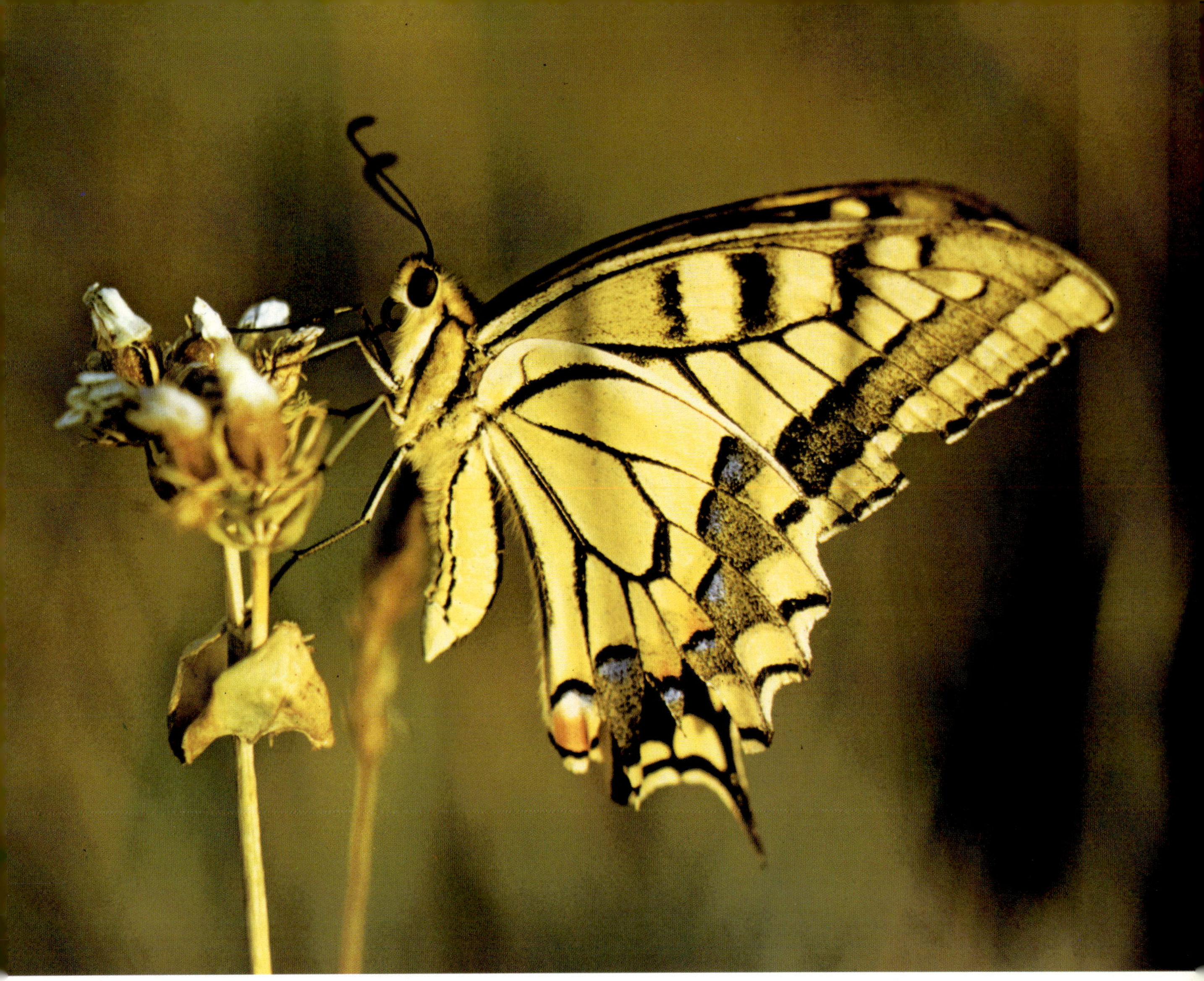

The guests which most ill-use the vegetation include plant-lice, minute insects related to the cicada; they live in close-packed colonies on twigs, which they surround with a living sheath. When observed closely, they appear literally staked to the plant by their proboscises and incapable of tearing themselves loose. But, if the twig supporting this immobile population is handled, the colony is pervaded with an air of panic. Each individual hastens to interrupt its meal of sap and, withdrawing its proboscis from the fleshy tissue of the plant, departs to seek a place where it can gorge more peacefully.

During the summer, plant-lice are viviparous and it is not unusual to find, among the individuals gathered on one twig, a female giving birth to a miniature plant-louse. This spectacle is not exceptional, due to the fact that during the high season the colony consists only of females. These are able to give birth to large numbers of progeny without being fertilized by males. Moreover, the generations succeed each other at an unrestrained rate since, even before their birth, the embryos already contain within themselves the next generation, like nests of boxes in which each contains one smaller than itself. When it is realised that each female can give birth to more than twelve young a

Swallowtail Butterfly (x 2).
One of the largest butterflies of Europe. Birds attacking it are attracted towards the orange-red patch on its rear wing, which is torn off by their beak. The vital parts of the body thereby escape injury.

Reproduction ratio: 0·5.
Lens: Macro 55mm.
Aperture: f/4-5·6.
Exposure time: 1/125th of a second.
Perched at the top of a ledge, the last rays of the sun are shining directly onto its wings. August, 7 o'clock in the evening.
Film: Kodachrome 25.

day, it becomes clear why plant-lice are so abundant.

Animals are most often found near their source of food; therefore, where plant-lice are found there will nearly always be ladybirds. The ladybird is, in fact, a great devourer of plant-lice, a fact which slows down the rapid increase in these plant parasites. Where crops cannot be protected from this scourge, man sees in the ladybird a chosen ally in the biological struggle. During the Second World War, to make up for the lack of insecticides, American farmers bought ladybirds by the gallon and distributed them in their orchards (up to five gallons, or fifty thousand ladybirds, for a single land-owner). Now that this type of treatment is no longer regarded as make-shift but is a popular remedy, ladybird 'factories' have been developed where these insects are raised on a large scale.

Certain climbers have recourse to remarkable subterfuges in order to escape attention and attack. In the spring one can often see among the plants small masses of white foam which commonly go under the name of cuckoo spit. This rather uninviting name is not a true indication of the origin of this froth. It is necessary to look inside the foam to find what was responsible for it – the small green, soft-bodied larva of the Froghopper. With the aid of its pointed rostrum it sucks the juicy sap of a plant, then secretes the surplus, mixed with hundreds of air bubbles, from the end of its abdomen. This light-weight covering, constantly replenished, hides it from the eyes of predators which, if they nevertheless attempt to penetrate the obstacle, find themselves woefully ensnared in the viscous and amorphous mass.

Other climbers seek their food right on the ground. The cattle which frequent the meadow leave behind them certain choice viands which attract numerous insects of affirmed tastes: there are those which are partial to cow-dung and which are rightly named dung-beetles. The

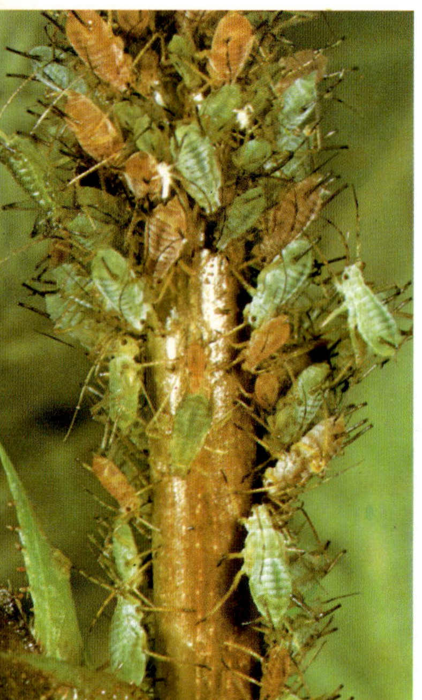

Colony of plant-lice on a rose bush stem (x 2·5).
In summer, the females give birth to young without being fertilized by a male. The fatherless offspring are all female. They, in turn, produce only females throughout the summer season.

Reproduction ratio: 1.
Lens: Macro 55 mm with extension ring.
Aperture: f/22.
Electronic flash.

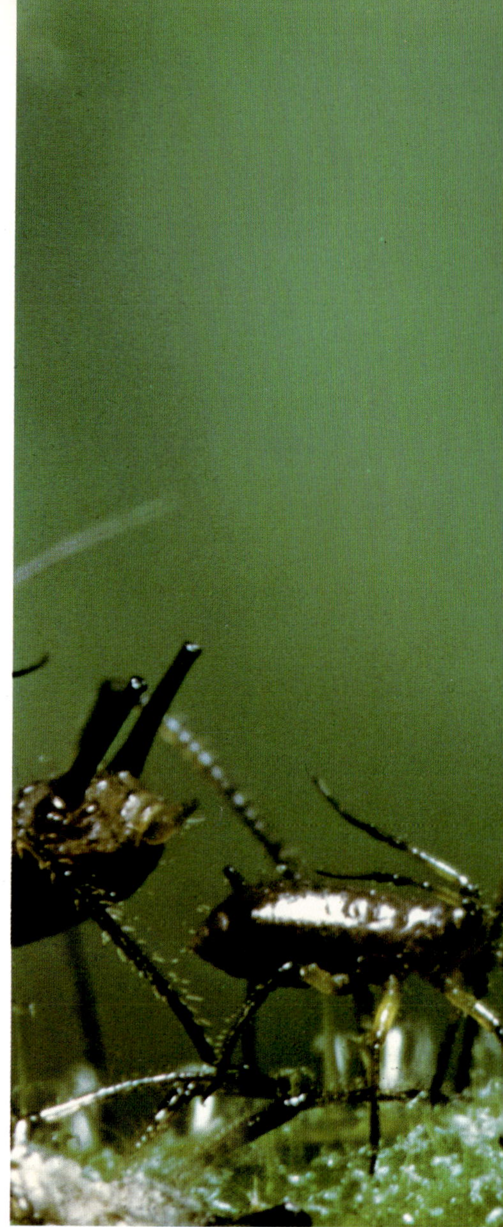

most famous of these is the Sacred Scarab, a somewhat rare Mediterranean species which the Egyptians venerated as a symbol of immortality; its profile has served as a decorative motif not only for the Egyptians but also for the Phoenicians, the Etruscans, the Romans, and others. This shows to what extent this small creature, the physical appearance of which provides no grounds for curiosity, has been able to fascinate man by its astonishing behaviour.

In summer one might be fortunate enough, on the path leading to the pasture, to come across a Sacred Scarab with its ball of dung, which it has carefully collected and fashioned

to provide a reserve of food that can be easily conveyed to its underground shelter. The sight is an impressive one: quite simply, this scarab has invented the wheel; it grips the ball with its rear legs, the claws of which provide the axis of rotation, and proceeds backwards at a surprising speed with the aid of its other two pairs of legs. The assembly operates no better than might be expected, like an eccentric wheel, but the obstinacy of the scarab always triumphs over the many obstacles in its path.

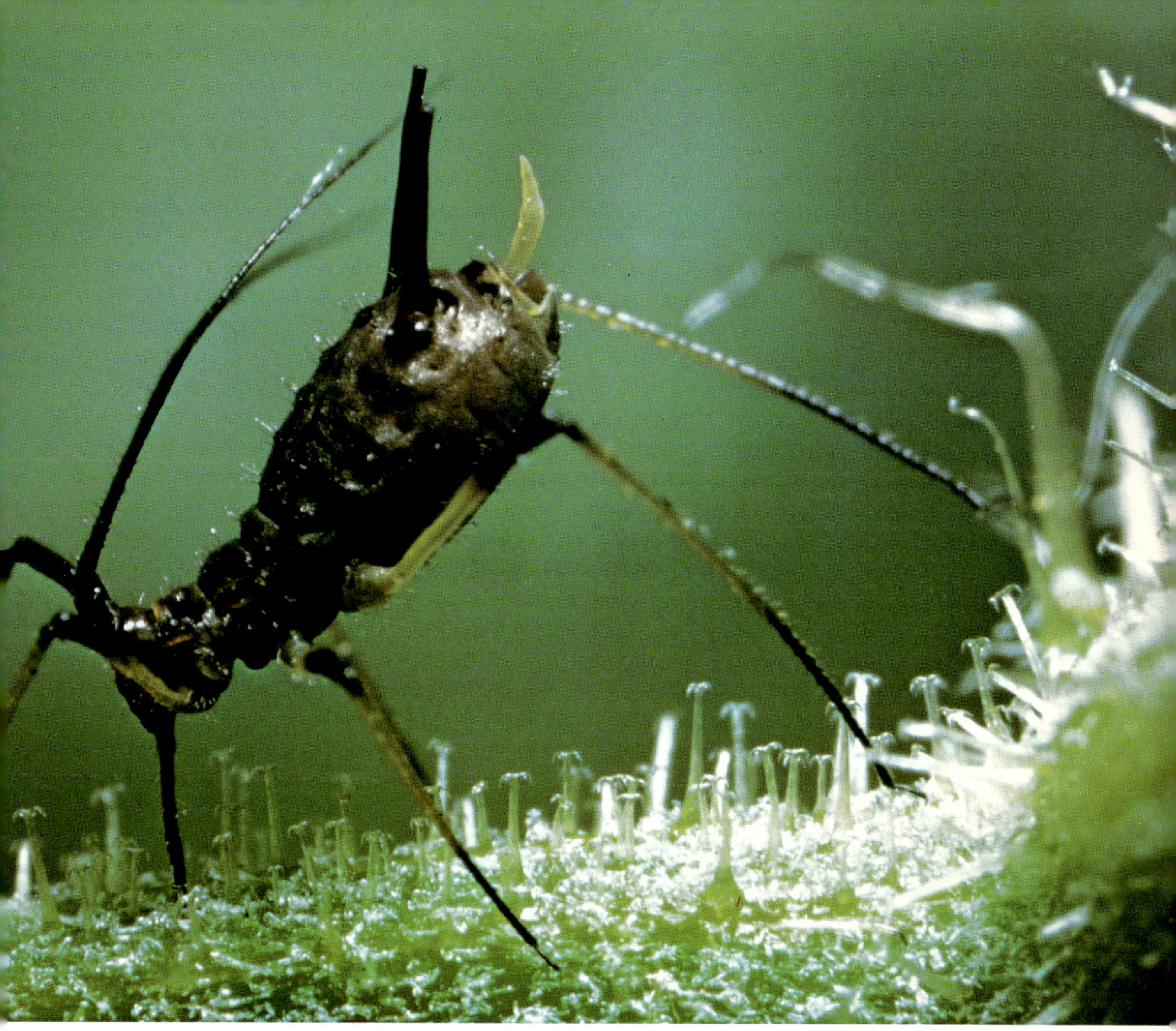

The climbers also include professionals that have a structure which forces them to adopt this method of locomotion: these are the reptiles. When it is not hot, in damp places one may encounter the Slowworm, which has become associated with so many names and beliefs because of its strange characteristics. Even though it is completely devoid of legs, this reptile is, in fact, not a snake but a lizard. The structure of the jaws, the scales and skeleton, and the presence of eyelids, which are much more important criteria than the absence of limbs, show that it should be classified in the latter group.

Like many lizards, the Slowworm is able to discard its tail voluntarily in order to escape from danger,

Plant-louse (× 31).
It is sucking the sap of a thistle through its proboscis, which is inserted into the stem.

Reproduction ratio: 4·2.
Lens: Macro mounted on bellows in reverse position.
Aperture: f/22-32.
Electronic flash.

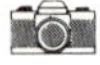

which explains why it is often called the 'Glass Snake'. The English call it the Blindworm, since it has a habit of closing its eyes when attacked, so that all that can be seen is a uniform surface of skin across the head. The Slowworm is a great devourer of slugs, but is rarely given credit for this useful habit, its serpentine appearance making it more often feared (unjustly) as a deadly animal; it is sometimes believed that its bite is more venomous than that of the Adder, though it is in fact harmless to humans.

The non-movers

Other inhabitants of the meadows are more difficult to discern among the tangle of low plants. This is because they remain completely motionless, swaying in the breeze on the plants where they are resting. Invisible to the photographer, they are also invisible to their prey, which passes close by without suspecting the lurking danger. The Praying Mantis is without doubt the most astounding of these secretive creatures in the grass. It has made such an impression on man that it is the subject of innumerable superstitions – in some it is a creature of the devil, whose very look brings bad luck, and in others it has been sent by Heaven (according to one legend it uses its legs to show lost children the right path to follow). In the South of France, where it is particularly numerous, it is called Prega-Diou (that which prays to God) because of the particular manner in which it holds its long front legs folded over, as though clasped in prayer. This attitude, however, has nothing to do with piety; it is rather that of a fierce carnivore lying in wait for its victim to pass. Just at that moment, the two front legs are rapidly extended towards the prey, close on it and draw it back to the mouth of the Mantis. The nervous centres are usually eaten first. The Mantis can then continue

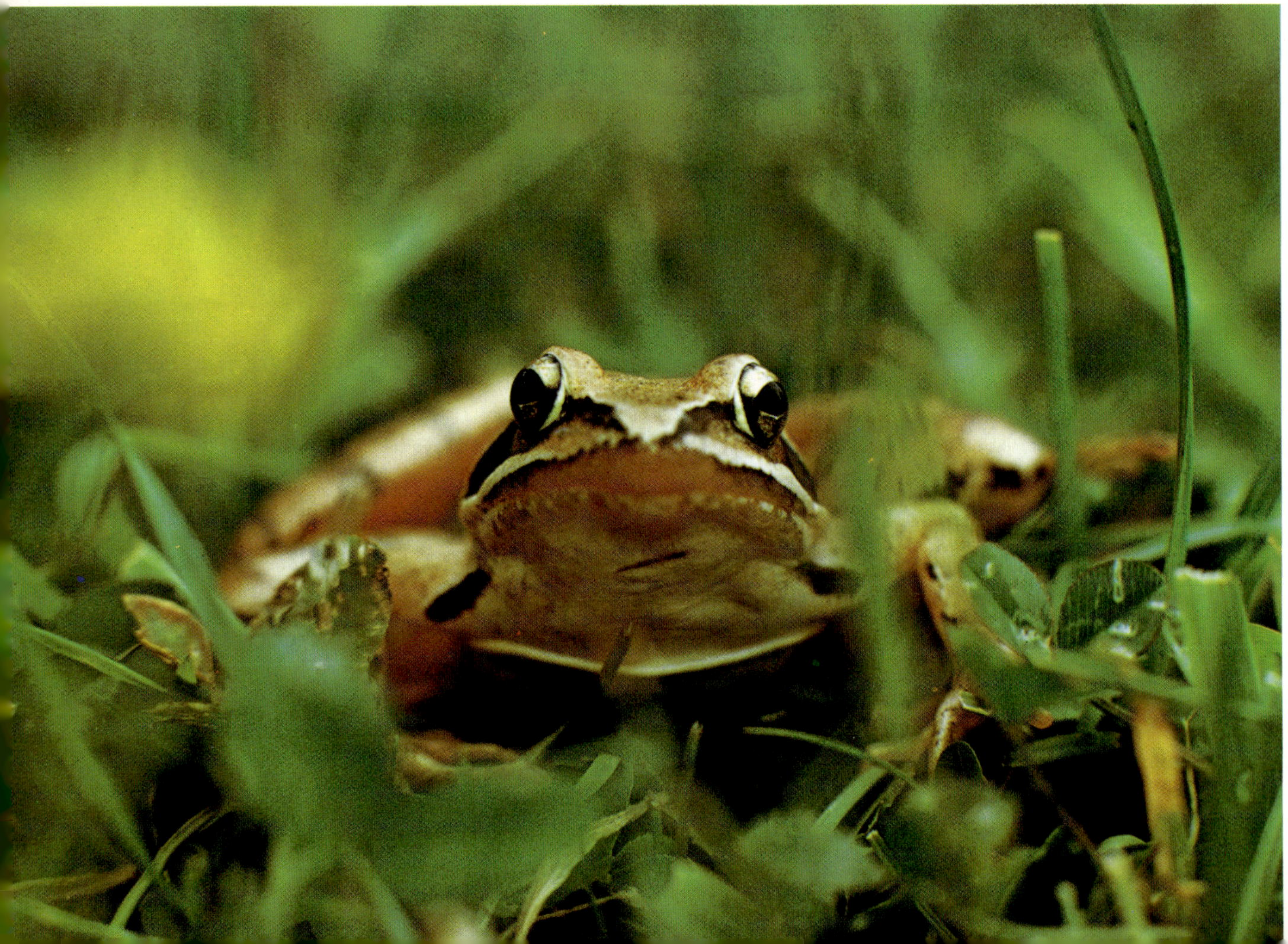

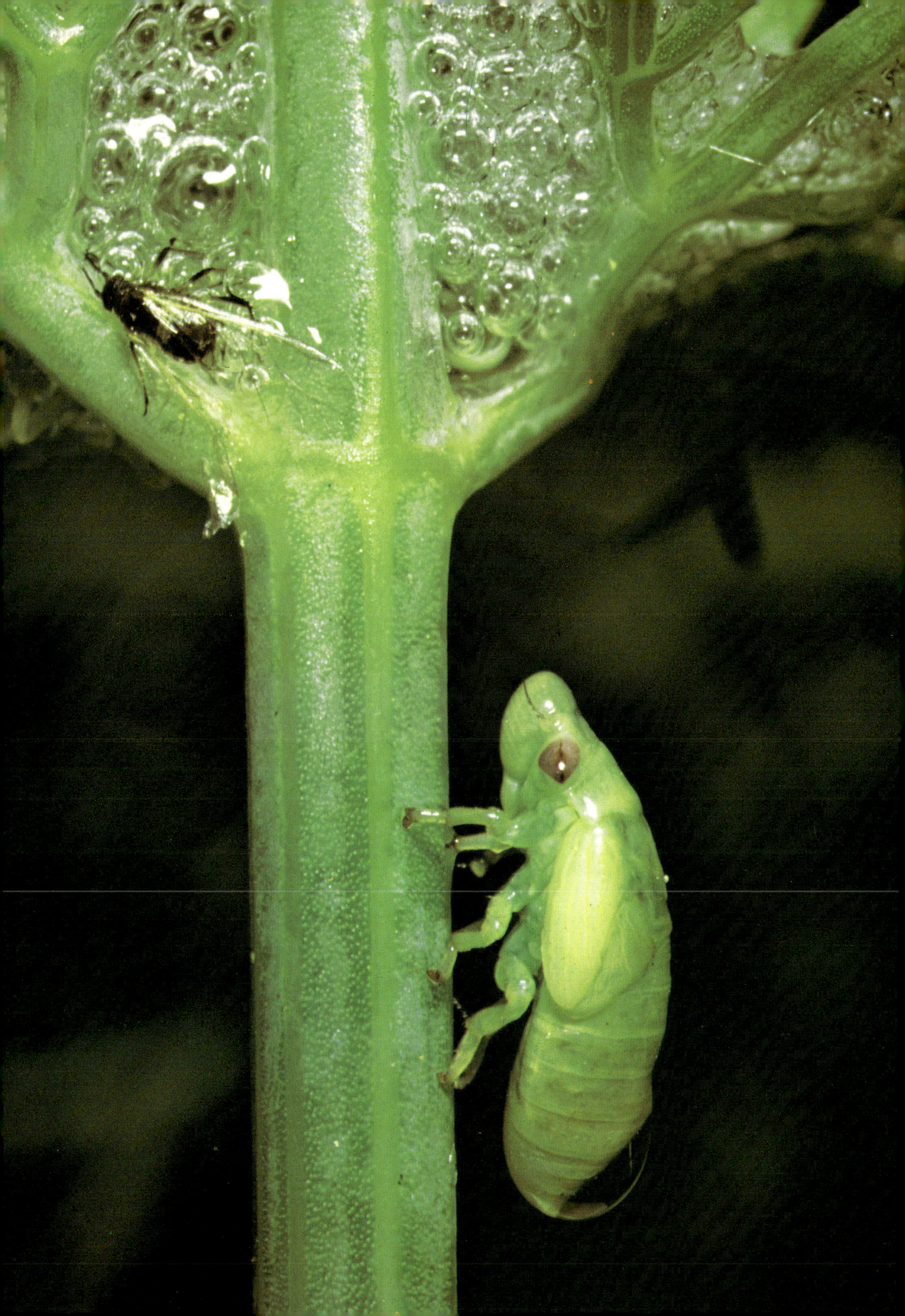

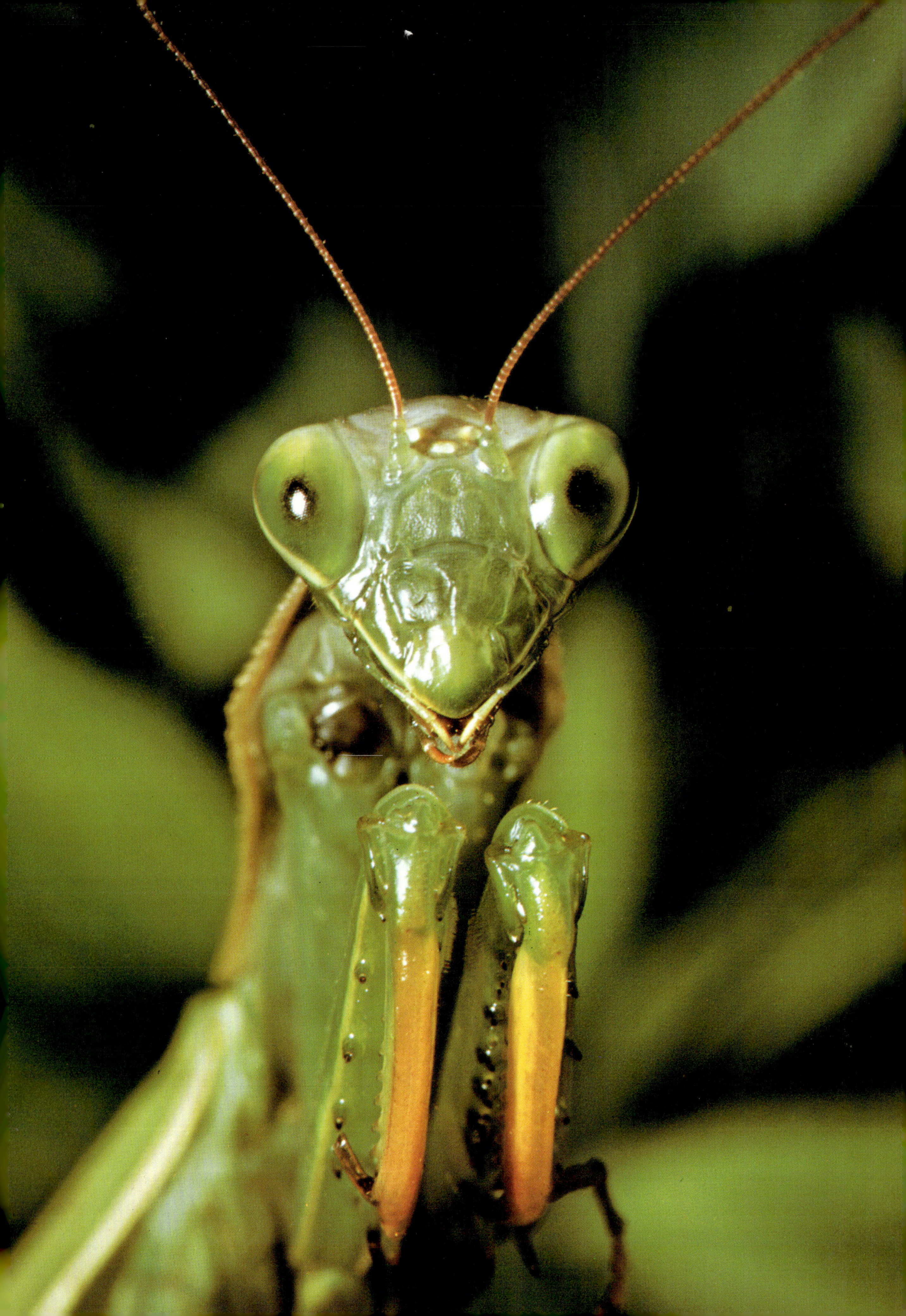

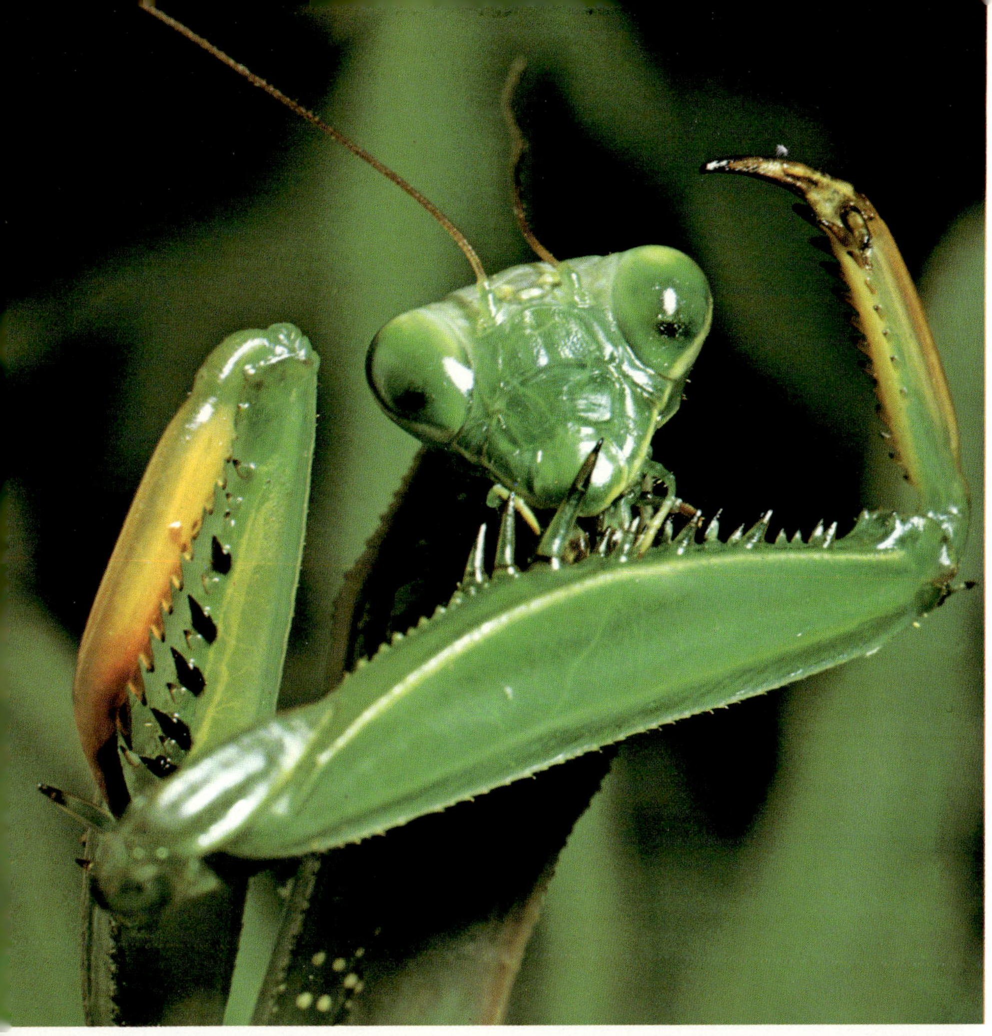

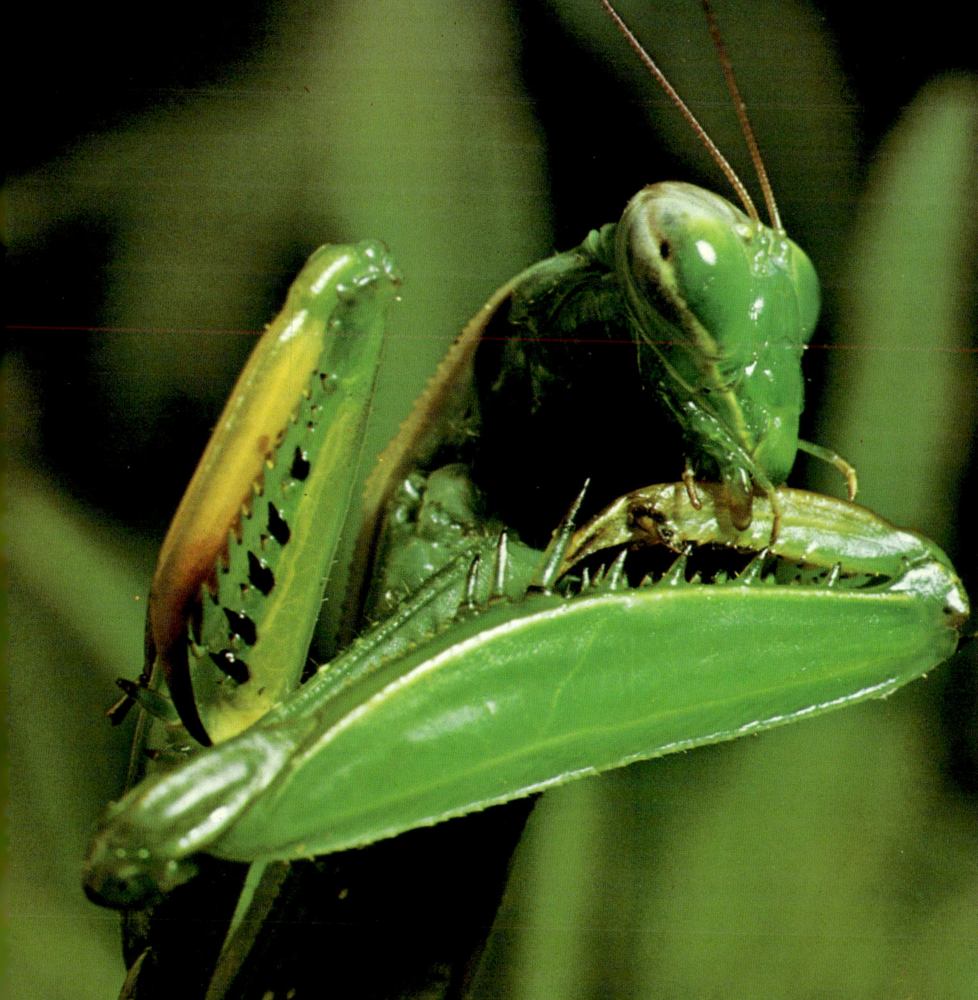

Opposite: Praying Mantis lying in wait (x 12).
Motionless, with its legs folded, the Mantis waits for a victim to pass within reach. The end claws are closed like two penknife blades to rest in a channel bordered by two rows of spines along the under side of the front legs. As the victim passes, this extremely efficient mechanism will enable the legs to be extended at very high speed, the operation taking only 1/20th of a second.

The Mantis hunts by sight. Its vision is most acute in the central area of its eyes. The surrounding area gives a more brilliant but less clear image. In order to look at something, it turns its head so that it can focus on the subject with both eyes.

On this page: The Mantis grooms its front legs with meticulous care. It proceeds methodically, without overlooking any part of these important organs.

Reproduction ratio: 1·6.
Lens: Macro 55 mm mounted on bellows in reverse position.
Aperture: f/16-22.
Electronic flash.

Cleg (x 20).
The gaudy colours of the eyes are not due to colour pigments but to light interference resulting from the actual structure of the eye, which consists of hundreds of transparent facets.

Reproduction ratio: 6·5.
Lens: Macro Summar 24 mm on bellows.
Aperture: f/11.
Two electronic flashlights, one on each side of the head.

its meal without being inconvenienced by the wild struggles of its victim.

The naturalist-photographer cannot wish for a better subject than the Praying Mantis. It is, without doubt, the most expressive insect there is. Thanks to its extraordinarily slender neck, which enables it to turn its head in all directions, and to its strange-looking predatory 'hands', it can provide the photographer with an infinite number of poses, often quite appealing, which give an impression of familiarity. It is as though a relationship is established between the photographer and his 'model', who literaliy exchange looks, as anyone will agree who has

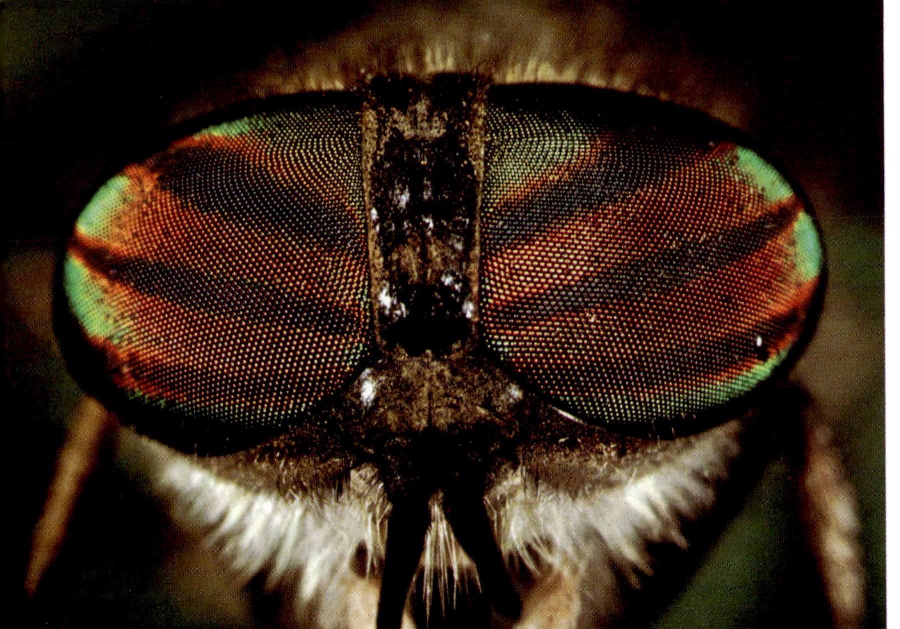

seen a Mantis hold its head on one side in an interrogative manner when it catches sight, through the lens aimed at it, of the movements of the photographer's eye held close to the viewfinder. After a few hesitant 'looks' the insect, overcome by curiosity, often jumps on to the rim of the lens.

In the presence of really big 'game', such as a Great Green Grasshopper, the Praying Mantis indulges in a

form of behaviour intended to terrify its adversary. It adopts an attitude of intimidation, with its wings spread out like a stately sail, its trembling abdomen curved upwards and striking against the wings with a curious noise like crumpling paper, the predatory front legs raised and widely extended, displaying their pattern of 'eyes'. If the photographer subjects the Praying Mantis to his presence for too long a time, it will invariably put on the same display. Adult Mantises are found from the beginning of August. The males can be identified by their smaller size, their more slender body and their disproportionately long antennae. If a gravid female is captured (the mass of eggs gives the abdomen a swollen appearance), it is possible to watch the eggs being laid towards the end of September. The female deposits, on a branch or in a crevice, a kind of whitish cream which hardens in the air to form an egg-case, a porous mass containing 150 to 300 eggs. Hatching takes place in spring. The new-born Mantises are miniature replicas of the adults, but without wings.

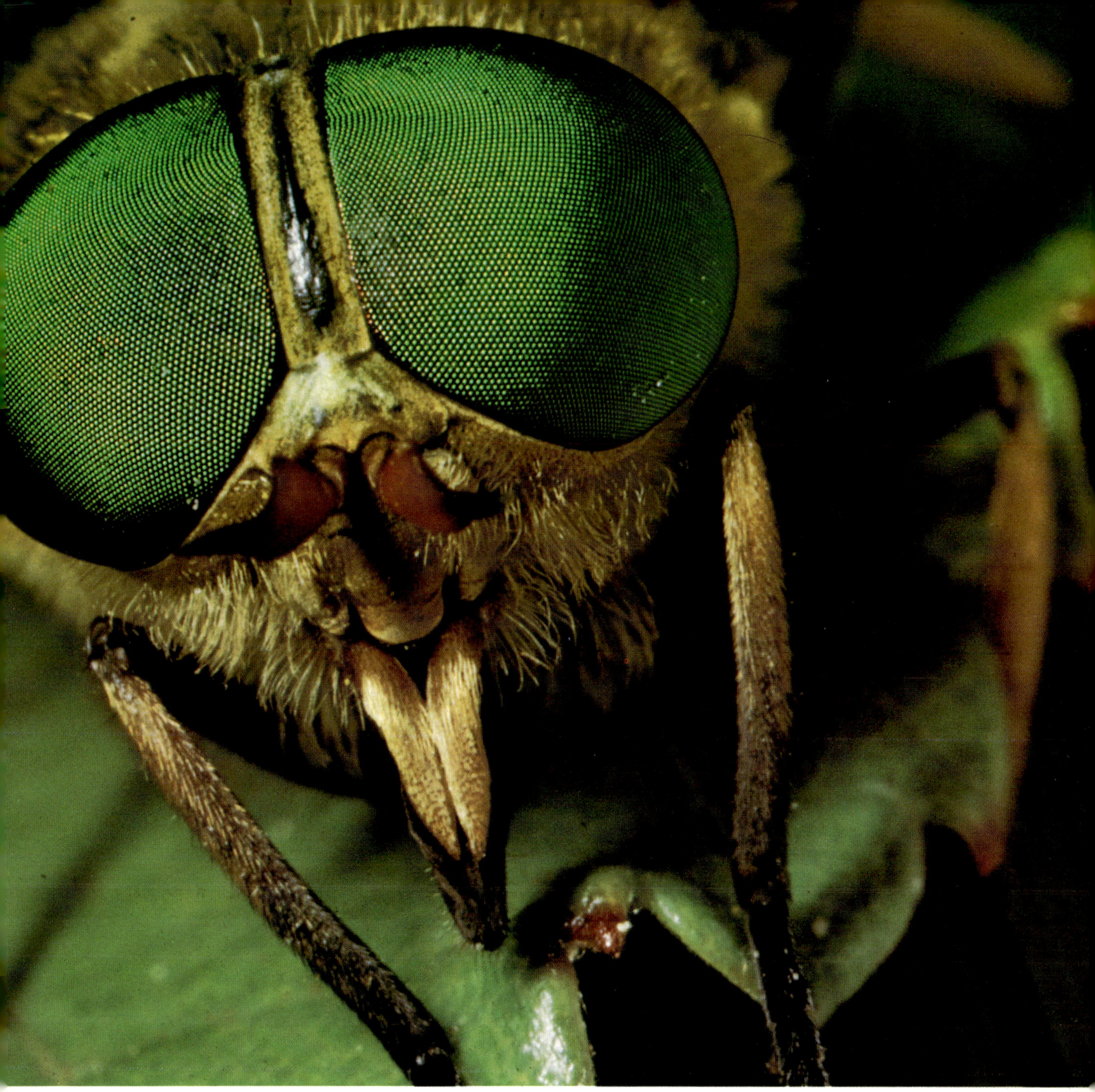

The acrobats

Other inhabitants spend most of their lives suspended between plants and

Ox Gad-fly (x 22).
To suck the blood of mammals, the insect pierces their skin with the aid of its powerful stylet.

Reproduction ratio: 3.
Lens: Macro Luminar 100 mm on bellows.
Aperture: f/11-16.
Two flashlights, one on each side of the subject.

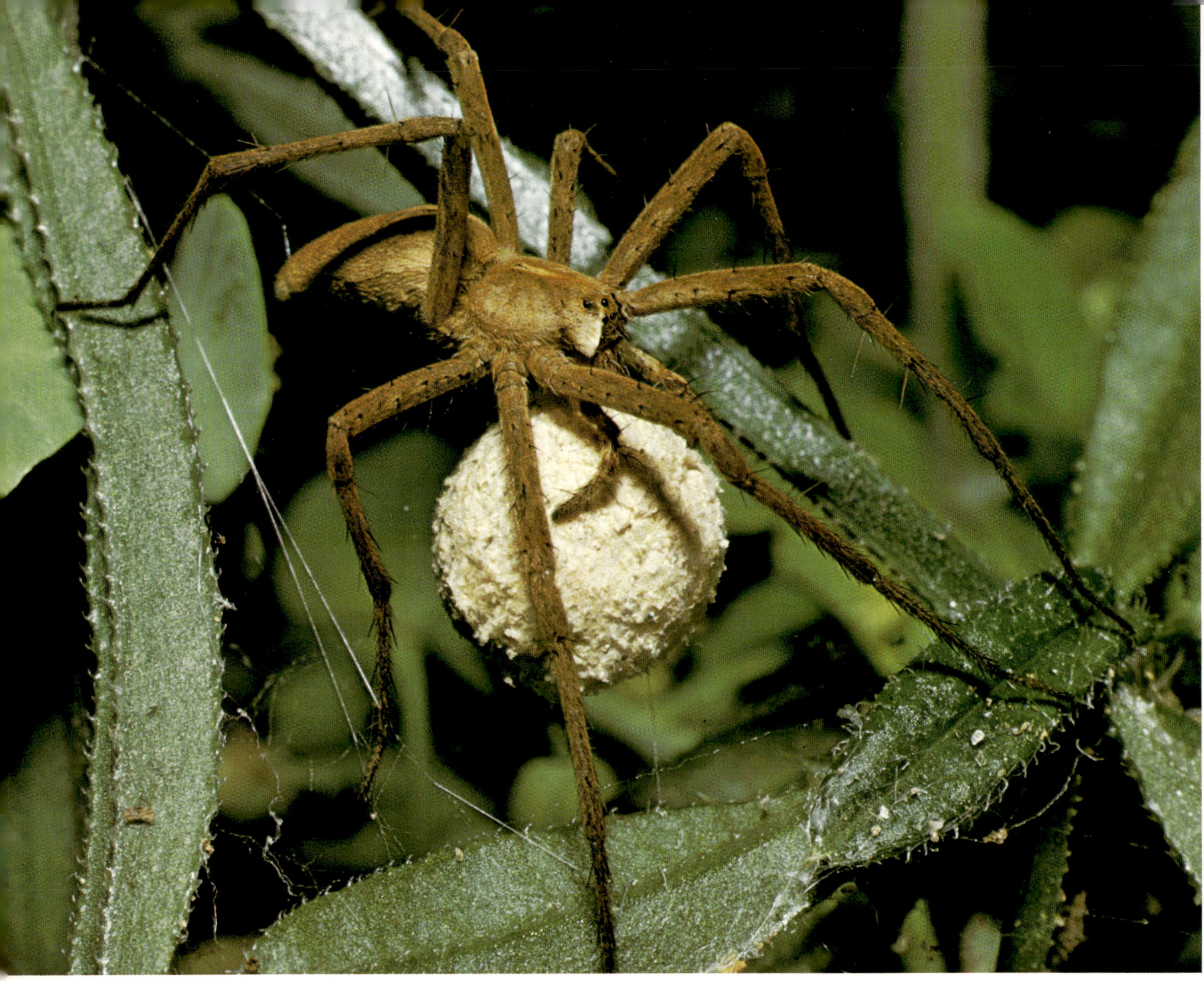

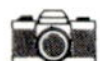

Hunting Spider carrying its egg-sac in its poison fangs (x 6). From this will come hundreds of minute spiders which the mother will watch over for about a week before they scatter.

Reproduction ratio: 0·9.
Lens: Macro 55 mm with automatic ring.
Aperture: f/22.
Electronic flash.

clinging to the delicate structure they have fashioned: these are the spiders. It is necessary to start out in search of them early in the morning, to get any opportunity of admiring their webs, then made clearly visible by innumerable small beads of dew, which evaporate as soon as the rays of the sun grow warmer. In photographs taken later in the day, the texture of the web is much less apparent. To correct this, artificial dew can be manufactured by spraying water on to the threads of silk with the aid of an atomiser.

The spider generally lies in wait for its prey in the middle of its web. Disturbed by the photographer, it will run away to hide in a neighbouring plant, but will soon return to its post. It is thus possible to use a tripod for framing and focusing in advance: the position that the subject will choose is already known. Sometimes the web is empty: the spider has taken up position on a neighbouring bush. But in this case it will have been careful to remain in contact with the centre of its snare by means of a warning thread. By tapping the web very lightly one can simulate the movements caused by a struggling insect to make the spider appear.

It often happens that the approach of the photographer coincides with the capture of an item of prey: without knowing it, he has acted as a beater by driving before him a number of insects which have finally hurled themselves into the web suddenly blocking their path. Ensnared in the sticky silk of the threads, each insect tries to free itself by repeated tugs. The spider then hastens to throw over it a flood of silk extruded from the spinnerets on its abdomen. After this, the spider rotates the insect rapidly, tying it into a neat package, which is then suspended from the web by a thread as a reserve of fresh food for the days to come. If the prey is dangerous (such as a wasp, armed with a sting), the spider uses its poison fangs to paralyze it before completely swathing it in silk.

The Garden Spider is very common in September. Its other name of Cross Spider refers to the ornamental design on its abdomen. The Banded Spider, the abdomen of which is striped in black and bright yellow, is mainly found in the south of Europe. Like the Garden Spider, it lays a cohesive mass of eggs in autumn which it surrounds with a very elaborate cocoon. Egg-laying can be observed in captivity. After this final act, on which she expends all her strength and physical reserves, the female quickly dies.

Small creatures of old walls, rocks and thickets

In autumn, when flowers have become scarce in the meadow, the honey-gatherers turn their attention to the late blossoms of the ivy. These small yellowish-green flowers attract a large number of insects to old walls,

Spider of the genus Dysdera (×19).
Eight small black eyes are set in its head. In this genus the extremely long and sharp poison fangs fold back like the blade of a penknife into a recess edged with fine hairs.

Reproduction ratio: 3.
Lens: Macro Luminar 100 mm mounted on bellows.
Aperture: f/16.
Electronic flash.

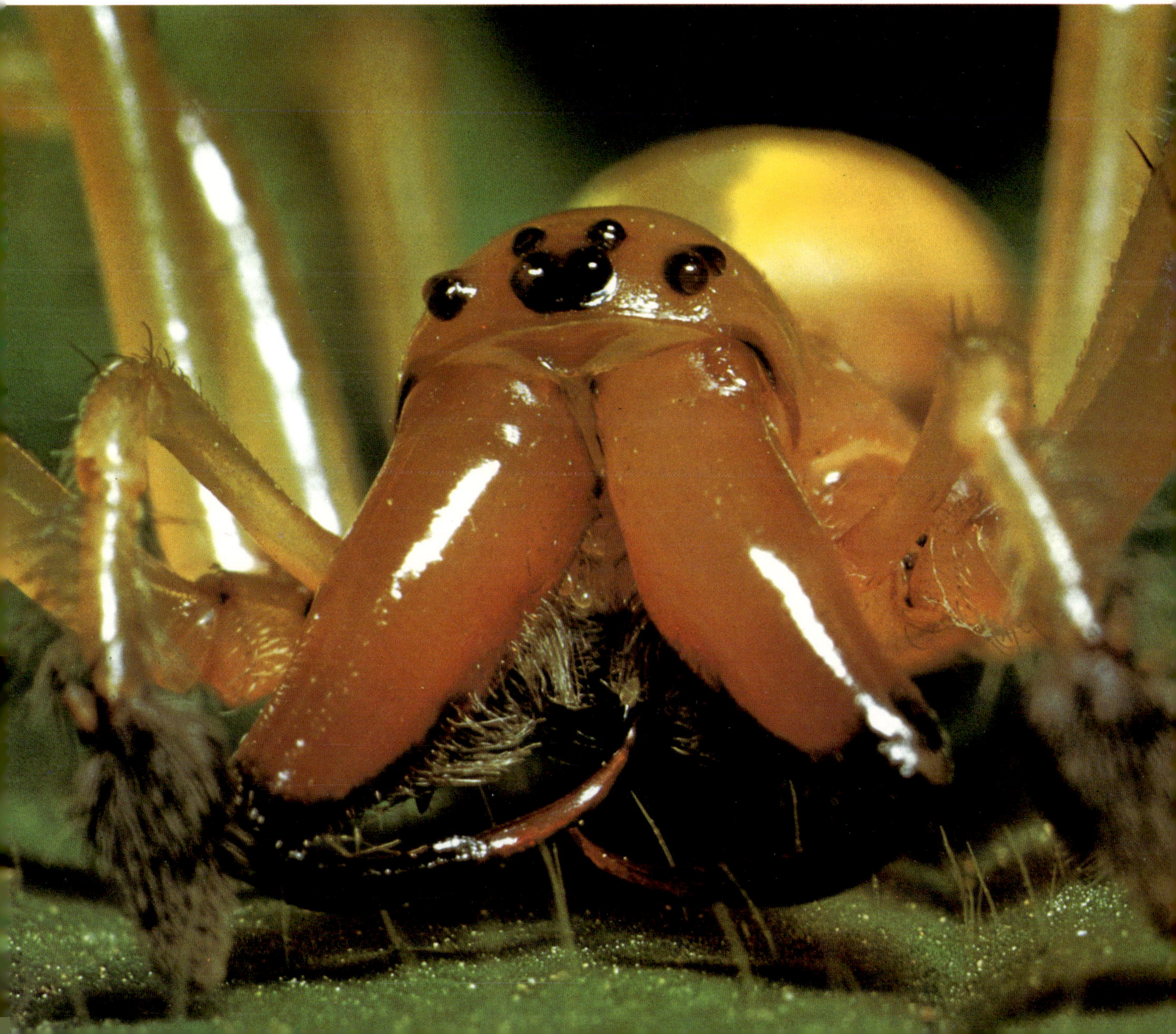

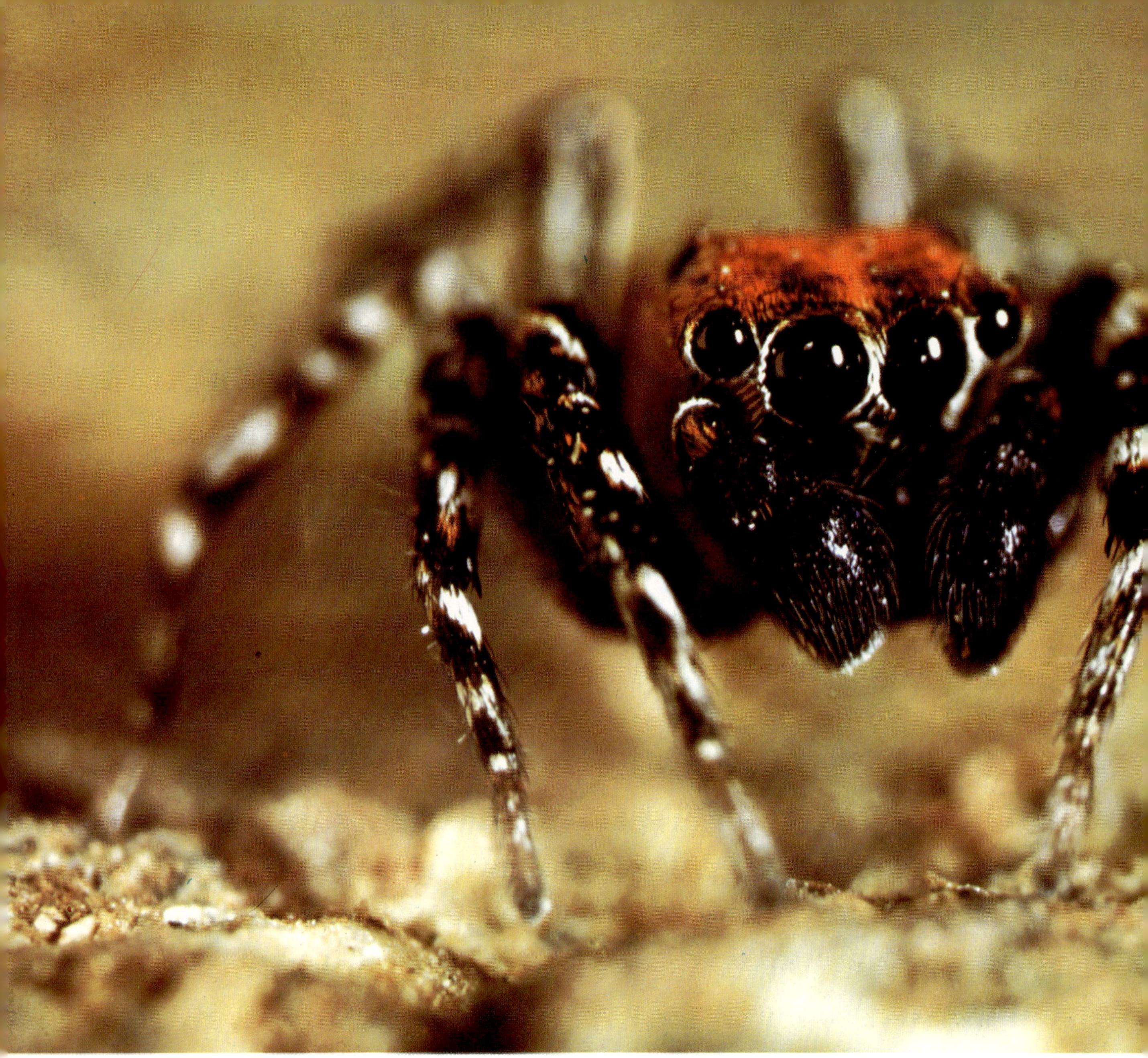

Jumping Spider (·x 32).
This minute spider escapes by performing jumps comparable to those of a flea. It has six eyes arranged around its head in a circle.

Reproduction ratio: 5.
Lens: Macro Summar 24 mm on bellows.
Aperture: f/8.
Electronic flash.

especially many species of fly: Syrphus, hovering Eristalus with yellow-striped bodies, enormous Volucella which look like hornets, and others.

At the foot of sun-bathed walls, on sandy soil, one can sometimes see little tunnels dug into the ground. If a closer look is taken at these tiny funnel-shaped excavations with gently sloping sides, two curved hooks can be seen protruding from the middle: these are the mandibles of the larva of the Antlion, buried at the centre of its trap. Its favourite prey is the ant, which in its endless wandering finds itself on the slope, starts to turn back and is suddenly bombarded by a deluge of sand which the larva directs towards it by a succession of head-movements; the ant then slides down the slope into the fangs waiting to close on it. It is easier to photograph this scene in captivity, the larva being placed in a terrarium filled with fine sand.

The numerous crevices in old walls are used for shelter by many small creatures. The spiders of the genus Segestria take up residence in small holes which they line with a tube of

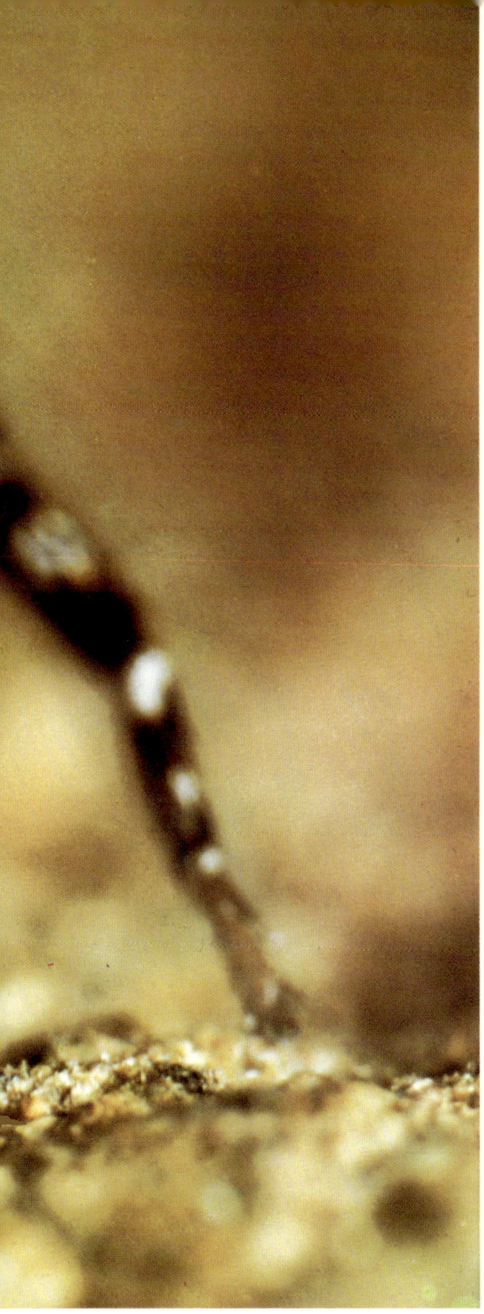

The Wall Lizard is undoubtedly the favourite inhabitant of these rocky abodes. Its home-loving nature makes it easy to record its movements. A lizard found sunning itself on a particular ledge will be there again in the same place on the following day, at around the same time. On the other hand, it knows the topography perfectly, and all the hiding-places into which it can disappear immediately if molested. It feeds mainly on flies and other small insects which its nimbleness enables it to catch, and if the observer keeps quiet he can have the privilege of witnessing its repast.

The stones which strew the ground

Zebra Spider (one of the Jumping Spiders) (x 25).
During their courting season, Jumping Spiders make use of an unusual system of gestures. Facing each other, the male and female raise and lower their palps in turn as though signalling by semaphore.

Reproduction ratio: 3·6.
Lens: 55mm mounted on bellows in reverse position.
Aperture: f/22.
Electronic flash.

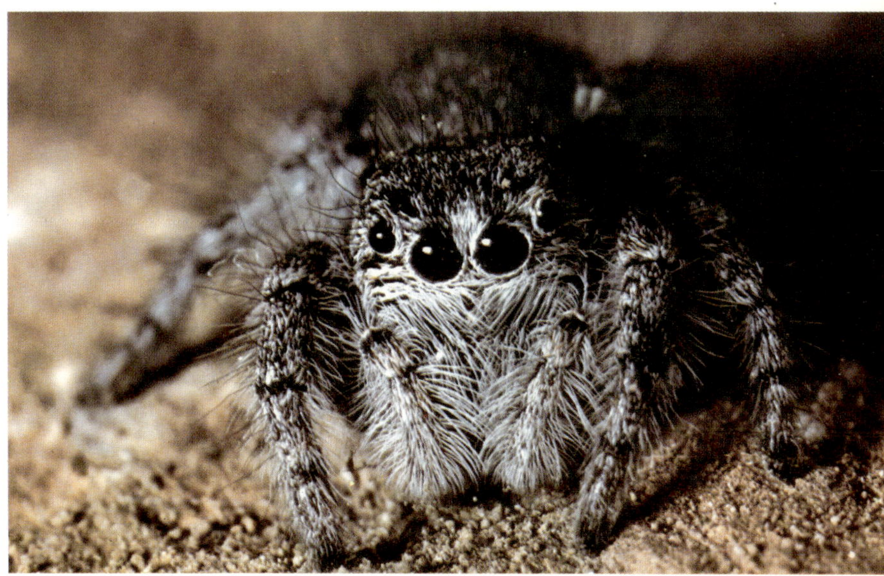

silk, the mouth of the tube being extended by means of long guy-lines radiating in all directions. Lying in wait in its tunnel, the Segestria is warned of the approach of prey by the vibration of the guy-lines, and emerges immediately. It is necessary for the photographer to allow for the considerable reflecting power of the nest (as is the case with all silk structures in general, such as cocoons) and to under-expose when using a flash-gun. The trick that one uses to make the spider appear is easy to guess.

provide a refuge for many creatures which become active only when night falls. One of the most interesting, in spite of its bad reputation, is the scorpion, the most widely distributed species in France being the little Yellow-tailed Scorpion. Although originally restricted to the South of France, this harmless creature owes the extension of its range to man and his countless means of transport, which sometimes carry stowaways. If it is possible to capture a gravid female, with her rounded sides, one can admire the maternal instinct she

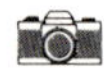

shows when her young are born; she helps them to escape from their envelope and then to climb on her back where they remain, all together and sheltered from danger, for about a week.

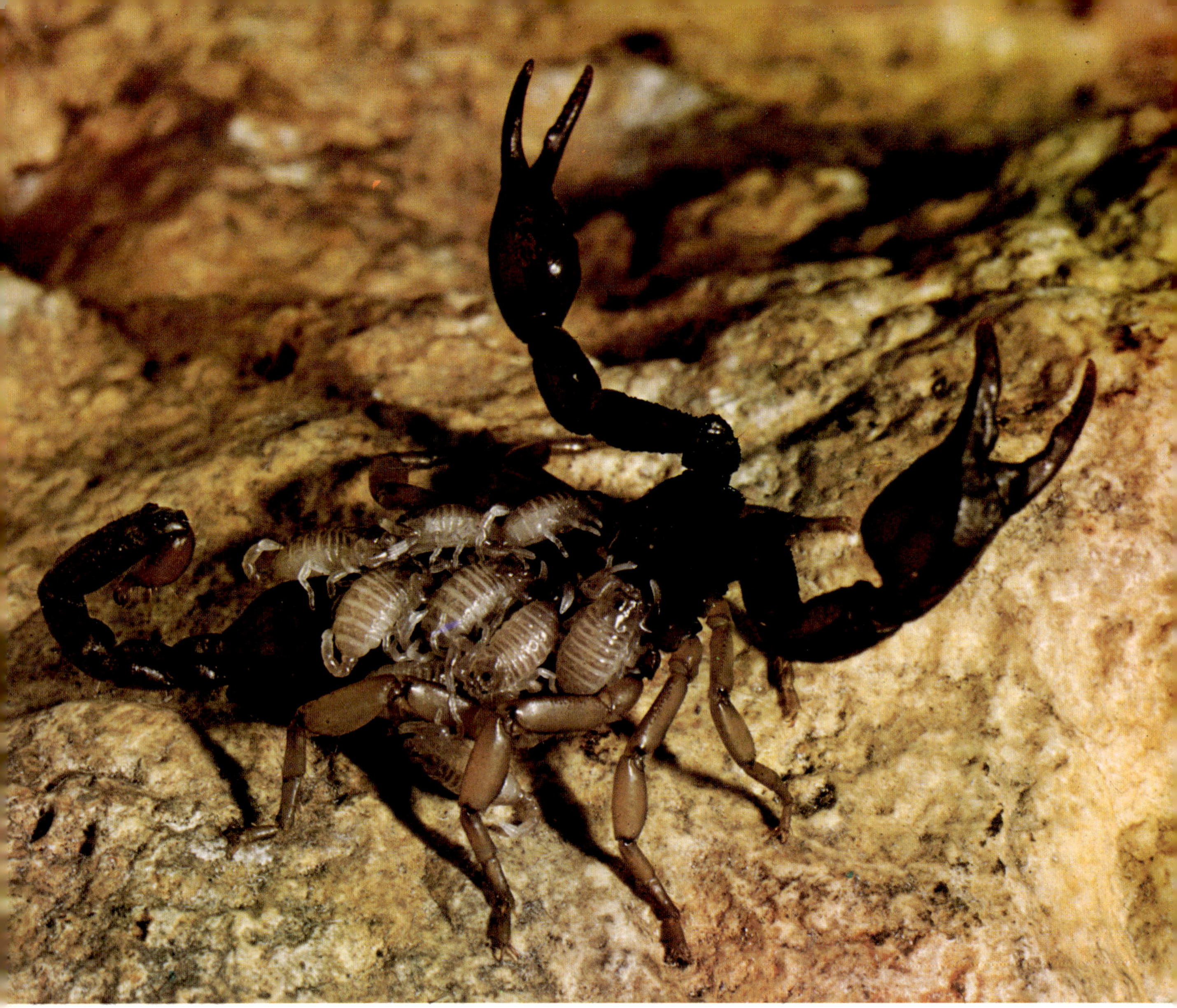

Thickets house numerous reptiles Their presence can be detected by the characteristic noise they make when moving about among the branches and dead leaves.

The large Green Lizard, which is very nervous and darts about, makes quite a lot of intermittent noise, by which its presence can easily be recognized. The male sports a beautiful turquoise blue throat. (Widely distributed in Southern Europe, this species is found in France as far north as a line drawn between Rouen and Belfort).

Snakes, on the other hand, betray their presence by a regular sound like something being dragged over the ground. In brushwood one can often find the Aesculapian Snake with its beautiful bronze-coloured scales (found as far north as the latitude of Switzerland), or the resplendent green and yellow European Whip Snake, which is common in Southern Europe. These two species readily climb trees.

The small Smooth Snake, by

contrast, widely distributed throughout Europe, is more likely to be
found in dry and rocky places.

These are all difficult subjects to
photograph in the field, particularly
in close-up. It is, therefore, better to
keep them in captivity for the period
of time necessary to obtain studio
photographs.

The mountains

Meadows on mountain slopes en-
compass so many unique features
that it is best to deal with each of
them separately.

It is in the mountains that the most
prodigious expanses of flowers and
the greatest variety of species can be
found. However, although it is possible, even at the beginning of spring,
to find the flowers of croci and Alpine
Snowbells pushing their way up
through the snow, it is necessary to
wait until some time in July before
this outburst of flowers can be seen
at the height of its glory.

The very nature of the topography
favours the greatest possible diversity of habitats. Depending on the
altitude, mountains can offer the
photographer quite an array of
characteristic zones over a distance
in height of a few hundred feet (the
mean annual temperature decreases
by one degree approximately every
650 feet [200m]).

Between about 2,500 and 4,500
feet (800–1,400m) is the 'upland'
range, where side-by-side with typi-
cally highland species there can still
be found a good proportion of lowland forms which are able to adapt
to the requirements peculiar to such
heights.

The 'sub-alpine' level, between
about 4,500 and 6,500 feet (1,400–
2,000m), is the region of large
forests of larch and spruce.

From 6,500 to 10,000 feet (2,000–
3,000m), on the other hand, there are
meadows of short grasses and low
plants: this is the 'alpine' level.
Finally, the zone above the snow-line
is characterized by permanent snow
(which in the past was often more
poetically referred to as the region of
eternal snows).

Within any of these levels, noticeable differences in the stage of
development of a given species can
be observed, depending on the altitude. Climbing towards the top, it

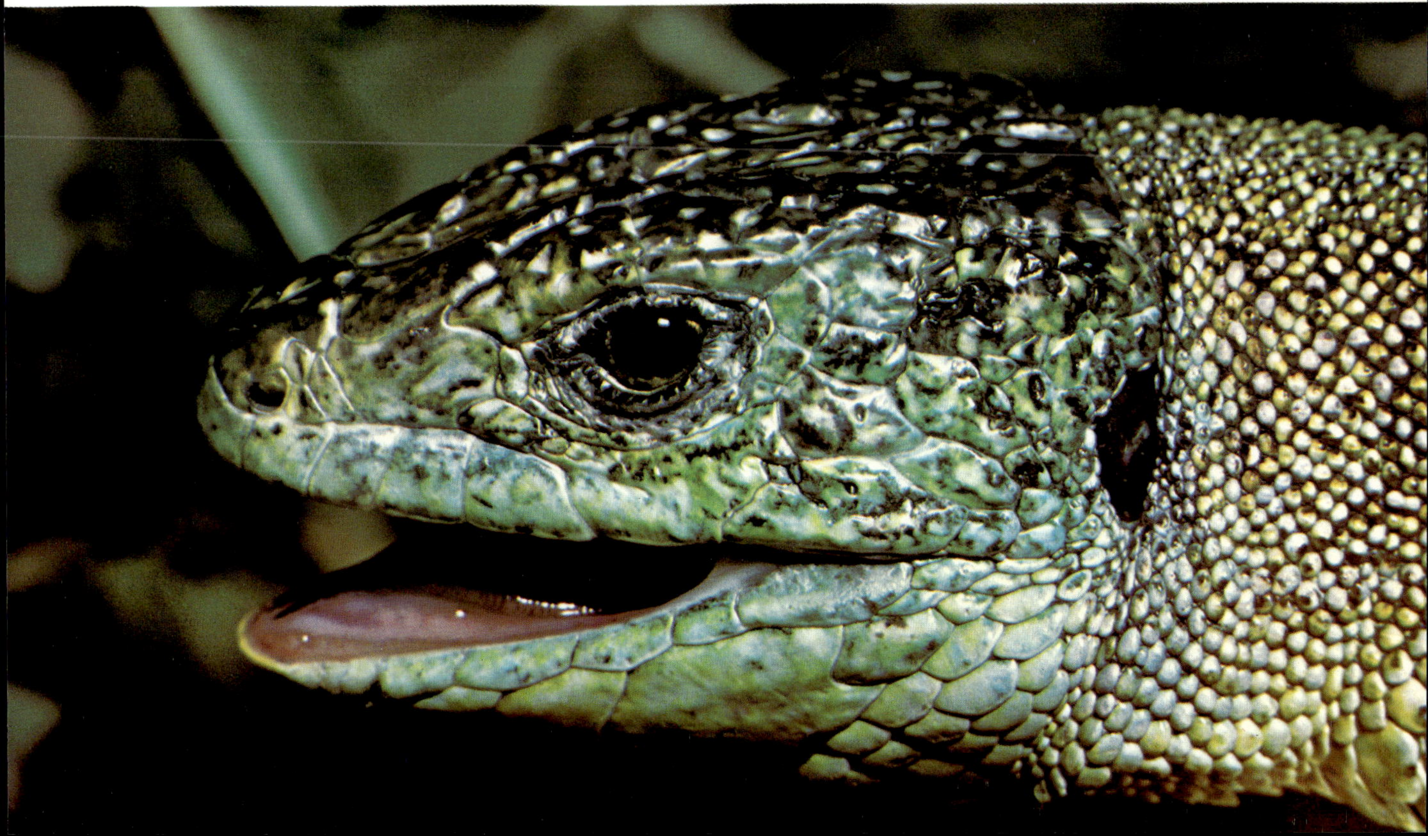

Green Lizard (x 0·5).
It is able to defend itself
vigourously against intruders.
Here it is shown with its jaws
half-open ready to bite.

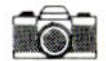

Reproduction ratio: 0·8.
Lens: 55mm with automatic
extension ring.
Aperture: f/22.
Electronic flash.

is as though one were travelling back in time during the season, finding flowers just opening which were already fading further down towards the valley.

Apart from the ubiquitous effect of altitude, there are also purely local features which are often decisive in determining the composition of the flora and fauna (north-facing slopes, for example, receive little sun and retain their humidity, while those facing south enjoy a lot of sunshine and tend to be much drier).

Light

High outcrops of rock, with their complex and distorted structure, tend to cut off the rays of the sun so that they strike the ground directly only during certain hours of the day, sometimes for a very short period. When carrying out his survey, therefore, the photographer must make it a strict rule to record precisely the periods of illumination of each of the locations he intends to revisit. This will enable him to arrange his daily programmes in such a way that his visits to different locations coincide with the times of day when sunlight can reach them. We would point out that when the sun disappears behind a peak, the reduction in light intensity is much more sudden and unexpected than during a normal sunset on the horizon.

Mountains receive a high level of solar radiation. The reduced density of the atmosphere results, in fact, in stronger light which is particularly rich in ultra-violet rays. The UV filter, however, is useless for close-up photography. On the other hand, if one wishes to include a few landscape pictures in a photographic recording, it is highly advisable to use it. The polarising filter, with which one can graduate the effects, is even better.

The light, which at low level is filtered by a thick atmospheric haze, becomes on the other hand very harsh on mountains. More than any-

Apollo Butterfly (x 2·5).
This large, snow-coloured butterfly frequents mountains. It is found up to about 8,000 ft (2,500 m) above sea level. It is seen here resting on a flowering stem of Cow-wheat one very misty morning in the Vanoise upland region of France.

Reproduction ratio: 0·5.
Lens: Macro 55 mm.
Aperture. f/3·5.
Exposure time: 1/30th of a second.
Natural light, sky very overcast, fine rain.
Film: Kodachrome 64.

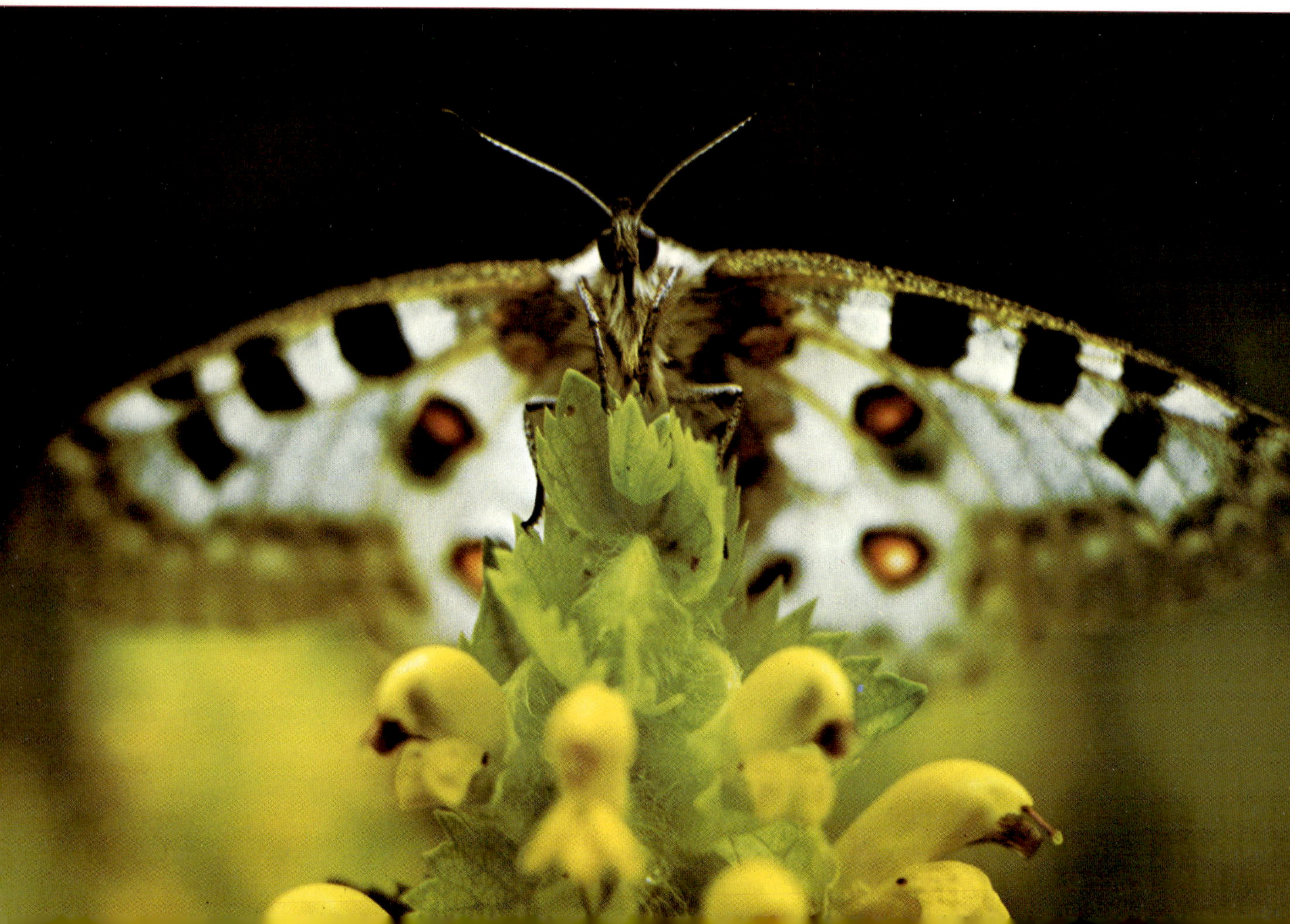

where else, it is necessary to avoid front-lit subjects and to look for side-lighting, the trajectory of which may well be close to the ground. General use should also be made of a reflecting screen to soften the shadows (it can also serve as a wind-shield). For these reasons, slightly overcast weather is an advantage when photographing in mountain areas, since clouds constitute an excellent light-diffusing screen.

Finally, we cannot too strongly emphasize that the photographic equipment to be carried should be strictly limited to essentials. Movement on mountains is slow and often difficult. It is essential not to carry too much for fear of not being able to reach the intended location. A rucksack is indispensible for moving about on steep slopes.

The subjects

It is undoubtedly among the plants that the amateur close-up photographer will find the most interesting subjects in mountainous country. The Turk's-cap Lily, Orange Lily, Nigritelle, Alpine Sea-holly, Edelweiss – these are only a few of the marvellous species which have become rare through being over-collected. It is, therefore, essential not to collect specimens but to be satisfied to observe and photograph them in their natural surroundings (which are often magnificent).

Among the countless insects which populate the mountain meadows, there will be found a large proportion of species also found at lower level. However, a number of new species of grasshopper will be found, as well as beetles of the Longhorn family (such as the Alpine Longhorn, which is grey-blue spotted with velvet-black).

The butterflies similarly include a few special representatives, such as the splendid Apollo Butterfly with semi-transparent white wings with red eye markings.

Amphibians are rare in mountains. Up to around 10,000 feet (3,000 m),

however, it may be possible to find the little Alpine Salamander, which is unusual in giving birth to living young which have already metamorphosed.

Among the reptiles, the Viviparous Lizard can be found at even greater heights. In this species, too, adaptation to the harsh conditions prevailing in mountains is apparent in their method of reproduction, which enables the newly-born young to confront the world in an advanced stage of development.

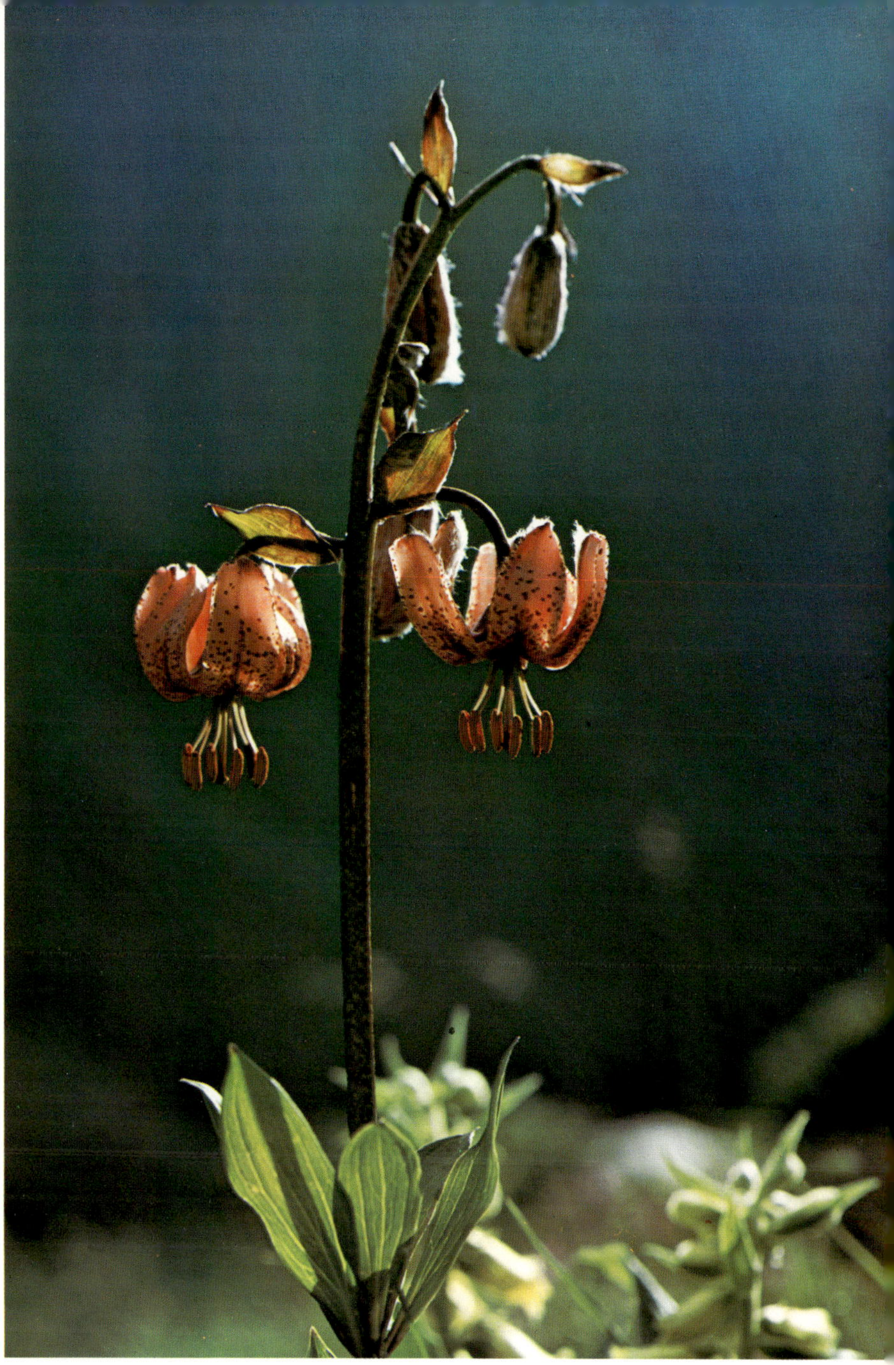

Martagon Lily, photographed in the Alps (x 0·5).
A victim of over-collecting, it has become increasingly rare. Unfortunately, it is protected only in parks and nature reserves.

Lens: Macro 55 mm.
Aperture: f/4-5·6.
Exposure time: 1·60 seconds.
Natural light, with the sun behind and just about to go down behind the mountains.
Film: Kodachrome 25.

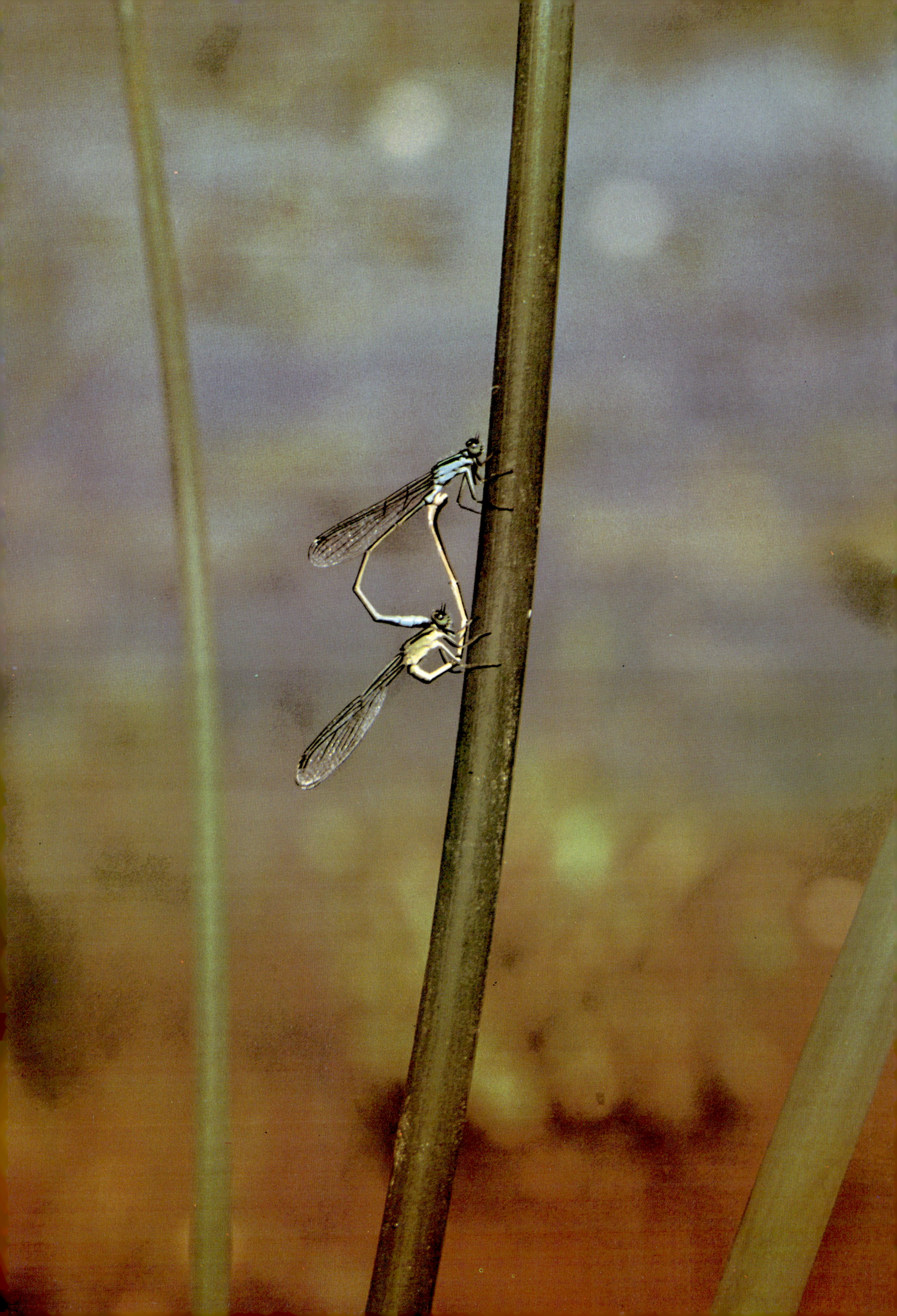

At the water's edge

The pond

A pond and its surroundings are a favourite location for the naturalist. Such a small area of standing water has the advantage of being easily accessible. Moreover, most species will be found concentrated around its periphery, in that sort of no-man's-land where a matter of a foot or so – about the distance a frog can jump – makes all the difference between being on dry land and being in the water. This mixed environment, half aquatic and half terrestrial, attracts many kinds of plants and animals which, depending on their particular affinities, take up residence on the bank, at the water's edge, in the shallows or in the open water in the middle of the pond.

The most productive method of carrying out 'pond hunts' is to arm oneself with a small-scale map of the region in which one wishes to operate – 1:50,000 G.S. maps or, better still, 1:25,000 Ordnance Survey maps. Maps on the same scales as these are published all over the world by national geographical institutes or government departments whose address may be obtained from the librarian in the reference department of any local public library.

In order to work in the field with greater freedom, it is not a bad idea to wear a pair of Wellington boots or even waders, as certain shots are undoubtedly more easy to obtain while standing in the water. This avoids the necessity for the dangerous acrobatics which often have to be indulged in by someone intent on keeping his feet dry, involving tricky balancing acts which may easily finish disastrously, particularly for the equipment!

Some wide-mouthed jars with perforated metal lids and a small-mesh hand-net complete the outfit; with them it is possible to collect aquatic specimens required for photographing back in the studio.

The abundance of creatures and the diversity of species found are not necessarily related to the size of the pond. We know a little pool in the Eure district of France which is not more than ten feet (3 m) across but provides a home for an amazing number of newts, frogs and dragonfly larvae, exhibiting a surprising range of species. A few hundred yards away an old gravel pit, which is now flooded and covers an area of nearly 50 acres, furnishes the sad spectacle of a complete aquatic desert, a sheet of water undisturbed by any form of animal life.

While we are on this subject, it should be pointed out that most bodies of water recently created by man show more or less the same features: in most cases it takes several decades for an intricate and balanced pattern of animal and vegetable life to develop in an environment of such recent origin. On the other hand, many ponds which we would now assume to be of natural origin were, in fact, created in the Middle Ages for fish-rearing purposes. Since then, Nature has had time to assert itself and endow these waters formerly reserved for fish-husbandry with teeming flora and

A pair of Damsel-flies (x 1·5). In this type of dragonfly, the male frequently claims possession of a hunting territory. He thereby reserves the sole right to capture gnats and mosquitos within this area, which he defends against all others of his own kind other than the female with which he will pair. Before mating, the male approaches his partner in a kind of dance in which he makes short, rapid flights around her.

Reproduction ratio: 0·25.
Lens: Macro 55 mm.
Aperture: f/5·6.
Exposure time: 1/250th of a second.
Natural light. A very sunny day, with the blue sky reflected in the pond.
Film: Kodachrome 64.

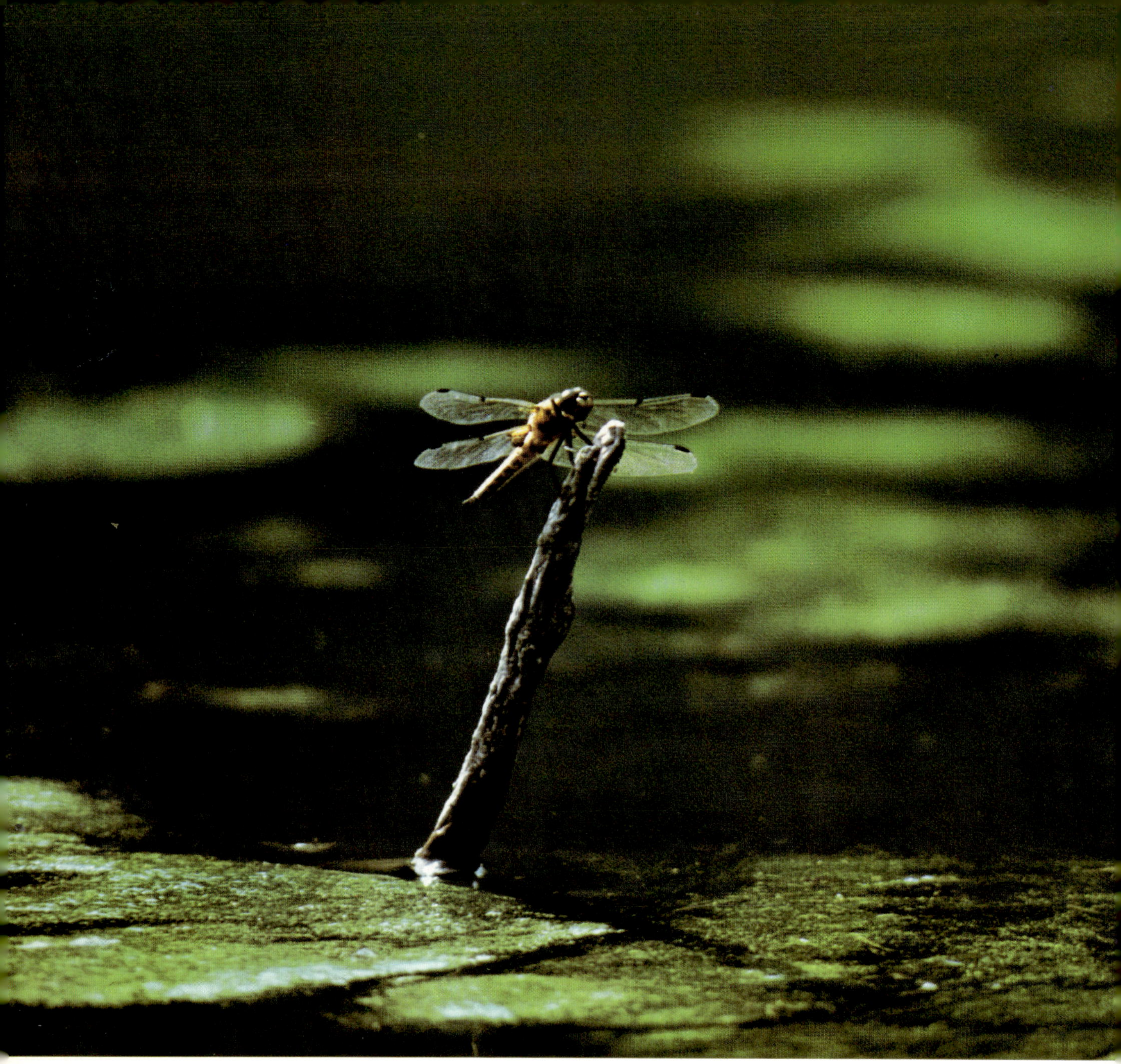

Broad-bodied Dragonfly (x 0·8).
Stationed on the end of a dead
branch protruding from the pond,
it waits for a victim to pass by,
ready to dart after it.

300 mm telephoto lens with 25 mm
extension ring.
Aperture: f/4·5.
Exposure time: 1/250th of a
second.
Natural light from behind, late
afternoon.

fauna.

What goes on in a pond depends almost entirely on the season. Winter is a period of reduced activity: many species lie buried in the mud, in a state of torpor. Life reawakens in the spring, but to some extent later than in the meadow, where the flowers and honey-gathering insects appear with the first fine days.

Over the years the physical appearance of a pond changes slowly: the constant deposition of mud (by the simple process of organic particles falling to the bottom and decomposing) gradually raises the bed and reduces the depth of the water. Because of this build-up of material, the vegetation on the banks slowly encroaches upon the pond, the area of which contracts like a piece of grained leather: the pond thus slowly dies a natural death, progressively invaded by vegetation from the land. There are, however, cases involving a more violent extinction: a pond is a biological entity the existence of which depends on a complex inter-

Denizens of the banks

Dragonflies

Holding sway as masters of the air-space above the pond and its surroundings, the large dragonflies seem at first sight to be very difficult subjects for photography. It is true that once they have taken wing, there is no longer any question of obtaining a picture: for some species, flying speeds reaching sixty miles per hour have been recorded, but most

Demoiselle Agrion (x 2).
It is holding a Mayfly that it has caught in flight. The pale skin of the Mayfly shows that it has just completed its metamorphosis. Its youthful inexperience has cost it its life.

Reproduction ratio: 0·4.
Lens: Macro 55 mm.
Aperture: f/5·6.
Exposure time: 1/125th of a second.
Natural light.

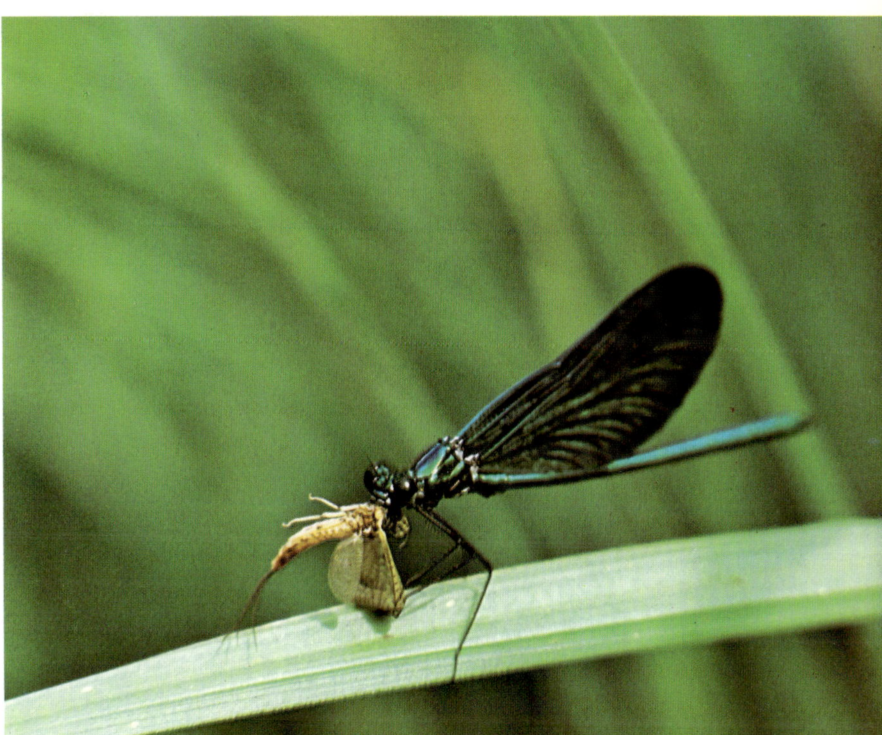

play of reciprocal forces in which the entire cast of performers is involved, from the microscopic algae suspended in the water to the heron feeding on frogs. All that is needed is the establishment, which man is quite capable of effecting, of some overwhelming factor, and the future of this autonomous universe is endangered. Such is the introduction of carnivorous fish (pike or perch) for angling, or the discharge of organic waste originating in some nearby urban centre.

of them are content with a cruising speed of twenty-five miles per hour, at a rate of thirty wing-beats a second.

Let us study the behaviour of a dragonfly: having traversed the surroundings in all directions, with a great display of aerial acrobatics, it generally returns to rest on the perch from which it took off. On this natural vantage point – the end of a rush or reed, or a convenient dead branch – it lies in wait almost completely motionless, its presence betrayed only by tiny abrupt movements of its head. In this respect it follows the example of birds of prey, which often take up their position on posts so that they can keep better watch over the ground and detect the movements of any prey.

The dragonfly possesses, if one may use the phrase, an eagle eye, at least on a scale appropriate to insects. Its two composite eyes are so well-developed that they form, as it were, a helmet enclosing the sides of the head, sometimes even joining at the top. No matter from which direction a potential victim may arrive, it can never escape these formidable panoramic eyes. The photographer must approach it cautiously, without making any sudden movement; the use of a telephoto lens will make it unnecessary to venture too close. If, in fact, the subject suddenly takes flight, it only remains for the photographer to take up his position close to the perch, adjust his framing and focusing, and unobtrusively await the return of the insect. The wait will rarely be in vain, and the dragonfly will sometimes return carrying a victim which it has captured in flight, perhaps a mayfly or a butterfly. This is bound to make the photograph even more interesting.

For the zoologist, the small dragonflies with a slender body and quiet flight, which are sometimes called 'damsel-flies', are not true dragonflies but 'agrions'. The Demoiselle Agrion, with a metallic blue body and wings which are smoke-coloured in the female and royal blue in the male, makes a particularly entrancing subject for the photographer. These fragile creatures have, however, the same carnivorous habits as the large dragonflies.

The mating of dragonflies is one of the most amazing spectacles in the insect world. While very violent among the large dragonflies, when it is preceded by considerable clashing of wings and aerial battles, it is easier to follow in the case of the agrions, which are less aggressive and more sedate. The male commences by seizing the female behind the head with the aid of his pincer-like claw which is situated at the end of his abdomen. Coupled in this way, they make a series of short flights in tandem and finally come to rest on some aquatic plant, the male clutching the support while the female hangs below him. Before long, she bends her abdomen forward until it is in contact with the forward body-rings of the male's abdomen, in order to receive the semen. Whilst this is going on, the bodies of the two insects form a striking heart-shaped figure. Even in this contorted position, which appears to be rather uncomfortable, the two partners are able to fly away if pestered. The photographer must, therefore, exercise a certain amount of care.

Having performed his duty, the male does not always release the female immediately. In certain

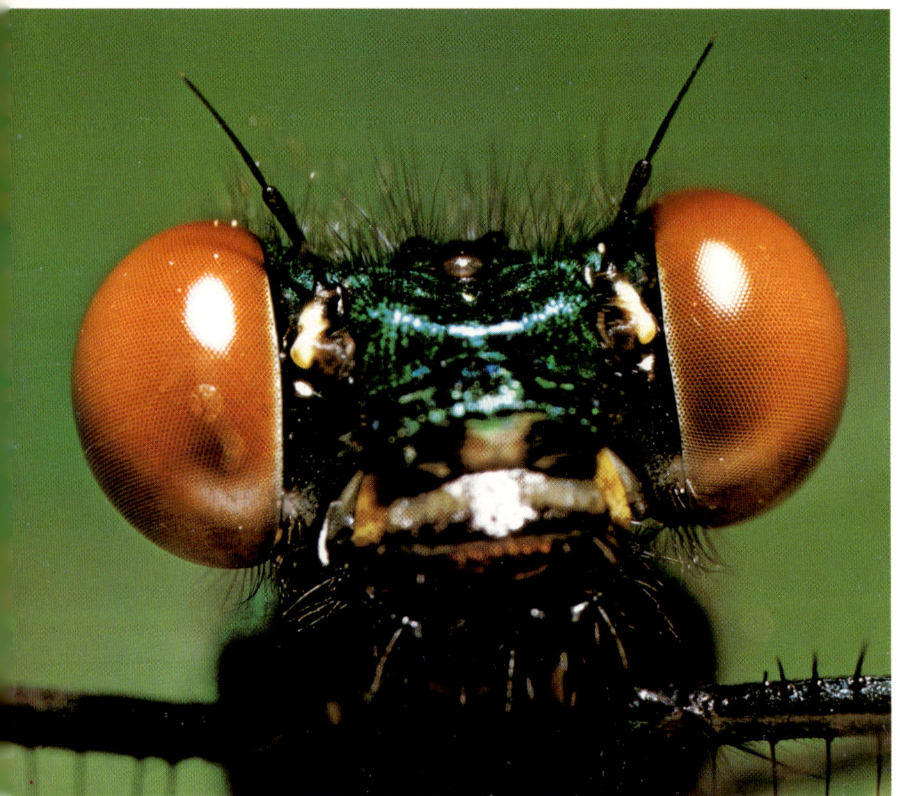

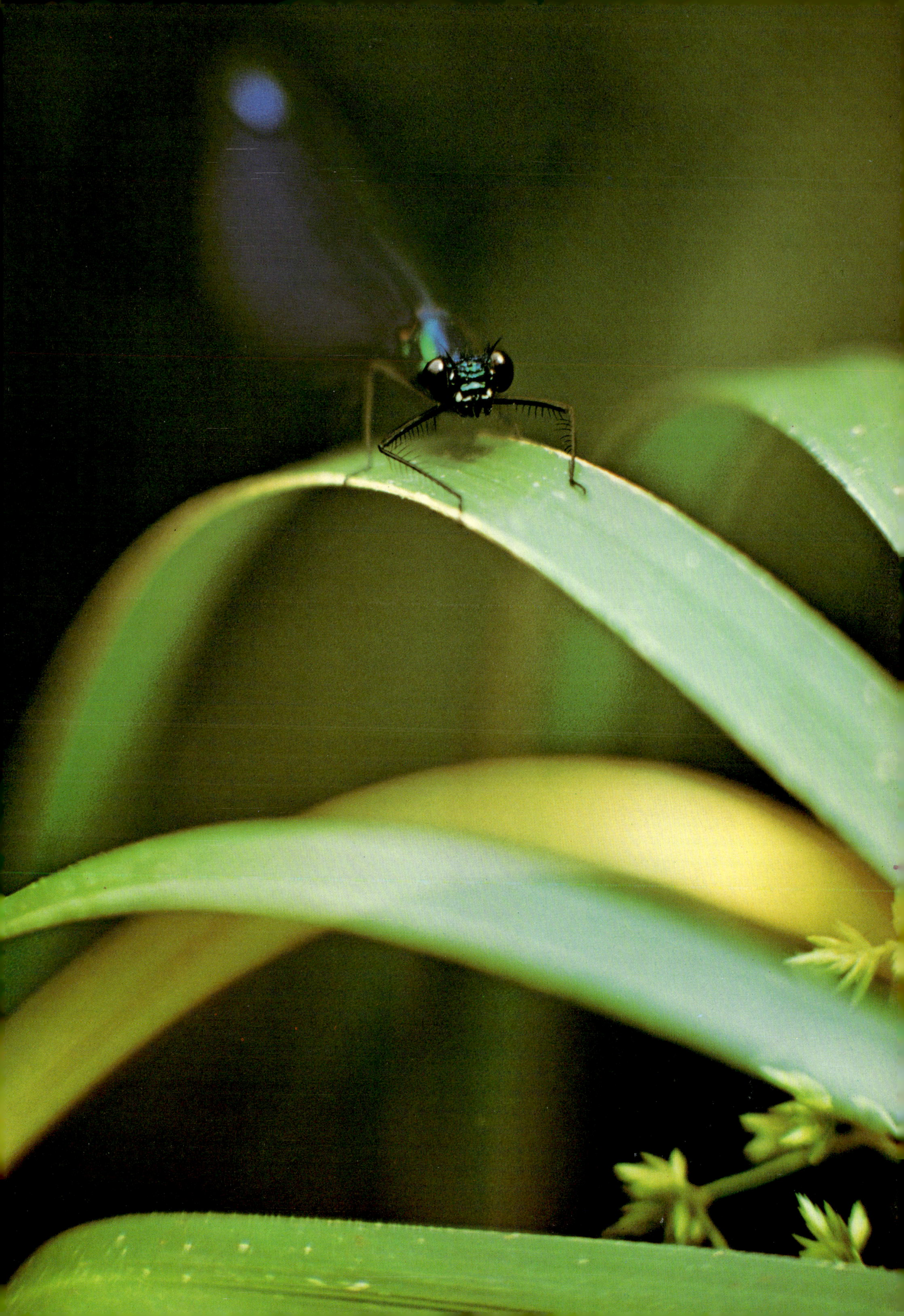

species, he remains attached to her until the eggs are laid. The female finally comes to rest on a half-submerged aquatic plant; she curves her abdomen down into the water to release her minute eggs, while the male holds himself rigidly upright with his legs folded, like an antenna mounted on the neck of his companion. This is another very strange double acrobatic trick which can be photographed if one wears a pair of waders and uses an angle or chest-level viewfinder so that it becomes possible to compose the picture at water-level while bending over the camera; the contortions of the photographer during this may well rival those of his subject!

Living clouds

Other insects that haunt the edges of ponds have, like the dragonflies, emerged from the water, where they have spent a long time as larvae, and it is to their original element that they return, after a brief aerial existence, to lay their eggs. Ephemera, or the Mayfly, owes its name

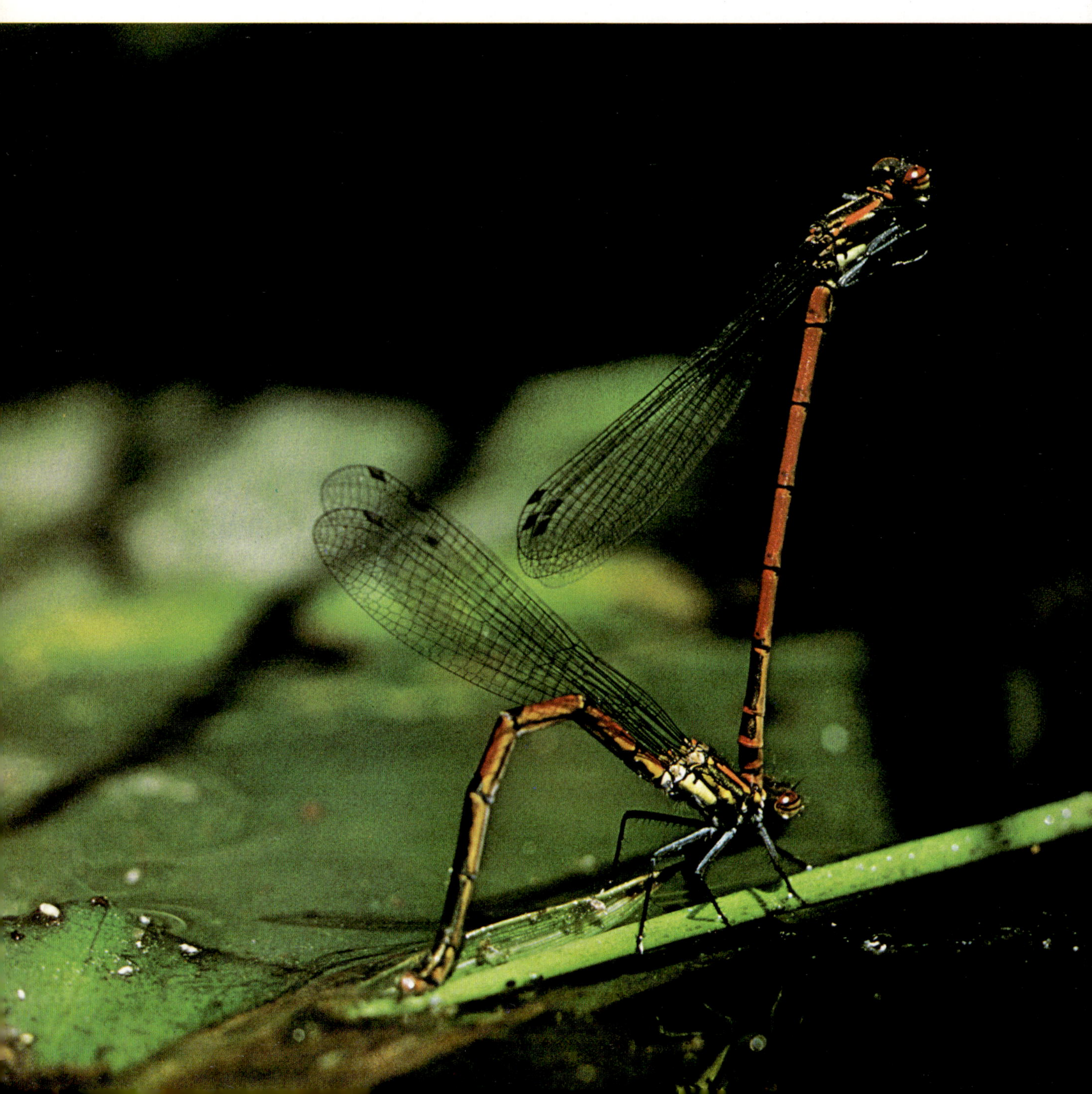

to the fact that it spends an extremely short time in the air. Its life as a winged adult often comes to an end after a few hours, which it has spent taking part in a collective nuptial flight, forming what appears to be a cloud moving over the water. The female consigns her eggs to the pond before falling exhausted on the bank. In the United States, in the region of the Great Lakes, millions of corpses lying on the roads can at times make them slippery for driving. To compensate for such a brief destiny, the larva of the Mayfly enjoys an aquatic existence which can last up to three years.

The life-span of mosquitoes is hardly more noteworthy: two or three weeks at the most. The dipteran Chironomus plumosus is one of the most fervent frequenters of pools of water. It has the advantage of not biting. Its larva is the well-known bright red mud-worm which is sold under the name of 'bloodworm' by dealers in angling shops. Only the male displays the two fine, feathery antennae which form, as it were, an impenetrable covering of down on its head. But this attractive creature is not merely an ornament: its antennae are vibration receivers used to pick up the 'note' emitted by females in flight. By beating their wings more than five hundred times per second, the latter produce, in fact, a sound of a special pitch (about five tones below 'la' in the musical scale) to which the male invariably responds by taking off in the direction of the originator of this seductive song.

The water's edge is also a haunt for other creatures of formidable appearance, like enormous mosquitoes with elongated legs – the crane flies. In spite of their appearance, however, these insects are incapable of biting. They are, in a way, the harvest-spiders of the air. Their long thread-like legs break easily. Although these cumbersome limbs seem to hang down uselessly during flight, they do in fact aid the movement of the insect in the air by enabling it to make use of atmospheric currents, like the long feathery appendages of certain seeds which are carried by the wind.

Resident hunters

There are certain creatures which take advantage of this incessant movement of insects in flight near pools of water. The spiders of the genus Tetragnatha, for example, have become specialists in hunting this abundant prey. They invariably

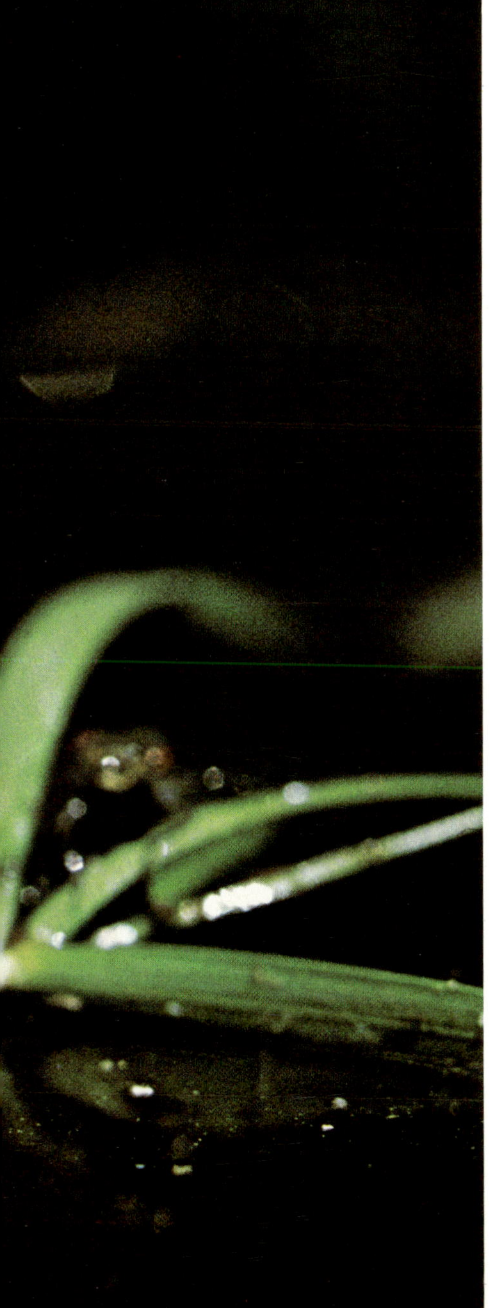

Red Agrions (x 3).
The female, with her body arched, is laying her eggs on an aquatic plant just below the surface of the water. Although his task of fertilization is complete, the male remains fastened by his abdominal claws to the rear of his partner's head, balanced in a vertical position. He will not release his hold until the eggs have all been laid.

Larger dragonflies behave in a much more agitated manner when laying their eggs. They execute dangerous acrobatic feats of low-level flying, brushing the surface of the pond with their abdomens. Following a curious, zig-zag flight-path, they touch the water repeatedly with the end of the abdomen, releasing at each contact a series of minute round eggs, which will ultimately produce aquatic larvae bearing little resemblance to the adults.

Reproduction ratio: 0·35.
Lens: Macro 55 mm.
Aperture: f/5·6-8.
Exposure time: 1/60th of a second.
A viewfinder with a hood was used to permit viewing at ground level.
Natural light, filtering through the leaves of aquatic plants.

take up residence on plants growing right next to the water, where they construct a large sloping web, which is quickly blanketed with countless victims. Occasionally one may find that, in this endeavour to keep as close to the aquatic world as possible, some of the supporting threads of the web have been fastened to a piece of dead branch protruding above the surface of the pond, and one wonders what daring feats of balance were involved in throwing these mooring-lines across the water. With the aid of our invaluable little folding magnifier – without which we are in the same state of confusion as a short-sighted person who cannot find his glasses – we can study at close-quarters the elongated physiognomy of this strange spider. Eight small black beads are set in a double row on the front of the cephalothorax: these are its eyes. Further forward still, two protruberances can be seen, which open to allow two long and extremely sharp-pointed poison fangs to emerge. When at rest, these remain folded back in a groove, like the blade of a penknife.

Water creatures

Other animals maintain a shuttle service between the dry land and the pond: these are the Edible Frogs. We call them 'water creatures' for the good reason that, driven from the bank by our approach, this is the environment into which they always escape with a single leap, resurfacing a few moments later, but ready to disappear into the depths at any further threat of danger. This frog is a typical 'telephoto lens animal'. In this instance there is no question of trying to take close-ups a few inches from its nose; when one realizes how well its large protruding eyes function, all movements are made as cautiously as possible. Because of their prominent position, these eyes act in the same way as periscopes: they allow the frog, while the rest of its body remains submerged, to see without being seen, for who would notice those two small green spheres protruding in the middle of a field of floating leaves? However, it is the mode of vision of this eye rather than its intriguing appearance which is of particular interest. Extensive research has elicited the fact that the frog sees only moving objects. These show up extremely clearly in the animal's visual field, since they appear against a black background corresponding to the motionless setting in front of which they are moving. From the pond the frog can, therefore, only see objects in motion or, in other words, the two things which are important in its world – prey (insects in flight) and enemies (herons, or possibly photographers). It should always be remembered that, to the frog, a photographer who does not move does not exist.

Two species of snake frequent ponds, the Grass Snake and especially the Viperine Snake. Although they can also be found in open country, finding them in an aquatic environment offers the advantage of avoiding any risk of confusion with a viper, which, as is known, prefers to avoid water. They are excellent swimmers and propel themselves by rapid undulations of the body, holding the head above water. It is mainly frogs which suffer from this association, not to mention fish, tadpoles and newts – an abundance of food items that easily explains the presence of snakes in such places. When trying to photograph these animals, one can be hindered by the reflection of the sky on the surface of the water, which conceals the submerged parts of the animal's body behind a sort of milky haze. The use of a polarising filter – the best position for which can be determined by turning it through one complete revolution while watching the result through the viewfinder – can dispel these surface reflections so that the underwater world suddenly becomes visible.

Agrions (x 3).
Found on a very large half-dry pond, together with thousands of other pairs, at the end of August. In spite of the very contorted position adapted during mating, the two partners will fly off at the slightest alarm to find a safer resting-place.

Reproduction ratio: 0·4.
Lens: Macro 55 mm.
Aperture: f/4-5·6.
Exposure time: 1/125th of a second.
Natural light from behind, in the morning.

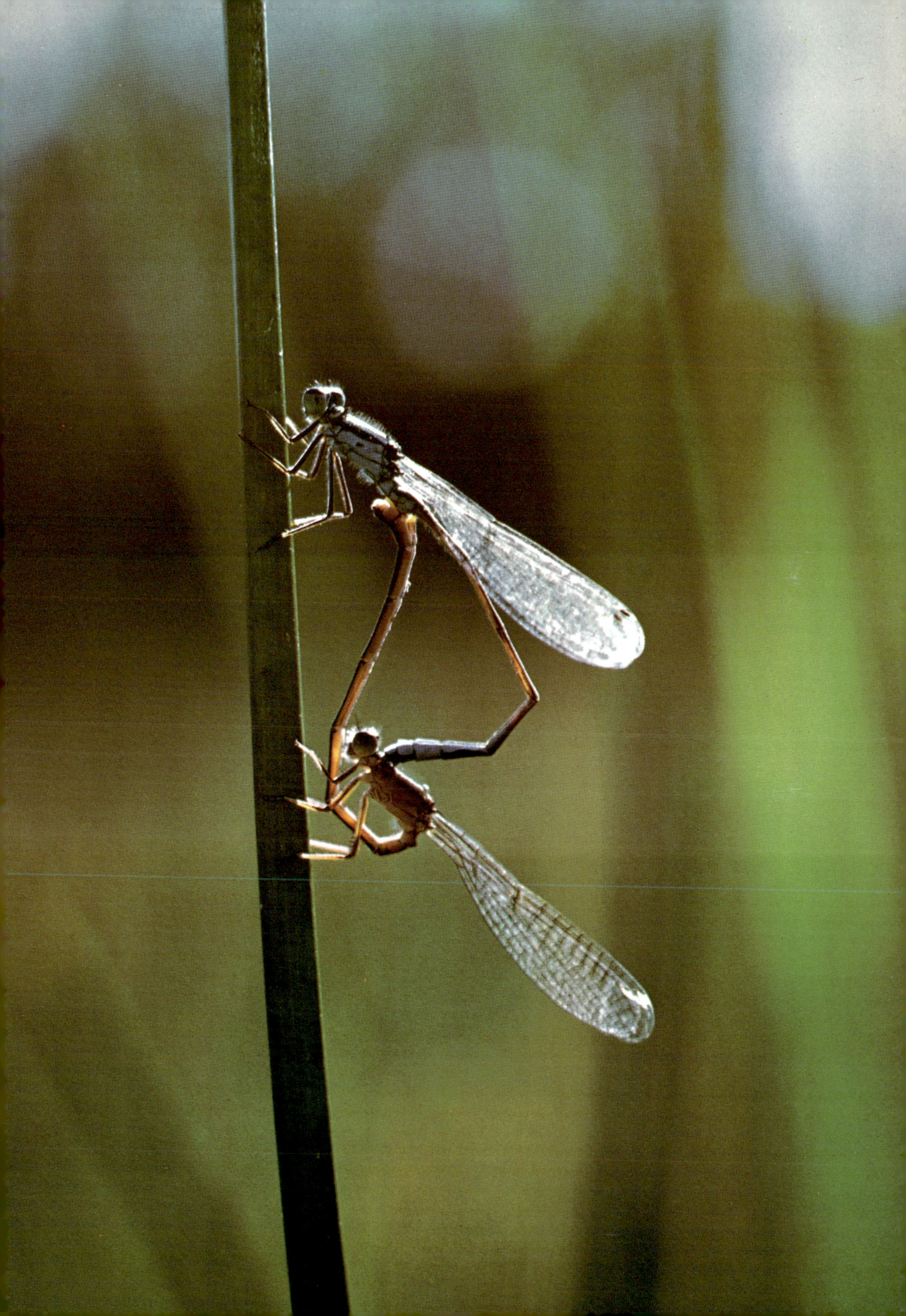

Demoiselle Agrion at the edge of
the water (x 1·5).
The sun's rays are reflected in the
rushing water of the small stream
as if by a multitude of shimmering
facets.

Reproduction ratio: 0·3.
Lens: Macro 55 mm.
Aperture: f/8.
Exposure time: 1/125th of a
second.
Natural light.

Below: Mayfly (x 3·5).

Reproduction ratio: 0·5.
Lens: 105 mm with 25 mm
extension ring.
Aperture: f/2·5.
Exposure time: 1/60th of a
second.
Natural light, in the morning, sky
overcast.

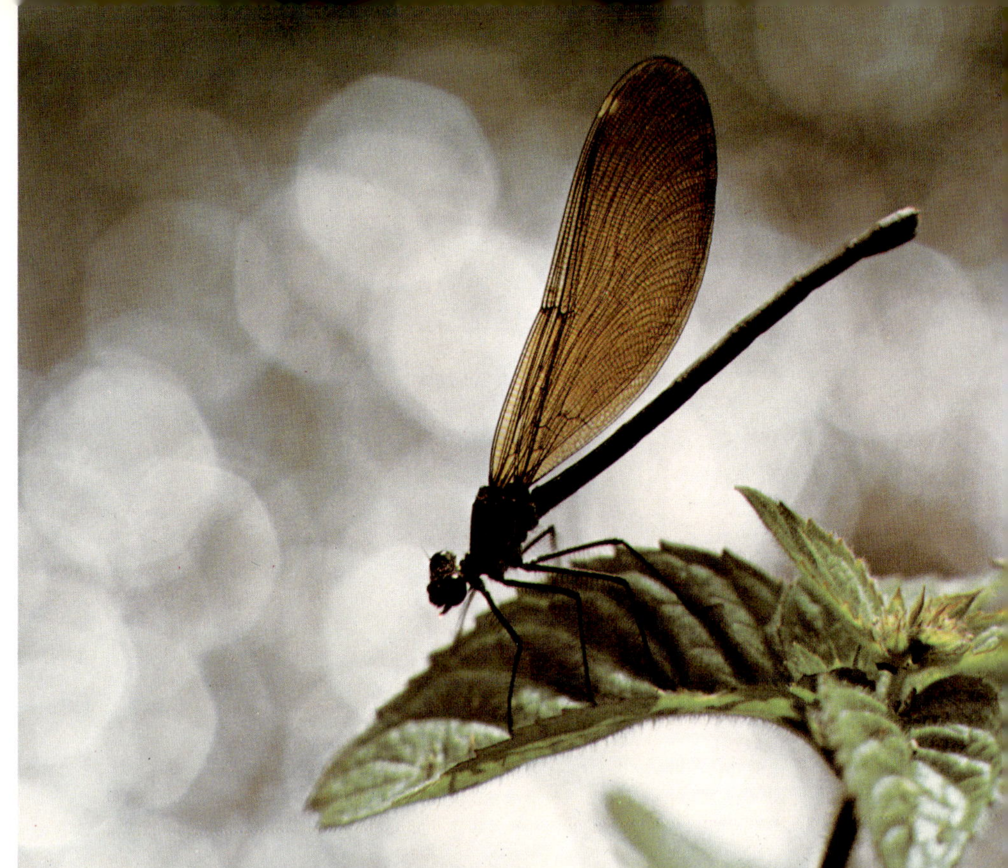

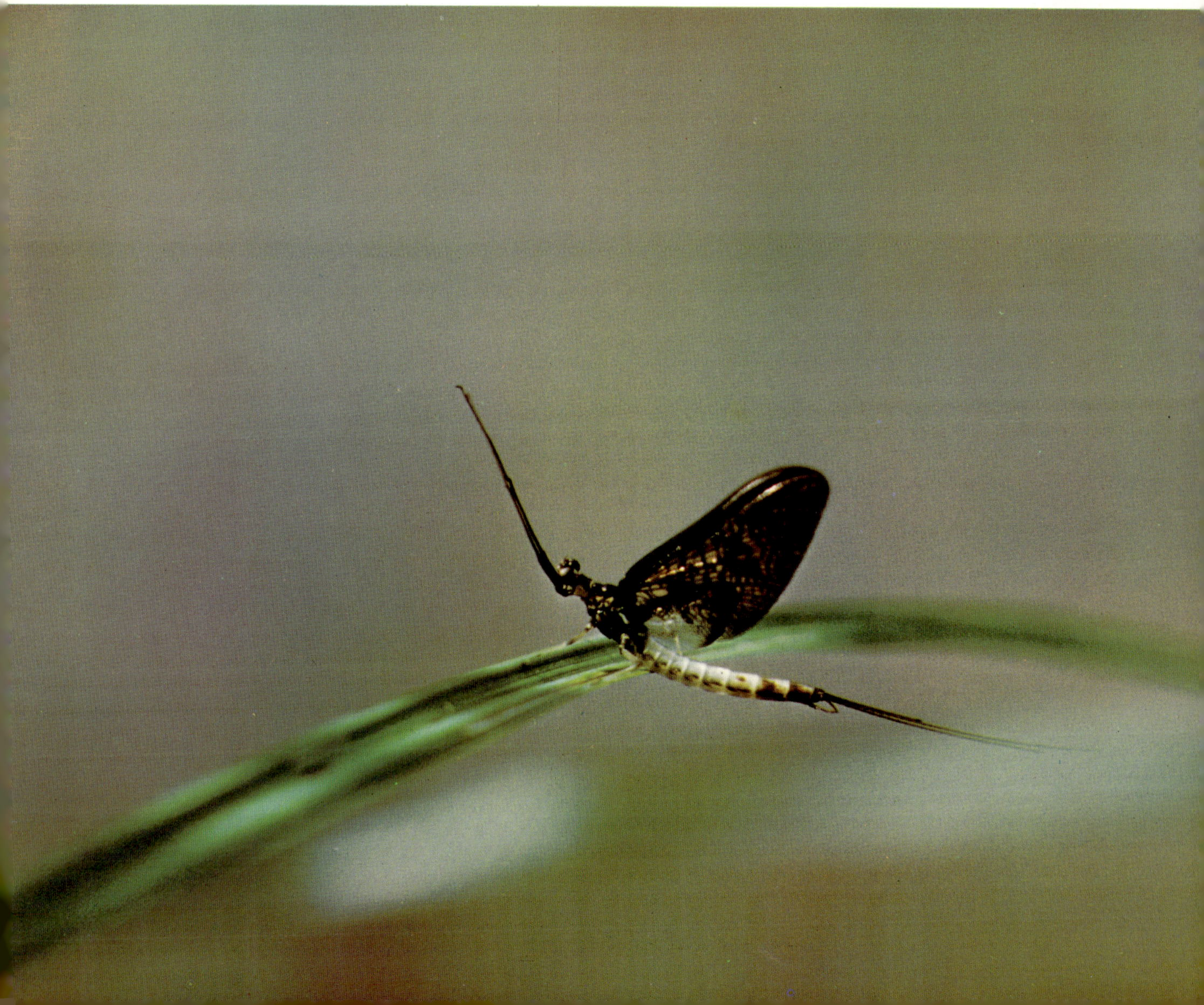

Insects of the water

Although insects have abandoned the marine environment to the care of crustaceans, they have not demonstrated the same aloofness as regards fresh water, which has become the preferred environment of numerous species perfectly adapted to aquatic life.

Some have adopted the surprising solution of walking on water. The Pond Skaters (which belong in fact to a hemipteran genus called Gerris) disturb the surface of the pond with their frenzied ballet. Due to the minute waterproof hairs covering their legs and body, they are able to glide over the water without fear of becoming wet. They prey upon flying insects which have been unfortunate enough to fall into the water and, not being so well equipped, can but struggle pitifully.

Apart from these unusual creatures, which spend their lives at the boundary between air and water, the search for aquatic insects must take place under water. Here, in particular, can be found other types of hemiptera, comprising the boat-flies, the water scorpions and the water stick-insects. The way in which boat-flies have adapted to aquatic life is apparent from their long rear legs fringed with hairs, which serve as oars. They are excellent swimmers and always swim upside down; for a carnivore feeding on living creatures under the water, it is not altogether a disadvantage for it to have its head permanently turned towards the depth of the pond. From time to time the boat-fly comes to the surface to renew its reserve of air by protruding the end of its abdomen, furnished with two respiratory spiracles, above the water. Should it wish to change its hunting ground, it still has the ability to fly to another pond.

Water scorpions and water stick-insects, on the other hand, are poor swimmers. Although they, too, are carnivores, they prefer to lie in wait for their prey. Like the Praying Mantis, the specialist in this method of capture on land, they are furnished with 'predatory feet' which close on their victims and carry them back to their mouth. Their method of respiration operates on the same principle as the snorkel used by skin-divers: the abdomen is extended by a long breathing tube. When protruded, it enables the animal to breathe while remaining under water.

Certain large aquatic insects can-

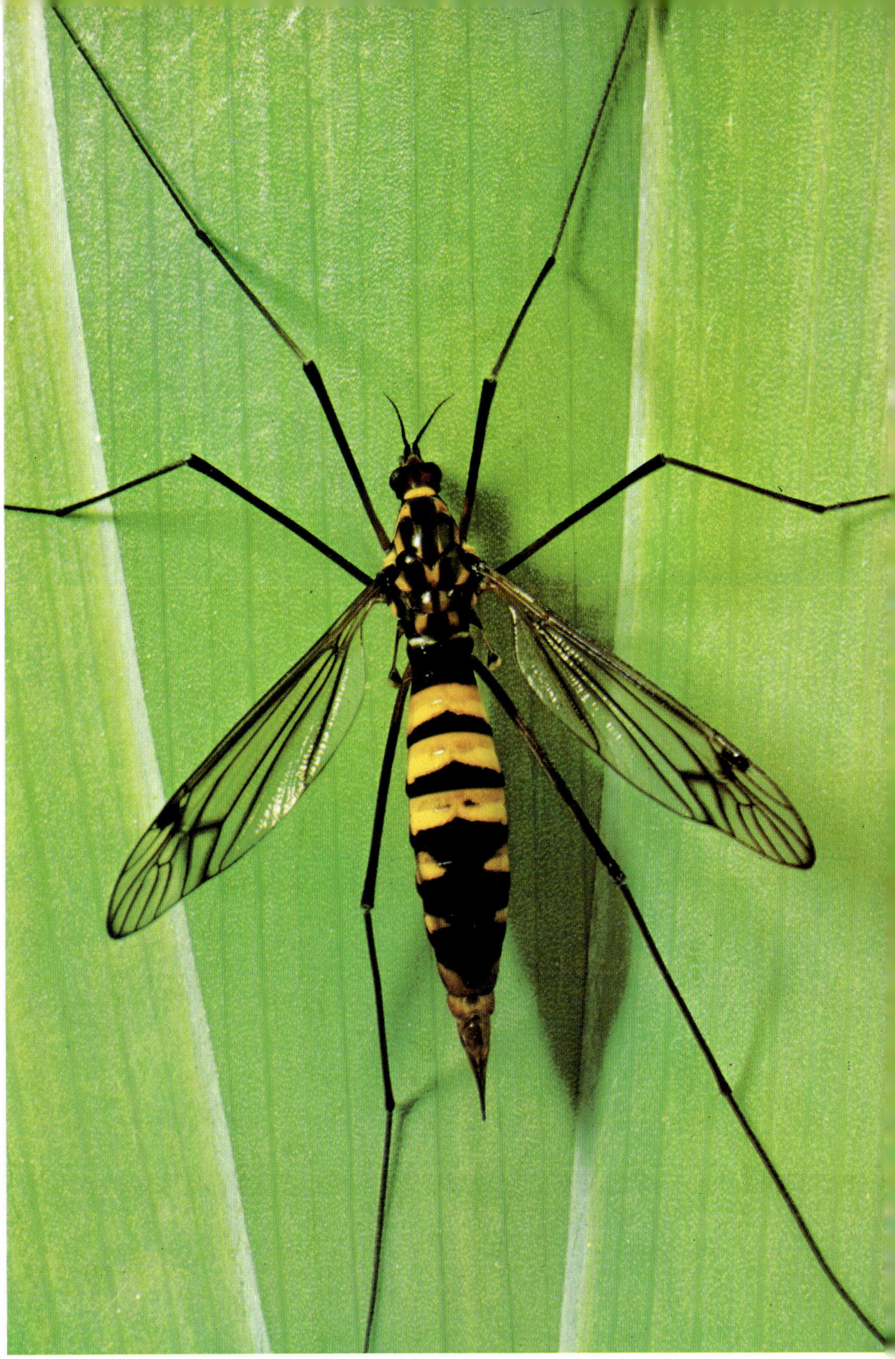

Yellow Crane-fly resting on an Iris Leaf (x 4).
A close relative of the mosquitoes, it does not sting. Its long legs provide purchase for the wind and help it to fly.

Reproduction ratio: 0·8.
Lens: 105 mm mounted on bellows.
Aperture: f/22.
Electronic flash with reflecting screen to reduce the shadows.

not fail to attract the attention of the naturalist. These are the diving beetles of the genera Dytiscus and Hydrophilus; the latter hold the record for size in their class with a length of two inches (5 cm). A sort of large aquatic beetle furnished with a thick, convex, black carapace, they too have solved the problem of underwater breathing by an original method.

In fact, Dytiscus holds its store of air in the flattened chamber formed by the space separating the wing-cases and the abdomen. The insect renews this reserve periodically by allowing the tip of its abdomen to emerge, the spent air being replaced by pure air.

Hydrophilus, on the other hand, carries its store of air on the under-side of its body in the form of a fine film held by numerous waterproof hairs, which give the lower surface of the insect a very attractive silvery sheen.

A diving spider

The same shiny appearance is also a feature of one of the strangest inhabitants of the pool, the Water Spider. This incredible aquatic spider – the only one of its group to have ventured into this environment – uses its skill as a weaver to construct what in view of its life-style is a very useful aid, the 'diving bell'. By virtue of its covering of waterproof hairs, it is able to carry down from the

Spider of the genus Tetragnathus (x 3).
It spins its web at the edge of the water and sometimes, as here, over a small stream.

Reproduction ratio: 0·4.
Lens: Macro 55 mm.
Aperture: f/5·6.
Exposure time: 1/60th of a second.
Natural light from behind, late afternoon.

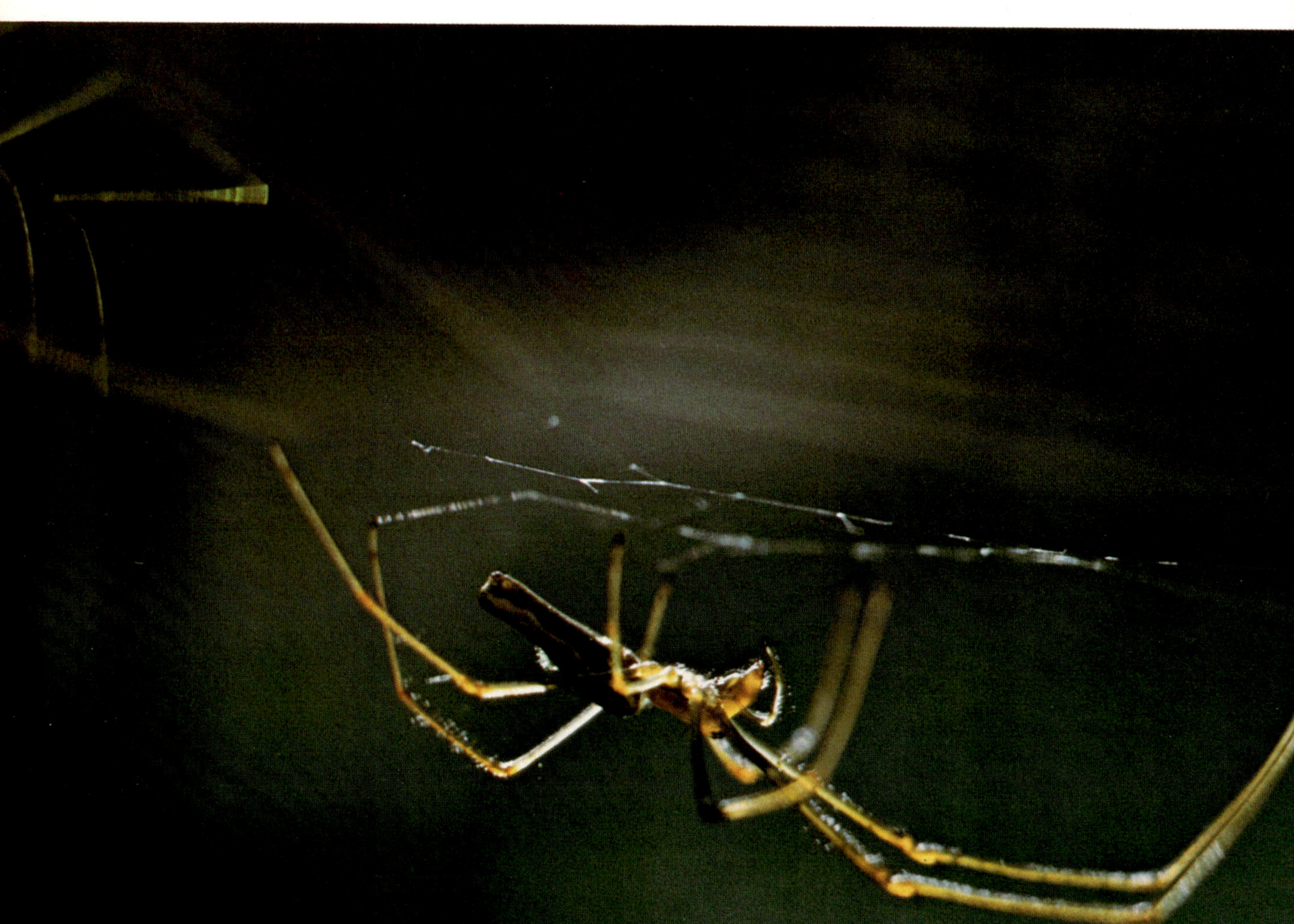

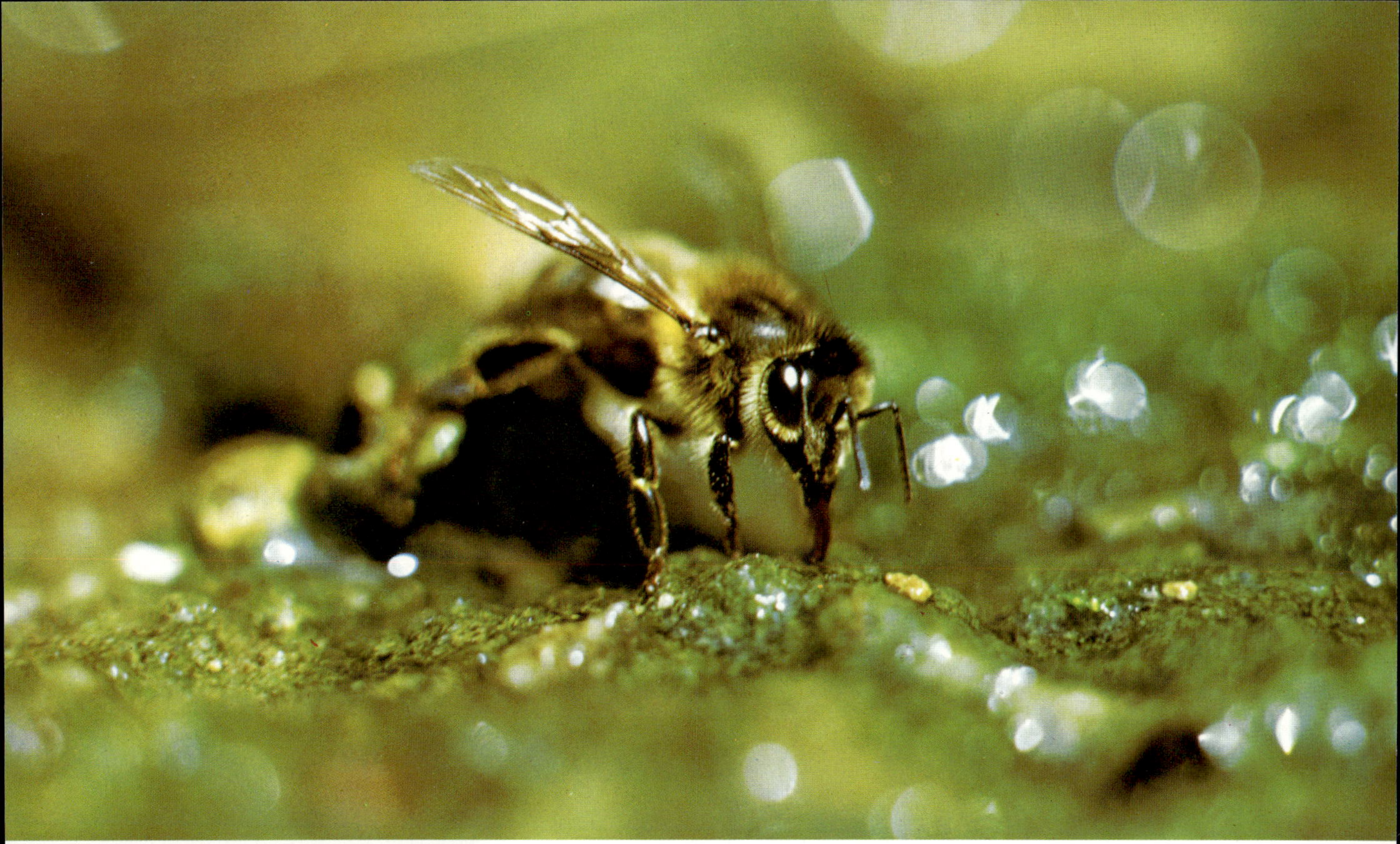

surface a gleaming sheath of air wrapped round itself, which it then releases under its web, already fastened between aquatic plants. After enough journeys, the web becomes inflated with an appreciable quantity of air, providing a comfortable residence where the spider can remain for several days without the laborious task of having to obtain further supplies.

Aquatic larvae

Not only the larvae of aquatic insects live in water but also those of numerous flying insects found near the pond. Raking the mud at the bottom of a pond with a hand-net will often produce a large mass of larval forms, mixed with aquatic plants.

One of the most remarkable of these is the large larva of the dragonfly, in which it is exceedingly difficult to recognize the buzzing insect which haunts the reeds. Among other bizarre features, this larva is equipped with a strange piece of

A bee drinking (x 5·5).
It is sucking the water exuded by wet moss near a pool.

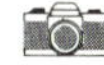

Reproduction ratio: 1.
Lens: Macro 55 mm with automatic extension ring.
Aperture: f/4-5·6.
Exposure time: 1/125th of a second.
Natural light, at midday.

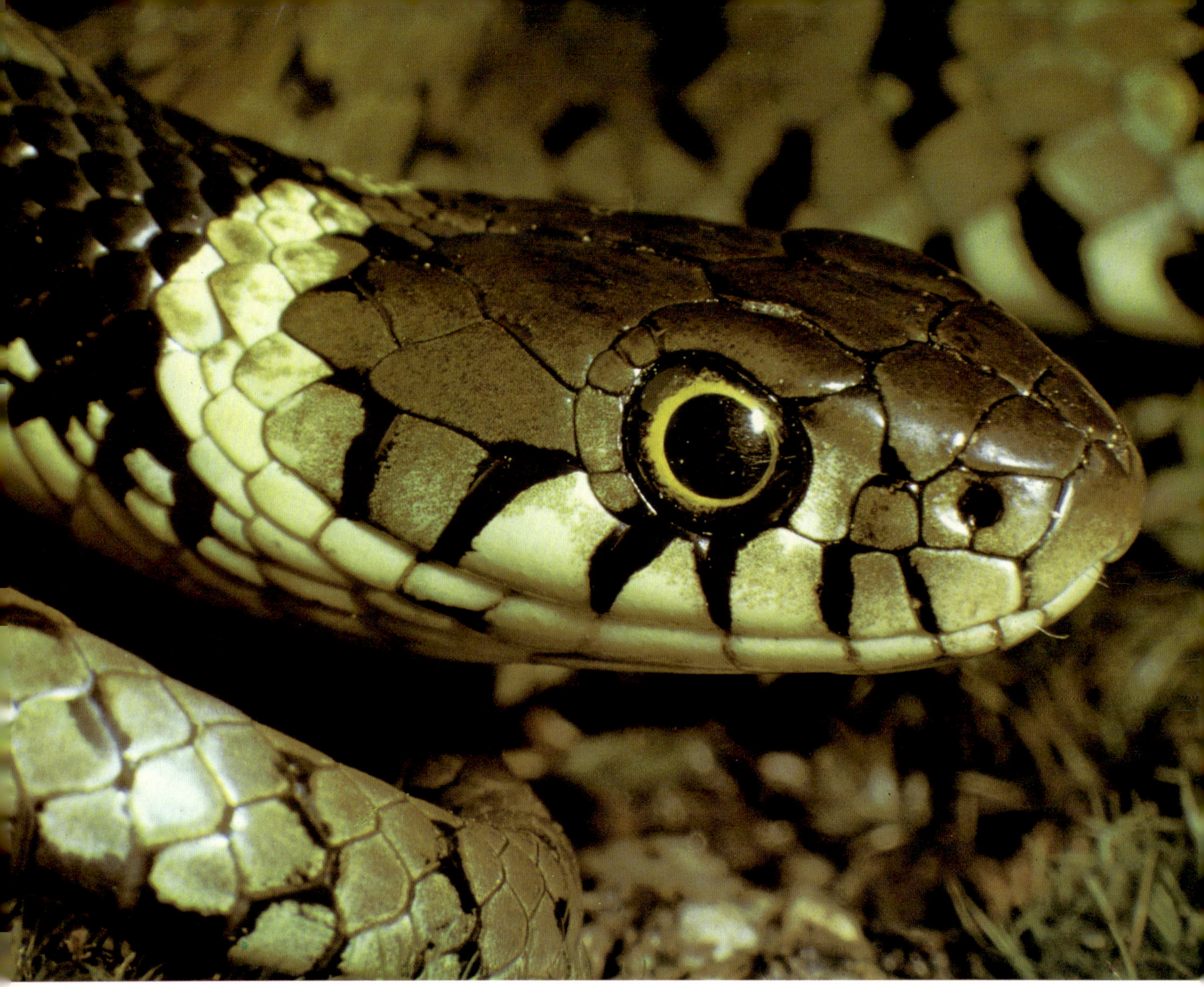

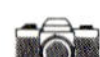

Young Grass Snake (x 7).
This snake frequents pools of
water, where it finds food such as
fish, tadpoles and frogs in
abundance.

Reproduction ratio: 1·2.
Lens: 105 mm mounted on
bellows.
Aperture: f/22-32.
Electronic flash. Reflecting screen
to reduce the shadows.

apparatus, the 'mask', with the aid of which it captures its prey. This appendage is normally folded back around the mouth. When it detects a potential victim, the larva slowly creeps towards it until, estimating that it has approached sufficiently close, it suddenly projects this natural grapnel, the two end claws-of which fasten on to the victim. Having performed its task, the mask retracts towards the mouth, which devours the food. The larva of the dragonfly, when molested, has recourse to an auxiliary method of propulsion – jet propulsion. By squirting a powerful jet of water from the anus, it can rapidly propel itself over a considerable distance.

The inexperienced naturalist·finding caddis-fly larvae in his net may well throw them back into the water, for who would imagine that this long agglomeration made of the most incongruous mixture of materials could possibly house an inhabitant? It is, however, the work of a 'caddis-worm' or larva of the caddis-fly, which has surrounded itself with a protective sheath made up of pieces of material fastened together by silk. Different species of the caddis-fly choose different materials: among those used are pieces of twig, leaves, shell, sand, gravel and dead wood.

The courtship of the Stickleback

It is seldom possible to explore the

water in a pond without finding any fish. The one most deserving of attention is undoubtedly the very common Stickleback. It is during the breeding season in May and June that it appears in its most flattering colours. The male is then adorned in sumptuous wedding apparel: with his back of green mixed with blue, orange-pink sides, bright red throat, and eyes spangled with emerald green, he has no need to envy the most beautiful ornamental fish. But his main talent is being able to build a nest! This takes the form of a hollow sphere of aquatic plants which the fish has glued together with the aid of a mucous secretion from its kidneys. When a female is persuaded to come and lay her eggs in this shelter, it is the male alone who assumes responsibility for guarding the young.

How can they be photographed?

In the case of all these aquatic creatures, the photographer must give up any idea of trying to photograph them in their natural environment. Imagine a frogman armed with a watertight camera trying to manoeuvre underwater in a pond! Rather than take a camera into the pond, it is better to take home a sample of this universe, collected with the aid of a hand-net, and to recreate the freshwater habitat in an aquarium. Both the photographer and the camera can then remain on the dry side of the glass. Incidentally, a lot of people on seeing our photographs have thought that we must have indulged in some kind of fresh-water diving activity to obtain them, and we have had to disillusion them. (See the last chapter for methods of aquarium photography.)

Microscopic fauna

On returning to the 'laboratory', it is also possible to find out, with the aid of a magnifying glass or a micro-scope, what the samples collected contain. In the field, it is merely necessary to collect aquatic plants, duckweed and bottom detritus, which are tipped all together into wide-mouthed jars filled with water obtained from the pond. Decanted as required into a more spacious aquarium, this tangle of plants will

Daphnia (x 30).
Reproduction ratio: 7.
Lens: Macro Summar 24 mm.
Aperture: f/8.
Flash positioned obliquely under the mini-aquarium.

Below: Female giving birth to young (x 60).
Photograph taken using a microscope.
Magnification 15.

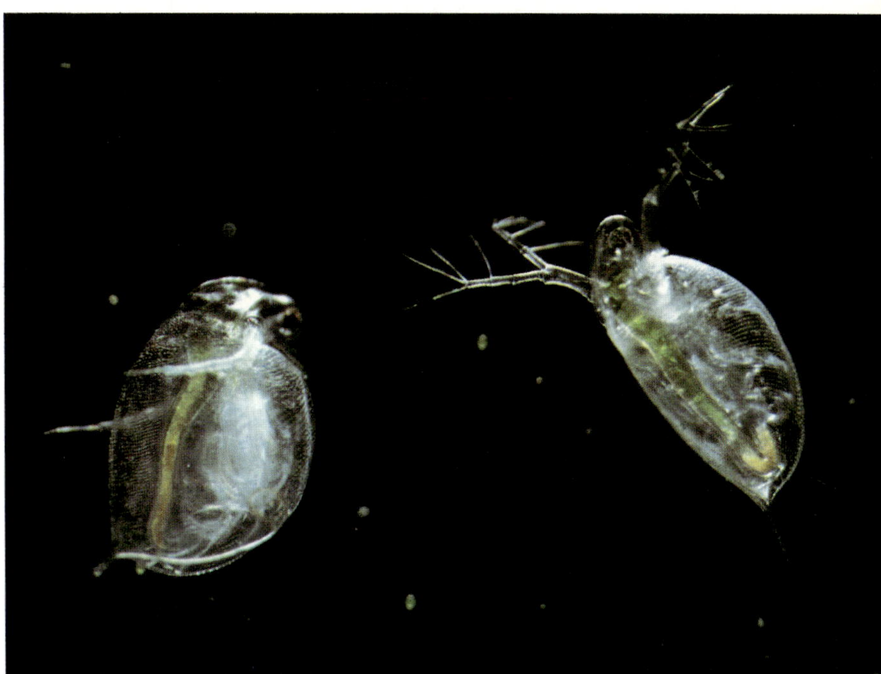

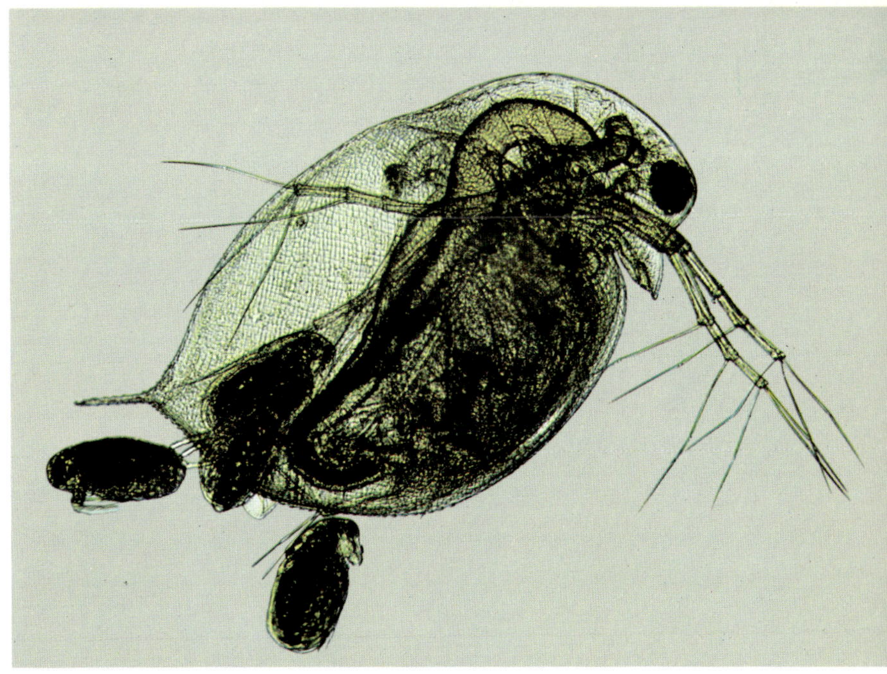

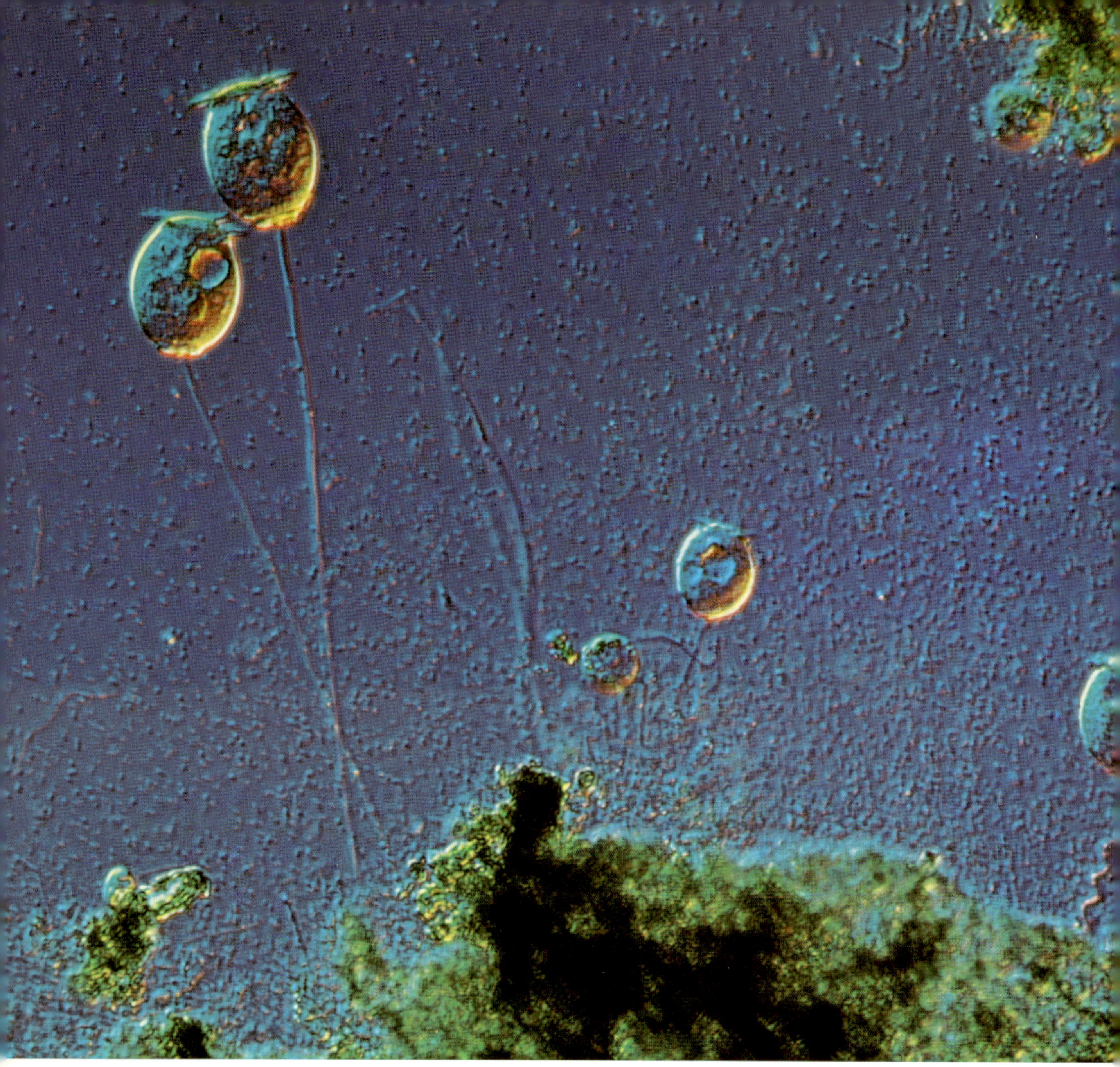

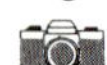

A colony of Vorticella (x 600). Each individual, consisting of a single cell, has a crown of vibratile cilia which draws into its mouth, in a vortex of water, the clouds of bacteria floating around it. The long stalk with which it is anchored to the vegetable debris retracts like a spring at the slightest alarm.

Reichert Zetopan microscope.
Magnification 80.
Exposure time: 1/30th of a second.
Kodachrome Type A.

gradually reveal – as the inumerable particles in suspension fall to the bottom – a swarm of minute animal forms moving in all directions. On this scale, which is even smaller than that of the tiny creatures found in the pond, a further incredible range of animal life appears before the eyes of the naturalist. Among the larger and more active ones, Gammarus (small crustaceans called fresh-water shrimps) and Asellus (close relatives of the woodlice) are the most useful guests in an aquarium, since they feed on vegetable and animal debris, and thus act as scavengers.

Smaller forms, Cyclops and Daphnia, are easily identified by their jerky methods of swimming. Daphnia moves by beating its antennae. Under a magnifying glass, its dorsally-positioned heart can be seen beating through its carapace. Further towards the rear, there is nearly always visible an incubating pouch filled with eggs arranged like the skins of an onion: during the warmer part of the year, in fact, there are

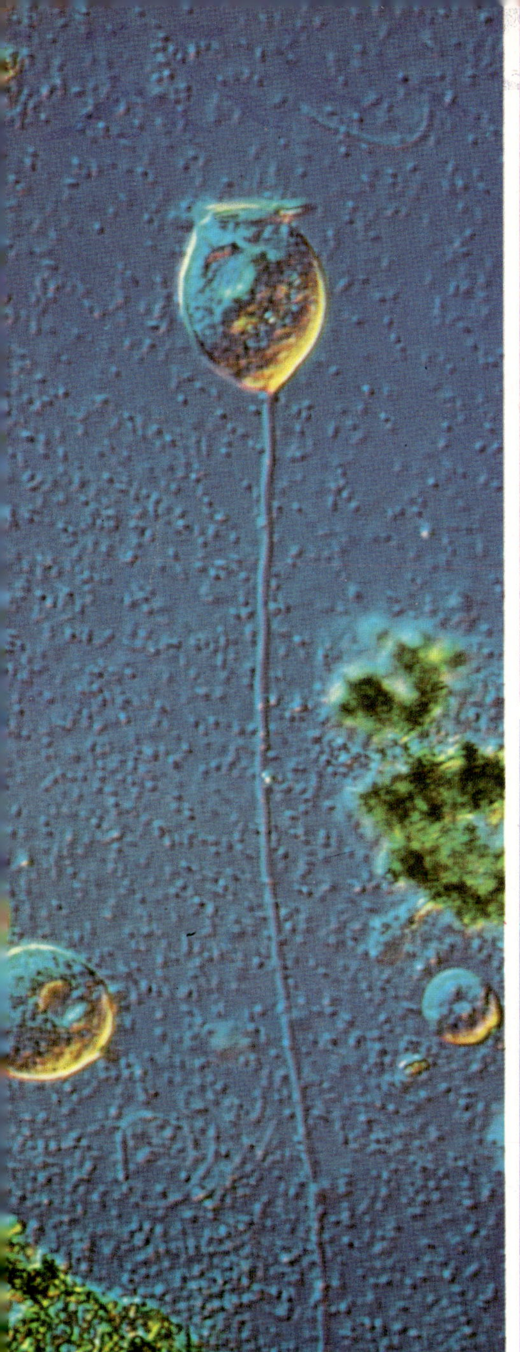

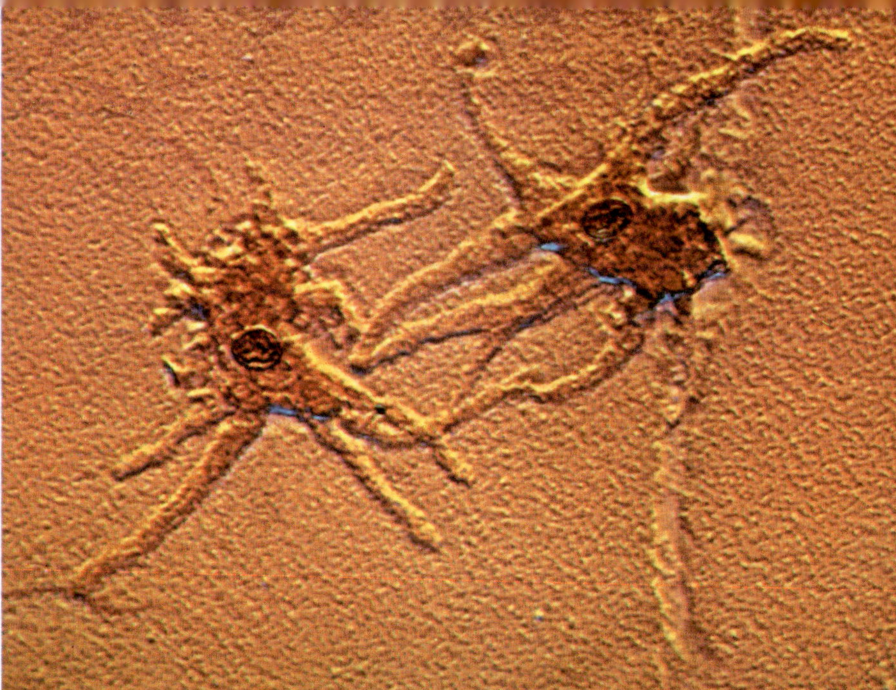

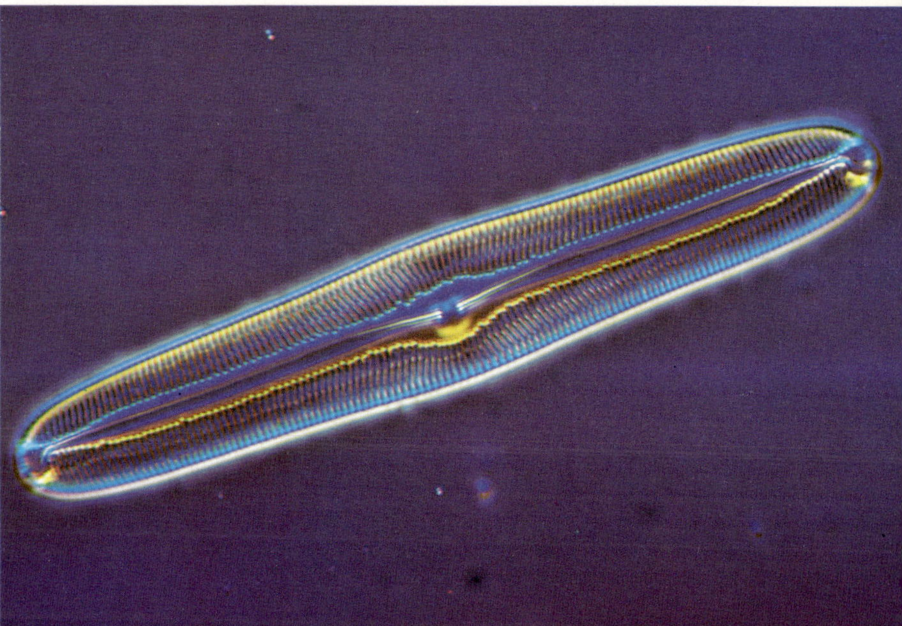

only females in existence, which reproduce themselves very rapidly by parthenogenesis. Cyclops owes its name to the single median eye which adorns its front end with a red spot; it carries its eggs in two small sacs attached to part of its abdomen.

Descending to the scale of the microscope, there is still no dearth of subjects. It is only necessary, with the aid of a pipette, to take a sample drop of liquid from the vicinity of an aquatic plant in the aquarium and to place it between the slide and cover-slip under the lens of the microscope. A fragment of decomposing submerged vegetable matter, torn apart by fine tweezers and placed in this drop of liquid, can populate this microscopic world with a surfeit of interesting species.

The organisms revealed in this way are of such variety that it would be impossible to try to describe them here. With the aid of a small handbook, one can learn to recognize the main species fairly easily. For our part, our favourites are the astonish-

Above: Amoeba (x 400).
These crawl over the bacterial film covering the surface of stagnant water by extending 'limbs' of constantly changing shape.

Below: Fresh-water diatom (x 1000).
Unicellular alga with a silicified membrane.

Reichert Zetopan microscope. Magnification 100 (above) and 250 (below).

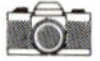

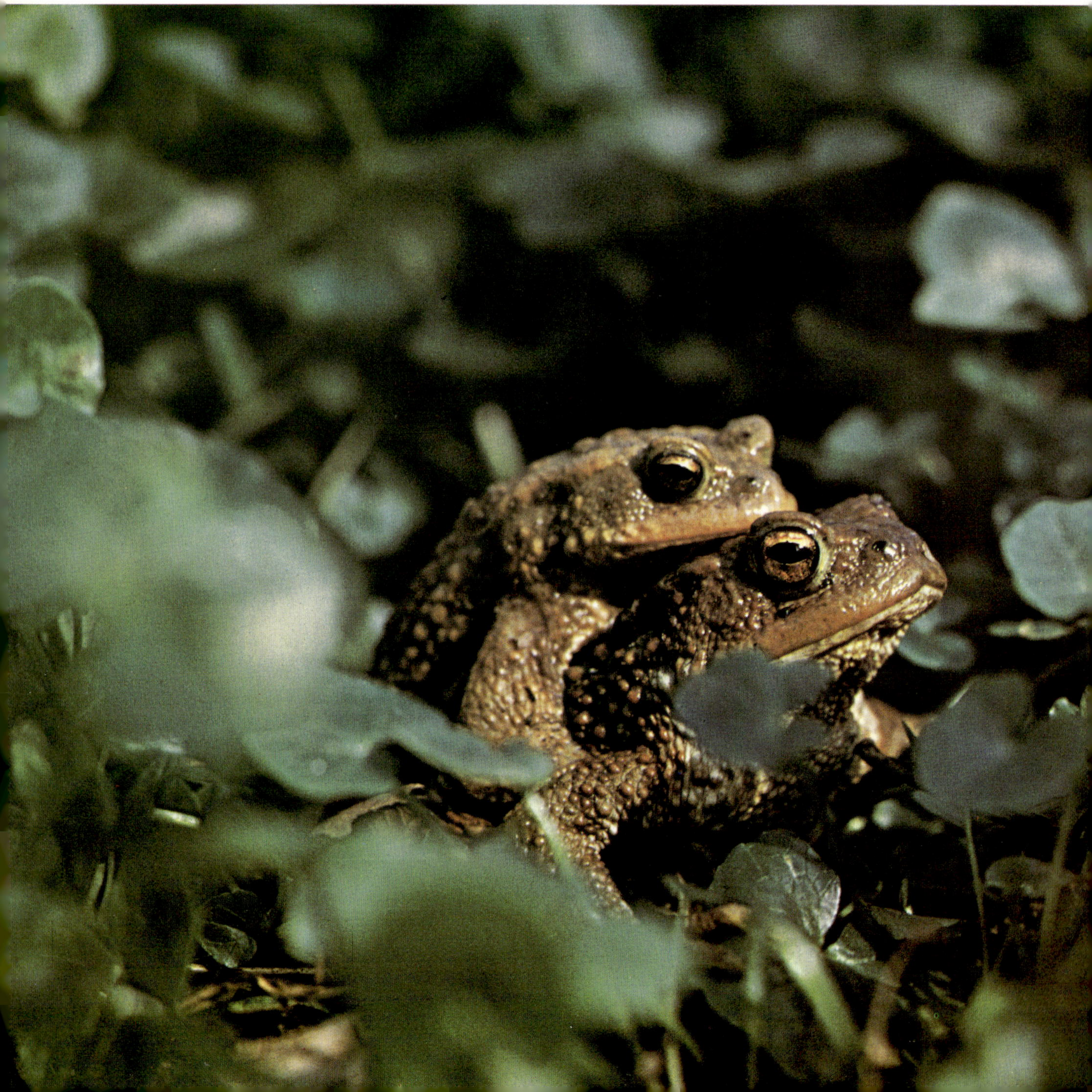

ing colonies of Vorticella, or bell-animalcules, which spread over the aquatic plants. These unicellular organisms, anchored by means of a long peduncle, have the appearance of a field of minute animated flowers. Their body is in the form of an inverted bell, fringed with a crown of vibratile cilia, the movement of which forms an eddy to draw in the particles in suspension. However, at the slightest sign of danger, these frail oscillating creatures rapidly withdraw, their peduncle shortening like a spiral spring. Afterwards, they slowly extend to their former position. The slightest tap on the lens panel of the microscope is sufficient to produce this phenomenon.

Seasonal visitors

Each year, following the first fine days of spring, the pond is the final stage in a grand migration which affects all the representatives of the group of amphibians. This is, in a way, a form of pilgrimage to the place of their birth which is made by frogs, toads, newts and salamanders.

They represent the 'living relicts' of the heroic era when life set out to conquer the dry land. From the fishes, nearly four hundred million years ago, came the first animals with four legs, large clumsy amphibians which represented a not altogether successful attempt to break away from their aquatic environment. The little amphibians of today have inherited these imperfections. Their thin, permeable skin forces them to remain in damp places in order to avoid being reduced to the state of a dessicated mummy, and at breeding-time they have to return to water to lay their eggs.

This renewal of activity in the pond during the first days of spring happily terminates the long period of enforced idleness suffered by the photographer during winter. Since, moreover, there is as much to hear as there is to see during these aquatic nuptials, a tape-recorder is by no means superfluous on this occasion.

Anurans (tailless amphibians) are particularly evident by their calls.

Spawn of the Common Toad
(x 1·2).
The string of eggs, wound among aquatic plants, can be up to 10 feet (3 m) long and may contain about 10,000 fertilized eggs looking like tiny black beads.

Photographed in an aquarium.
Reproduction ratio: 0·35.
Lens: Macro 55 mm.
Aperture: f/16.
Electronic flash.
A second flash was used to illuminate the background.

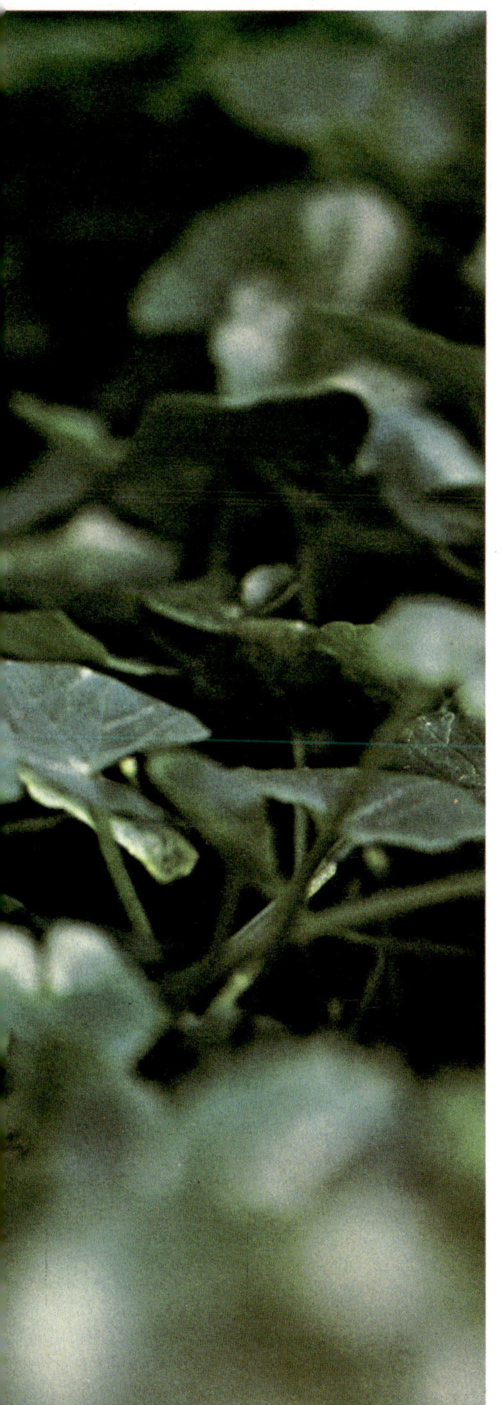

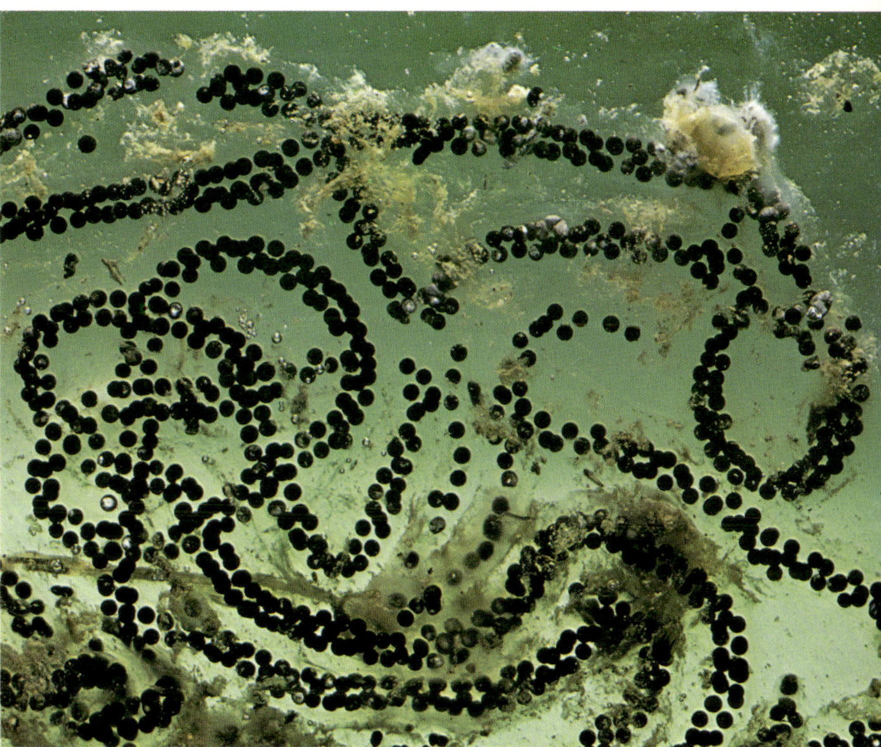

Among the first arrivals in this dash for the pond are the toads, somewhat clumsy swimmers which quickly seize a partner with a view to mating. In his eagerness to find a female, the male demonstrates little discrimination in his choice, and one can sometimes find clumps of seven or eight toads feverishly clutching each other, though they finally succeed in disentangling themselves in a ferment of movement punctuated by urgent

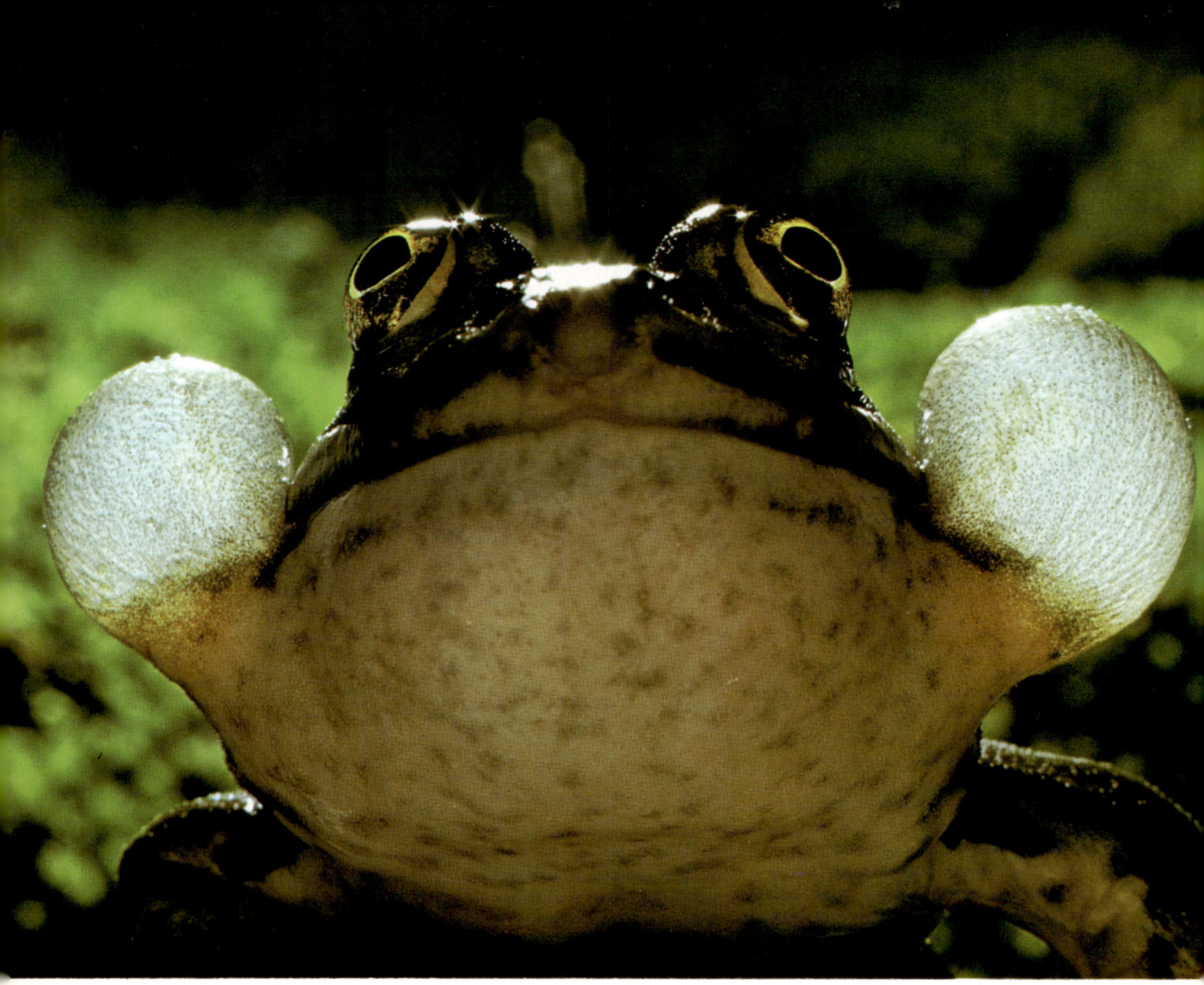

Edible Frog (x 4·5).
The use of an electronic flash has made it possible to capture the moment when, with its vocal sacs distended, the frog is croaking. The backlighting shows how extremely thin the skin of these resonators is when filled with air.

Reproduction ratio: 0·8.
Lens: Macro 55 mm with extension ring.
Aperture: f/16-22.
Flash directed downwards behind the subject.

little cries in a thin, high-pitched voice. Having found his female, the male clasps her as tightly as he can with the aid of his two front legs, and nothing can separate them until the eggs are laid. The spawn consists of a gelatinous cord several yards long containing about ten thousand eggs, which the male fertilizes with his semen.

The Common Frog has a more resonant call. This is because it has two internal vocal sacs which serve as sound-boxes. It lays several thousand eggs the size of a grape-pip, glued together in a gelatinous floating mass.

The real tenors in the group, however, are the Edible Frog and the Green Tree Frog, which enter the pond in May. When the Edible Frog makes its powerful, rhythmic call, two vocal sacs ludicrously resembling bubble-gum can be seen to inflate rapidly on either side of its mouth. With these efficient amplifiers, it can be heard several hundred yards away.

The croaking of the little Green Tree Frog easily competes with that of its more corpulent cousin. This is because, though it has only a single vocal sac under its throat, it is of much more than comparable size. When inflated, it is half as large as the frog's body! Like the Edible frog, the Green Tree Frog enjoys quite a repertory – a 'rain' call, a mating call, a distress call, etc. – and it has a habit of calling in chorus, the sound of which can reach deafening levels.

The fancy-dress ball of the newts

Urodeles (amphibians with tails) are voiceless. They have devoted all their talents to their appearance. At the time when they enter the water to breed, male newts acquire a nuptial livery which is as dazzling as it is transitory. The Crested Newt, for example, can only really justify its name at this time of the year, when a high serrated crest waves like a banner along the whole length of its back. Its stomach is a brilliant orange-yellow, while its tail, accentuated by a silvery stripe, increases considerably in size to become a powerful swimming organ. In order to attract his partner successfully, the male performs an ardent dance around her, arching his back strongly and lashing his sides with his tail. (The photographer can very easily observe this dance in an aquarium.) When the nuptials are over, all these imposing features of the newt

Frog embryo in the egg, shortly before hatching (x 35).
When this time comes, the young tadpole will secrete from the area of its mouth a substance which will dissolve the transparent membrane of the egg.

Photograph taken in a mini-aquarium.
Reproduction ratio: 4·5.
Lens: Macro Summar 24 mm, on bellows.
Aperture: f/11.
Electronic flash directed horizontally.

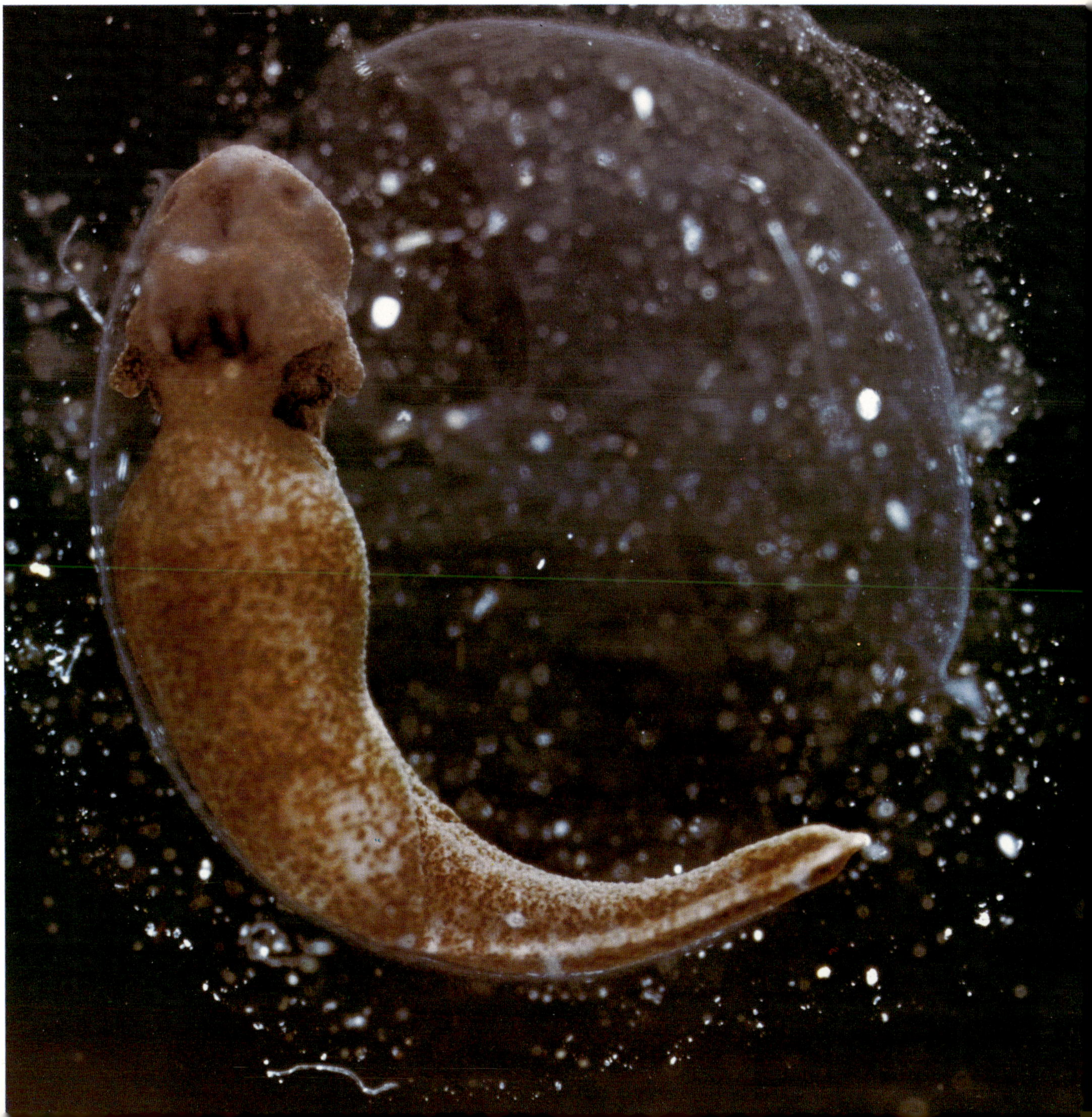

Male Alpine Newt (x 2·6).
Its magnificent nuptial colours will
fade at the end of the breeding
season.

Photograph taken in an aquarium.
Reproduction ratio: 0·35.
Lens: Macro 55 mm.
Aperture: f/16.
Electronic flash.
A second flash was used to
illuminate the background.

gradually disappear. Having returned to being an ordinary land newt, it hoists itself out of the water to search for a mossy branch under which to hide, and which will from now on be its home.

Occasional visitors

On the African plains even the smallest pool of water, at certain hours of the day, attracts herds of mammals which go there to drink. Though on a different scale, a pond has the same attraction for the clouds of insects which can take their fill of water there. Wasps, bees and hornets arrive in turn on the edge of the bank, with all the bustle of an airfield. Some are even brave enough to land on a piece of floating branch in order to drink undisturbed.

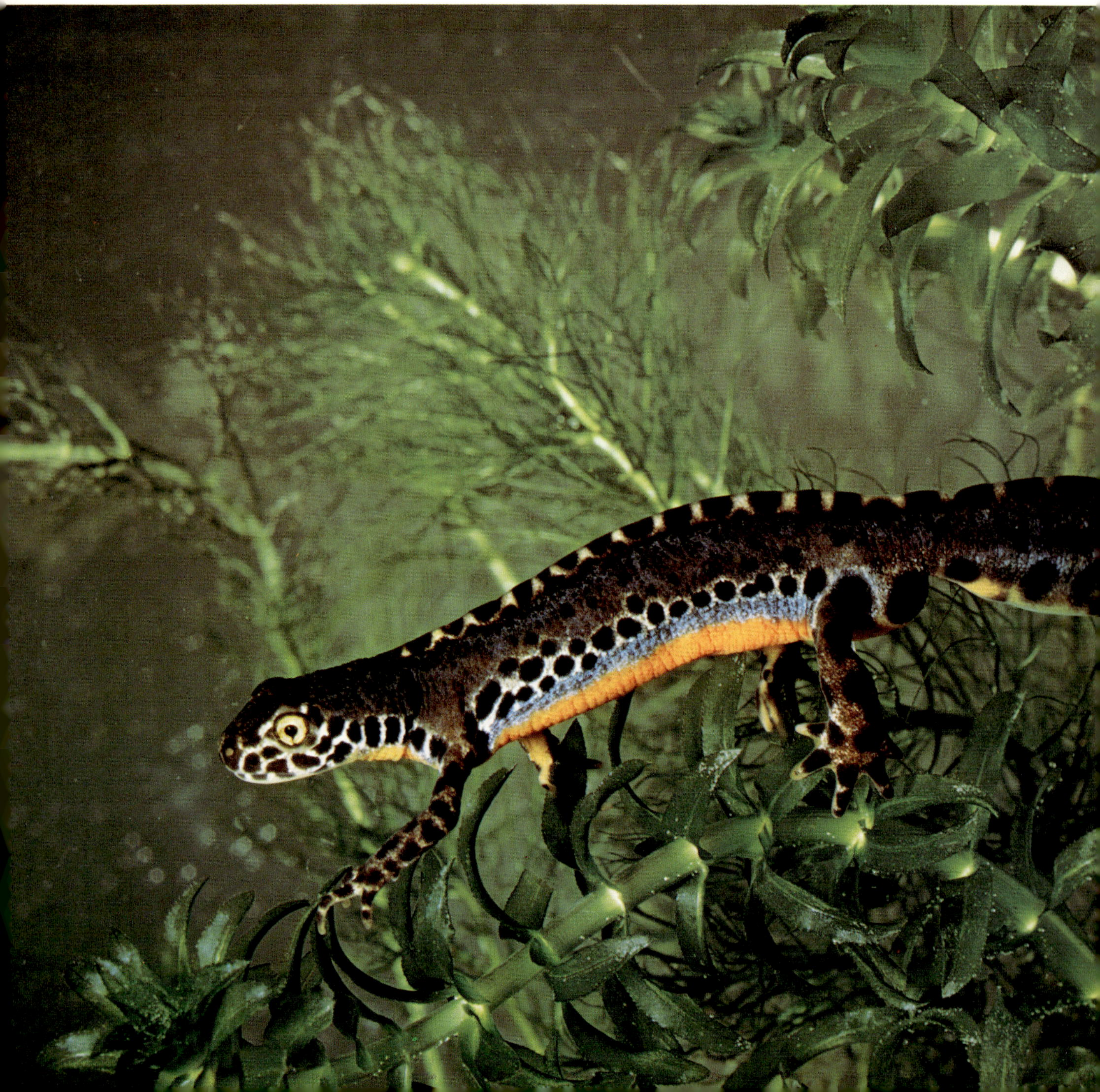

The rich flora along the edge of a pond is constantly visited by innumerable honey-gathering insects. The golden-yellow crowns of the Marsh Marigold, the long erect clusters of the Purple Loosestrife and the dense beds of Mint provide tempting reserves of nectar for butterflies and bees. The Purple Loosestrife is even obliging enough to display a conspicuous pattern on its corolla – formed by dark veins converging towards the base of the petals – to indicate the exact location of its nectar to the insect.

Not all plants, however, are so well-disposed towards insects. It is, in fact, on peaty soil that one of the few insectivorous plants in Europe is found, the Sundew. Because its leaves are covered with tentacles tipped with a droplet of sticky liquid reflect-ing a thousand colours, it acts as a source of attraction for insects, which find themselves ensnared in this deadly dew. Dozens of tentacles curve towards the new victim, which is slowly engulfed as the entire rim of the leaf folds in on itself. A few days of digestion, and the leaf opens again to receive its next victim. It has been calculated that in this manner a single plant can consume about two thousand insects each summer.

Small fresh-water crustaceans are also exposed to similar misfortune brought about by certain plants. The

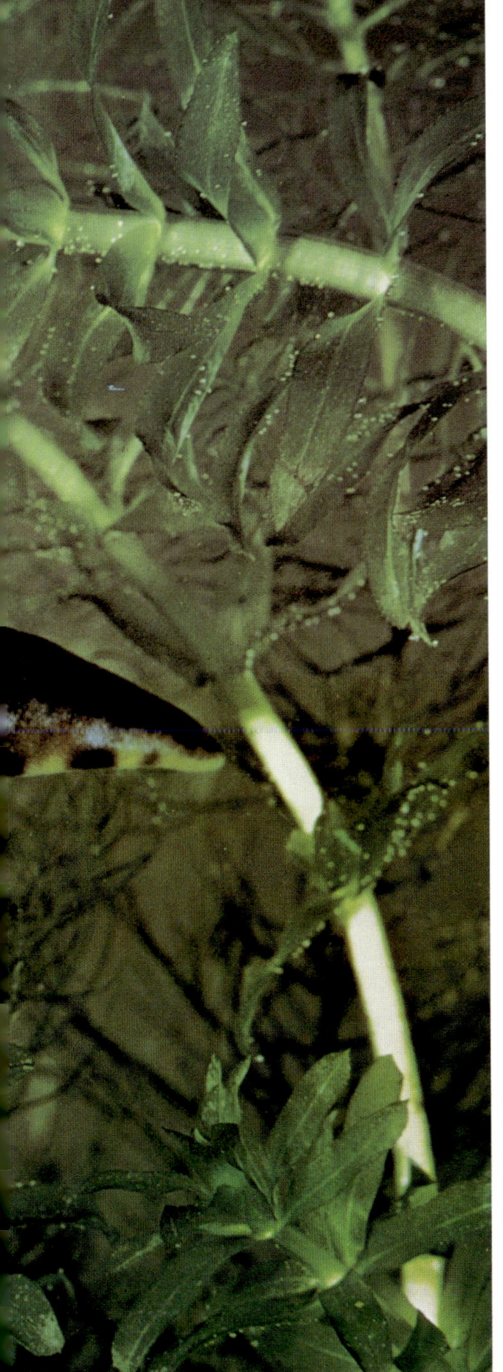

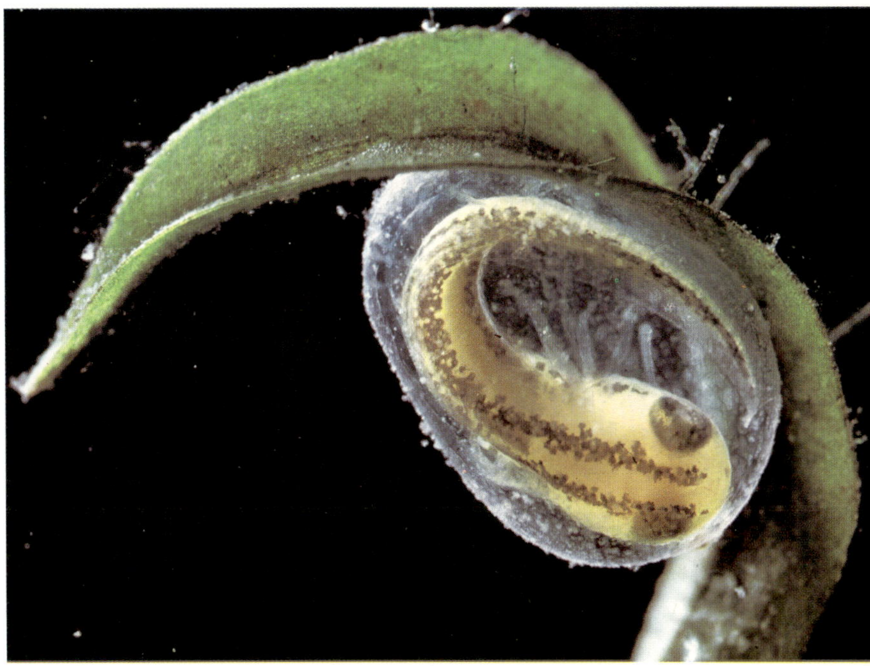

Pond Bladderwort, which raises its bunch of yellow flowers above the water, has long, finely ramified, submerged branches which carry hundreds of minute flask-shaped appendages. These peculiar organs are traps, which can be seen in action under a low-power microscope. If a small crustacean comes into contact with one of the hairs fringing the opening of a flask, a sudden intake of water draws it inside, while the flap which seals the entrance closes on it. The mechanism is so perfect that no escape is possible.

Embryo of the Palmate Newt in its egg, shortly before hatching (x 15).
The eggs are fastened separately by the female to the leaves of aquatic plants.

Photograph taken in a mini-aquarium.
Reproduction ratio: 4.
Lens: Macro Summar 24 mm.
Aperture: f/11.
Electronic flash positioned laterally and behind.

Marine diatom seen through a microscope (x 700).
Diatoms are minute algae consisting of a single cell. They are protected by the frustule, a rigid shell impregnated with silica. This covering consists of two parts joined together like a box and its lid. The world of diatoms includes an incredible variety of shapes. The delicacy and complexity of their ornamentation are such that even today the frustules of certain diatoms still provide the best subjects for testing the quality of microscope lenses. The spindle-shaped shell of the species Amphipleura pellucida bears an extraordinary close-packed series of parallel transverse ridges: about 4,000 can be counted in only 1/25th of an inch (1 mm). The distance between each one is a quarter of a micron (1/1000th mm), which is smaller than can be distinguished by the best optical microscope. Only sophisticated methods of observation make it possible to see such fine detail clearly.

Magnification of the microscope: 280.
Exposure time: 1 second.
Lighting: 100 watt, 12 volt incandescent lamp.
Film: Kodachrome Type A.

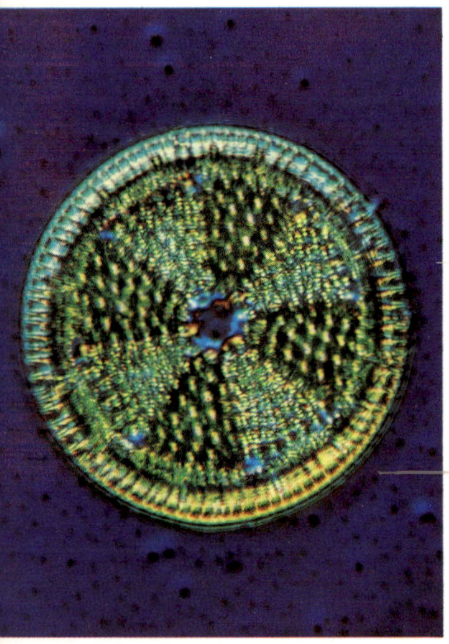

At the edge of the sea

The littoral zone shelters a rich biological community, certain representatives of which are of interest to the close-up photographer. In this narrow area, which is subject to the rise and fall of the tides, there live some quite unique plants and animals which are specially adapted to the ceaseless disorder of their environment.

Low tide

Strangely enough, the opportunities for photography in the field – which naturally means at low tide – are comparatively limited. In fact, all the animals which the ebbing of the tide exposes to the open air take refuge in damp places, in the sand, under stones or simply in their shells.

Even though it is always possible to dislodge them from their hiding-places, it must be admitted that they make a sorry spectacle at such times. Apart from crabs, there is very little worth photographing (the Common Crab, which assumes very striking attitudes of defence, makes an excellent subject).

It is, however, an altogether different matter as regards the scenes which can be captured in the countless pools of water dotted about among the rocks. These natural aquaria provide a refuge for small communities of the most diverse nature, which are able to carry on their normal lives in spite of the sea having temporarily abandoned them. These include Actinia (sea anemones), shrimps, hermit crabs, limpets, small shore-crabs, rock barnacles and starfish. In order to photograph them, it is essential to use a polarising filter to suppress the images reflected by the surface of the water (especially that of the photographer leaning over his subject).

It is, moreover, as well to remember that the conditions prevailing at the edge of the sea may expose your equipment to rough treatment if you do not take a few simple precautions. In fact, the spray and more generally the high salinity of the atmosphere have a corrosive effect on both optical and mechanical equipment. Grains of sand can prove even more damaging to the lens, and may seep into the camera when the film is being changed and jam the shutter mechanism. It is, therefore, advisable to protect your equipment by carrying it in a flexible airtight plastic bag, and to remove it only for the purpose of taking a photograph.

The marine aquarium

It is obvious that the small creatures inhabiting the shoreline can best be photographed in their aquatic environment. It is, however, impossible to photograph them in close-up in the sea: the exigencies of under-water swimming would simply not permit the necessary accuracy of framing and focusing. There remains, however, the alternative of using an aquarium: all the excellent photographs which appear in various publications, showing marine species in very large close-up, are in fact obtained by this means. Very careful reconstruction of the natural environment of the animal provides the illusion of the scene having been photographed under the sea.

By observing and photographing them in an aquarium, many species can be seen in a new light: scallops, the half-open valves of which allow countless tentacles to emerge, under which can be seen shining a double row of blue eye-spots; sea urchins with their multiple legs which assist the spines as locomotory appendages; rock barnacles and tube-worms, with a limy sheath (often living together on the same hermit crab), waiting to be submerged in order to spread their delicate branchial tufts, and so on.

To obtain good photographs, it is important that the water shall be as clear as possible, so it must be collected at a place which is not

exposed to surf movement. It will, in any case, be necessary to filter the water with the aid of a piece of fine linen, to remove all extraneous debris. The sand, rocks and algae to be placed in the aquarium should be well washed. After the aquarium has been filled, it should be left standing for half a day to allow any remaining impurities to settle. See *Photographing aquatic species* on page 139.

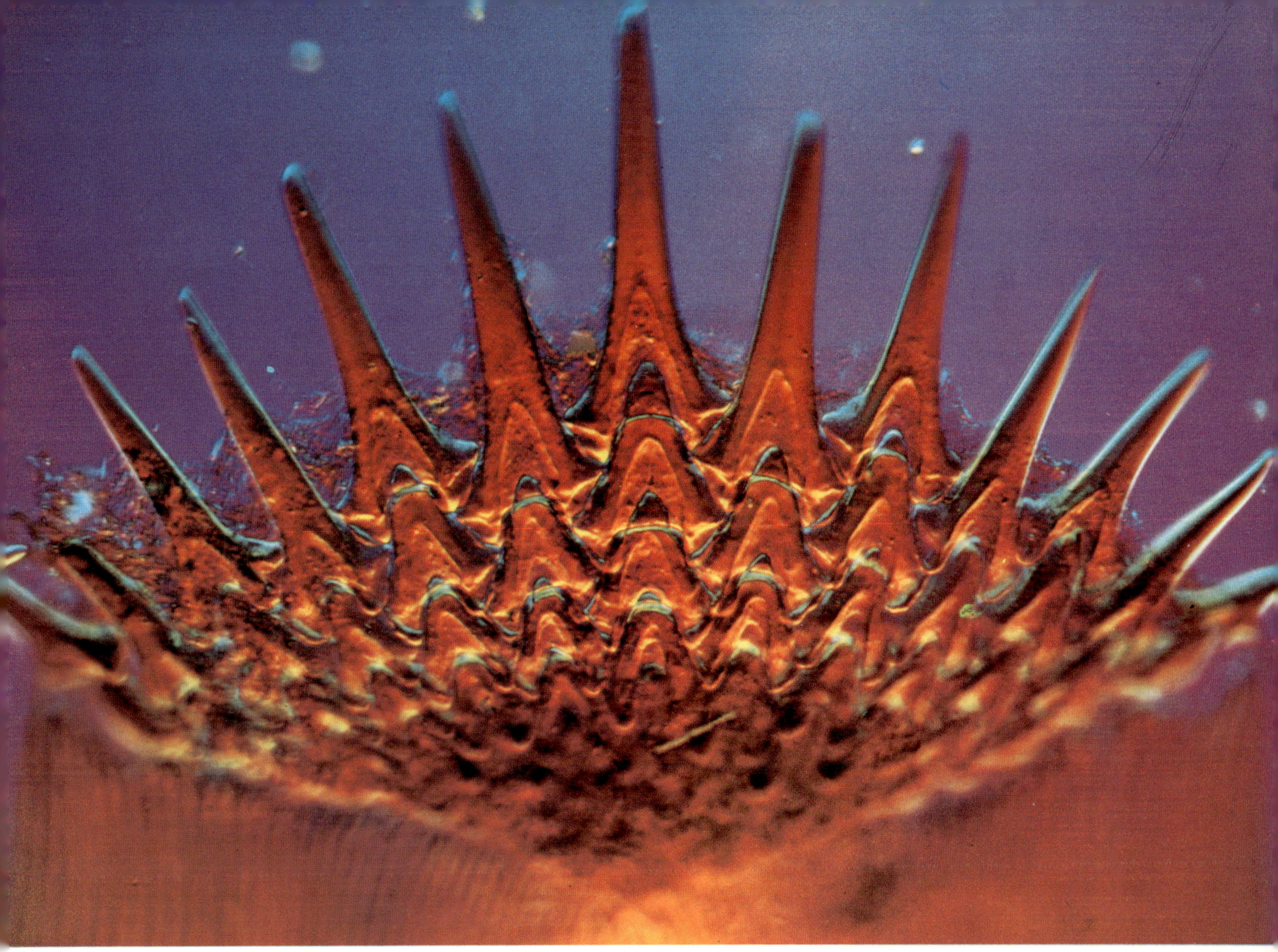

Plankton

Finally, for the owner of a microscope, there still remain to be discovered the varied forms of fauna and flora constituting the plankton.

These can be collected with the aid of a conical net of silk or fine muslin, towed along the surface behind a boat moving at low speed, when the sea is very calm. After a few minutes a sort of thick soup, more or less transparent, will have collected at the bottom of the cone, which can then be transferred on board to a small jar of sea-water. It is possible in this way to obtain a representative sample of the microscopic algae – including the beautiful diatoms with their beautiful siliceous carapaces – as well as small crustaceans, various eggs and larvae, and certain of the *Foraminifera*, unicellular organisms protected by a minute shell.

Similar collections can be made more easily at low tide. To obtain diatoms, all one has to do is collect shellfish – especially mussels and oysters – and brush their shells over a vessel of water. Brown and red algae also often carry diatoms, which form brownish encrustations on them.

A scale of the Sole (x 350). Detail of the minute spines found on the end, which is the only part of the scale to be exposed on the surface of the skin of the fish.

Reichert Zetopan microscope.
Magnification: 63.
Exposure time: 1/15th of a second.
Film: Kodachrome Type A.

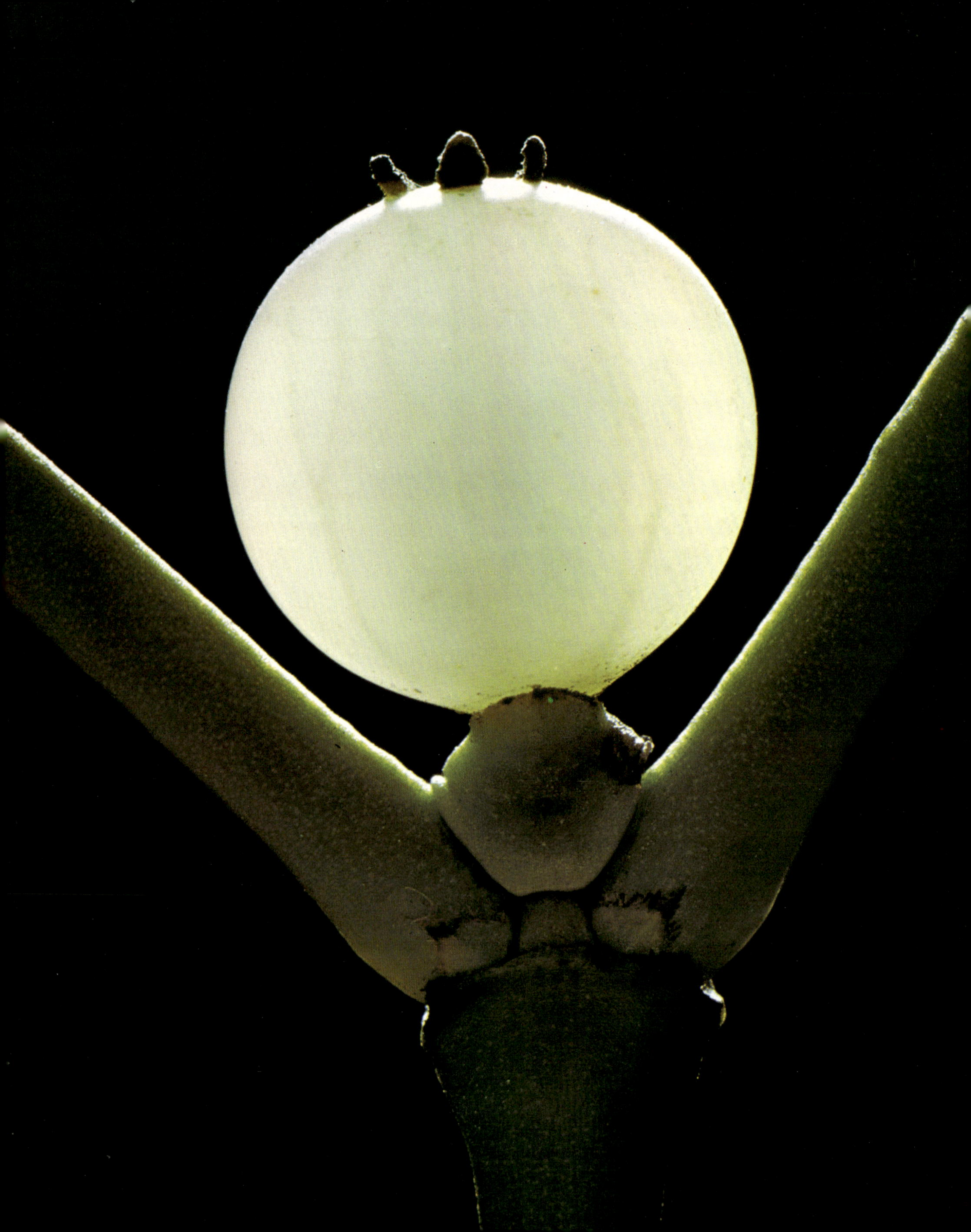

The forest

The forest represents the pinnacle of the plant world. For the ecologist, it constitutes the most highly developed stage which can be reached by a living community – a balanced population of animals and plants occupying the same habitat – at the end of a period of gradual adjustment.

The forest is a vertical universe and its considerable height provides certain features which are unique among terrestrial habitats. This constant striving upwards, which decides the fate of a forest, results in the formation of successive levels of life – the level of the mosses, the level of the grasses, the level of the bushes and the level of the trees. These four levels also act as four successive screens between the ground and the atmosphere above the forest: screens which not only keep out the rain and the wind, but also the sun and thus heat and light.

The forest is, in fact, a multi-level world providing a range of superimposed climates. It is up to the animals to choose the one that best suits them to live in.

This immense cloak of vegetation is also the best natural protection against erosion of the soil. In the U.S.A., it has been calculated that the time required for normal run-off to remove a layer of soil of about eight inches (20 cm) thick would be 174,000 years in a forest zone and 15 years in a region where maize was grown as the only crop.

Finally, the forest acts as an air purifier by absorbing carbon dioxide and releasing oxygen in considerable quantities. The entire forests of the world represent the reserves of oxygen for humanity. It would be wise not to regard them merely as reserves of timber.

It is difficult to imagine now that Spain and Greece were once covered with forest. Today, the names of these countries evoke for us an image of a bare countryside with scarce, low vegetation which seems to have existed for all time. There, as elsewhere, man has carried out for centuries a vast programme of deforestation in order to make room for his flocks, herds and crops, or to make use of the felled timber.

More recently, a truce seems to have been called in the havoc being wrought in forests, at least in those countries where their disappearance is causing concern: in Europe, for example, only 28% of the total area is still wooded (25% in Switzerland, 21% in France, 21% in Belgium, and 7% in Great Britain). In Canada, the forests which still cover 43% of the country are threatened by felling for the purpose of making pulp for paper.

There is, moreover, a new danger which threatens these natural sanctuaries. The hasty reafforestation now being practised is being carried out almost entirely with conifers, which offer the advantage of rapid growth. If this practice continues, tomorrow's forests may consist of nothing but artificially created plantations, with pines or firs succeeding each other monotonously and having nothing in common with the temperate forest we still know, the home of a great living community of countless species.

Life in rhythm with the seasons

The effect of the seasons on all forms of life can be most clearly seen in the forest. The winter is the season of

Fruit of the Mistletoe (x 7). The white, semi-transparent berry exudes a viscous substance which was formerly used to make glue. Birds sometimes feed on these fruits, and help to spread the seeds by excreting them in their droppings. The seed of this parasitic plant germinates on the branch of an apple or poplar tree. It inserts its suckers into the tissues of its host and feeds at the latter's expense, thereby obtaining the water and mineral substances it requires.

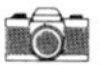

Reproduction ratio: 1·2.
Lens: Macro 55 mm mounted on bellows.
Aperture: f/16.
Electronic flash positioned above to illuminate the Mistletoe berry from behind.

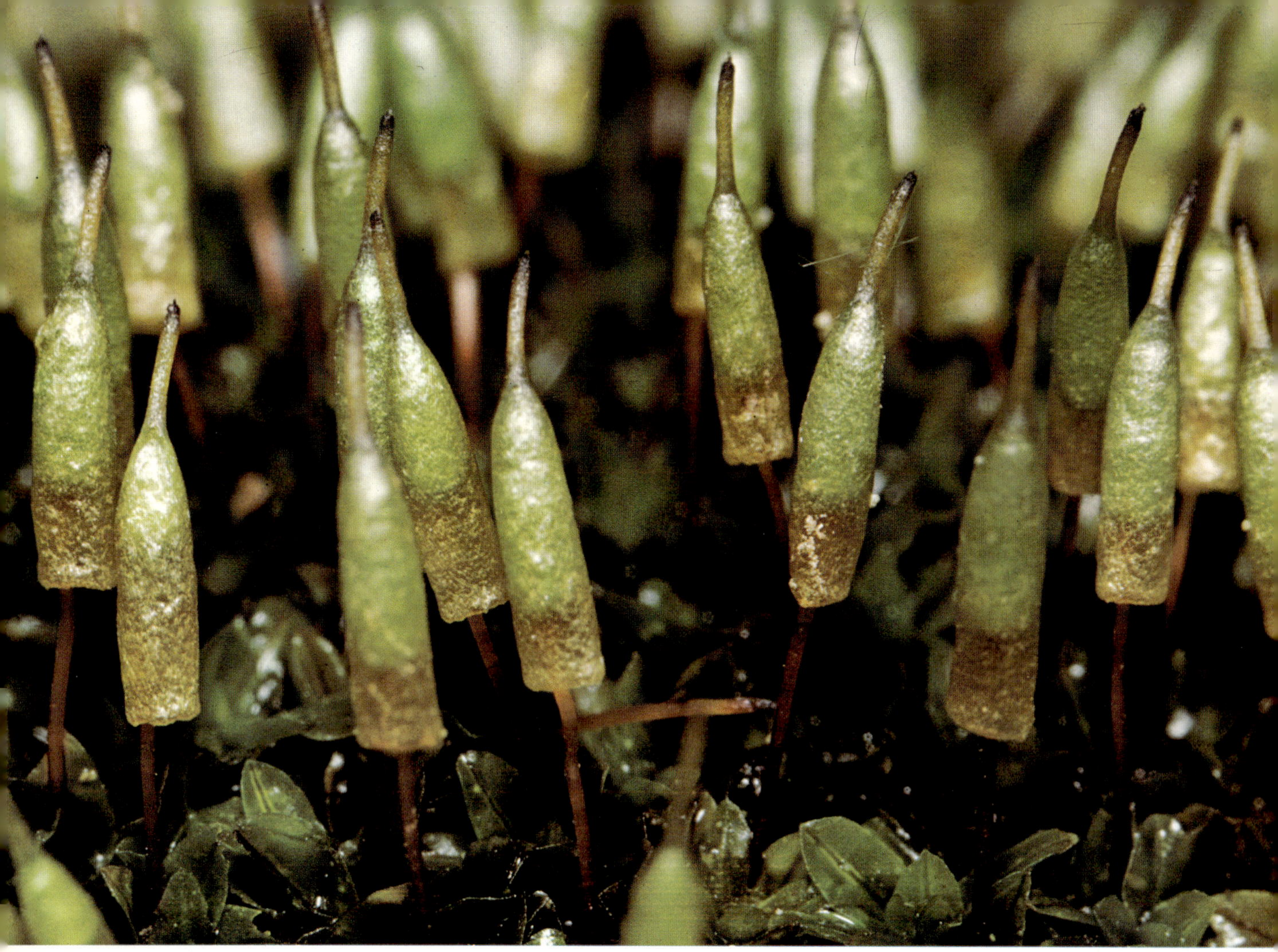

Reproduction ratio: 2·7.
Lens: Macro 55 mm mounted on
bellows in reverse position.
Aperture: f/22.
Electronic flash.

anticipation, with life holding itself back. The trees are already covered with minute scaly buds, the dormant buds.

With the first days of spring, the flowers of the forest floor hasten to take up the offensive. This is because it is necessary for them to blossom and set their seeds before the leaves of the trees form a screen to keep out the light of the sun. Immense carpets of Wood Anemones and Lesser Celandines then cover the ground.

The photographer can also take advantage of this respite before the foliage darkens the sky, in order to work by daylight. Later, when the buds have burst, there is that lighting effect which is such a special feature of the forest, an alternation of zones of shadow and splashes of bright light, which often holds unpleasant surprises for the photographer. Most of the time, colour films are unable to reproduce such pronounced contrasts and, if it is necessary for the photographer to take his pictures in a shaded area, there is a risk of their being insufficiently sensitive.

Therefore, when making an expedition into the forest, it is best to take flash equipment, at least for close-ups. If the photographer prefers not to go to all this trouble, he can, if necessary, use highly sensitive emulsions (100 to 400 ASA). Finally, we would point out that the screen of leaves is not neutral, but coloured: the light it lets through is particularly rich in green rays. For this reason, one should not be surprised to find certain colour casts appearing in photographs taken in natural daylight, which can in any case be quite attractive and express the prevailing glaucous shade of the undergrowth.

While the upper canopy is filling out, intense activity is also taking place in the soil: this is the time of germination. Every fallen fruit spared by parasites gives birth to a plantlet, the rapid growth of which is always interesting to observe. Acorns, sweet chestnuts, horse chestnuts and pine-seeds open to release stems and roots. Ferns, scolopendriums and polypodiums join in the upward surge by raising their yellow leaves, coiled like scrolls. At the same time, the mosses form thick cushions from which there soon emerge reddish stalks crowned by a capsule, like a little box full of spores.

In summer, growth is followed by ageing. The leaves are worn out, ravaged by the weather and above all by attack from insects.

Autumn sweeps away these dessicated vestiges. It is then that there follows the explosive outburst of fungi. The rough-skinned pear-shaped puff-balls, the imposing speckled sunshades of the parasol mushrooms, the slender bell-tufts of Mycena – the most varied shapes and colours are found side by side. In birchwoods, one can sometimes even find the scarlet hat of the Fly Agaric, a genuine warning signal of the plant world, advising all who might pick it of its poisonous nature.

Parasites and leaf-eaters

The new leaves on the trees have hardly finished opening out, giving

Germination of a Stone Pine (x 2·5).
As it starts to grow, the young shoot breaks through the hard cover of the seed and lifts it off the ground. When the cover falls off, the first leaves unfold like the ribs of an umbrella.

Reproduction ratio: 0·85 (0·35 below).
Lens: Macro 55 mm.
Aperture: f/16. Flash.

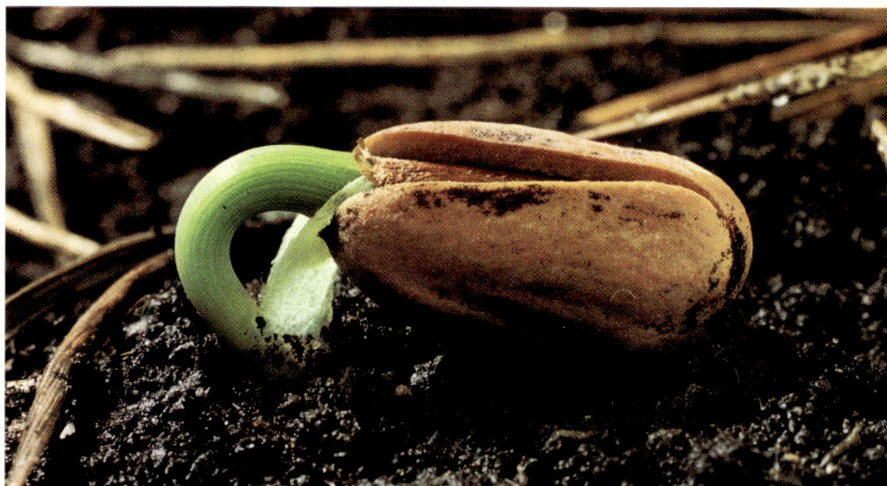

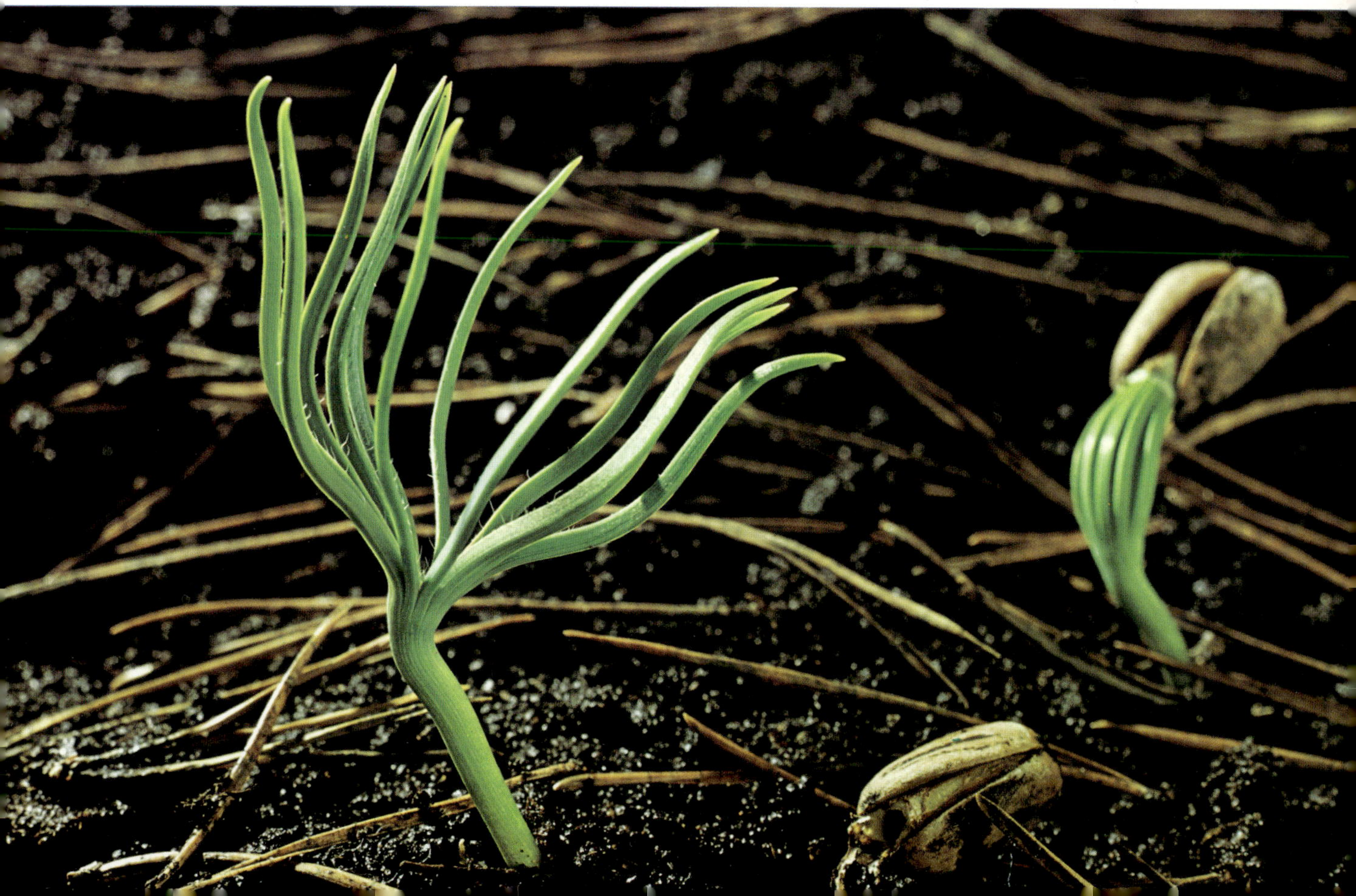

the forest that fugitive, tender green shade of colour which marks the beginning of spring, when a crowd of small creatures rushes to attack this readily available source of food.

Some leaves can then be seen to break out into strange growths of all shapes and colours. These are not some kind of eruption resulting from a disease of the plant, but galls, the tiny homes of minute larvae. Certain adorned with galls shaped like orange pips, of a purplish red colour, which are the work of tiny flies. As for the oak, it has the doubtful privilege of accommodating some thirty species of parasite, and a corresponding number of different types of gall.

Leaves can also suffer quite different transformations. The looper caterpillars of the Great Winter Moth,

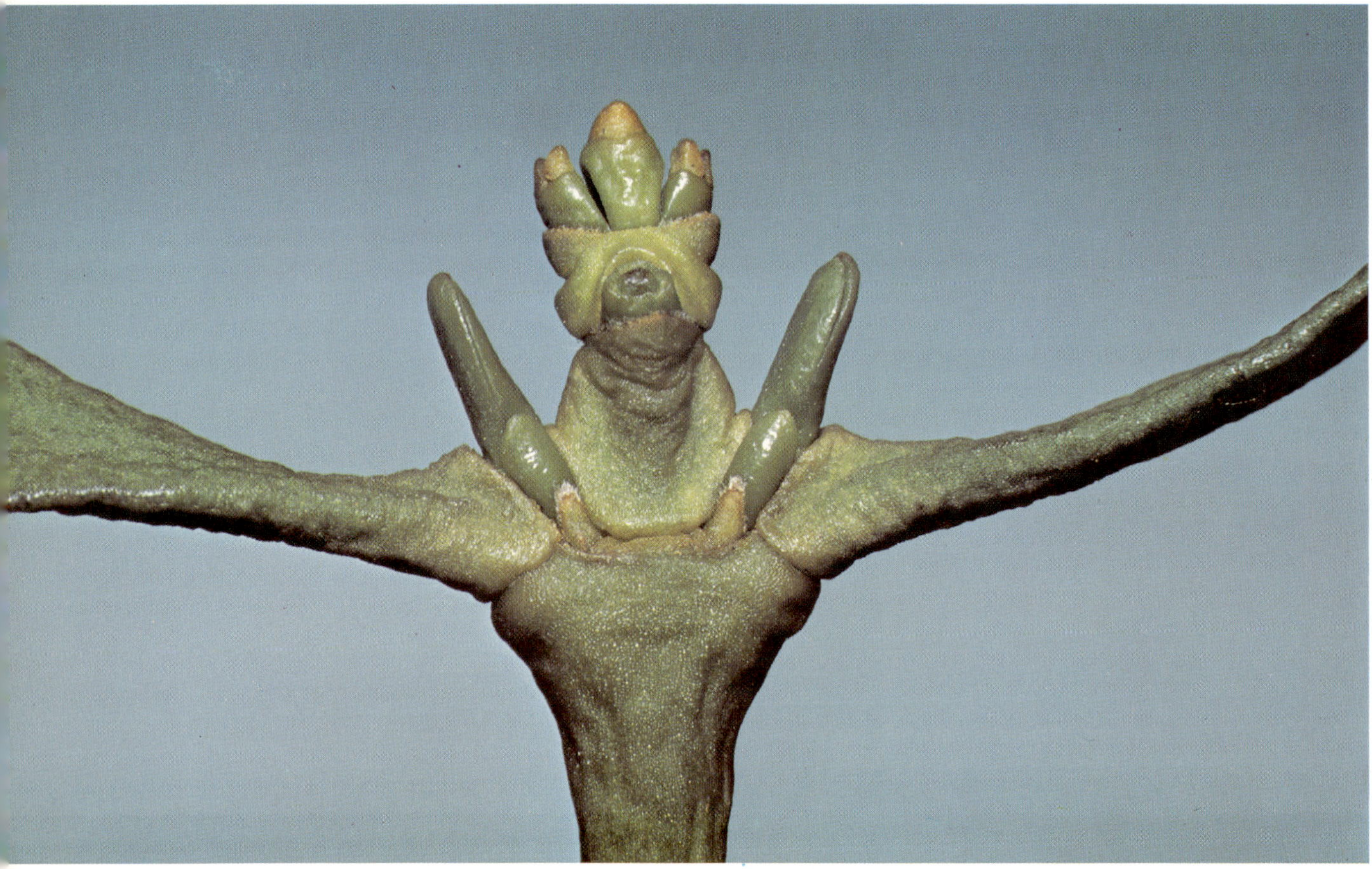

Mistletoe bud (x 6·5).

Reproduction ratio: 1·2.
Lens: 55 mm mounted on bellows.
Aperture: f/22.
Electronic flash.
The background, positioned about 70 cm (27 inches) behind the subject, is illuminated by a second flash.

substances secreted by these larvae, which arise from eggs laid inside the leaf, result in each larva becoming surrounded by a gall, the swollen tissues of which provide it with both board and lodging at the same time. Each species attracts its own particular parasites, each of which produces a different type of gall. On the leaves of lime trees appear the cornute galls caused by a mite (a relative of the spider), while the leaf of a beech is not content with stripping the trees, create a hiding-place for themselves between two leaves which they join together with the aid of silken threads.

As for leaf-rollers, small coleoptera with sharp snouts, their particular practice can be guessed from their name: the females roll the leaves to make, as it were, small cigars in which they lay their eggs. The larvae start to devour their home as soon as they are born.

Hard fruit such as acorns, hazelnuts and chestnuts are attacked by nut weevils, which are closely related to the leaf-rollers. In this case, however, the pointed snout is converted into an elongated proboscis, sometimes as long as the body. By using this imposing instrument, the female is able to bore a tunnel to reach the kernel of the nut. Having reached a sufficient depth, she turns round and applies the end of her abdomen to the newly-made opening, and protrudes a sort of fine probe which carefully deposits a single egg at the end of the tunnel. This ensures that one more larva will not have to look far for food.

In the case of May-bugs, the assault on the trees is even more serious, since it attacks successively at two levels. During the three years

Dormant bud of the Ash (x 12). The buds, which start to develop at the beginning of summer, remain dormant throughout the winter. In the spring, the terminal bud is the one which first shows signs of renewed growth.

Reproduction ratio: 1·25.
Lens: Macro 55 mm.
Aperture: f/16-22.

Flash directed downwards on bud.
Reflecting screen under subject.

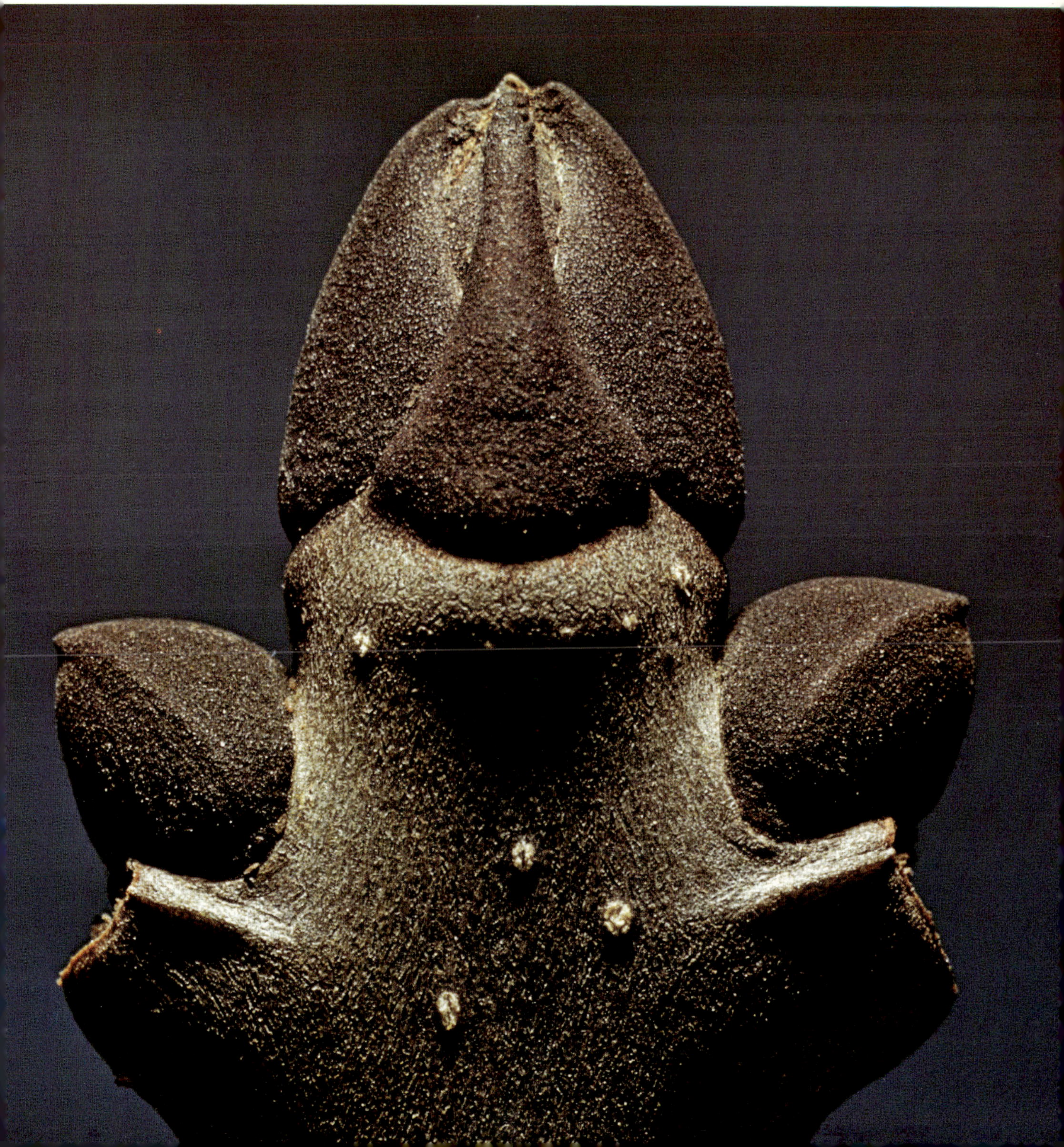

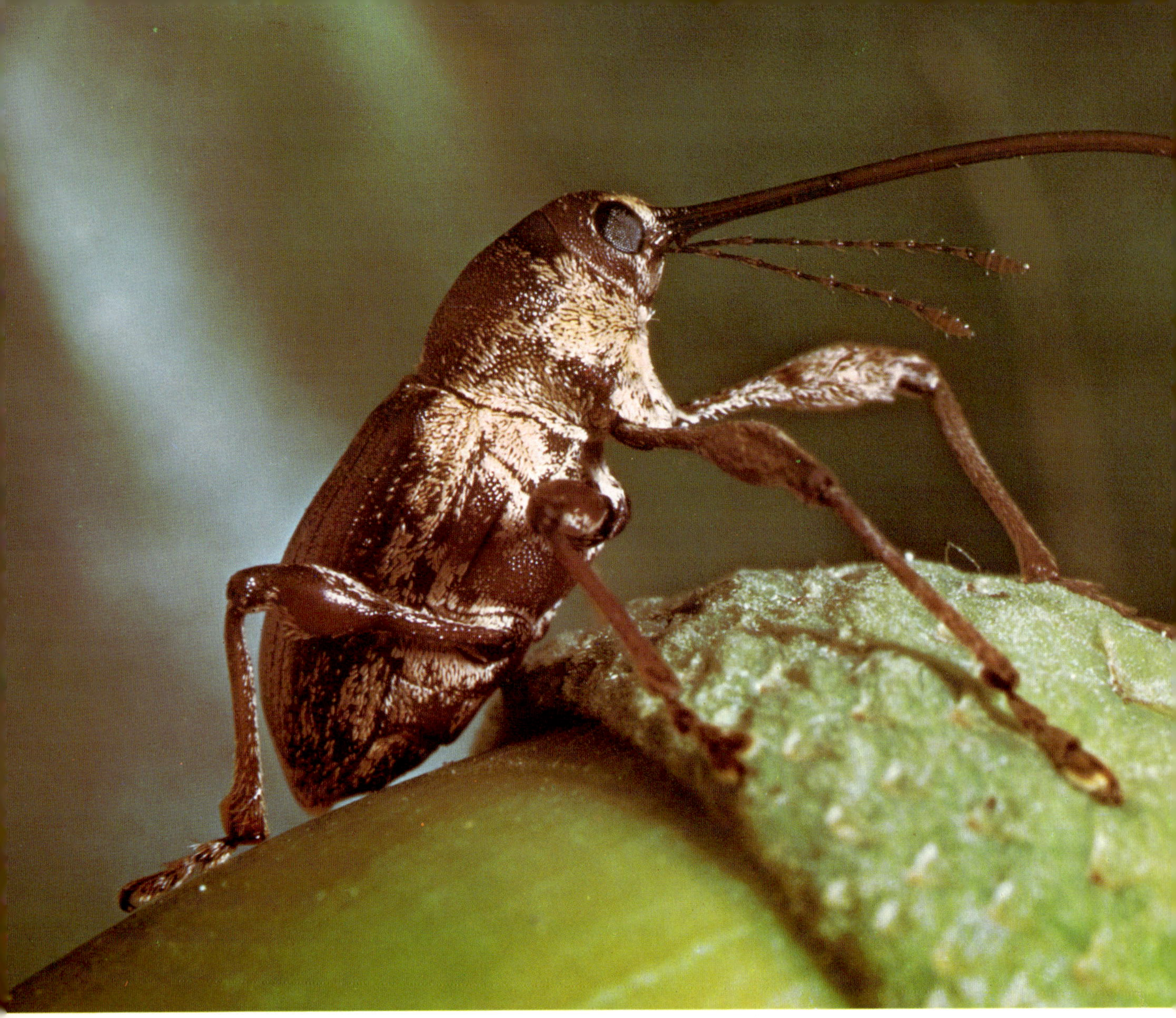

Acorn Weevil or Elephant Weevil
(×13).
Using her proboscis as a drill, the
female digs a tunnel to the pulpy
part of the acorn. She then turns
round and lays a single egg in the
tunnel. On hatching, the larva
will be assured of a supply of
food in the heart of the acorn.

Reproduction ratio: 1·7.
Lens: Macro 55 mm mounted on
bellows in reverse position.
Aperture: f/22.
Electronic flash with reflecting
screen.

it spends as a larva, in the shape of a white grub, it attacks the roots. The winged adult appears in May or June, often in very large numbers. In spite of its short life – less than a month – it has time to devastate entire trees, which are soon completely stripped of their leaves. As a corollary to their life cycle, May-bugs emerge in force every three years: these are what are often referred to as 'May-bug years'.

Finally, the processionary caterpillars provide an example of perfect organization in devastating trees. They live in a group on oaks or pines, hiding during the day inside their silk nests, which look like large white balls fastened to the branches. At dusk, they leave their shelter in single file and descend from the branches in a slow-moving, undulating procession to spread out over the leaves which have so far escaped damage. In the morning, the last procession can be seen on its return journey, carefully following the path taken by the leading caterpillar. The latter has no difficulty in finding its way, as all it has to do is to climb back along the ribbon of silk formed by each member of the colony adding its own personal thread when leaving the nest – a sort of railway track for

the worst as regards the future of our forests. In fact, though, their populations are not free to increase completely without restraint. Their numbers are limited by the presence of predators which survive at their expense, including not only large numbers of birds but also certain species of insect, which are often of interest to the photographer.

The caterpillar hunters of the

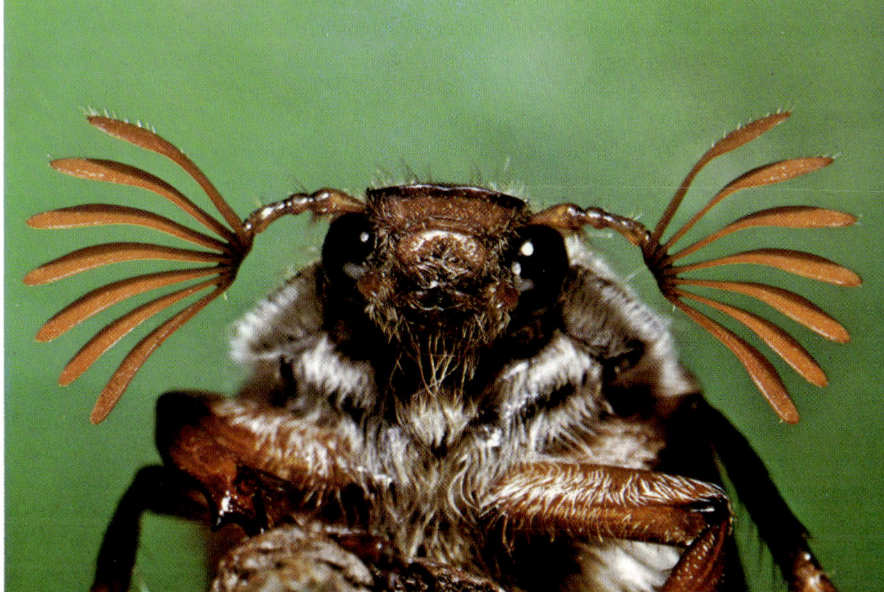

caterpillars. One word of advice – do not try to stroke the furry coat of these insects; the sting of a nettle is nothing compared to what you will suffer. Their stinging hairs are like hundreds of minute needles which will become embedded in your skin, where they will break off and release very active toxins. One does not immediately feel the pain, but on the other hand it lasts quite a long time.

Carnivores

This rapid but impressive glimpse of cohorts of insects setting out to attack the trees might make one fear

genus Calosoma, for example, the broad striated wing-cases of which produce magnificent rainbow reflections, are responsible for the slaughter of many processionary caterpillars.

Ground beetles compete with them in the richness of their colours: the Violet Ground Beetle, the Gleaming Red Ground Beetle, the Resplendent Ground Beetle and the Gold-flecked Ground Beetle are the evocative names of some of their species. They are also endowed with a less attractive facility: when annoyed, the beetle emits an acrid liquid from the end of its abdomen. These 'prima-

May-bug (x 7).
The antennae of insects, which are sense organs with many functions, appear in a wide variety of shapes. Those of the May-bug are composed of segments which can fold together like a fan.

Reproduction ratio: 1·8.
Lens: Macro 55 mm mounted on bellows in reverse position.
Aperture: f/16.
Electronic flash.

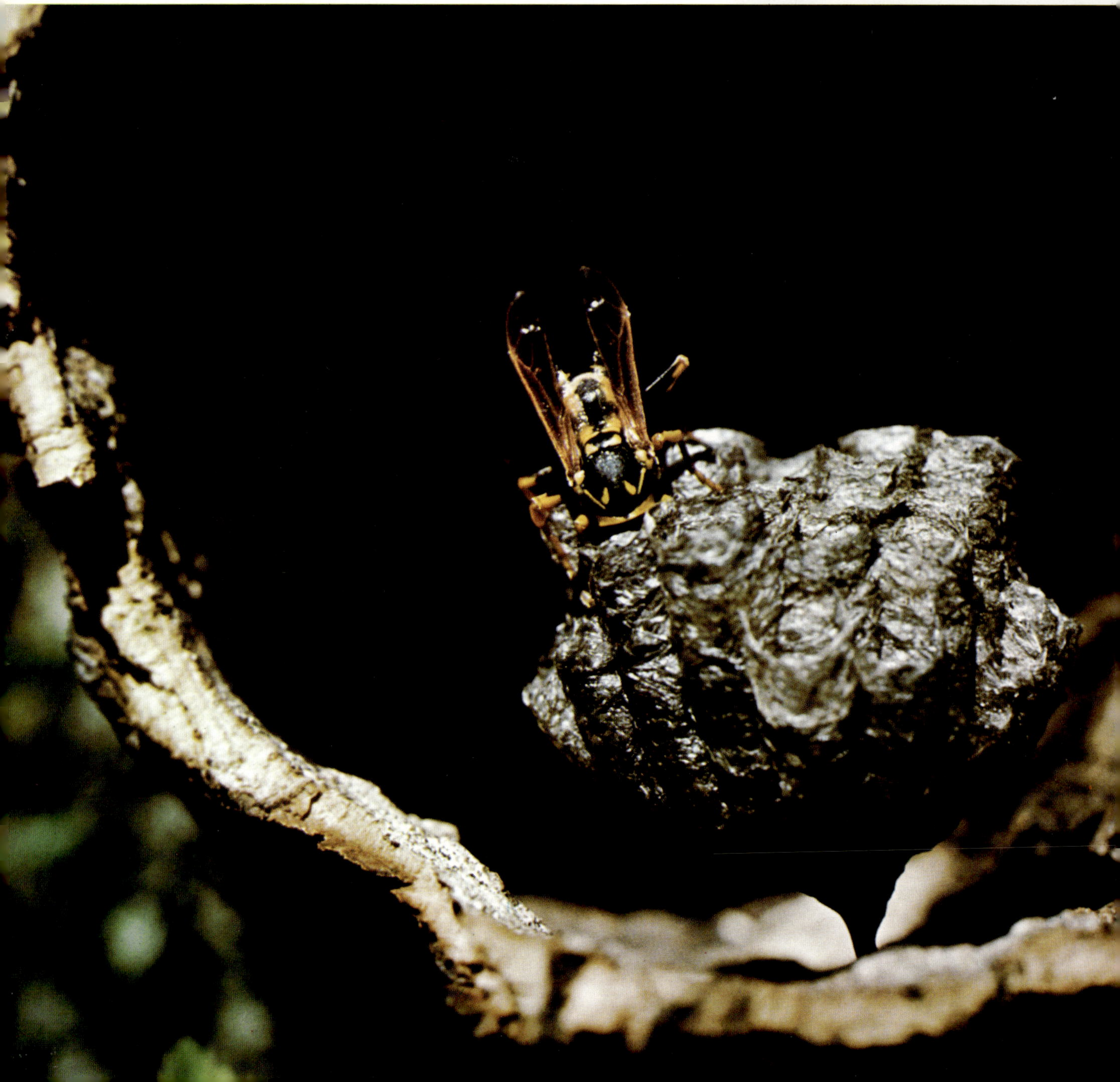

donnas' must, therefore, also be treated with the greatest respect. The photographer will also have to overcome a few further problems before being able to record them on film. These insects are, in fact, quite tireless runners. The only way to stop them in their tracks is to offer them a favourite item of food, such as a caterpillar, earthworm, snail or slug. Moreover, the fascinating colours of the carapace may not come out very well on film, since they are of a very special nature: they are caused by the microscopic structure of the wing-cases, which gives rise to light

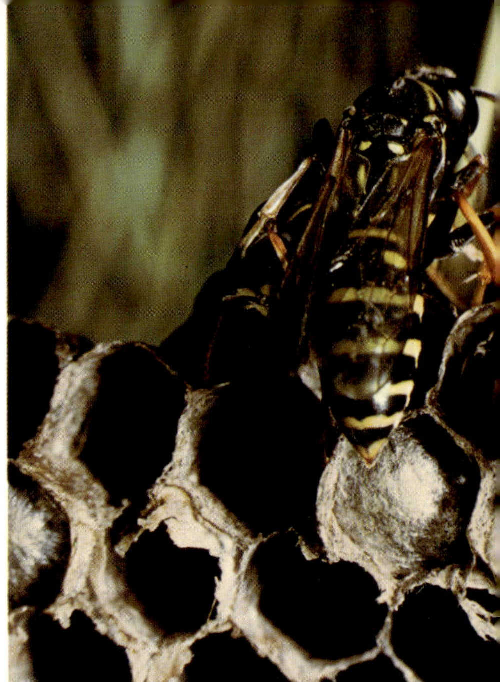

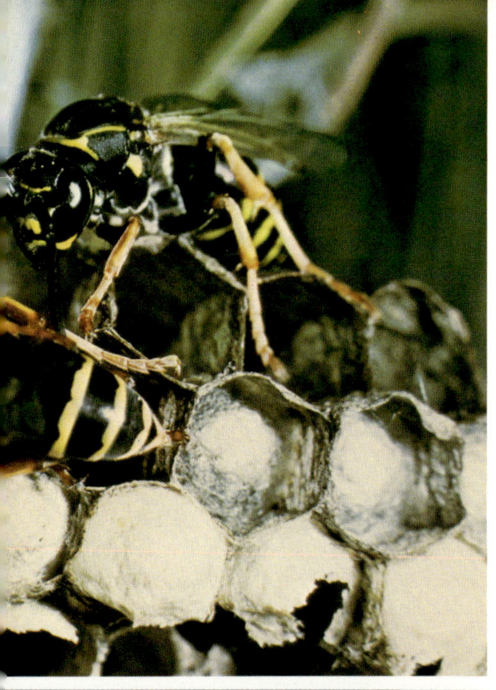

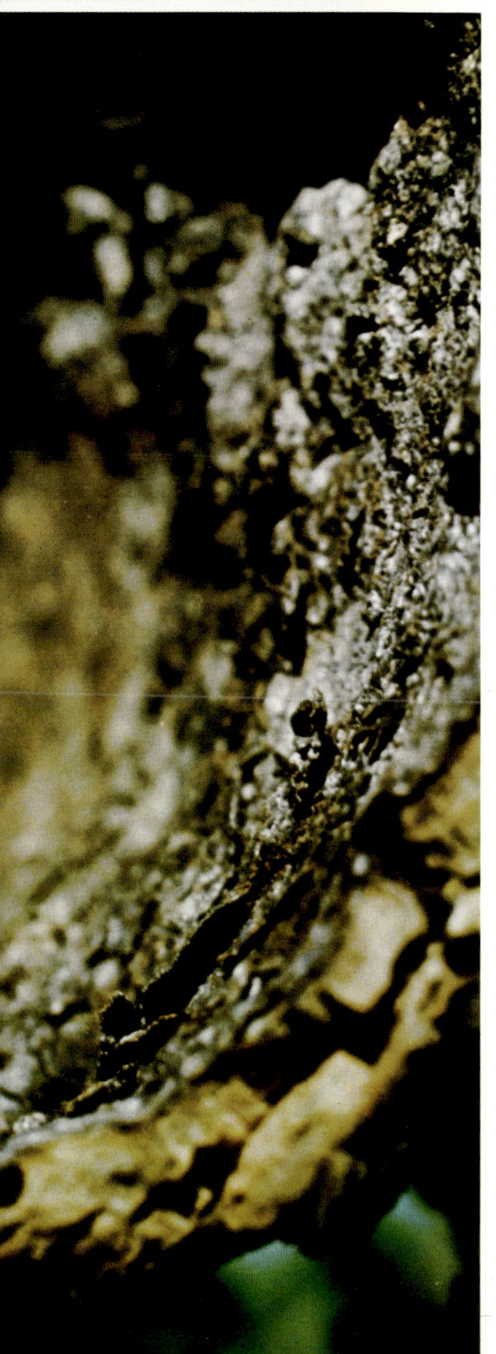

interference producing iridescent metallic reflections. The same phenomenon is produced, for example, on the surface of soap-bubbles, where multicoloured areas can sometimes be seen. The highly directional light of an electronic flash gun may diminish the richness of colouring by limiting the rays striking the carapace to a narrow lighting angle. A diffusing screen positioned in front of the flash aperture may overcome this difficulty.

Sap-suckers

In most countries, it is in the forests that the largest wild mammals find refuge. They are also the place where one meets what might be called the 'big game' of the insect world.

The largest of these, Lucanus cervus, which can reach a length of over three inches (8 cm), has been very suitably named the Stag-beetle. Strictly speaking, this somewhat surrealistic name should be applied only to the male, which (like its quadruped namesake) alone carries an impressive pair of 'antlers'. The female Lucanus, of more modest size and appearance, is thus logically sometimes referred to as the 'hind'. Although there is a striking similarity between the antlers of the stag and the armament of Lucanus, the two structures are of entirely different origin. In the case of the Stag-beetle, it is the mandibles which have enlarged to become enormous armoured claws, which are in fact more impressive than formidable. They can only be regarded as a somewhat useless ornament, as cumbersome as a false nose worn at a fancy-dress ball. At the most, they are of use during brief battles between males, and very little even then. The males use them to seize each other quite forcibly, but without inflicting the slightest harm. The fact that they fail to kill each other should not, however, be held against them. If you pick up a Stag-bettle,

Left: Two wasps communicate by touching antennae (x 4).

Reproduction ratio: 1.
Lens: 105 mm mounted on bellows.
Aperture: f/22.
Electronic flash.

Below: Nymph of the Bush Wasp in its cell (x 4.5).

Reproduction ratio: 1.4.
Lens: 55 mm mounted on bellows.
Aperture: f/22.
Electronic flash.

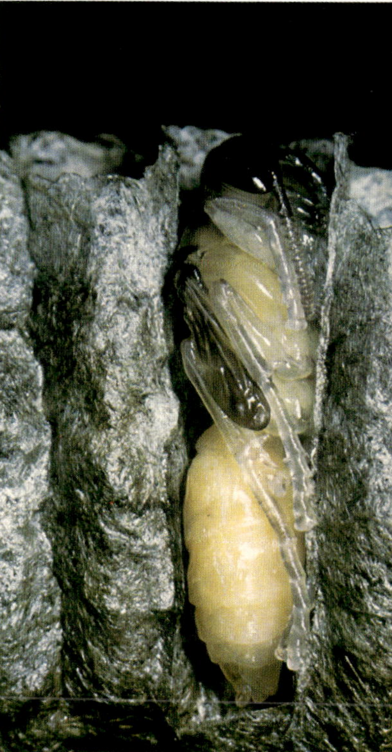

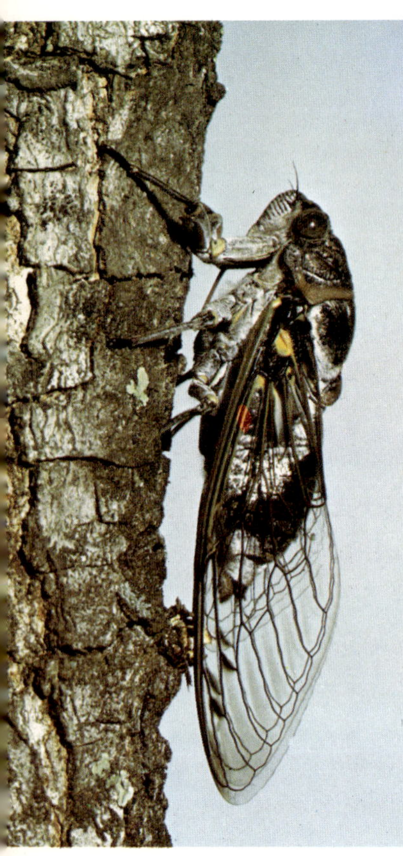

you can find out for yourself that it has ridiculously little strength in its mandibles.

The Stag-beetle can be found abroad in June and July. Unfortunately, during the daytime it remains on the trunks of trees, lapping up the sap which oozes from them, and its leather-coloured carapace makes it difficult to detect. At dusk, the males take to the air in search of females. At such times it is impossible not to notice their noisy and laboured flight, which makes it easy to follow the insect in the air and capture it when it lands.

Another giant of the air is the Great Longicorn Beetle, which measures two inches (5 cm) in length, not including its antennae, which are at least as long as the body. This insect also flies at dusk, when it looks like some winged devil as it buzzes through the air with its enormous antennae turned up like horns.

Found in southern Europe, the Cicada is a lover of sap and is much better equipped to satisfy its passion. A close relation of plant-lice, it has like them a long, straight proboscis, which it inserts into the trunks of pines or olive-trees in order to suck the sap. Being easier to hear than see – at least the male, which alone can sing – the Cicada is of particular interest for sound-recording. As for the photographer who wants to get close to it at all costs, he must record precisely the point of origin of the sound (which is not as easy as one might think, particularly when there is a chorus of several hundred insects) and then probably use a ladder to get within range of the creature.

Woodland butterflies

Being insects which like full sunlight, butterflies do not usually enter forests. However, certain species of the family *Satyridae*, like the satyrs of mythology after whom they are named, prefer the half-light of the undergrowth.

The Woodland Grayling, Scotch Argus and Great Banded Grayling are large brown butterflies which might almost be called ghost butterflies, because, although they are easy to observe while flying, one cannot fail to be surprised at their ability to disappear as if by magic. Experts in camouflage, they forsake the flowers to settle on the trunks of trees and fold their wings, the pattern of which completely matches that of the bark.

Moreover, woodland contains a great many species of moth. During

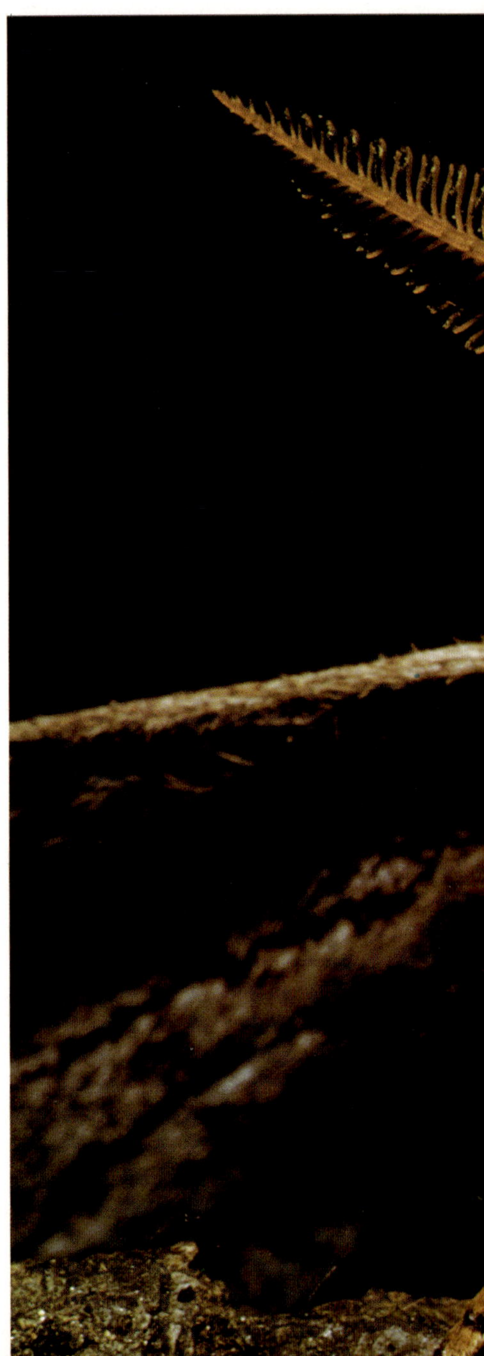

the daytime, there is little opportunity of finding them: they are distributed high among the branches, pressed against the bark, motionless and asleep, where they remain waiting for the night to bring them to life.

Without doubt the most effective method of attracting them is by a light trap – a powerful electric bulb, of about 250 watts, installed in front of a piece of white cloth stretched vertically on a wooden frame about six feet (2 m) square. The moths soon arrive and strike against the cloth, without risk of injury from the heat of the lamp. It is, in fact, the nature of their system of location which delivers them into the trap. Moths direct their flight by maintaining their visual image of the moon at a constant angle. A sufficiently bright light-bulb can replace the moon as a marker-beacon, but, as it is much nearer to the moth, the latter is forced to correct its course continuously and ends up by describing an ever-diminishing spiral around the false moon.

Under the dead wood

Dead branches lying on the ground

Emperor Moth (x 7).
The male moth has large feathery antennae capable of detecting the odour of a female up to a distance of seven miles (11 km).

Reproduction ratio: 0·9.
Lens: Macro 55 mm with extension ring.
Aperture: f/22.
Flash positioned centrally above the moth.

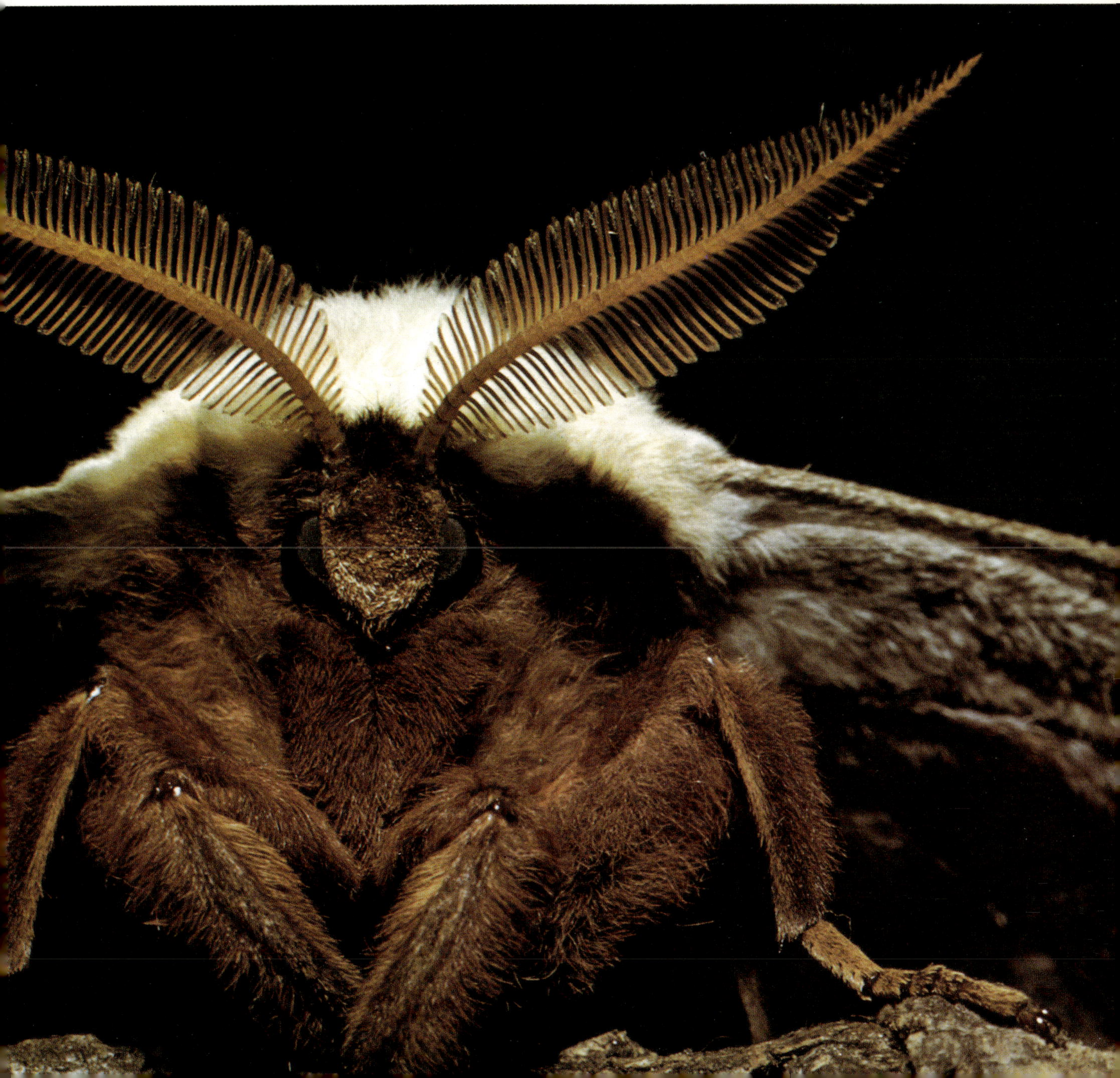

are like a mini universe swarming with life, providing food and shelter for a very varied fauna and flora.

By removing some decayed wood with the aid of a knife-blade there is every chance of finding, in the bend of a tunnel, a few xylophagous (wood-eating) larva gnawing at the fibres with their strong mandibles. The large larva of the Stag-beetle spends four or five years tunnelling through old fallen oaks in this way.

The bark of decayed trunks can easily be pulled off by hand. Here, too, there is a possibility of bringing to light colonies of small creatures such as wood-lice, earwigs and millipedes, which have come in search of somewhere damp and dark.

Finally, if branches on the ground are turned over carefully, this will often reveal the hiding-places of nocturnal species (which shelter under them during the daytime) such as ground beetles, for example (the Calosoma beetles, on the other hand, are diurnal), the presence of which is betrayed immediately by their brilliant corselets; or even a splendid amphibian with an equally conspicuous colour pattern, the Fire Salamander.

Its black skin dotted with irregular patches of bright yellow might, it is true, call to mind the appearance of some frightfully poisonous toadstool, and country people still tell the most alarming stories about this peaceful amphibian. Sometimes (they say) its bite is deadly, and sometimes it is sufficient merely to touch it. There is a grain of truth in these beliefs: the salamander actually produces two different venoms. However, these are secreted by its skin, and it is thus incapable of injecting them. There is no risk in handling a salamander, as the venoms can take effect only if injected directly into the bloodstream. There is just one precaution which should be taken – to avoid temporary irritation of the

European Fire Salamander (x 4). Because it dislikes dry conditions, it hides during the day in the shelter of old tree-stumps.

Reproduction ratio: 0 75.
Lens: Macro 55 mm with automatic extension ring.
Aperture: f/11.
Electronic flash.

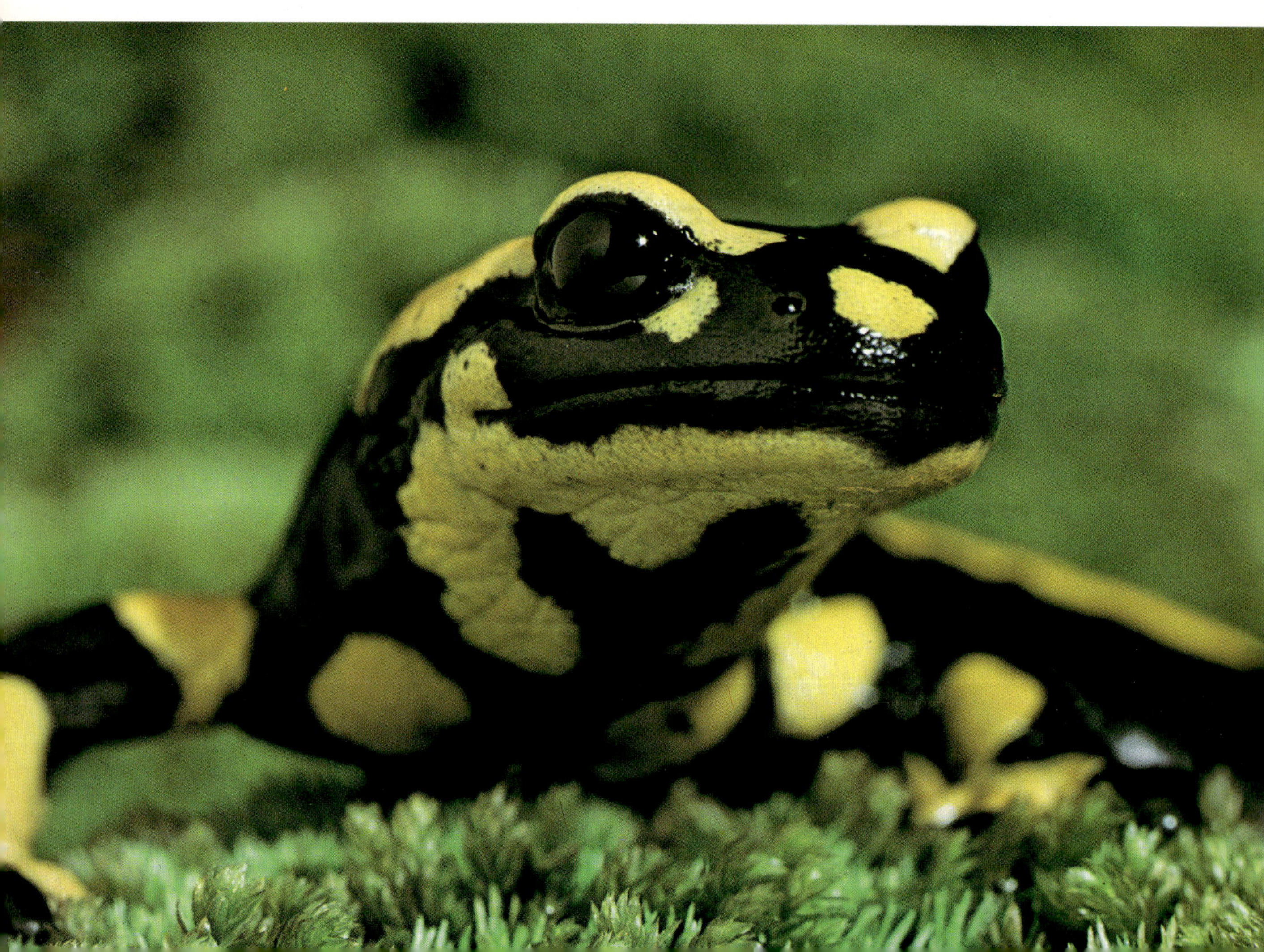

cornea, do not let your hands come into contact with your eyes after having handled a salamander, without washing them first.

Lastly, a piece of advice – do not forget to replace in their original positions the branches and stones you have turned over, after you have finished your examination: there is no point in condemning to death by dessication a whole host of small animals, larvae and eggs which play an active part in the life of the forest.

Insect societies

Insects represent 80% of the animal species living in a forest. If, however, one were to count the number of individuals, there is no doubt that ants would be amongst the most numerous.

The Wood Ant, for example, builds cone-shaped heaps consisting mainly of an accumulation of pine needles, which can reach a height of four to five feet (1·50m). Each nest of this type might house two to three million individuals. It should be added that the tunnels are much longer and more convoluted below ground than they are above. Such a mass of insects swarming in all directions may discourage the photographer, but it is, in fact, a rich field of activity. The ultra-rapid flash of the electronic flashgun makes it possible to capture these restless subjects on film without risk of blurring the picture; the small size of the ants requires, moreover, a maximum depth of field (the flash making it possible to use a smaller stop). One can quickly record workers engaged in dragging an outsize load towards the colony, such as a twig or a dead insect (just over 2 lbs [1 kg] of insects, including processionary caterpillars, are killed every day and taken to the nest). When alarmed, the Wood Ant assumes an unusual attitude of defence, with its jaws held wide open and its abdomen swung forward ready to squirt a jet of formic acid towards

its assailant – a scene which the photographer can easily provoke.

Small black and yellow ants often set up their nests under stones. When the location of such a nest has been discovered, it is a good idea to replace the lifted stone immediately and then to get the equipment ready for taking the photograph. When everything is prepared, the stone should be quickly rolled away and the maximum possible number of photographs taken before the workers have dragged into their dark tunnels all the white larvae which a few minutes before were strewn over the surface of the ground.

In the case of wasps and hornets, the photographer finds himself faced with even more fascinating structures, but also more dangerous individuals (although the Red Ant Myrmica rubra is best avoided, as it is able to inflict stings which are just as painful as those of wasps). It is wise to take a few precautions to spare oneself unnecessary pain by wearing leather gauntlets reaching well above the wrists and a wide-brimmed hat surrounded by a fine net falling below the shoulders, by avoiding any sudden movement, and by using a telephoto lens in order to be able to maintain a reasonable distance. Even if these measures of protection are taken, we advise against approaching the nests of hornets (the sting of a hornet is very painful, and being stung by an entire enraged colony even more so). The nest is also often inconveniently located in a hollow tree.

The Bush Wasp of the genus Polistes is without doubt the most interesting of the group, as its nest (unlike that of other wasps) has no covering and its compartments are completely exposed to view. The life of the colony is, therefore, in this case particularly easy to observe: one can watch the workers attending to the eggs and larvae, which can be clearly seen at the bottom of each cell. It would almost seem that the architecture of this nest was especially designed to facilitate photography!

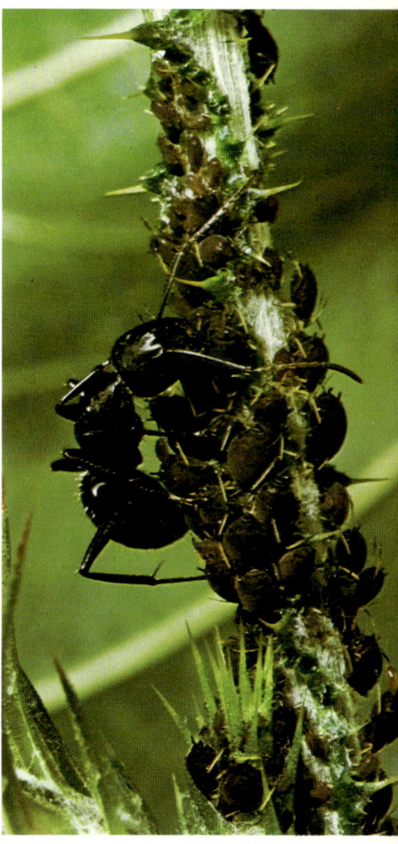

An ant engaged in milking a plant-louse (×3·8).
With its antennae it taps the rear of the plant-louse, which then secretes a drop of sugary substance of which the ant is very fond.

Many species of ant raise plant-lice in their nests. For this purpose they construct proper stables located at the foot of a tuft of grass or even below ground in the middle of the nest. They are careful to place the plant-lice around roots into which they can plunge their probosces and suck the sap on which they feed. The ants watch over their 'cattle' and protect them against aggressors. They clean them meticulously and look after the newborn young, which increase the size of the herd. They value their stock highly and ants from two neighbouring nests have been seen to fight over their plant-lice.

Reproduction ratio: 1·4.
Lens: Macro 55mm mounted on bellows.
Aperture: f/16-22.
Electronic flash.

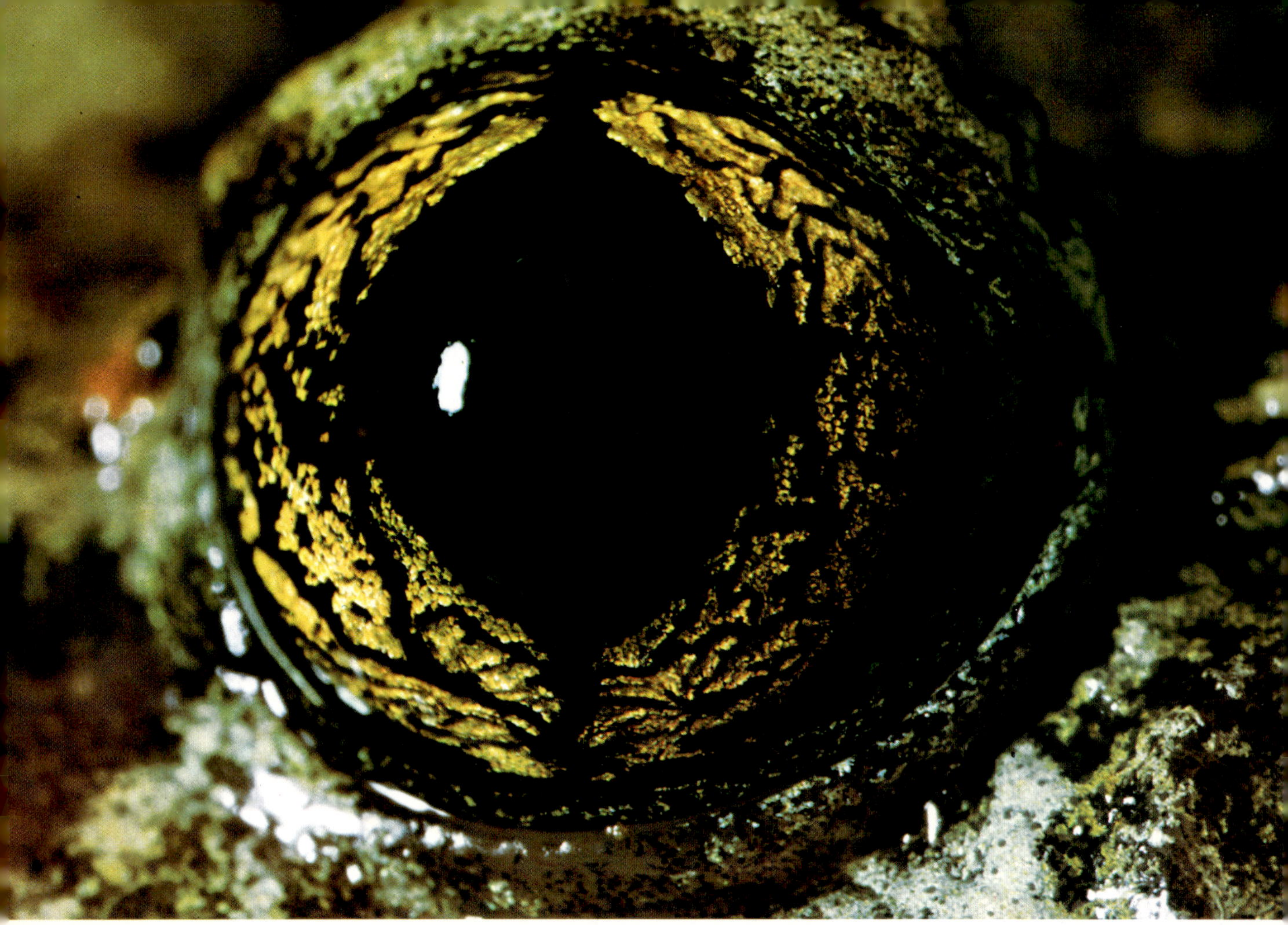

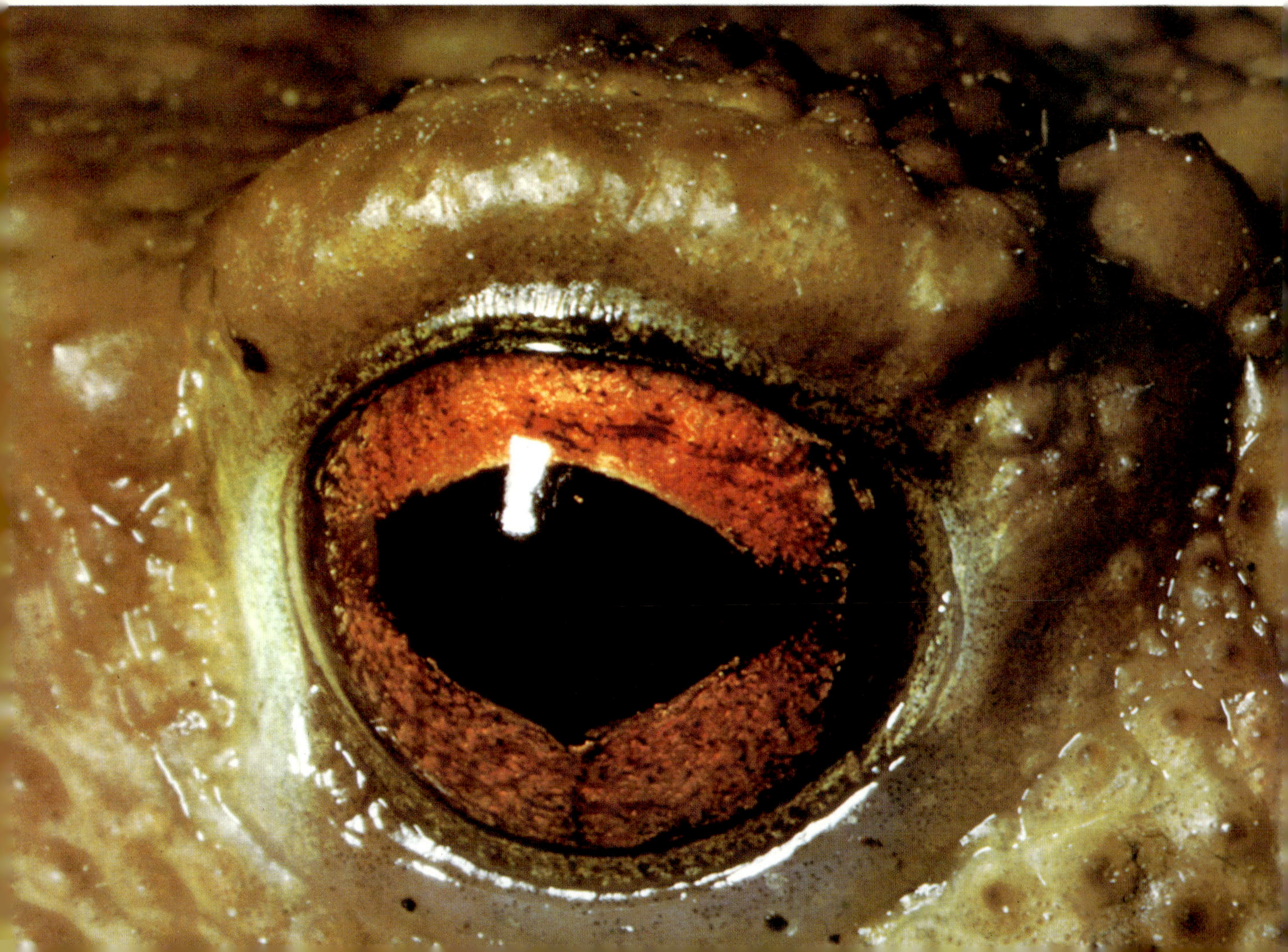

The 'animal laboratory'

The 'animal laboratory' – it was this slightly ironical expression which the great entymologist Jean-Henri Fabre used to indicate his place of work in his *Entomological Reminiscences*. In fact, the simple furnishings of this room bring to mind a kitchen or studio rather than a laboratory with its complex and expensive equipment. A large table cluttered with glass bottles, wire dish-covers and the occasional test-tube – this was all the equipment Fabre required for the research with which he filled the four thousand or so pages of his extra-ordinary memoirs.

The naturalist photographer may take comfort from this illustrious example – his 'laboratory' can be limited to a corner of a room, furnished with a few shelves to hold aquaria and vivaria, and a board resting on two very rigid trestles for photographic use. He will then be completely equipped to record spec-tacular scenes, under what will, moreover, often be memorable cir-cumstances.

Keeping and rearing specimens

Meadow, field and forest offer the rambler an apparently inexhaustible wealth of things to see. What is the point, therefore, of collecting a few specimens of this diverse fauna in the narrow confines of a room in order to keep and raise them? What are the advantages to be gained from indoor observation?

Certain particularly fleeting stages in the life of small animals can rarely be observed outdoors. A caterpillar-skin splitting open to reveal the shell of a chrysalis, a chrysalis opening to release a butterfly, a dragonfly extri-cating itself from the skin of its final-stage nymph – these are all events which last only a few minutes.. The best way of making sure to be there at the right time is to follow the daily progress of these animals in-doors and to watch for the signs of impending metamorphosis.

To obtain good pictures of snakes, lizards, frogs and insects, it is essen-tial that framing and focusing should be carried out with extreme accuracy, and the right conditions for this can be provided only by studio photo-graphy. Moreover, having been kept for a while in a vivarium, the 'models' will have become a little more accustomed to humans. It will have been possible to keep them under observation for a period and to note their reactions, their likes and dis-likes – all of which will help to ensure their co-operation when the time comes for them to sit for their portraits.

Some small creatures which are normally so timid that there is no possibility of obtaining pictures of them in their natural habitat, even as a long-distance shot, will happily submit to being photographed after having been brought in for observa-tion for a few days. The Tiger-beetle, an elegant little carnivorous coleop-ter in beautiful metallic colours, which can be seen running along forest paths, is a typical 'studio' animal: to catch this insect outdoors it is best to use a butterfly-net, as it takes flight at the slightest alarm. In captivity, even if the Tiger-beetle

Top: The eye of a Midwife Toad (x 20).

Reproduction ratio: 3·6.
Lens: Macro Summar 24 mm mounted on bellows.
Aperture: f/11.
Electronic flash.

Bottom: The eye of a Common Toad (x 13)..

Reproduction ratio: 2·4.
Lens: Macro 55 mm mounted on bellows in reverse position.
Aperture: f/22.
Electronic flash.

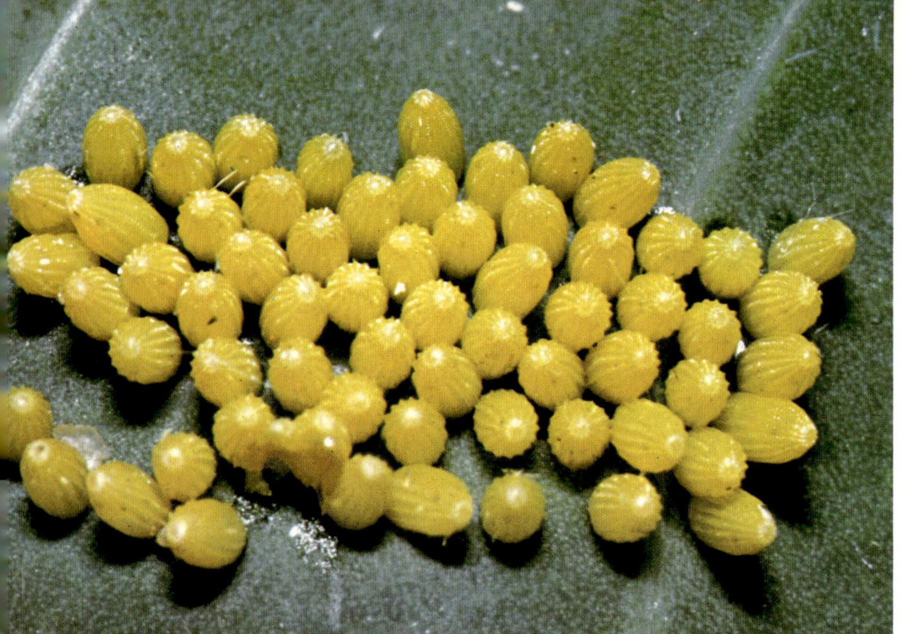

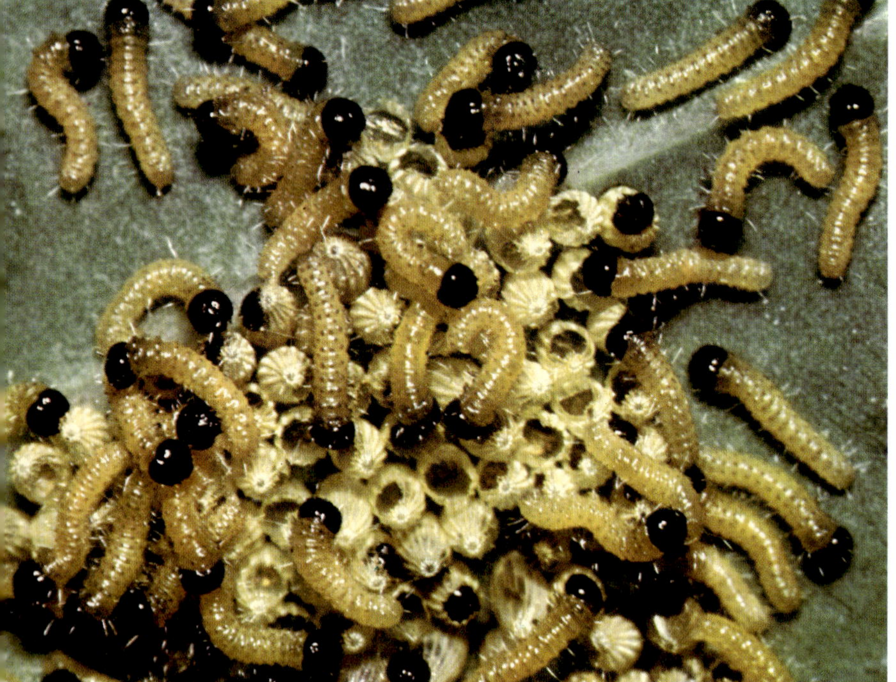

Terrestrial species

Example: Rearing the Large White Butterfly.

The eggs or caterpillars of this butterfly can easily be obtained by collecting them from cabbages. The eggs appear as small, bright yellow beads adhering in tightly-packed clumps to the lower side of leaves. There is no difficulty in providing a regular supply of food, as it is merely a matter of buying an occasional cabbage in the market.

The leaves should be placed in a narrow-necked vessel filled with water, which will stop them withering. When the caterpillars have succeeded in reducing them to rags, a new supply of food should be provided in the immediate vicinity so that the caterpillars can transfer themselves direct from the bare stems to the as yet untouched leaves.

Three weeks after its birth, the caterpillar is ready to undergo pupation (transformation into a chrysalis). However, well before this time arrives, it is advisable to place the colony in the cage intended for the future butterflies, to make sure that none of them escape (see the drawing of a cage on page 138). A few pieces of branch and bark should also be placed in the cage to assist the impending pupation.

When it is ready to metamorphose, the caterpillar stops feeding and wanders around for a time, searching for a suitable support to which to attach itself. Strangely enough, most caterpillars are likely to choose the netting stretched over the sides of the cage, but some will choose a branch or a piece of bark and will thereby be suitable for a good series of photographs when transforming into a chrysalis (after the caterpillar has fastened itself to the support by its silk girdle, the branch can be removed from the cage to a position more suitable for photography).

The chrysalis stage likewise lasts about three weeks. When the case of the pupa becomes semi-transparent

The eggs of a Large White Butterfly, fastened on to the leaf by their mother (x 14).

Below: the caterpillars hatching. As soon as they have devoured the envelope of the egg, they start to eat into the leaf, carefully avoiding the veins.

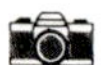

Reproduction ratio: 3·5.
Lens: 55 mm mounted on bellows in reverse position.
Aperture: f/22.
Electronic flash.

remains very active, advantage can always be taken of one of its rare moments of immobility to photograph it, without having to risk seeing it disappear into the air (see the section on *Photography in the laboratory* further on in this chapter).

Finally, it is necessary to use an aquarium when photographing any aquatic species (cf. *The water's edge* and later *Photographing aquatic species*).

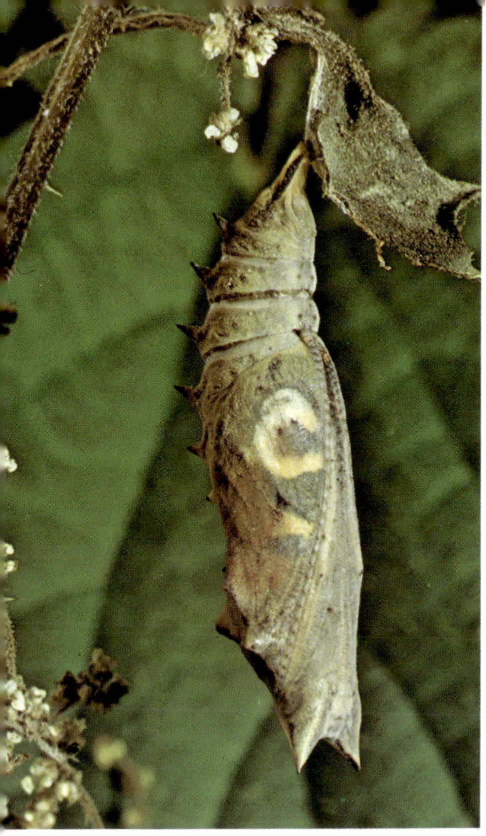

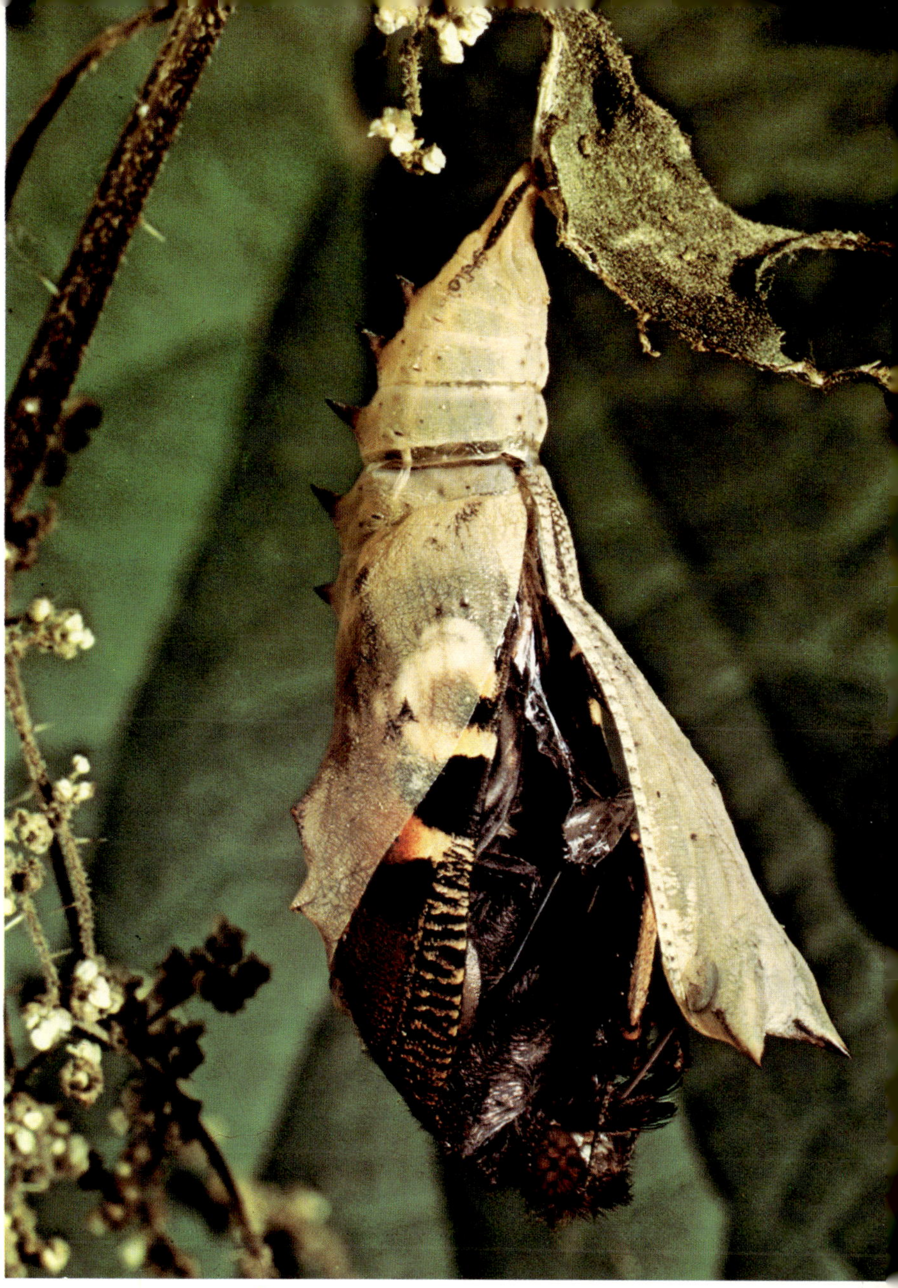

so that the folded wings, tinted bright yellow, of the butterfly can be seen, the imago is ready to emerge. Now is the time to attend to lighting, framing and focusing, and to settle down to wait – a few minutes or a few hours – until the event takes place.

Breeding from adults is the most difficult stage to achieve. A 500 watt tungsten lamp positioned above the cage will act as an artificial sun, dispensing light and heat (a temperature of 25°–30°C or 80°F is suitable). The butterflies should be fed on sugar-water with added honey, which they can sip from containers serving as artificial flowers (see drawing on page 138). A few cabbage leaves should be available, on which the females can lay their eggs.

It is essential to know exactly on which plants caterpillars collected in the wild will feed; most species have, in fact, very precise food requirements. It is merely necessary to record the plant species on which the caterpillars were found. The caterpillar of the Swallowtail will feed only on umbellifers (Wild Carrot, etc.) and that of the Peacock Butterfly only on nettles; though their tastes are certainly conservative, their preferred food is by no means difficult to find.

Amphibian species

Example: Breeding newts.

Adult newts can be captured in a net in March, when they crowd into the ponds to breed. A single pair is all that is required for breeding purposes: they will lay their eggs quite readily in captivity, and there is therefore no point in capturing more in order to increase the chances of success, and thereby depopulating the ponds to no purpose.

A Peacock Butterfly emerging. The chrysalis is suspended from the leaf of a nettle by a silken girdle. The colour of the wings can already be seen through the semi-transparent wall (on the left, x 3). It opens (on the right, x 5) to release the butterfly.

Reproduction ratio: 0·9.
Lens: Macro 55 mm with extension ring.
Electronic flash.

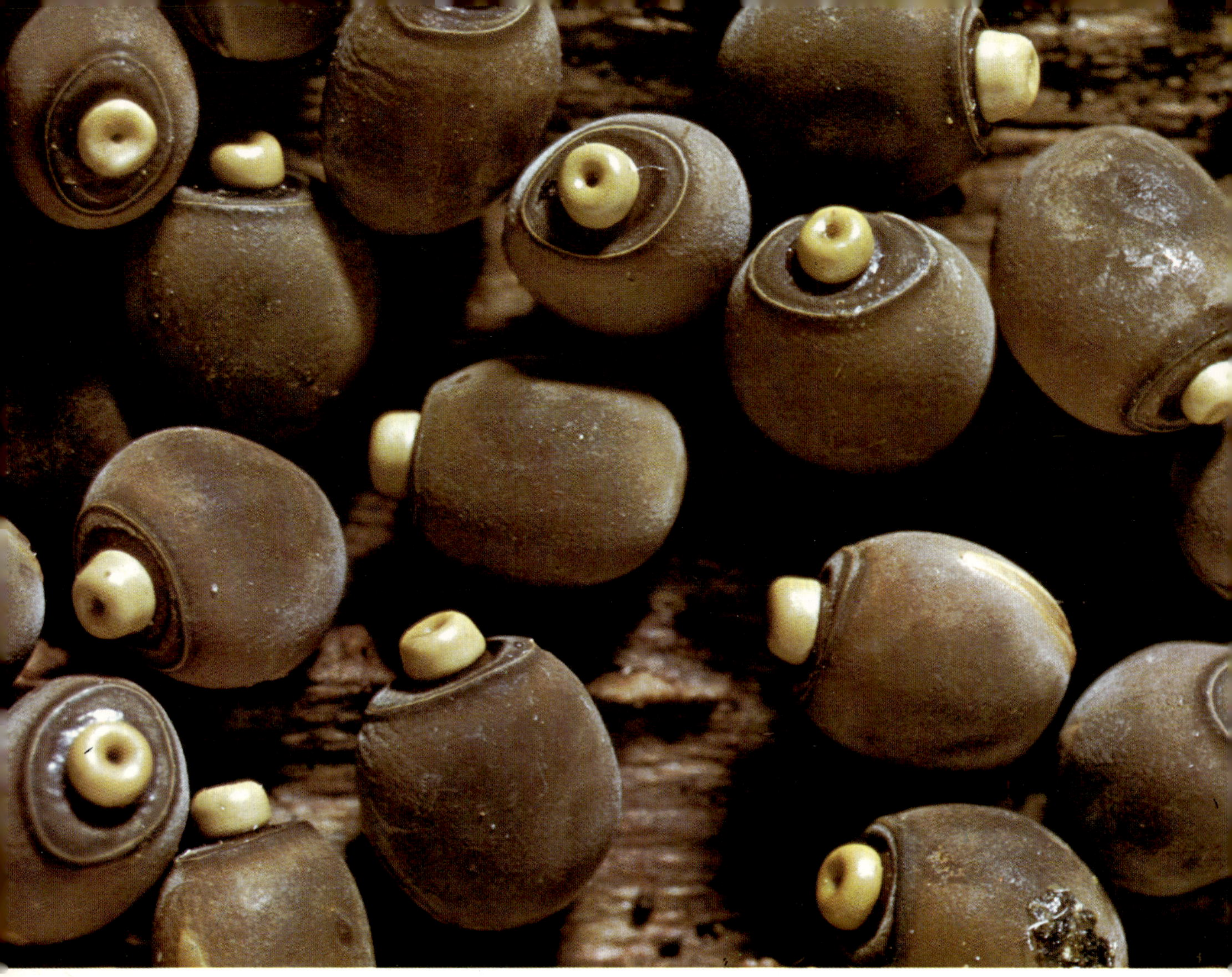

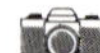

Eggs of a Stick Insect (×18). The insect lays them on the bare ground, where they look like seeds.

Reproduction ratio: 3.
Lens: Macro Summar 24 mm on bellows.
Aperture: f/11.
Electronic flash.

They can be fed on mud-worms or Tubifex. A few clumps of aquatic plants – Elodea is particularly suitable – should be provided, on which the female can lay her eggs. The plants should be held to the bottom of the aquarium by lead shot. (All these requisites can be obtained in a good angling shop.)

After a spectacular courtship dance, the male deposits a gelatinous mass on the bottom: this is the spermatophore, which contains the semen. A few moments later, the female picks it up in her cloaca, and is thereby fertilized. She lays her eggs one by one, over a period of several days, on submerged leaves to which she carefully attaches them with the aid of her hind legs.

The young larvae of the newt have large feathery tufts on either side of their head: these are the gills. The front legs appear first, then the hind-legs. The larvae can be fed on small fresh-water crustaceans such as Cyclops and Daphnia, and, when they have grown sufficiently large, on mud-worms. Around midsummer they start to lose their gills and adopt air-breathing: this completes their metamorphosis into land animals, so that it is time to transfer them to a vivarium for amphibians, or an aquarium that has a land area furnished with pebbles and moss.

As regards the parents, as soon as egg-laying is over, they endeavour to leave the water, constantly approaching the surface to find a way out. This is the time to return them to their natural habitat, or to prepare a suitable vivarium, if it is intended to keep them in captivity a little longer.

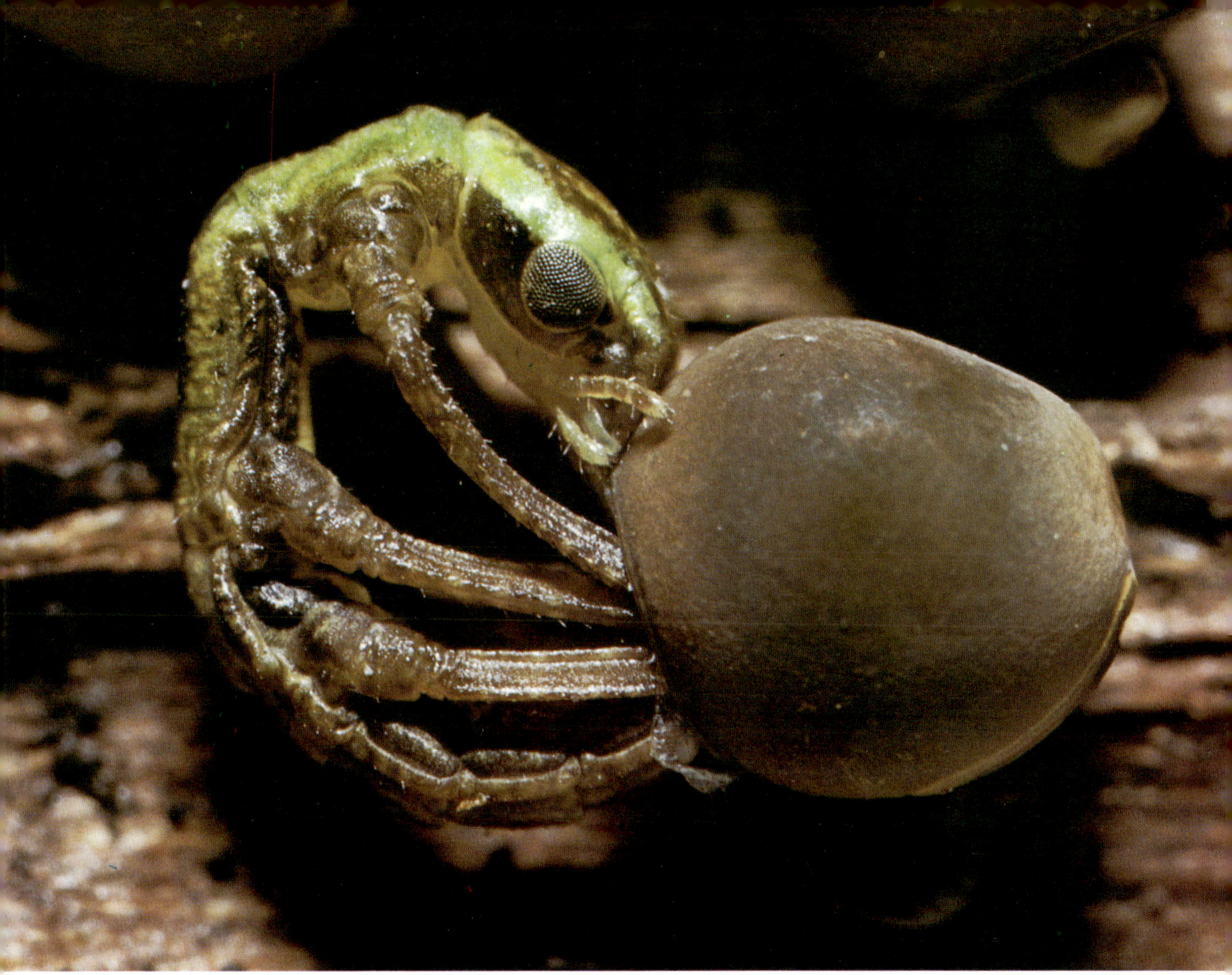

Aquatic species

Example: Dragon-fly larvae.

The large larva of Aeshna (the largest of the pond dragonflies) is one of the most common and most interesting. It is best to capture only the largest specimens (the maximum length is just under two inches [45 mm]) if you do not wish to wait too long to witness metamorphosis, as they take five years to develop. Extremely carnivorous, these larvae have a liking for mud-worms. When approaching metamorphosis, the larva stops feeding and endeavours to leave the water: a branch should then be placed in the aquarium in such a way that it protrudes for some distance above the surface. As soon as the larva starts to crawl on to this 'perch', it is necessary to take up position ready to record the metamorphosis, with the consolation of knowing that a few hours of patience will be rewarded by an unforgettable spectacle. (It is necessary to provide for several rapid changes in reproduction ratio on a decreasing scale, as the adult dragon-fly is significantly larger than the larva.)

Photography in the laboratory

Animals which live on the ground

In the case of small creatures found crawling on the ground in their natural state, photography in the

Birth of a Stick Insect (x 30). Having pushed back the lid of its egg, the young Stick Insect uses the shell as a support while withdrawing its long legs.

Reproduction ratio: 5.
Lens: Macro Summar 24 mm on bellows.
Aperture: f/8.
Electronic flash.

Example of cage to build

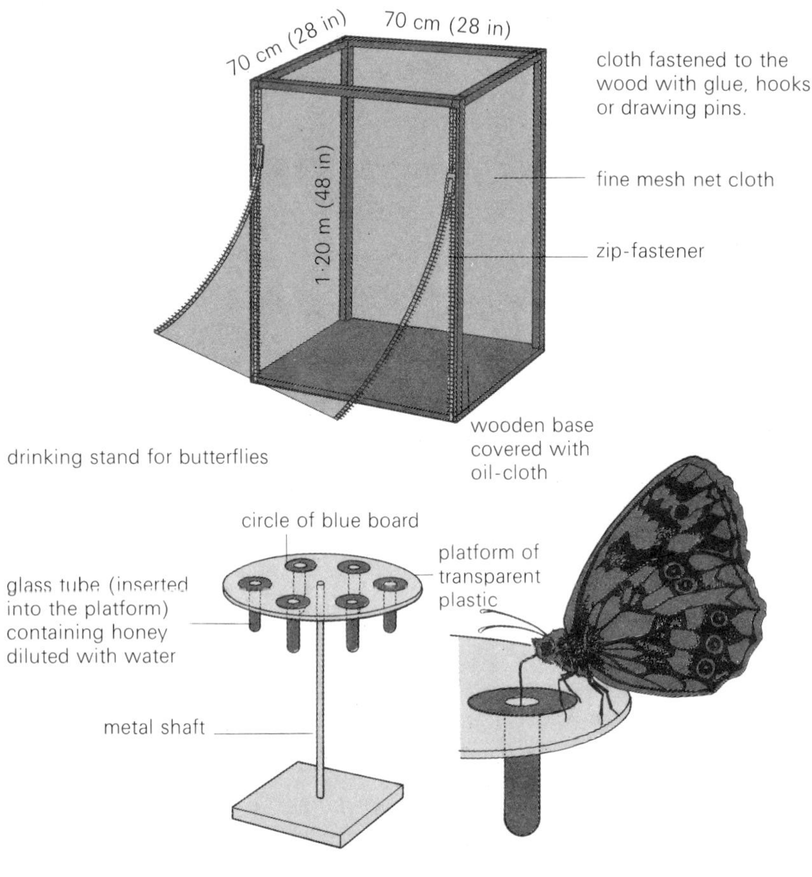

drinking stand for butterflies

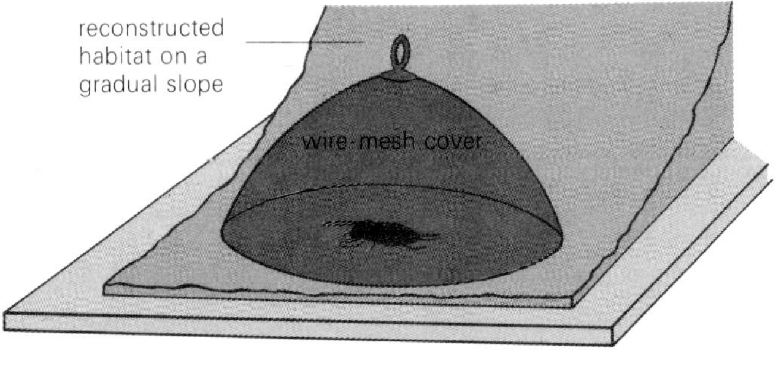

ARRANGEMENT FOR INDOOR PHOTOGRAPHY
OF GROUND-LIVING SPECIES

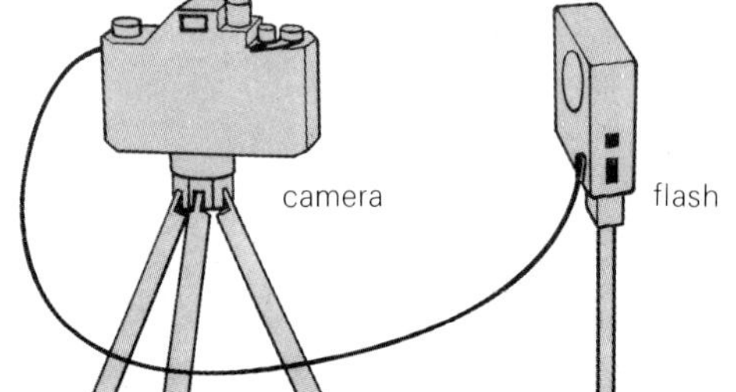

laboratory offers the immediate advantage of being able to raise, as it were, the ground level to a convenient height, on the working table: this makes it much easier to take pictures.

The habitat can be reproduced with the aid of soil, dead leaves, moss, bark, stones and other materials, which should be chosen to match the locations frequented by the animal in its wild state. They should be arranged on a tray (a suitable size for this in most cases would be 16 ins × 30 ins or 40 cm × 60 cm), the position of which on the table can be adjusted, if necessary, to assist in framing (it is, in fact, easier to move the subject than to move the equipment, which is awkwardly mounted on a heavy tripod).

In order to ensure that the background does not come out dark on the photograph (see *Observer and photographer* regarding electronic flash), it is necessary only to raise the rear part of the 'set' slightly to form a slope which completely blocks out the perspective.

To restrict the movement of the animal, it should be placed under a wire cover (see left). As soon as it stops moving, it can easily and accurately be brought into focus through the wire-mesh. The cover should be lifted just before exposure and replaced immediately.

Animals which live on plants

The choice of the plant to act as a support for the animal when being photographed should not be left to chance if one wishes to avoid taking unnatural photographs combining two organisms which would normally have no connection.

The simplest method is to keep the plant on which the subject has been found. Some caution is nevertheless indicated, as the creature might have been merely passing through from one place to another. It is, therefore, best to check that it was not there purely by chance, by referring to the recorded habits of the species.

The plant chosen should be placed in a flask full of water to keep it sufficiently fresh. Other plants, arranged as a background in similar flasks, will help to reconstruct a natural environment without the confused tangle of stalks and leaves which is sometimes a nuisance when working in the field, and which can detract from the clarity of the photograph.

A stiff sheet of green paper placed vertically about eighteen inches (50 cm) behind and illuminated by a second flashlight will make it possible to avoid the unsightly 'black holes' which might otherwise appear between the various items in the composition.

Photographing aquatic species

To show them in their proper environment, aquatic species must be photographed through the glass of an aquarium.

The range of aquaria commercially available is perfectly suitable for species of moderate size. For small-sized species, on the other hand, it is necessary to construct aquaria on a scale suited to that of the subjects, in order to avoid the latter being lost from view in an unduly large quantity of water. Glass 1/10th of an inch (2 mm) thick (as used for picture-mounting) and cut to the dimensions shown in the adjoining diagram can be used for this purpose. The various parts are glued together by means of a special adhesive for use with glass, ensuring that the joints will be perfectly watertight.

For very small species (fresh-water crustaceans, mosquito larvae, etc.) a mini-aquarium made from microscope slides (about 1/20th of an inch or 1 mm thick) joined together is even better (see diagram).

Except in the last case, a sheet of glass slightly smaller than the front of the aquarium should be provided for the purpose of confining very

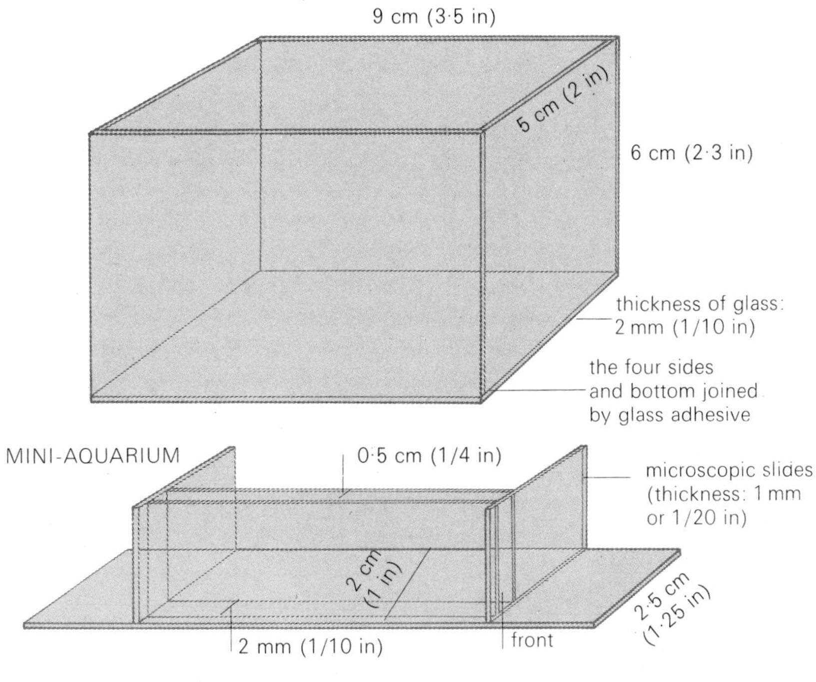

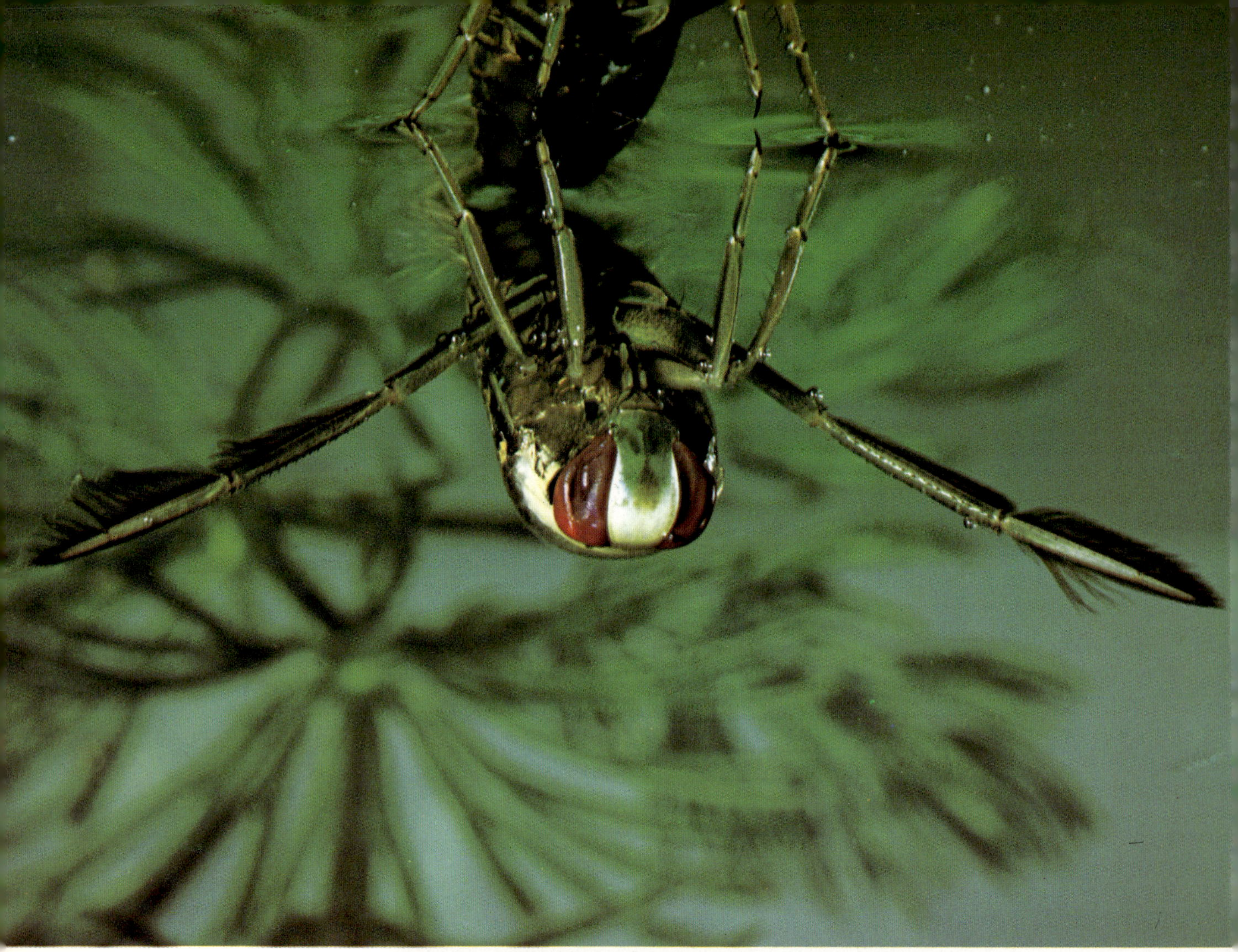

Water Boatman below the surface
of the water (x 7).
This aquatic insect swims on its
back, its two long rear legs
serving as oars.
   Photographed in an aquarium,
the background (blue-green stiff
paper) being submerged against
the rear side.

Reproduction ratio: 1·1.
Lens: 105 mm on bellows.
Aperture: f/22.
Electronic flash.

Right: Aquatic larva of a
Chaoborus Mosquito (x 12).
Its inflated 'water-wings' enable it
to control the level at which it
floats.

Mini-aquarium.
Reproduction ratio: 2·8.
Lens: Macro 55 mm on bellows.
Aperture: f/22.
Electronic flash.

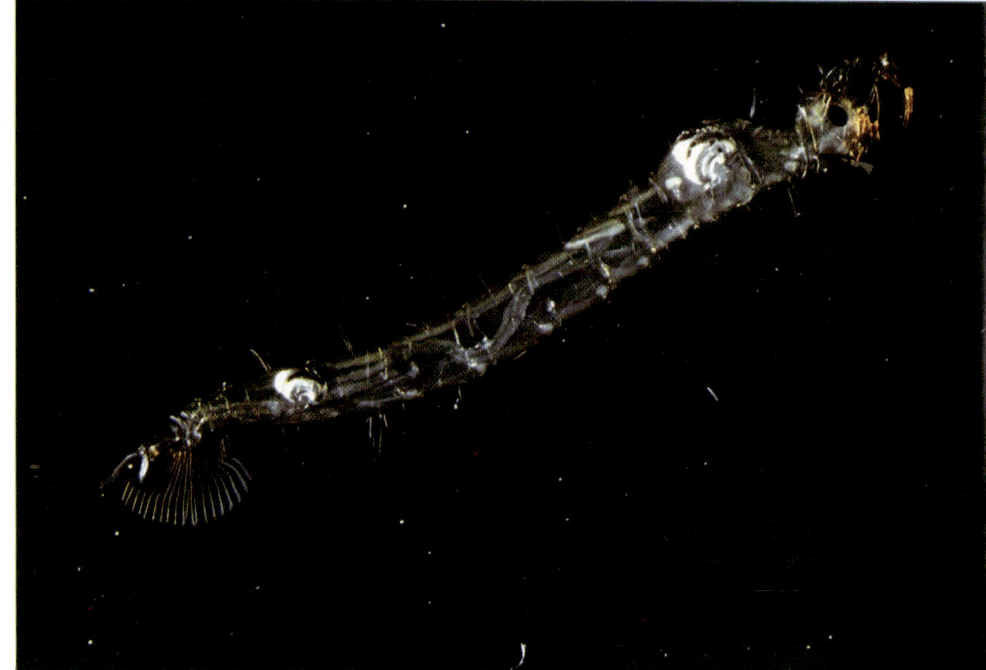

active subjects to the narrow front sector of the container to facilitate focusing, as the movements of the animal will be virtually limited to one pane.

It is essential for the front panel of glass to be perfectly clean both outside and inside, since this will naturally affect the quality of the photograph.

To prevent the light from the flashgun appearing in the picture, reflected by the glass at the front, it is best to align the gun at an angle of 50° to the axis of exposure of the camera (perpendicular to the front panel), checking this angle carefully with the aid of a protractor.

Under these conditions, only part of the light emitted by the flashgun penetrates the aquarium (the remainder being reflected outside the angle of aperture). This loss of light should be corrected by bringing the flashgun nearer, determining the amount of this by a series of tests at different distances (the loss is generally in the neighbourhood of 50%, in which case it is merely necessary to divide by 1·4 the distance normally used between the flashgun and the subject).

A reflecting screen (of white cardboard) submerged in the aquarium on the side opposite the flashgun will diminish the imbalance in lighting resulting from the flash being placed well to one side.

The background (of stiff paper) should be positioned either in the water against the rear wall of the aquarium or vertically, well behind the aquarium, at a distance of at least eighteen inches (50 cm), and illuminated by a second flashlight.

Finally, to avoid the image of the camera (and the photographer's hands) appearing in the picture, reflected by the front panel of glass, the photograph should be taken through a large piece of matt black cardboard with a hole through which to pass the lens (see layout drawing on page 139).

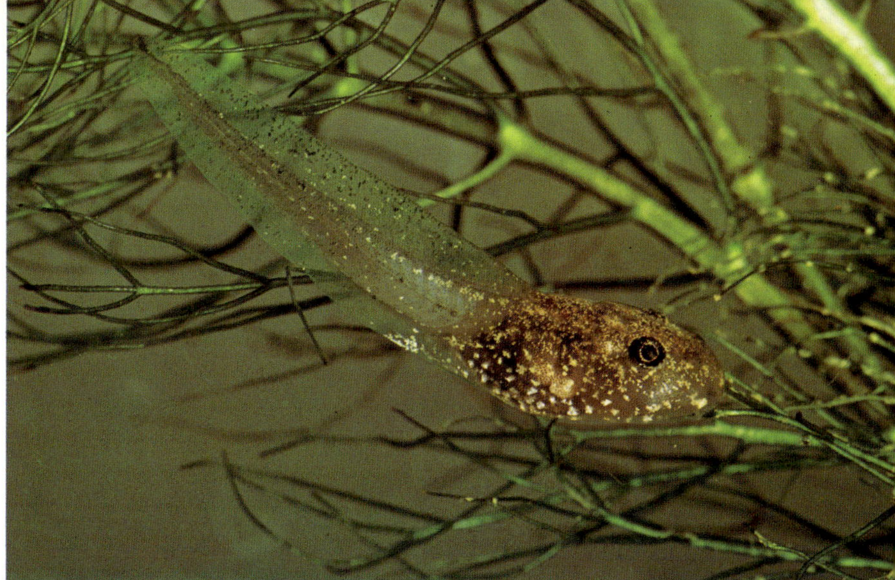

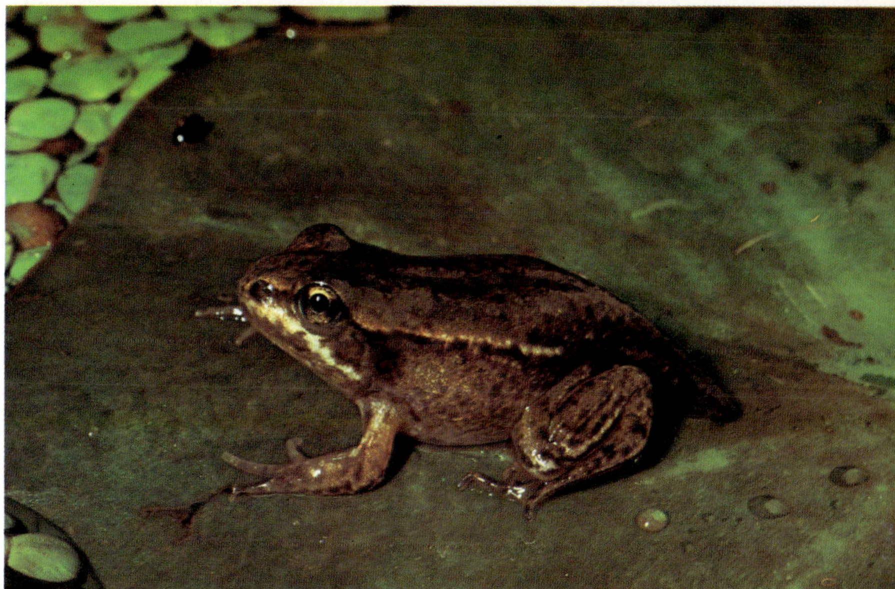

The fate of the models

A final word to draw attention to the fate of the 'models' after being photographed. It must be remembered that these animals are nothing other than prisoners, their comfort depending on the aquaria or vivaria in which they are housed.

Once the series of observations and photographic sessions has been satisfactorily completed, it is important to return these creatures, the interests of which we claim to have at heart, to their proper environment. It would take a very thoughtless

Above: Young frog tadpole (x 2·5).
Photographed in an aquarium.

Reproduction ratio: 0·3.
Lens: Macro 55 mm.
Aperture: f/22-32.
Green background set behind the aquarium and illuminated by a second flash.

Below: Final phase of metamorphosis (x 3). The tadpole has almost completely reabsorbed its tail.

Reproduction ratio: 0·6.
Lens: Macro 55 mm.
Aperture: f/22-32.
Electronic flash.

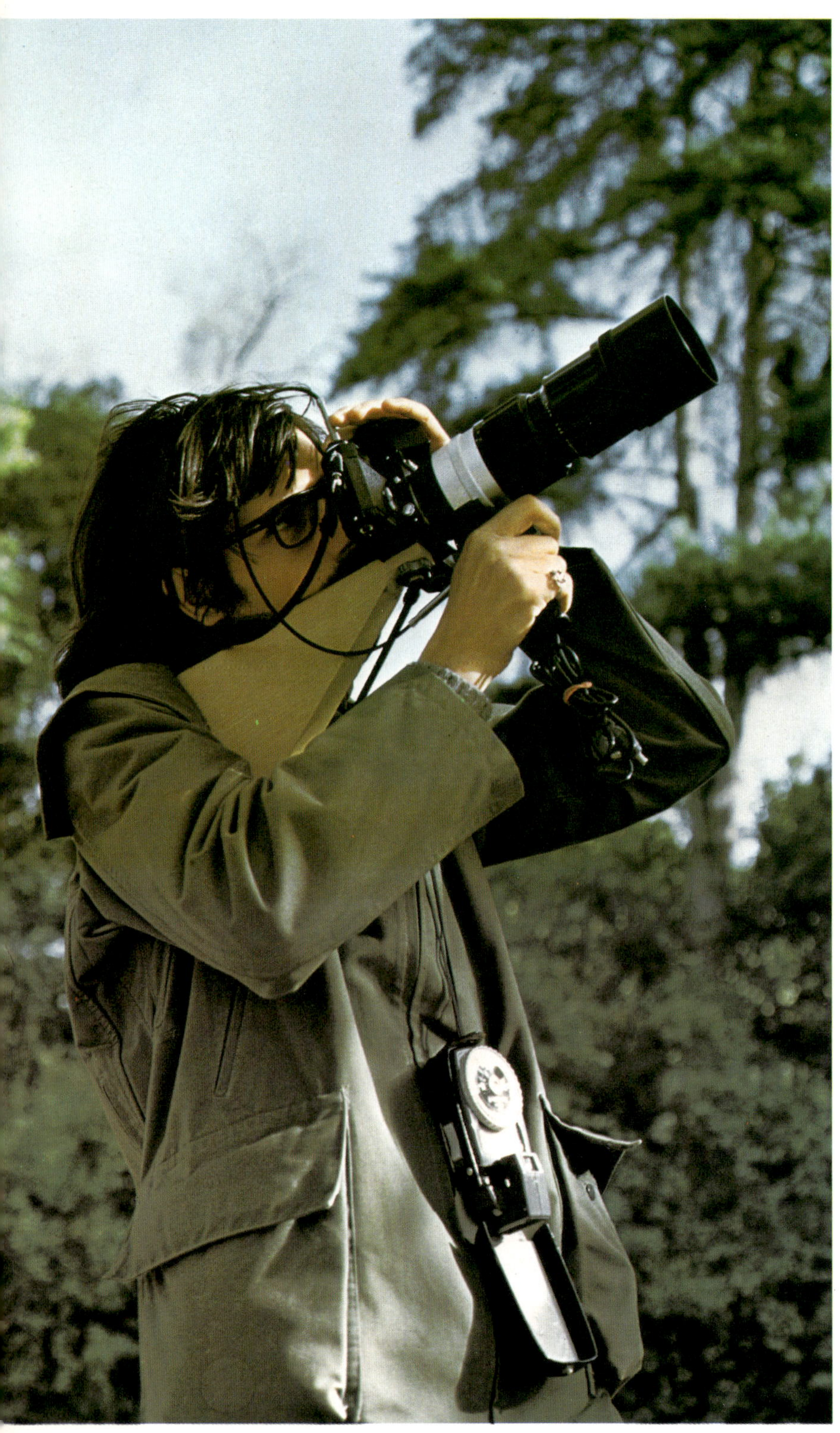

Photographing with a telephoto lens (300mm). Useful for timid species such as butterflies, dragonflies and reptiles. A shoulder-piece, made to measure from a piece of wood, improves stability. A pistol grip is used for shutter release. A sports-type viewfinder is used for focusing. Exposure meter: Lunasix 3 with telephoto accessory.

person to assume that all the life requirements of an animal can be satisfied in such a restricted space.

Conclusion

In summarising the results presented here, we would be entitled to claim that the entire collection of photographs appearing in this book is the fruit of five years of work, but, while five years of incessant activity have certainly elapsed between the oldest photographs and the most recent ones, we think the word 'work' is quite inadequate to describe what we have experienced in the process.

The reader may wonder whether we have had to call upon endless reserves of patience, but we have never felt that we were practising this virtue, which presupposes a rather unenthusiastic form of resignation.

In our particular field of activity it is sufficient merely to accept that the only attitude to adopt is one of keeping to the pace set by the animals: it is necessary to forget one's natural tempo – or at least that imposed on us by modern life – and then gradually to adopt that of one's subjects. We have always admired the determination with which animals decide what pattern of behaviour to follow (even though, for us, it has meant some unprofitable days as far as photography is concerned). If, for reasons of convenience, the photographer tries to change the behaviour, itinerary or position of his subject, he will find that he is powerless to make it accept these changes, and that it will always revert to its original decisions. Only after having remained for a long time in close contact with certain species is it possible occasionally to bring about an effective change in the behaviour of the subject, and in such cases we prefer to regard this as a matter of 'exchange' or 'collusion' with the animal, rather than a photographer's trick.

We are always subject to the whims of Nature, and rain and wind can sometimes cause the collapse of projects which have been built up over a number of days. However, it is also the unexpected which sometimes furnishes us with a valuable discovery that might perhaps never have been revealed to us by systematic and devoted research.

Finally, the slow progress of the seasons imposes on us its cyclic rhythm. This succession of climatic patterns, each with its own accompaniment of animals and plants, is what decides our programme of activities during the course of the year. This ceaseless change in the living world has, moreover, sometimes made it necessary for us to repeat for several years at a stretch the efforts we had made to photograph certain very fleeting seasonal occurrences. Photographing the breeding behaviour of toads, for example, several times produced disappointing results. Each set-back meant that the next attempt had to be postponed until the following year. It was only in the fourth year that we were successful in obtaining photographs worthy of the event.

But what can be more logical, when wishing to photograph the living world, than to submit to its laws and to come to terms with its customs, as practised by animals and plants? Is this not an indication of our true concern for the things of Nature?

The first set-backs experienced merely express our ignorance of a world which we had expected would accept us right away.

Endeavouring over the years to achieve an increasingly faithful photographic expression of this universe, we see Nature's apparent resistance to us begin to disappear. Doubtless the obstacles were mainly within ourselves.

Having got thus far, it remains only for us to prove that we are capable of matching the grandeur of the scenes before us – an ideal we must never tire of pursuing.

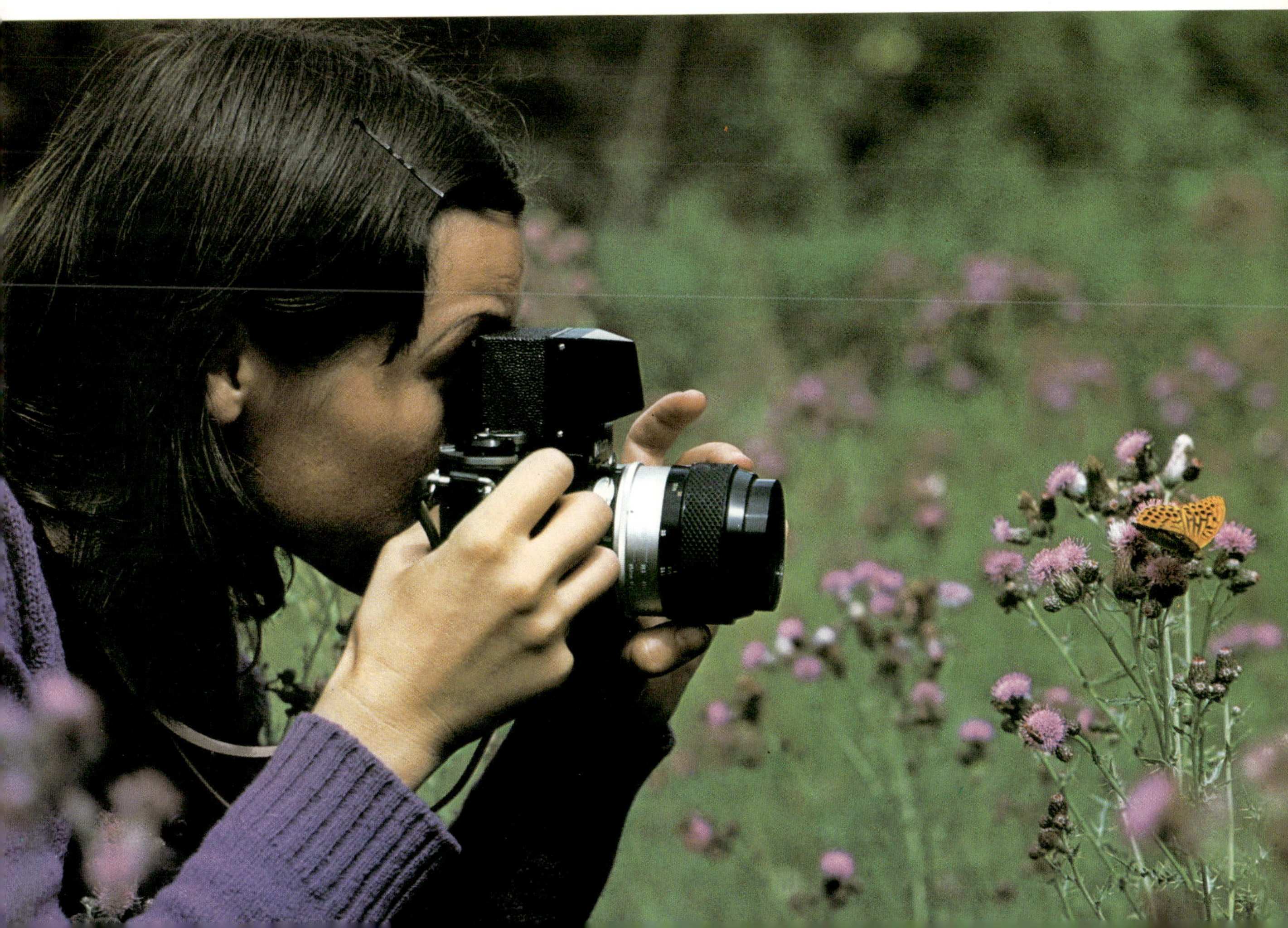

Approaching a butterfly busy sipping nectar. Micro Nikkor 55 mm mounted directly on the camera. Sports-type viewfinder.

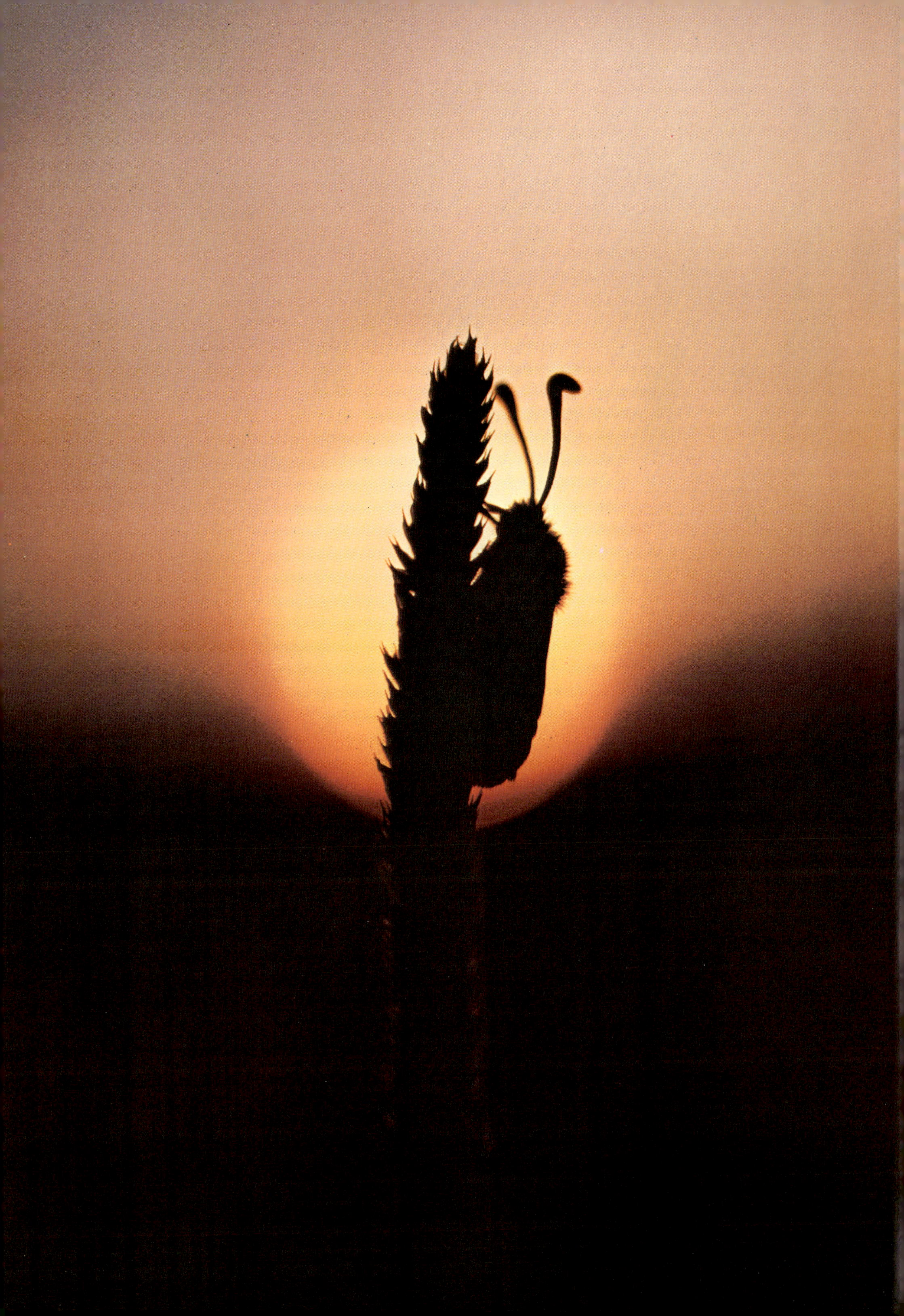

Practical information

Index of Technical Terms

The naturalist's calendar

This calendar gives only general information on the sequence of events which can be observed. It applies particularly to temperate lowland regions.
In mountainous areas and in Canada winter lasts noticeably longer, at the expense of spring. Activity is compressed into a period of four to five months.

meadow

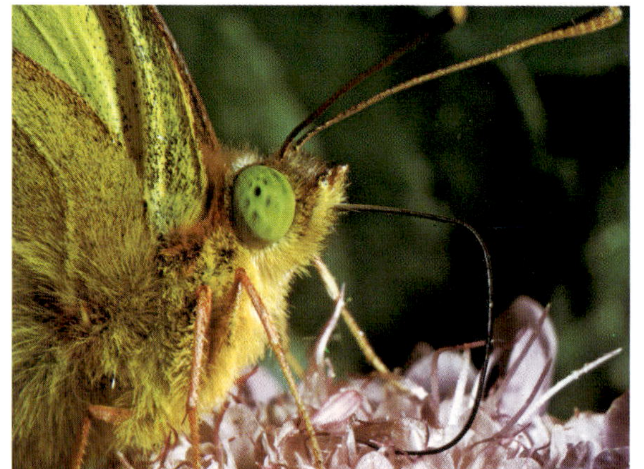

First generation of butterflies and moths hatch out.

Honey-bees, Bumble-bees, Rose-chafers, etc. appear.

Mating of Green Lizards and Wall Lizards.

Eggs of Banded Spider hatch.

Young Mantises hatch.

pond

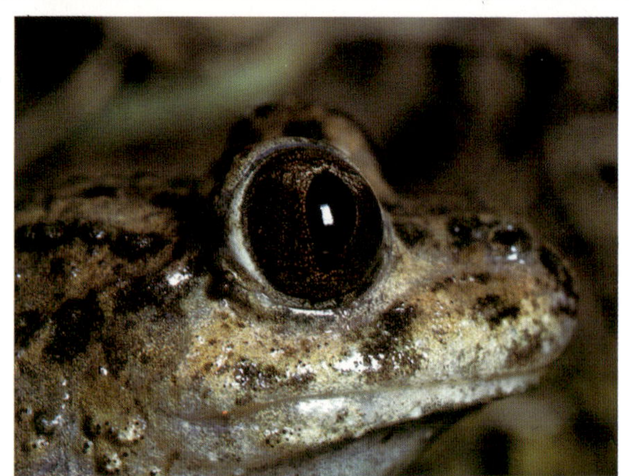

Frogs and toads mate and spawn.

Courtship dance of newts.

Sticklebacks build their nests.

Dragonfly larvae metamorphose.

Flight of the Mayfly.

Caddis-fly larvae.

forest

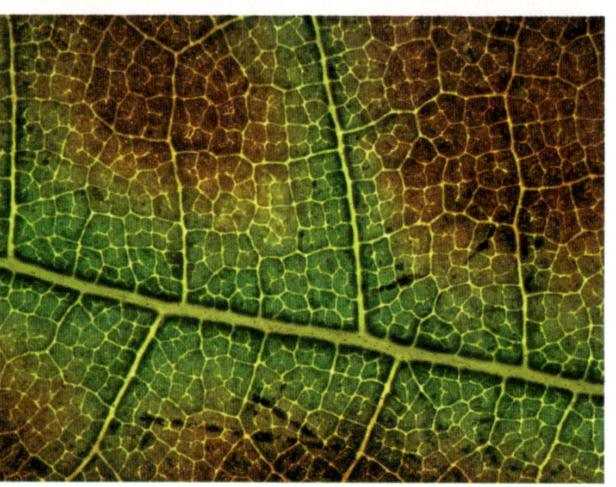

Germination of seeds (acorns, chestnuts, etc.).

Ferns produce their first shoots ('crosiers').

Caterpillars of geometrid moths.

Tiger Beetles.

May-bugs.

summer	autumn	winter
Crickets and grasshoppers. Common Frogs. Tree Frogs (in the bushes). Umbelliferous plants flower (attracting numerous insects in search of nectar). Praying Mantis (at the end of summer).	Garden Spiders. Banded Spiders (at the end of summer). Honey-seeking insects visit Ivy flowers.	Specimens can be collected under stones.
Edible Frogs (tadpoles and adults). Metamorphosis of tadpoles of Common Frog (at the beginning of summer). Crane-flies. Mating of Agrions (late spring and throughout summer).	Aquatic beetles (Hydrophilus and Dytiscus) particularly abundant.	Specimens can be found hibernating in the mud.
Stag-beetle (also in late spring). Cicadas. Buprestid beetles. Birth of the Longicorn Beetle. Nut-weevils.	Spore-cases under the leaves of ferns. Mushrooms.	Dormant buds. Specimens found torpid under stumps and moss.

Some 24 x 36 reflex cameras available on the market grouped by price

MODEL	EXPOSURE METER	VIEWFINDER	MOTOR	MACRO LENS	PRICE RANGE (approx.) equipped with 50 mm lens
Zenith E	No. Selenium exposure meter on camera, over lens.	Fixed prism	No	Takes all lenses with standard 42 mm thread.	**Less than £100 (U.S. $200)**
Zenith EM	No. Selenium exposure meter on camera, over lens.	Fixed prism	No	Takes all lenses with standard 42 mm thread.	
Praktica L	No	Fixed prism	No	Takes all lenses with standard 42 mm thread.	
Praktica LTL	Yes, measuring with diaphragm closed	Fixed prism	No	Takes all lenses with standard 42 mm thread.	
Praktica LLC	Yes, measuring at full aperture	Fixed prism	No	Takes all lenses with standard 42 mm thread.	
Mamiya MSX 500	Yes, measuring at full aperture	Fixed prism	No	Macro-Sekor 2·8/60 mm	
Topcon IC-1	Yes, measuring at full aperture	Fixed prism	No	Macro-Topcor 3·5/50 mm, 3·5/30 mm and 4/135 mm.	
Asahi Pentax Spotmatic 1000	Yes, measuring with diaphragm closed	Fixed prism	No	Macro-Takumar 4/50 mm and 4/100 mm.	
Miranda Sensomat RE-II	Yes, measuring with diaphragm closed	Interchangeable prism (4 different viewfinders)	No	Macron 2·8/52 mm.	**£100-£150 (U.S. $200-300)**
Canon TLbn	Yes, measuring at full aperture	Fixed prism	No	Macro-Canon 3·5/50 mm.	
Miranda Auto-Sensorex EE	Yes, measuring at full aperture	Interchangeable prism (4 different viewfinders)	No	Macron 2·8/52 mm.	
Asahi Pentax Spotmatic F	Yes, measuring at full aperture	Fixed prism	No	Macro-Takumar 4/50 mm and 4/100 mm.	
Mamiya DSX 1000	Yes, measuring at full aperture	Fixed prism	No	Macro-Sekor 2·8/60 mm.	
Fujica ST 701	Yes, measuring with diaphragm closed	Fixed prism	No	Takes all lenses with standard 42 mm thread. Macro-Fujinon 3·5/55 mm.	
Minolta SRT 101	Yes, measuring at full aperture	Fixed prism	No	Macro-Rokkor 3·5/50 mm and 3·5/100 mm.	
Nikkormat FT2	Yes, measuring at full aperture	Fixed prism	No	Macro-Nikkor 3·5/55 mm and 4/105 mm.	**£150-£200 (U.S. $300-400)**
Asahi Pentax KM	Yes, measuring at full aperture	Fixed prism	No	Takes 'K'-mount lenses.	
Asahi Pentax KX	Yes, measuring at full aperture	Fixed prism	No	Takes 'K'-mount lenses.	
Olympus OM1	Yes, measuring at full aperture	Fixed prism. Interchangeable viewing screens	Yes	Zuiko-Macro 3·5/50 mm.	
Topcon Super DM	Yes, measuring at full aperture	Interchangeable prism (5 different viewfinders) Interchangeable viewing screens	Yes	Macro-Topcor 3·5/58 mm, 3·5/30 mm and 4/135 mm.	
Minolta SRT 303	Yes, measuring at full aperture	Fixed prism	No	Macro-Rokkor 3·5/50 mm and 3·5/100 mm.	

MODEL	EXPOSURE METER BEHIND LENS	VIEWFINDER	MOTOR	MACRO LENS	PRICE RANGE (approx.) equipped with 50 mm lens
Fujica ST 801	Yes, measuring at full aperture	Fixed prism	No	Takes all lenses with standard 42 mm thread. Macro-Fujinon 3·5/55 mm.	
Nikkormat EL	Yes, measuring at full aperture	Fixed prism	No	Macro-Nikkor 3·5/55 mm and 4/105 mm.	£200 (U.S. $400) and over
Asahi Pentax K2	Yes, measuring at full aperture	Fixed prism	No	Takes 'K'-mount lenses.	
Nikon F2 Photomic	Yes, measuring at full aperture	Interchangeable prism (4 different viewfinders). Interchangeable viewing screens	Yes	Micro-Nikkor 3·5/55 mm and 4/105 mm.	
Canon F1	Yes, measuring at full aperture	Interchangeable prism	Yes	Macro-Canon 3·5/50 mm.	
Nikon F2	Yes, measuring at full aperture	Interchangeable prism (5 different viewfinders). Interchangeable viewing screens	Yes	Micro-Nikkor 3·5/55 mm and 4/105 mm.	
Nikon F25 Photomic	Yes, measuring at full aperture	Interchangeable prism (5 different viewfinders). Interchangeable viewing screens	Yes	Micro-Nikkor 3·5/55 mm and 4/105 mm.	
Minolta XM	Yes, measuring at full aperture	Interchangeable prism including auto-electric viewfinder permitting automatic exposure in conjunction with electronic shutter. 4 different viewfinders. 9 interchangeable viewing screens.	Yes, on Motor Drive model	Macro-Rokkor 3·5/50 mm and 3·5/100 mm.	
Leicaflex SL2	Yes, measuring at full aperture	Fixed prism	No. Yes, on motorised	Macro-Elmarit 2·8/60 mm, Macro-Elmar 4/100 mm.	
Olympus OM1	Yes, measuring at full aperture	Fixed prism. Interchangeable viewing screens.	Yes	Zuiko-Macro 3·5/50 mm.	

Specimen purchase programme

	EQUIPMENT	PERFORMANCE
STAGE 1	24 × 36 reflex camera + 50 mm 'macro' lens.	Outdoor (daylight) shots up to R = 1. Indoor (photoflood) shots of motionless subjects.
STAGE 2	Electronic flash.	High-power light available everywhere: sharp increase in depth of field in all cases. Removes risk of blurring.
STAGE 3	Bellows + reversing ring and tripod + focusing rail.	Exposures at R greater than 1 (up to 4 or 5). Accurate focusing and framing.
STAGE 4	100 mm lens (if possible 'macro').	Facilitates approach to subject outdoors and in the studio.
STAGE 5	Photomicrographic lens (24 mm).	Exposures at R of from 2 to greater than 10.
	2nd electronic flash.	Better-quality lighting (control of shadows and background illumination).

Dimensions of the subject: these indicate the maximum dimensions of the subject which can be photographed at the proposed reproduction ratio; at a reproduction ratio of 1, they are equal to the size of the negative, or 24 × 36 mm.

Other reproduction ratios are determined by dividing the dimensions of the negative by the R value: for R = 2, they are

$$\frac{24}{2} \times \frac{36}{2} \text{ or } 12 \times 18 \text{ mm, etc.}$$

To decide what extension tube or bellows to use to arrive at a given R, the formula used is A = F × R in which

A = Extension
F = Focal distance of lens used
R = Reproduction ratio

Calculation of exposure factor F_{exp} :

$$F_{exp} = (R + 1)^2 \text{ in which R = Reproduction ratio}$$

Subject distance, reproduction ratio, dimensions of field and exposure factor in terms of extension

50 mm LENS				
Extension (in mm)	Subject distance (in mm)	Reproduction ratio	Dimensions of field (in mm)	Exposure factor
5	550	0·1	240 × 360	1·2
10	300	0·2	120 × 180	1·4
15	217	0·3	80 × 120	1·7
20	175	0·4	60 × 90	2
25	150	0·5	48 × 72	2·3
30	133	0·6	40 × 60	2·6
35	121	0·7	34 × 51	2·9
40	113	0·8	30 × 45	3·2
45	106	0·9	27 × 40	3·6
50	100	1	24 × 36	4
55	95	1·1	22 × 33	4·4
60	92	1·2	20 × 30	4·8
70	86	1·4	17 × 26	5·8
80	81	1·6	15 × 23	6·8
90	78	1·8	13 × 20	7·8
100	75	2	12 × 18	9
110	73	2·2	11 × 16	10·2
120	71	2·4	10 × 15	11·6
130	69	2·6	9 × 14	13
140	68	2·8	9 × 13	14·4
150	67	3	8 × 12	16
170	65	3·4	8 × 11	19·4
180	64	3·6	7 × 10	21·2
200	63	4	6 × 9	25
220	61	4·4	5 × 8	29

100 mm LENS				
Extension (in mm)	Subject distance (in mm)	Reproduction ratio	Dimensions of field (in mm)	Exposure factor
5	2,100	0·05	480 × 720	1·1
10	1,100	0·10	240 × 360	1·2
15	767	0·15	160 × 240	1·3
20	600	0·20	120 × 180	1·4
25	500	0·25	96 × 144	1·6
30	433	0·30	80 × 120	1·7
35	386	0·35	69 × 103	1·8
40	350	0·40	60 × 90	2
45	322	0·45	53 × 80	2·1
50	300	0·50	48 × 72	2·3
55	282	0·55	44 × 65	2·4
60	267	0·60	40 × 60	2·6
70	243	0·70	34 × 51	2·9
80	225	0·80	30 × 45	3·2
90	211	0·90	27 × 40	3·6
100	200	1·00	24 × 36	4
110	191	1·10	22 × 33	4·4
120	183	1·20	20 × 30	4·8
130	177	1·30	18 × 27	5·3
140	171	1·40	17 × 26	5·8
150	167	1·50	16 × 24	6·3
170	159	1·70	14 × 21	7·3
180	156	1·80	13 × 20	7·8
200	150	2	12 × 18	9
220	145	2·20	11 × 16	10·2

Using the exposure factor

$F_{exp.}$	open aperture by:	or divide the distance from flash to subject by:
1·5	$\frac{1}{2}$ stop value	1·2
2	1 stop value	1·4
3	$1\frac{1}{2}$ stop values	1·7
4	2 stop values	2
6	$2\frac{1}{2}$ stop values	2·5
8	3 stop values	2·8
12	$3\frac{1}{2}$ stop values	3·5
16	4 stop values	4
24	$4\frac{1}{2}$ stop values	5
32	5 stop values	5·7

Table of depths of field (mm)

in terms of reproduction ratio R and lens aperture d

R \ d	5·6	8	11	16	22	32
0·1	41	59	81	117	160	235
0·2	11	16	22	32	44	64
0·33	4·5	6·4	8·8	12·8	17·6	25·6
0·5	2·2	3·2	4·4	6·4	8·8	13
0·66	1·7	2	3·3	4	6·6	8
1	0·8	1·1	1·5	2·1	3	4·2
1·5	0·41	0·6	0·8	1·2	1·6	2·4
2	0·28	0·4	0·55	0·8	1·1	1·6
3	0·16	0·25	0·32	0·47	0·64	1
4	0·11	0·16	0·22	0·32	0·44	0·64
5	0·09	0·13	0·18	0·25	0·36	0·5

The depth of field is doubled each time the aperture is closed by two stops.
The shaded area indicates the zone in which diffraction can affect definition.

Specimen record card

This card gives details of the conditions under which each photograph was obtained. Its use makes it possible to avoid repeating certain mistakes, and to choose the most suitable method of operation for each subject.

The number of the film followed by that of the negative should be recorded on the slide mount to enable technical data relating to each photograph to be retrieved.

Date:				Number of film	
Emulsion type					
No. of photo	Lens	Aperture	R	Lighting: daylight or flash	Special remarks (reflectors, etc.)

Colour temperature

The colour temperature (CT) is expressed in kelvins (K). A light having a low CT appears more or less yellow (such as ordinary electric light-bulbs, at about 2,500K).

A light of higher CT appears white or bluish (daylight, up to 10,000K).

It is easy to bear this relationship in mind if it is remembered that a piece of hot metal emits first red light, then yellow, then white as its temperature is raised: the Kelvin scale is based on this correspondence.

'Daylight' films are colour-balanced for a CT of about 6,000K (the CT of the sun overhead, in summer, with a clear sky) but can in fact accept a fairly wide variation on either side of this figure.

'Artificial light A' films (Kodachrome II Type A) are balanced for a CT of 3,400K (the CT of stepped-up incandescent photofloods).

'Artificial light B' films (High Speed Ektachrome, Tungsten) are balanced for a CT of 3,200K (the CT of stepped-up 'half-watt' lamps).

Kodak colour correction filters positioned in front of the lens make it possible to expose these different types of film at a colour temperature for which they were not designed:

CT of light source	Use with Type B film	Use with Type A film	Use with daylight film
3,200K (half-watt lamps, slide projector)	Yes	+82A filter (open by 1/3 stop)	+80A filter (not advised*) (open by 2 stops)
3,400K (photofloods)	+81A filter (open by 1/3 stop)	Yes	+80B filter (not advised*) (open by 1 and 2/3 stop)
6,000K (daylight, electronic flash)	+85B filter (open by 2/3 stop)	+85 filter (open by 2/3 stop)	Yes

*Except for microscope photography, when colour accuracy is not so important as in ordinary photography.

Electronic flash

Colour temperature of flash 6,000K (equal to that of daylight). Used with normal-type 'daylight' films.

Duration of flash approximately 1/1,000th of a second.

Used with a precise shutter speed, called the 'synchronization speed', of 1/60th to 1/125th of a second.

Power: indicated by the guide number (G.N.). This is supplied by the manufacturers for use with a film having a sensitivity of 50 ASA (18 DIN) or, increasingly for 100 ASA (21 DIN).

G.N. = Distance from flash to subject (in metres) × lens aperture.

Knowing the G.N. for a given film speed $G.N._a$, it is possible to calculate the corresponding G.N. for a different film speed $G.N._x$ by means of the formula:

$$G.N._x = G.N._a \times \sqrt{\frac{x}{a}}$$

in which a = reference film speed (in ASA).
x = film speed for which the new G.N. is required.

Example: If the G.N. of a flash unit is 20 for a 50 ASA film, then for a 200 ASA film its G.N. will be:

$$G.N. = 20 \times \sqrt{\frac{200}{50}} = 20 \times \sqrt{4} = 20 \times 2 = 40$$

Film speed	G.N.										
50 ASA	8	10	12	14	16	18	20	22	24	26	28
25 ASA	5·6	7	8·4	9·8	11·2	12·6	14	15·4	16·8	18·2	19·6
100 ASA	11·2	14	16·8	19·6	22·4	25·2	28	30·8	33·6	36·4	39·2
160 ASA	13·6	17	20·4	23·8	27·2	30·6	34	37·4	40·8	44·2	47·6
400 ASA	16	20	24	28	32	36	40	44	48	52	56

If the distance from flash to subject is divided by $\sqrt{2}$, or 1·4, the quantity of light illuminating the subject is doubled (which is equivalent to opening the aperture by one stop).

If it is divided by $\sqrt{1·5}$, or 1·2, the quantity of light is increased by 50%, which is equivalent to opening the aperture by half a stop.

Conversely—Distance from flash to subject × 1·4 → 2 times less light.
Distance from flash to subject × 1·2 → 25% less light.

Calculation of guide number resulting from combination of 2 flash units:

$$G.N. \text{ total} = \sqrt{(G.N. \text{ flash 1})^2 + (G.N. \text{ flash 2})^2}$$

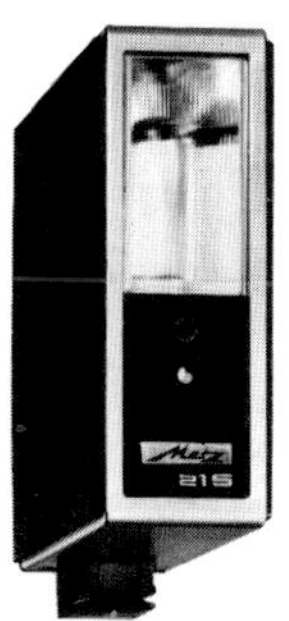

Metz Mecablitz 215 flash.
Disconnectable computer flash,
programmable for 3 stops.
Guide number: 22 for 50 ASA.
Interval between flashes:
7 seconds.
Duration of flash: 3/1,000th to
1/50,000th of a second.
Weight: 380 grams.

Braun 2,000 28 BVC flash.
Disconnectable computer flash,
programmable for 2 stops, and
economiser ('Vario-computer').
Guide number: 20 for 50 ASA.
Interval between flashes: 6 to 0·3
seconds.
Duration of flash: 1/600th to
1/30,000th of a second.
Weight: 240 grams.

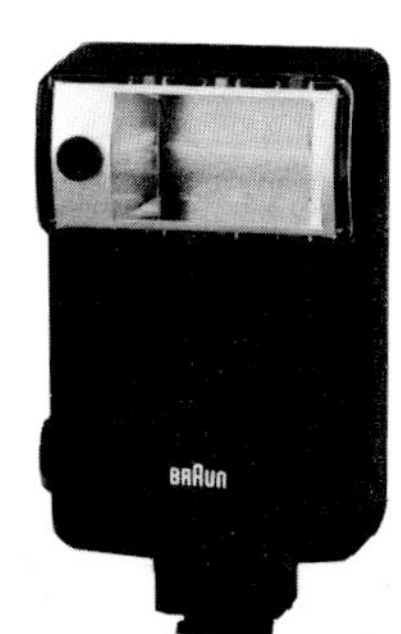

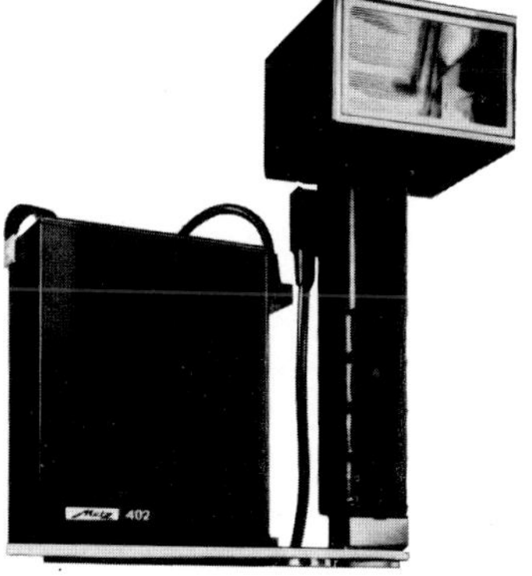

Metz Mecablitz 402 flash.
Disconnectable computer flash,
programmable for 5 stops, and
economiser ('Vario-computer').
Guide number: 40 for 50 ASA.
Interval between flashes:
5 seconds to 1 second.
Duration of flash: 1/250th to
1/40,000th of a second.
Weight: 2·2 kg.

Flash-subject distances

(in centimetres)
To be used in terms of reproduction ratio R and guide number G.N. of flash used.

APERTURE f/16

G.N. / R.	8	10	12	14	16	18	20	22	24
0·1	46	56	68	80	91	102	113	126	136
0·2	42	51	63	73	83	93	104	115	125
0·3	38	47	58	68	77	86	96	106	115
0·4	35	44	53	63	71	80	89	97	107
0·5	33	41	50	59	67	75	83	92	100
0·6	31	38	47	55	63	70	78	86	93
0·7	29	36	44	52	59	66	73	82	87
0·8	27	34	41	49	56	62	69	78	83
0·9	26	32	39	46	52	59	65	74	79
1	25	31	37	44	50	56	62	69	75
1·2	23	28	34	40	46	51	57	63	68
1·4	21	26	31	36	42	47	52	57	63
1·6	19	24	29	33	39	43	48	53	58
1·8	18	22	27	30	36	40	45	50	54
2	16	20	25	28	33	37	42	47	50
2·5	14	18	21	25	29	32	36	40	43
3	12	15	19	22	25	28	31	35	37
3·5	11	14	17	19	22	24	28	30	33
4	10	13	15	17	20	22	25	27	30

APERTURE f/22

G.N. / R.	8	10	12	14	16	18	20	22	24
0·1	33	42	50	60	67	74	83	90	99
0·2	30	38	46	55	60	68	75	83	91
0·3	28	35	42	50	56	63	70	77	84
0·4	26	32	40	47	52	59	65	71	78
0·5	24	30	37	44	48	55	60	66	73
0·6	23	28	35	41	45	52	57	61	68
0·7	21	27	32	39	43	48	54	58	64
0·8	20	25	30	36	40	45	50	56	60
0·9	19	24	29	34	38	43	48	53	57
5	18	22	27	32	36	41	45	50	54
1·2	16	20	25	30	33	38	41	46	49
1·4	15	19	23	27	30	34	38	41	45

APERTURE f/32

G.N. / R.	8	10	12	14	16	18	20	22	24
0·1	23	28	34	40	46	51	57	63	78
0·2	21	25	31	36	42	47	52	58	63
0·3	19	24	29	34	39	43	48	53	58
0·4	18	22	26	32	36	40	45	49	54
0·5	17	21	25	30	34	38	42	46	50
0·6	16	19	24	28	31	35	39	43	47
0·7	15	18	22	26	30	33	37	41	44
0·8	14	17	20	25	28	31	35	39	42

All these distances have been calculated by means of the formula:

$$\text{Flash-subject distance} = \frac{\text{G.N.} \times 100}{\text{f/stop} \times (R + 1)}$$

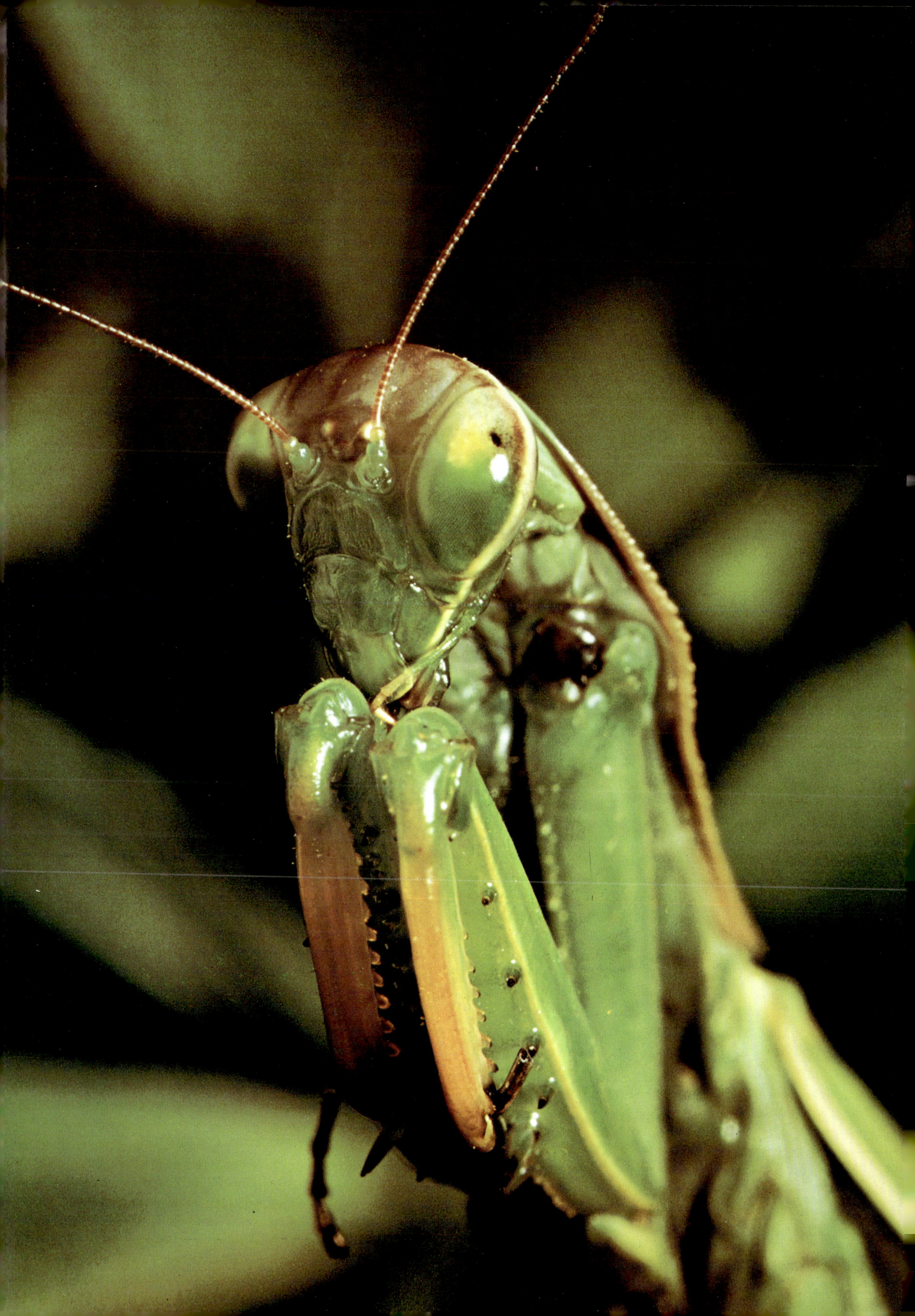

Bibliography

Insects and small creatures

J. W. STEWARD
The Tailed Amphibians of Europe
David & Charles

J. W. STEWARD
The Snakes of Europe
David & Charles

W. M. BLANEY
How Insects Live
Elsevier-Phaidon, Oxford

D. M. COCHRAN
Living Amphibians of the World
Hamilton, London

K. P. SCHMIDT AND R. F. INGER
Living Reptiles of the World
Hamilton, London

A. LOVERIDGE
Reptiles of the Pacific World
Macmillan, London

V. SERVENTY
Wildlife of Australia
Nelson, London

R. FITTER
Vanishing Wild Animals of the World
Kaye & Ward, London
Franklin Watts, New York

L. G. HIGGINS
Field Guide to the Butterflies of Britain and Europe
Collins, London

P. SMART
An Illustrated Encyclopaedia of the Butterfly World in Colour
Hamlyn, London

L. LYNEBORG
Moths in Colour
Blandford, London

The Beetles of America
Yoseloff/Tantivy, London
Arco, New York

Botany

P. MORNS AND G. JONES
The Encyclopaedia of the Plant Kingdom
Hamlyn, London

F. H. PERRING AND S. M. WALTERS
The Atlas of British Flora
E. P. Publishing, London

P. H. DAVIS
The Mosses of Southern Australia
Academic Press, London

BLOMBERY
Guide to Native Australian Plants
Angus & Robertson

GLEASON
Plants of the Vicinity of New York
Hafner

RYDBERG
Flora of the Prairies and Plains of Central North America
Hafner

E. KREBS AND H. GOHL
Living Forests
Kaye & Ward, London
Oxford University Press, New York

Photography

J. M. BAUFLE AND J. P. VARIN
Photographing Wildlife
Kaye & Ward, London
Oxford University Press, New York

Filters and Lens Attachments for Black and White and Colour Pictures
Patrick Stephens, London
Kodak, USA

P. PETZOLD
The Photoguide to Existing Light Photography
Focal Press, London

R. KINGSLAKE
Applied Optics and Optical Engineering
Academic Press, New York

T. TOWERS
Electronics and the Photographer
Focal Press, London

L. GAUNT
Electronic Flash Guide
Focal Press, London

M. I. WALKER
Amateur Photomicrography
Focal Press, London

A. AND I. TOLKE
Macrophoto and Cine Methods
Focal Press, London

Microscope as a Camera
Focal Press, London

PAPERT
Photomacrography: Art and Techniques
Amphoto, London and New York

J. BERGNER, E. GELDKE, W. MEHLISS
Practical Photomicrography
Focal Press, London

156

KODAK
Applied Infra Red Photography
P. Stevens, London
Kodak, USA

Infra Red and Ultra Violet Photography
P. Stevens, London
Kodak, USA

Basic Scientific Photography
P. Stevens, London
Kodak, USA

Close-up Photography
P. Stevens, London
Kodak, USA

Photography through the Microscope
P. Stevens, London
Kodak, USA

Photomacrography
P. Stevens, London
Kodak, USA

D. F. LAWSON
Photomacrography
Academic Press, New York

H. ANGEL
Nature Photography: its Art and Technique
Fountain Press

O. R. CROY
Creative Photomicrography
Focal Press, London

H. M. MALIES
Applied Microscopy and Photomicrography
Fountain Press

Useful Addresses

World Wildlife Fund (Head Office), 1110 Morges, Switzerland.

World Wildlife Fund, Panda House, 29 Greville Street, London EC1N 8AX.

World Wildlife Fund, Suite 619, 910 17th Street N.W., Washington, D.C. 20036.

World Wild Fund, Suite 353, 2100 Drummond Street, Montreal 25, Canada.

Royal Photographic Society, Nature Group, 14 South Audley Street, London W1Y 5DP.

National Parks Association, 1300 New Hampshire Avenue N.W., Washington D.C. 20036.

Society for the Promotion of Nature Reserves, c/o British Museum (Natural History), Cromwell Road, London SW7.

Australian Conservation Foundation, P.O. Box 804, Canberra City, ACT 2601.

Royal Forest and Bird Protection Society of New Zealand, P.O. Box 631, Wellington, New Zealand.

Biological Photographic Association, P.O. Box 333, Station A, Ottowa, Ontario, Canada KIN 8V3.

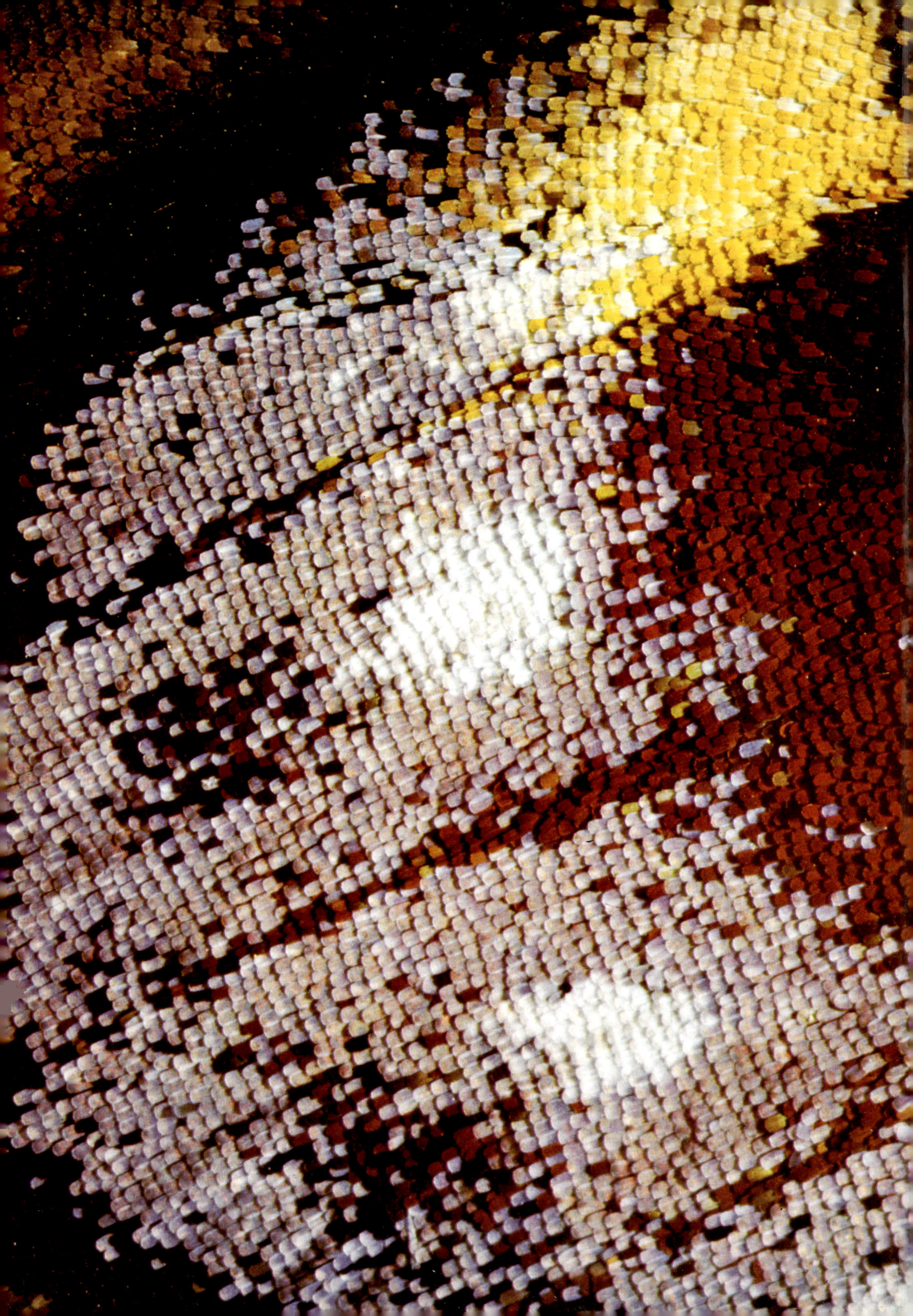